Canadian Politics

Canadian

Politics

FIFTH EDITION

edited by
James Bickerton
Alain-G. Gagnon

 **UTP** University of
Toronto Press

LIBRARY AND ARCHIVES CANADA CATALOGUING IN PUBLICATION

Canadian politics / edited by James Bickerton, Alain-G. Gagnon. — 5th ed.

Includes bibliographical references and index.
ISBN 978-1-4426-0121-5

1. Canada—Politics and government. I. Bickerton, James II. Gagnon, Alain-G.
(Alain-Gustave), 1954–

JL65.C35 2009   320.971   C2009-903388-7

We welcome comments and suggestions regarding any aspect of our publications —
please feel free to contact us at news@utphighereducation.com or visit our Internet site
at www.utphighereducation.com.

North America
5201 Dufferin Street
North York, Ontario, Canada, M3H 5T8

2250 Military Road
Tonawanda, New York, USA, 14150

ORDERS PHONE: 1-800-565-9523
ORDERS FAX: 1-800-221-9985
ORDERS E-MAIL: utpbooks@utpress.utoronto.ca

UK, Ireland, and continental Europe
Plymbridge Distributors Ltd.
Estover Road, Plymouth, PL6 7PY, UK
TEL: 44 (0) 1752 202301
FAX ORDER LINE: 44 (0) 1752 202333
enquiries@nbninternational.com

This book is printed on paper containing 100% post-consumer fibre.

The University of Toronto Press acknowledges the financial support for its publishing
activities of the Government of Canada through the Book Publishing Industry
Development Program (BPIDP).

Book design by Metapolis.

Printed in Canada

Contents

Part III: Democracy and Representation

Part IV: Canada in the World

Preface

The new, fifth edition of *Canadian Politics* continues the work of earlier editions in offering a comprehensive introduction to Canadian government and politics by a widely recognized and highly respected group of political scientists, writing on subjects on which they are acknowledged experts. For this edition, the editors have organized the book into four sections: Part I: *Citizenship, Identities, and Values*; Part II: *Institutions*; Part III: *Democracy and Representation*. Part IV: *Canada in the World*, comprised of three chapters, develops a new focus on the diverse and increasingly important influences of globalization on the Canadian polity, the environment, and the role of Canada in the world. Of the 18 chapters, those retained from earlier editions have been revised and updated. This edition adds several new authors and nine completely new chapters.

Notes on Contributors

About the Editors

James Bickerton is Professor of Political Science at St. Francis Xavier University. His research interests are in the areas of federalism and regionalism, as well as party and electoral politics. His publications include co-authorship of "Regions" in Danielle Caramani, ed., *Comparative Politics*; *Freedom, Equality, Community: The Political Philosophy of Six Influential Canadians*; and *Ties That Bind: Parties and Voters in Canada*.

Alain-G. Gagnon holds the Canada Research Chair in Québec and Canadian Studies at the Université du Québec à Montréal. His most recent books include *Quebec: State and Society, third edition*; *Contemporary Canadian Federalism*; *Canadian Parties in Transition* (with Brian Tanguay); *The Case for Multinational Federalism*; and *Federal Democracies* (with Michael Burgess).

About the Contributors

Yasmeen Abu-Laban is Professor and Associate Chair (Research) in the Department of Political Science at the University of Alberta. Her publications include *Gendering the Nation-State: Canadian and Comparative Perspectives*; *Politics in North America: Redefining Continental Relations* (with Radha Jhappan and François Rocher); and *Selling Diversity: Immigration, Multiculturalism, Employment Equity, and Globalization* (with Christina Gabriel).

Raymond Bazowski is Associate Professor in the Department of Political Science at York University. He researches and writes on the subject of law and politics and the administration of justice. His research interests include the philosophy of law, comparative constitutionalism, and the effect of law on public policy.

Mark R. Brawley is Professor of Political Science at McGill University where he specializes in international political economy and international security. He is currently researching connections between trade liberalization and domestic adjustment during globalization. He is the author of *Political Economy and Grand Strategy: A Neoclassical Realist View*.

Stephen Brooks is Professor of Political Science at the University of Windsor and Adjunct Professor of Political Science at the University of Michigan. His most recent books include *Understanding American Politics* and *Canadian Democracy*, 6th ed.

Andrew F. Cooper is Associate Director and Distinguished Fellow at the Centre for International Governance Innovation (CIGI) and Professor in the Department of Political Science at the University of Waterloo. His recent books include *Celebrity Diplomacy*, and as co-editor (with D. Rowlands) *Minorities and Priorities: Canada Among Nations 2006*.

William Cross is the Honourable Dick and Ruth Bell Chair for the Study of Canadian Parliamentary Democracy in the Department of Political Science at Carleton University. His recent publications are in the areas of party democracy, democratic institutions, and democratic reform.

Roger Gibbins joined the Canada West Foundation in 1998 as its President and CEO. He has authored, co-authored, and edited over 20 books, most dealing with Western Canadian themes and issues and constitutional politics.

Will Kymlicka holds the Canada Research Chair in Political Philosophy at Queen's University. His books include *Finding Our Way: Rethinking Ethnocultural Relations in Canada* and *Multicultural Odysseys: Navigating the New International Politics of Diversity*.

Samuel LaSelva is Professor of Political Science at the University of British Columbia. He is the author of *The Moral Foundations of Canadian Federalism*. His articles have appeared in the *Canadian Journal of Political Science, Dalhousie Review, BC Studies, Supreme Court Law Review*, and elsewhere He is currently at work on human rights and the ethics of constitutionalism.

Éric Montpetit is Associate Professor of Political Science at the Université de Montréal. *The Politics of Biotechnology in North America and Europe: Policy Networks, Institutions and Internationalization* (with Christine Rothmayr and Frederic Varone) is among his recent publications.

Martin Papillon is Assistant Professor at the School of Political Studies at the University of Ottawa. His research focuses on Indigenous governance and policy in Canada, the United States, and Australia, and on the reconfiguration of citizenship regimes in multinational states. He has published widely on Indigenous politics and federalism in Canada.

Ian Robinson teaches international and comparative political economy at the University of Michigan-Ann Arbor. His research and publishing has focused mainly on how the neoliberal model of economic globalization reshapes our lives and our societies, and how worker and other social movement organizations are attempting to reshape globalization.

Donald J. Savoie holds the Canada Research Chair in Public Administration and Governance at the Université de Moncton. He has published numerous books on public policy, public administration, and federalism. His latest publication is *Court Government and the Collapse of Accountability in Canada and the United Kingdom*.

Richard Simeon is Professor of Political Science and Law at the University of Toronto, and a Fellow of the Royal Society of Canada. His works include *Federal-Provincial Diplomacy: The Making of Recent Policy in Canada*; *State, Society and the Development of Canadian Federalism* (with Ian Robinson); and *Re-designing the State: The Politics of Constitutional Change in Industrial Democracies*.

Jennifer Smith is Professor of Political Science at Dalhousie University. She wrote the Canadian Democratic Audit's volume on *Federalism* and edited *The Democratic Dilemma: Reforming the Canadian Senate*.

Peter Stoett is Associate Professor of International Relations and Chair of the Department of Political Science at Concordia University. Recently published books include *Environmental Challenges and Opportunities: Local-Global Perspectives on Canadian Issues* (co-edited with Chris Gore); *International Ecopolitical Theory: Critical Reflections* (co-edited with Éric Laferrière); and *Bilateral Ecopolitics*.

A. Brian Tanguay is Professor of Political Science at Wilfrid Laurier University. His current research focuses on electoral reform in liberal democracies and the evolving division of labour between political parties and organized interests. He drafted the Law Commission of Canada's report entitled *Voting Counts: Electoral Reform in Canada* and co-edited *Canadian Parties in Transition, third edition.*

Lisa Young is Professor of Political Science at the University of Calgary. Her publications include *Feminists and Party Politics* and *Advocacy Groups* (with Joanna Everitt).

PART I

Citizenship, Identities, and Values

Understanding Canada's Origins: Federalism, Multiculturalism, and the Will to Live Together

SAMUEL V. LASELVA

"More than most other countries, Canada is a creation of human will. It has been called a 'geographical absurdity,' an 'appendage of the United States,' a '4,000-mile main street' with many bare stretches. Nevertheless this country has existed for a long time, because its people have never stopped willing that there be a Canada."
—*Preliminary Report of the Royal Commission on Bilingualism and Biculturalism* 144

Introduction: The Canadian Enigma

Canada has existed for a long time, but Canada is a difficult country to understand and also a difficult country to govern both in times of constitutional crisis and in periods of constitutional stability. Even if Canadians "have never stopped willing that there be a Canada," the near successful sovereignty referendum in Quebec and the Supreme Court secession reference suggest that Canada's continued existence cannot be taken for granted. The sovereignty referendum and the secession reference focused on Quebec and reveal its complex relationship to the rest of Canada, a relationship that is not fully or easily encapsulated within Parliament's recent, ambiguous, and aspirational declaration that the Québécois form a nation within a united Canada. The difficulties that confront Canadians are by no means confined to the French-English question. Aboriginal nationalism, with its demand for Aboriginal sovereignty, raises equally difficult questions. There are also multicultural groups. These groups — together with women, gays, lesbians, and the disabled — do not threaten the unity of Canada, but they seek to shape its identity, and their demands can conflict with those of other political actors. The failed Meech Lake and Charlottetown Constitutional Accords demonstrate that the very pluralism of Canada can sometimes result in "mosaic madness" and may yet compel Canadians to "look into the abyss" (Bibby, 1990; Cairns, 1997). When the focus is shifted away from mega-constitutional matters to issues like health care or the Canadian social union or the federal spending power, problems of disunity and fragmentation are just as evident, and Canada continues to be both a difficult country to understand and a difficult country to govern (Adam, 2007: 32-34; Petter, 1989: 463-68).

Consequently, Canada is often regarded as a "geographical absurdity" or even an "impossible country." Canada, it has been urged, "preserves nothing of value. It is literally nothing. It is the *absence* of a sense of identity, the absence of a common life" (Horowitz, 1985: 363). When such a view is taken, Canada is regarded as a country without a future and Canadians are urged to begin the process of deconfederation. But not everyone favours the fragmentation of Canada, or the creation of regional and ethnic solitudes, or absorption into the United States. Many Canadians believe that Canada does preserve something of value and that the Canadian experiment differs from the American union. But why is Canada worth preserving? Historically, one of the most evocative expressions of Canadian distinctiveness has been the motto, "true north, strong and free." As a northern country, Canada was held to differ from the United States and to express unique character values. Canada's cold climate was also used to explain its adherence to British liberty and its rejection of American-style democracy (Berger, 1966: 15). Just as evocative is the celebration of Canadian multiculturalism that often occupies pride of place in contemporary accounts of Canada's uniqueness. In his *Conversation with Canadians* (1972), Pierre Trudeau contrasted Canada with the American melting pot and insisted that a vigorous policy of multiculturalism formed the basis of fair play for all Canadians. Of course, Trudeau attached even greater significance to the Canadian Charter of Rights and Freedoms. In his *Memoirs*, he emphasized that his search for the Canadian identity "had led [him] to insist on the charter" (Trudeau, 1993: 323).

However, the adoption of the Charter has not settled the most difficult questions about the Canadian identity. If anything, Canadians are more divided than before on the most fundamental questions. Charter patriotism has come into conflict with the other particularisms that define Canada, with the result that Canada has become an even more difficult country to govern and a more difficult country to understand. Trudeau believed that the Charter would provide Canadians with a new beginning and a foundation for the future. Yet Canada existed for a long time before the Charter was adopted in 1982, and Trudeau took too little account of this fact. The Canadian nation, a distinguished historian has written, "is fragile indeed, and one reason ... might well be the lack of a history that binds Canadians together. It is not that we do not have such a history. It is simply that we have chosen not to remember it." He goes on to say: "If we have no past, then surely ... we have no future" (Granatstein, 1998: xvii, xviii). Others, like Janet Ajzenstat, are more specific. They warn that "we have lost the Fathers' insight," they pray that Canada will not "be wracked by the terrible passions that have inflicted such damage on European nations in the twentieth century," and they hope "that our shortsightedness never catches up with us" (Ajzenstat, 2007: xii, 109). Not only do Canadians have a past, but their past has demonstrated their will to live together. If they assume, as Trudeau often did, that "the past is another country," they lose the opportunity to reflect more deeply on the distinctiveness of their country, the values it has come to represent, and the challenges that bedevil it. Canada may never become an easy country to govern, but it can become a less difficult country to understand.

Confederation and Canadian Federalist Theory

Unlike Canadians, Americans do not need to be told about the importance of their history; they revere their past and draw sustenance from it even in times of crisis. In the Gettysburg Address, delivered during the American Civil War, Abraham Lincoln prayed for a "new birth" of freedom so that government by the people would not perish (Current, 1967: 284–85). But Lincoln began his address by invoking the Declaration of Independence and by remembering that the American founders had brought forth a new nation conceived in liberty and dedicated to equality. The paradox of Lincoln is that he was able to utter "the words that remade America" by appealing to the spirit of its most important founding document (Wills, 1992: 120). In contrast, no theme of Canadian history seems better established or more often retold than the failure of the Macdonald Constitution. In textbook accounts, the Confederation Settlement of 1867 is identified almost exclusively with Macdonald and his failed dream of creating a highly centralized state that reduced the provinces to little more than administrative units and that conferred almost imperial powers on Ottawa. Where constitutional scholars diverged is with respect to the reasons for the failure. Some blame the Judicial Committee of the Privy Council (JCPC), and believe that its decentralizing judicial decisions undermined the original understanding of Confederation. Others insist that Macdonald's vision was flawed from the outset because it underestimated the pluralism of Canada, a pluralism that initially manifested itself though a strong provincial rights movement and eventually incorporated Quebec's Quiet Revolution, as well as the demands of new Canadians. If such accounts of Confederation are sound, then Canada's constitutional past is little more than a lesson in failure and, unlike American history, hardly worth remembering.

But there is more to the Constitutional Settlement of 1867 than Macdonald's understanding of it (Gwyn, 2007: 5, 322–33). Nor is the failure of his vision tantamount to the defeat of Confederation. In the debates of 1865, Macdonald announced that he favoured a strong unitary state for Canada because "it would be the best, the cheapest, the most vigorous, and the strongest system of government we could adopt" (Canada, 1865: 29). Macdonald was, after all, a Tory and he had a Tory vision of Canada. As a Tory, he celebrated the British connection, admired the unlimited sovereignty of the British Parliament, and exalted the nation. "The nation," Donald Creighton wrote in his account of Macdonald's idea of union, "transcends the group, the class, or section" (Creighton, 1972: 217). Macdonald dreamed of Canada as "a great nationality commanding the respect of the world, able to hold our own against all opponents." But even Macdonald had to admit that his dream of a Tory Union was "impracticable." It was impractical, he said in the debates of 1865, because it did not meet with the assent of Quebec, which feared that its nationality, language, religion, and code of law might be assailed in a legislative union. And even the Maritime provinces rejected the idea of a unitary state. As a result, Macdonald modified his views and accepted the project of a federal union. However, Macdonald still claimed victory. Canada would be a federal union, but the Parliament of Canada would have all the great powers of legislation as well as the residual power. By so strengthening the central government, he insisted, "we make ... the Confederation one people and one government" (Canada, 1865: 41).

For Macdonald, the important contrast was with the United States and its federal experiment. Federalism is often regarded as an American invention. It is just as often praised for guaranteeing freedom. But in 1865, many Canadians viewed federalism with suspicion, partly because it was regarded as inconsistent with parliamentary institutions and partly because of its association with the American Civil War. In response, Macdonald's bold tact was both to praise the American Constitution and to insist that its framers "had commenced at the wrong end." They had made each state "a sovereignty in itself" and had conferred too limited powers on the general government. By so doing, they made "states rights" the defining feature of their federation and prepared the way for the Civil War. Moreover, the American president, Macdonald added, was merely a party leader and incapable of representing the whole of the American people. In contrast, Canadian Confederation accepted the monarchical principle and elevated the sovereign above the rivalry of political parties. Confederation would also confer the criminal law power on the central government, thereby correcting the American mistake of allowing every state to enact its own criminal code. It would establish lieutenant-governors for the provinces and create a unified judicial system controlled primarily by the central government. Macdonald even boasted that Canadian Confederation so successfully arranged the powers of government that, unlike the American union, it would eliminate "all conflict of jurisdiction and authority." By centralizing power rather than dispersing it, Confederation would create a new dominion of the North, one demonstrably superior to its southern neighbour because it solved the difficult problems of federalism (Canada, 1865: 33).

Such, in outline, was Macdonald's understanding of Confederation. Its importance is difficult to exaggerate. Canada's first century was, in constitutional terms, little more than an engagement with it. Moreover, its eventual failure made a second constitutional beginning almost inevitable. But why did the Macdonald Constitution fail? Macdonald himself provided one answer. Less than two years after Confederation, he complained, "It is difficult to make the local Legislaures understand that their powers are not so great as they were before the Union." He then added: "In fact, the question that convulsed the United States and ended in Civil War, commonly known as the 'States Rights' question, has already made its appearance in Canada" (Rogers, 1933: 17-18). For Macdonald, it was the refusal of the provinces to accept the subordinate position assigned to them that shattered the original understanding of Confederation and, if pressed still further, would spell its failure. Not only did the provinces press their demands, but the JCPC was often sympathetic to them, so much so that in 1937 it struck down much of Prime Minister Bennett's "New Deal" legislation. Critics of the JCPC believe that its decentralizing decisions were largely responsible for the failure of the Macdonald Constitution, a failure that had severe economic and social consequence during the Great Depression of the 1930s. Its decisions also facilitated "province-building," which countered Macdonald's project of nation-building. Writing in 1979, Alan Cairns believed that province-building had produced "big governments" capable of embarking on policies usually reserved for sovereign nations. Province-building, he insisted, had turned the Canadian Constitution into "a lame-duck constitution." It had made Canadian federalism into a game similar to "eleven elephants in a maze" and just as self-defeating (Cairns, 1988: 183, 188).

The defeat of the Macdonald Constitution can also be explained in a way that does not privilege Macdonald's understanding of Confederation. In the debates of 1865, Macdonald's vision of Canada met with skepticism and even derision from critics of Confederation. Christopher Dunkin rejected Macdonald's boast that there would be no conflicts of jurisdiction and authority under Confederation. He not only accused Macdonald of failing to respect the distinction between a legislative and a federal union, but he also predicted the early demise of Confederation. The allocation of powers under the proposed Constitution, he said, would fuel quarrels rather than quell them. The Senate would not perform the functions assigned to it, and lieutenant-governors, if they acted to control provincial legislatures, would provoke open resistance. Nor would judges appointed by the central government earn the confidence of the local legislatures. The provinces, he added, "cannot possibly work harmoniously together long; and so soon as they come into collision … the fabric is at an end." Dunkin was not alone in refusing to "prophecy smooth things" (Canada, 1865: 487, 508, 530). Joseph Perrault warned that although French and English had come to a new world, they had brought their old hostilities with them. He recalled Lord Durham's assimilation proposals and complained that the real object of Confederation was, like Durham's, the obliteration of the French-Canadian nationality. He warned that French-Canadian patriots would defend their cultural heritage and predicted that racial tensions would disrupt Confederation (Canada, 1865: 596, 600, 612). For the critics of Confederation, it was the very pluralism of Canada that rendered Macdonald's constitutional vision untenable. For them, the Macdonald Constitution had failed even before it was adopted.

The story of Canada is a story of failure so long as Confederation is understood as Macdonald's attempt to remedy "states rights" and other errors of American federalism by creating a highly centralized state. But there is more to Confederation. Confederation was also intended as a solution to Canadian problems, and it was hardly achieved by Macdonald alone. "Canadians," wrote Carl J. Friedrich, "… had a very special problem to deal with which found no parallel in the American experience: that was how to arrange a federal system that would satisfy their French-speaking citizens" (Friedrich, 1967: 60–61). In the debates of 1865, Dunkin surmised that "the two differences of language and faith … were the real reasons" for the supposed federal union, whose purpose it was to meet a "probable clashing of races and creeds" (Canada, 1865: 509). If French Canadians provided the "real" reason, the Maritime provinces were the "other" reason, for they too rejected Macdonald's initial plea for a unitary state based on their concern to preserve their local identities and distinct destinies. Not the specter of the American Civil War but the deep pluralism of Canada was the problem that most engaged Canadians in 1867. Moreover, when Confederation is understood as a response to the pluralism of Canada, pride of place belongs not to Macdonald but to his political co-equal, Georges Etienne Cartier. It was Cartier who, despite Macdonald's misgivings, insisted on significant autonomy for Quebec and thereby guaranteed that Quebec and the other provinces would have exclusive and substantial powers of their own. Without him, Confederation would have remained a political dream.

In Cartier's understanding of it, Confederation represented a novel engagement with the pluralism of Canada, one that rejected both assimilation and cultural solitudes and envisaged the creation of a new political nationality (LaSelva, 1996: 39–41, 156–60; Azjenstadt, 2007: 88-109). In response to

Lord Durham and other advocates of assimilation, Cartier insisted that the project of racial unity was not only utopian but impossible, because diversity was "the order of the physical world and of the moral world." He also rejected the creation of cultural solitudes and the belief that cultural peace was impossible without them. On the contrary, he insisted that the racial, cultural, and religious diversity of Canada was a benefit rather than otherwise. "We were of different races," he observed, "not for the purpose of warring against each other, but in order to emulate for the general welfare." Moreover, unlike Macdonald, Cartier was an unequivocal federalist; he believed that federalism, when responsive to cultural and local differences and combined with a suitable scheme of minority rights, made Canada possible. In his view, Canadian federalism did not presuppose the Canadian nation but created it. Confederation, he said, would bring into existence a new Canada and a new nationality, "a political nationality with which neither the national origin, nor the religion of any individual, would interfere" (Canada, 1865: 60). While Macdonald worried about "states rights" and the American Civil War, Cartier reflected on the pluralism of Canada and imagined a new kind of nationality. But Cartier died in 1873, and his understanding of Confederation was nearly forgotten. Macdonald lived until 1891 and struggled to realize his vision of Canada, only to witness the emergence of a strong provincial rights movement as well as the compact theory of Confederation, both of which countered his Constitution and worked to defeat it.

A Second Beginning: Charter Canadians, Multicultural Citizenship, and Trudeau's Canada

In contemporary Canada, almost no one worries much about the fate of the Macdonald Constitution. The past — and certainly Macdonald's idea of Tory Union — almost seems a different country, and the Canadian model is now increasingly identified with multiculturalism and the Charter of Rights (Igartua, 2006: 1, 164-92). That such a change has occurred is due in no small measure to Pierre Elliott Trudeau. For more than a century, Canadians struggled with Macdonald's vision of Confederation. But with the adoption of the Charter of Rights and the other changes of 1982, they increasingly live in a constitutional world reshaped by the liberal universalism of Pierre Trudeau. Trudeau's constitutional world is not Macdonald's. Macdonald was a Tory; Trudeau, a liberal. Macdonald cherished the past and valued the British connection; Trudeau looked to the future and admired the American constitutional system. For Macdonald, sovereignty ideally resided in Parliament; for Trudeau, in the individual. Macdonald feared federalism; Trudeau celebrated the pluralism that federalism brings. Moreover, Trudeau also embraced multiculturalism, and multiculturalism bears no resemblance at all to Macdonald's idea of Tory Union. If Canadians increasingly neglect their past, only part of the reason is the failure of the Macdonald Constitution. Just as important is the extent to which Trudeau's vision of the future has captured the public imagination of Canadians. In Trudeau's constitutional vision, the past *is* another country and the future is a liberal utopia (LaSelva, 2007: 11–18). But Trudeau's constitutional vision has not been embraced by all Canadians, and it has not produced a more harmonious Canada. His vision has replaced Macdonald's, but Canadians struggle with it just as much.

Trudeau is an enigmatic figure, and recent revelations about his youthful political activities have made him even more so (Nemni and Nemni, 2006: 173–74, 266–73). A philosopher turned politician, he initially warned against fundamental constitutional change but then introduced, as prime minister, the most important innovations since Confederation. His motto was "reason over passion," yet he had passionate commitments to a reconstructed federalism, to a charter of human rights, and to Canada itself. In his earlier years, he rejected patriotism only to embrace it when he felt in his bones the vastness of his country. He regarded the Canadian mosaic as superior to the American melting pot and insisted that no such thing as a model or ideal Canadian existed. For him, multiculturalism made Canada "a very special place" because it offered every Canadian "the opportunity to fulfil his own cultural instincts and to share those from other sources" (Trudeau, 1972: 32). Moreover, he regarded Canadian federalism as an experiment of major proportions. If French and English cooperated to create a truly pluralistic state, Canada could serve as an example for the new Asian and African states on "how to govern their polyethnic populations with ... justice and liberty." Such a Canada, he insisted, would have the best reason possible for rejecting "the lure of annexation to the United States" (Trudeau, 1968a: 178–79). Trudeau's commitment was to a Canada that differed fundamentally from the United States; yet he also believed that Canada required a fully entrenched Charter of Rights and Freedoms that, like the American Bill of Rights, secured the "primacy of the individual" and the "sovereignty of the people." For Trudeau, such a Charter would secure "inalienable rights" and express the "purest liberalism." It would provide "a new beginning for the Canadian nation" and bring into existence a Canada with which all Canadians could identify (Trudeau, 1990: 363).

Trudeau attached the utmost importance to his proposed Charter and pinned virtually all his hopes for Canada on it. Even before he entered politics, he strongly favoured the adoption of a Charter of Rights while warning Canadians that other constitutional changes, such as modification of the division of powers or a reformed Senate, were either not pressing or too perilous to undertake. When he became minister of justice, he called on both Ottawa and the provinces to restrict their powers in favour of the basic human values of all Canadians — political, legal, egalitarian, linguistic. With such a constitutional innovation, he said, "we will be testing — and, hopefully establishing — the unity of Canada" (Trudeau, 1968a: 54). Shortly after becoming prime minister, he renewed his call for an entrenched Charter and insisted that constitutional reform should take as its starting point the rights of the people rather than the rights of government. The principal objective of constitutional reform, he said, should be to "construct a Canada in which the prime strength is … in the people; a country which is knit [together] by persons confident of their individual rights wherever they might live; a Canada with which the people may identify" (Trudeau, 1972: 91, 94). After the Charter was adopted but well before such incidents as the Maher Arar terrorism case exposed additional concerns about the protection of rights in Canada, Trudeau reminded Canadians of its crucial importance: it embodied a set of common values and ensured that all Canadians had the same rights. "All Canadians," he wrote, "are equal, and that equality flows from the Charter" (Johnston 1990: 34). In his *Memoirs* (1993), Trudeau even surmised that the adoption of the Charter had solved the long-standing problem of the Canadian identity.

In Trudeau's conception of it, the Charter embodies common values and guarantees the equality of Canadians thereby expressing the identity of Canada and securing its unity. But the fundamental fact about Canada is its many-sided pluralism, and Trudeau knew as much. Why else did he sponsor official multiculturalism or remind Canadians, in a speech on Louis Riel, that a democracy is ultimately judged by the way the majority treats the minority. Trudeau went further still. "Canada's population distribution," he noted as early as 1971, "has now become so balanced as to deny any one racial or linguistic component an absolute majority. Every single person in Canada is now a member of a minority group" (Trudeau, 1972: 32). What, then, is to be done about minority rights? And how are minority rights to be reconciled with the equality of Canadians? Trudeau provided an answer to these questions, and his answer is rooted in his commitment to liberalism. Trudeau said that because Canada was a mosaic rather than a melting pot, the Charter protected both individual rights and minority rights. In protecting the rights of minorities, however, the Charter sought, whenever possible and even in the case of the official languages, "to define rights exclusively as belonging to a person rather than a collectivity." Trudeau went on to say: "the spirit and substance of the Charter is to protect the individual against tyranny — not only that of the state but also any other to which the individual may be subjected by virtue of his belonging to a minority group" (Trudeau, 1990: 365). Put in another way, the Charter treats all Canadians equally because it does not privilege minority rights but treats them as derivative of individual rights. Had Trudeau's liberalism solved the problem of minority rights and envisioned a Canada with which all Canadians could identify?

This is a difficult question. The answer can be partly gleaned from Trudeau's opposition to the Meech Lake Constitutional Accord, which had as its basic purpose the recognition of Quebec as a distinct society within Canada. Such recognition was deemed necessary partly because the government of Quebec regarded the Charter as unduly restrictive of its autonomy. The Accord was almost ratified but eventually failed. In rejecting it, Trudeau both defended the Charter and reformulated his long-standing opposition to special status for Quebec. According to Trudeau, the Meech Lake Accord would require Canadians to "Say Goodbye to the Dream of One Canada." "For Canadians who dreamed of the Charter as a new beginning for Canada," he wrote, "… where citizenship [is based on] commonly shared values, there is to be nothing left but tears" (Johnston 1990: 10). He felt that the spirit of the Meech Lake Accord conflicted with the spirit of the Charter and that special status for Quebec *of any kind* destroyed the dream of one Canada (Cook, 2006: 151–62). But such a position encounters a host of difficulties, not the least of which is the fact that the Confederation Settlement of 1867 accommodated Quebec and even used Quebec's distinctiveness to shape the Canadian federation. If Trudeau's vision of the Charter cannot accommodate Quebec, then his conception of minority rights is problematic: Trudeau's Canada is not a Canada with which all Canadians can identify.

Trudeau's vision of Canada contains a number of unsettling ironies. His most basic objective was to de-legitimate Québécois separatism by creating a truly pluralistic Canada with which Quebecers and other Canadians could identify. The formula he initially embraced was "multiculturalism within a bilingual framework" (Trudeau, 1985 [1971]: 350). What his Charter adds to the formula is the theme of equality: Canadians are equal citizens in a multicultural society that exists within a bilingual framework. If the revised formula captures Trudeau's vision of Canada, then the first irony is that it does nothing at all to satisfy the historic demand of Quebec, namely, the recognition of Quebec's distinctiveness so that the French-Canadian homeland can flourish within Canada (Laforest, 2001: 304–05). And even if Canada is conceived without Quebec, the formula remains untenable because it does not adequately accommodate Aboriginal Canadians. In the *Statement on Indian Policy*, the Trudeau government had asked Aboriginal peoples to move off their reserves and become full members of Canada's multicultural society. They were told that different status was "a blind alley" (Government of Canada, 1969: 5, 9; Trudeau, 1972: 13–15). But Aboriginal peoples rejected this proposal. As Canada's First Nations with historic entitlements to self-government, they struggled to have their rights recognized first by the courts and then again in sections 25 and 35 of the Constitution Act, 1982. Later, the Government of Canada also apologized to Aboriginal peoples for the treatment they received in residential schools and initiated a Truth and Reconciliation Commission. Taken together, these facts created the second irony for Trudeau's vision of Canada. Aboriginal peoples were accommodated within Canada only when their claim to special status was recognized; but if their claim was (as it should have been) recognized, then Quebec's claim to distinct status is and should be no less imperative and no less capable of explicit recognition and accommodation in the text of the Constitution.

Trudeau said that the Charter protects minority rights; it would be more accurate to say that it brings minorities into conflict and thereby challenges the dream of one Canada (Cairns, 1991: 108). The Charter does not protect the right of French Canadians to a homeland within Canada or the right of Aboriginal Canadians to self-government. But it does protect the rights of "Charter Canadians" (women, gays, lesbians, the disabled) and multicultural citizens (new immigrants). In *The Charter Revolution and the Court Party*, Morton and Knopff argue that the Charter has transformed the Canadian constitutional system by transferring power from legislatures to courts. Moreover, although Trudeau often portrayed the Charter as a victory for minority rights over majority tyranny, they insist that the Charter revolution is not about tyranny at all. Canada, they write, would remain a liberal democracy "regardless of the outcome of such Charter issues as whether Sikhs in the RCMP are allowed to wear turbans or the legal definition of spouse is read to include homosexuals" (Morton and Knopff, 2000: 36). For them, the most sinister aspect of Charter litigation is that it enables special interest groups to advance their agendas under the guise of inalienable rights and at the expense of democratic politics. Will Kymlicka takes a more benign view. In *Multicultural Citizenship*, he argues that the recognition of multicultural or polyethnic rights is nothing less than a requirement of liberal justice. Such minority rights deserve recognition, he insists, partly because individual choices are made in a cultural context and partly because to deny them is to unfairly privilege the dominant culture. But Kymlicka stops short of saying that the recognition of multicultural or polyethnic rights has made Canada an easier country to understand or govern. In fact, he believes that Canadians lack a theory of what holds their country together (Kymlicka, 1995: 76, 109, 192). In a later essay, Kymlicka reflected again on Canada and insisted that the Canadian model of pluralism should be judged a success, at least when compared to European nations where ethnic and cultural pluralism has frequently resulted in reactionary policies, secession, and even civil war (Kymlicka, 2007: 69, 79–81).

As for Trudeau, he became less sanguine about Canada's future, as can be seen from his reflections on the Charlottetown Constitutional Accord of 1992, which provided him with a final opportunity to discuss minority rights and to explain his vision of Canada. If the Charter is, as he called it, the "people's package," then the Charlottetown Accord was the "Canada round." Its purpose was to recognize the rights of Charter Canadians and multicultural citizens alongside the right of Aboriginal peoples to self-government and Quebec's status as a distinct society. The Accord also contained provisions for the reform of central institutions such as an elected Senate, outlined a comprehensive social and economic union for the country, and modified aspects of the division of powers as well as the amending formula. When Canadians voted on the Accord, they rejected it, and Trudeau believed that they made the only choice possible. In a speech delivered before its defeat, Trudeau described the Accord as "A Mess That Deserves a Big 'NO.'" He insisted that the Accord was nothing less than a recipe for dictatorship and a prelude to civil war because it undermined equality, established a hierarchy among citizens, and privileged collective rights over individual rights. Moreover, he reminded Canadians that his own constitutional vision was based on inalienable rights and he reiterated his admiration for the American Constitution. He urged Canadians to read Madison's Number 10 of the *Federalist Papers*, informed them that the American Supreme Court had been established to defend individual rights, and reminded them that the American system had "worked out well" (Trudeau, 1992: 57–58, 44, 47–48). Trudeau regarded the Charlottetown Accord as such a mess that it almost drove him to abandon the Canadian mosaic and embrace the American model.

The Will to Live Together:
Pluralism in Canada and the United States

What followed the defeat of the Charlottetown Accord was a near successful sovereignty referendum in Quebec and then a landmark reference case in the Supreme Court on the secession question and the break-up of Canada. The Secession Reference is now part of Canadian constitutional history, but it also has an enduring and practical relevance because of the fundamental constitutional principles that the Supreme Court announced in it. In the Secession Reference, the most immediate and pressing question was whether or not Quebec had a unilateral right of secession under the Canadian Constitution. The Supreme Court ruled that Quebec had no such right, but it also insisted on the duty of all concerned parties to negotiate constitutional change, including the possible dissolution of Canada. The federalism principle, together with the democratic principle, the Court held, "dictates that the clear repudiation of the existing constitutional order … would give rise to a reciprocal obligation on all parties to Confederation to negotiate constitutional changes." The Court's ruling is important, partly because it denies that secession is purely a political matter and brings it within the pale of the Constitution. It is also important for a different reason. In order to arrive at its decision, the Court had to analyze the Canadian Constitution, but instead of adopting a narrow or legalistic approach, it attempted to uncover nothing less than the Constitution's "internal architecture" and its fundamental principles. In fact, the Court identified four such principles: federalism, democracy, constitutionalism and the rule of law, and respect for minorities. The Court insisted that these four principles of Canadian constitutionalism were as new as the Charter and as old as Confederation (Supreme Court of Canada, 1998: 424, 410, 403). The Court's opinion is much more than a discussion of the secession question. It is also an innovative exploration of the Canadian Constitution and the pluralism of Canada.

In the Secession Reference, the Court quietly corrected several widespread fallacies of Canadian constitutionalism and attempted to replace them with sounder positions. The first fallacy did not originate with Trudeau but is best exemplified by him. Trudeau never tired of insisting that the Charter provided a new beginning for the Canadian people. Others have described Canada before the advent of the Charter as a "lost constitutional world" (Cairns, 1995: 97). The Court did not deny the importance of the Charter or underestimate the changes that had come with it. It recognized that the Charter significantly restricted Parliament and the provincial legislatures while considerably enhancing the authority of the judicial branch. But it also insisted that, with respect to minority rights, the Charter represented a continuance of Canada's constitutional past rather than a break with it. "Although Canada's record of upholding the rights of minorities is not a spotless one," the Court wrote, "that goal is one towards which Canadians have been striving since Confederation, and the process has not been without successes." The Court insisted that even the "recent and arduous" achievement of Aboriginal rights was "consistent with this long tradition of respect for minorities, which is at least as old as Canada itself" (Supreme Court of Canada, 1998: 422). In the opinion of the Court, the goal of protecting minority rights did not suddenly emerge with the adoption of the Charter but was an integral part of the Confederation Settlement of 1867 and a defining feature of the Canadian identity.

The second fallacy corrected by the Court also relates to Confederation and, in particular, the interpretation of it as the Macdonald Constitution. When the focus is on Macdonald, the emphasis is on the unitary features of the Canadian Constitution and the dream of a Tory Union. What is remembered is the desire of the Fathers of Confederation to create a constitution similar in principle to that of the United Kingdom, and it is almost forgotten that, in the very same preamble to the Constitution, they first expressed their desire to be federally united. Canada becomes lost in the British connection, and the Canadian identity becomes almost impossible to comprehend. Such has been the influence of Macdonald. The Court did not so much deny Macdonald's influence as largely ignore it and drew attention instead to the importance of Cartier and his goal of creating a Canadian federal state that solved Canadian problems. The Court quoted at length Cartier's belief that Canadians had come together to contribute to the common welfare and to create a new political nationality with which neither the national origins nor the religion of any individual would interfere. Far from regarding federalism as an aberrant or incidental feature of the Canadian Constitution, the Court insisted that "the significance of the adoption of a federal form of government cannot be exaggerated." Federalism was the "lodestar" of the Constitution. The federal-provincial division of powers was "a legal recognition of the diversity that existed among the initial members of Confederation, and manifested a concern to accommodate that diversity within a single nation" (Supreme Court of Canada, 1998: 405, 412, 407).

By thus focusing on Cartier's vision of Canada, the Court reinterpreted Confederation and revealed its significance as the foundational event of Canadian constitutionalism and the defining moment in the evolution of Canadian pluralism. When so interpreted, Confederation is not a lost constitutional world, nor is it part of a past that is another country. Macdonald's idea of a Tory Union may be a failed constitutional experiment, but Cartier's vision of Canada is one that has yet to be achieved or even fully understood. What seems clear enough, though, is that Cartier's vision of Confederation differed from Macdonald's and also differed from the American understanding of constitutional pluralism. At Canada's founding, the leading exponent of constitutional pluralism was Cartier. In the United States, it was James Madison. He is commonly regarded as the Father of the American Constitution and also the author of the theory of the compound republic that underpins it. Less accurately referred to as the theory of checks and balances, the kernel of Madisonian pluralism is aptly stated in his own summary of it: "In the compound republic of America, the power surrendered by the people is first divided between two distinct governments, and then the portion allotted to each subdivided among distinct and separate departments." Madison then added, "Hence a double security arises to the rights of the people. The different governments will control each other, at the same time that each will be controlled by itself" (Hamilton, Madison, and Jay, 1961: 323). Writing almost 80 years before Cartier, Madison outlined a theory of pluralism that did for the United States what Cartier would attempt to do for Canada.

But Madison's theory is not Cartier's and the United States is not Canada. For Americans of the founding generation, the most pressing problem was how to guarantee republican liberty while garnering the military and economic benefits of a large commercial empire. Moreover, Americans appeared to be caught in a dilemma. They could either remain as they were after their War of Independence in a weak and ineffectual confederal system, incapable of securing economic prosperity and military defence, or they could adopt a unified and strong government that secured their prosperity without protecting their liberty. Based on their experience as colonies, they had come to associate empire with tyranny and small republics with self-government. Such was their predicament until Madison's famous theory of the compound republic challenged and reversed some of their most cherished assumptions. In the *Federalist Papers*, Madison argued that small republics, far from protecting liberty, were hothouses of oppression and that a compound republic was in fact the best guarantee of liberty. At the centre of his ingenious theory was the idea of a faction and his belief that a single self-interested faction could oppress a small community but not a large society composed of a multiplicity of factions. If factions were the enemies of liberty, then the solution, so Madison reasoned, was to dilute their strength by multiplying their numbers in an extended territory and then to render them incapable of oppression by dividing and re-dividing the powers of government. "In the extent and proper structure of the Union," Madison concluded, "we behold a republican remedy for the diseases most incident to republican government" (Hamilton, Madison, and Jay, 1961: 84; Adair, 1998: 132–51).

Madison's theory was not without its critics. Anti-federalists complained that it conferred too many powers on the central government. They defended local government and states' rights, and they demanded a Bill of Rights to curb any further centralization of power. But not even anti-federalists denied in 1787 that Americans formed one people (Storing, 1981: 24). Both federalists and anti-federalists took the American nation for granted and debated the kind of government that best preserves liberty. Therein rests the crucial difference between the United States and Canada. With the exception of the Civil War and the slavery issue that fuelled it, Americans have never questioned that they belong to the same nation (LaSelva, 1999: 771). Canada is different, because Canadians have never been able to take their nationhood for granted in this way. "The disadvantage of a synthetic state like ours," wrote John Holmes about Canada in the mid-1960s, "is that it lacks the visceral drive to achievement" and engenders "anxiety about national survival [based on] fear of our own failure of will." He then added that the "central problem" for Canada "is to find a reason for the country's existence" (Holmes, 1966: 204).

Unlike Canadians, Americans have almost no difficulty at all understanding the reason for the existence of their country. There is an American civil religion and an American constitutional faith, and the American people form one nation dedicated to liberty. "Faith in America," wrote an influential Chief Justice of the United States, "confirms the hope that we shall preserve for our children all that our fathers ... secured for us; that our heritage of liberty will not dwindle, but increase" (Kammen, 2001: 12–13). Canadians also value liberty, but Canada was not conceived in a quest to preserve liberty or in a revolution against tyranny. If not liberty, what then does faith in Canada confirm? For Cartier, it meant that Canadians could form one country and live under a common constitution provided they also made adequate provision for their linguistic, ethnic, and regional differences. Such a belief may seem uninspiring, until it is recalled that Lord Durham could see in Canada nothing but a war of races and that Christopher Dunkin forecast the early dissolution of Confederation based on the inability of the provinces to cooperate for very long. More recently, Canadian federalism has been compared to two scorpions in a bottle and 11 elephants in a maze. But Cartier had a different vision of federalism and Canada. For him, the existence of Canada represented the will of Canadians to live together under a common political nationality that presupposed mutual obligations and collective goals but did not require them to submerge their allegiances and identities in a monolithic and all-embracing nationalism. Canadian federalism, with its scheme of minority rights, allowed multiple loyalties and multiple identities to flourish; it thereby enabled Canadians both to live together and to live apart in one country.

Conclusion: Understanding Canada

To understand Canada it is necessary to comprehend both the challenges that confront Canadians and the values that have grounded the Canadian experiment at least since Confederation and possibly, though very tentatively, as early as the Royal Proclamation of 1763 or the Quebec Act of 1774. For Canadians, the most basic challenge is to come to terms with their own diversity. Writing in 1946, W.L. Morton insisted that "the Canadian state cannot be devoted to absolute nationalism [because] the two nationalities and the four sections [regions] of Canada forbid it" (Morton, 1967: 49). Canada is still composed of the two nationalities and the four (or more) regions described by Morton, but it now contains self-governing territories as well as provinces, multicultural citizens, Charter Canadians, and French- and

English-speaking Canadians, as well as Aboriginal and Québécois nationalists. For some Canadians, this explosion of pluralism has called the existence of Canada into question; at the very least, it has made Canada an even more difficult country to govern. Other Canadians seek to re-imagine Canada. They imagine a three-nations Canada composed of English Canada, Quebec, and Aboriginal peoples. Or, believing that strong fences make for good neighbours, they have called for the creation of a more autonomous Quebec, as well as sovereign Aboriginal nations within a highly decentralized Canada. There are also those who concentrate on articulating a theory of multicultural justice and redesigning the Canadian state to meet its quite different requirements. Reflecting on the explosion of pluralism, Robert Fulford has called Canada a post-modern dominion and has insisted that it can be best understood as a post-modern state. The key to post-modernism, he suggests, is the absence of a master narrative and the questioning of any notion of a coherent, stable, autonomous identity (Fulford, 1993: 118). "What," he asks, "could be more Canadian than that?"

But Canada is not merely an ever-changing association of particularisms. Its very existence presupposes values that are seldom made explicit or fully understood. In *Lament for a Nation*, George Grant insisted that Canada was a country without a future because its foundational values conflicted with modernity. "To be a Canadian," he said, "... was to build a more ordered and stable society than the liberal experiment in the United States." He identified Canada with the values of British conservatism; he also insisted that Canada could not survive the encounter with technological progress and the American dream. For Grant, modernity meant the disappearance of local cultures and the emergence of a homogeneous universal state centred on the American empire (Grant, 1970: 4, x, 54). Four decades after Grant wrote his book, a world state has not appeared, local cultures flourish, and Canada has not been absorbed into the United States. Grant did not simply fail to predict the future, he also misunderstood Canada's past and its foundational values. He identified Canada with Macdonald's idea of a Tory Union, yet it was Cartier's rejection of cultural assimilation and his faith in a new kind of political nationality that grounded the Canadian experiment (Smiley, 1967). Macdonald identified Canada with order and stability; Cartier viewed it in terms of mutual recognition, the cooperative virtues, and the many faces of amity or fraternity. Cartier's vision is deeply rooted in Canada's past, but it also speaks to the complex issues of mutual recognition that confront Canadians as they attempt to come to terms with the Aboriginal Truth and Reconciliation Commission, as well as new experiments in Aboriginal self-government, with greater demands for provincial autonomy and decentralized federalism, and with the multicultural anxiety that non-Western ways of life can create, not only for Quebec but for the rest of Canada. Canada may yet disappear if Canadians fail to overcome the limitations inherent in Trudeau's constitutional vision, or if they experience a failure of political will in the face of new challenges of diversity. "Other people besides Canadians," Michael Ignatieff writes, "should be concerned if Canada dies. If federalism can't work in my Canada, it probably can't work anywhere" (Ignatieff, 1993: 147). In a post-modern world increasingly characterized by competing nationalisms and multicultural identities, the fate of Canada concerns more than just Canadians.

References and Suggested Readings

Adair, Douglass. 1998. *Fame and the Founding Fathers*. Indianapolis: Liberty Fund.

Adam, Marc-Antoine. 2007. "Federalism and the Spending Power: Section 94 to the Rescue." *Policy Options* (March): 30–34.

Ajzenstat, Janet. 2007. *The Canadian Founding: John Locke and Parliament*. Montreal: McGill-Queen's University Press.

Bailyn, Bernard. 1967. *The Ideological Origins of the American Revolution*. Cambridge, MA: Harvard University Press.

Berger, Carl. 1966. "The True North Strong and Free." In Peter Russell, ed., *Nationalism in Canada*. Toronto: McGraw-Hill, 1966. 3–26.

Bibby, Reginald W. 1990. *Mosaic Madness*. Toronto: Stoddart.

Bissoondath, Neil. 1994. *Selling Illusions: The Cult of Multiculturalism in Canada*. Toronto: Penguin.

Cairns, Alan C. 1988. "The Other Crisis of Canadian Federalism." In Alan C. Cairns, *Constitution, Government, and Society in Canada*. Toronto: McClelland and Stewart. 171–91.

Cairns, Alan C. 1991. "Citizens (Outsiders) and Governments (Insiders) in Constitution-Making: The Case of Meech Lake." In Alan C. Cairns, *Disruptions*. Toronto: McClelland and Stewart. 108–38.

Cairns, Alan C. 1995. "The Constitutional World We Have Lost." In Alan C. Cairns, *Reconfigurations*. Toronto: McClelland and Stewart. 97–118.

Cairns, Alan C. 1997. *Looking into the Abyss*. Ottawa: C.D. Howe Institute.

Canada. 1865. *Parliamentary Debates on the Subject of the Confederation of British North American Provinces*. Quebec: Hunter, Rose. Photographically reproduced. Ottawa: King's Printer, 1951.

Cook, Ramsay. 1969. *Provincial Autonomy, Minority Rights, and the Compact Theory, 1867–1921*. Ottawa: Information Canada.

Cook, Ramsay. 2006. *The Teeth of Time: Remembering Pierre Elliott Trudeau*. Montreal: McGill-Queen's University Press.

Cooper, John Irwin. 1942. "The Political Ideas of George Etienne Cartier." *Canadian Historical Review* 23: 286–94.

Creighton, Donald. 1972. *Towards the Discovery of Canada*. Toronto: Macmillan.

Current, Richard N., Ed. 1967. *The Political Thought of Abraham Lincoln*. Indianapolis: Bobbs-Merrill.

Friedrich, Carl J. 1967. *The Impact of American Constitutionalism Abroad*. Boston: Boston University Press.

Fulford, Robert. 1993. "A Post-Modern Dominion: The Changing Nature of Canadian Citizenship." In William A. Kaplan, ed., *Belonging*. Montreal: McGill-Queen's University Press. 104–19.

Government of Canada. 1969. *Statement on Indian Policy, 1969*. Ottawa: Queen's Printer.

Granatstein, J.L. 1998. *Who Killed Canadian History?* Toronto: Harper Collins.

Grant, George. 1970. *Lament for a Nation: The Defeat of Canadian Nationalism*. Toronto: McClelland and Stewart.

Gwyn, Richard. 2007. *John A.: The Man Who Made Us*. Vol. 1: *The Life and Times of John A. Macdonald, 1815–1867*. Toronto: Random House Canada.

Hamilton, Alexander, James Madison, and John Jay. 1961. *The Federalist Papers*. Ed. C. Rossiter. New York: Mentor Books.

Holmes, John. 1966. "Nationalism in Canadian Foreign Policy." In Peter Russell, ed., *Nationalism in Canada*. Toronto: McGraw-Hill. 203–20.

Horowitz, Gad. 1985. "Mosaics and Identity." In H.D. Forbes, ed., *Canadian Political Thought*. Toronto: Oxford University Press. 359–64.

Igartua, Jose E. 2006. *The Other Quiet Revolution: National Identities in English Canada, 1945–71*. Vancouver: University of British Columbia Press.

Ignatieff, Michael. 1993. *Blood and Belonging: Journeys into the New Nationalism*. Toronto: Penguin.

Ignatieff, Michael. 2000. *The Rights Revolution*. Toronto: Anansi.

Johnston, Donald, Ed. 1990. *Pierre Trudeau Speaks Out on Meech Lake*. Toronto: General Paperbacks.

Kammen, Michael. 2001. *Spheres of Liberty: Changing Perceptions of Liberty in American Culture*. Jackson: University of Mississippi Press.

Kymlicka, Will. 1995. *Multicultural Citizenship*. Oxford: Clarendon Press.

Kymlicka, Will. 2007. "The Canadian Model of Multiculturalism in a Comparative Perspective." In Stephen Tierney, ed., *Multiculturalism and the Canadian Constitution*. Vancouver: University of British Columbia Press. 61–90.

Laforest, Guy. 1995. *Trudeau and the End of a Canadian Dream*. Montreal: McGill-Queen's University Press.

Laforest, Guy. 2001. "The True Nature of Sovereignty." In Ronald Beiner and Wayne Norman, eds., *Canadian Political Philosophy*. Don Mills: Oxford University Press. 298–310.

LaSelva, Samuel V. 1996. *The Moral Foundations of Canadian Federalism: Paradoxes, Achievements, and Tragedies of Nationhood*. Montreal: McGill-Queen's University Press.

LaSelva, Samuel V. 1999. "Divided Houses: Secession and Constitutional Faith in Canada and the United States." *Vermont Law Review* 23: 771–92.

LaSelva, Samuel V. 2007. "To Begin the World Anew: Pierre Trudeau's Dream and George Grant's Canada." *Supreme Court Law Review* 36 (2D): 1–30.

Levinson, Sanford. 1988. *Constitutional Faith*. Princeton: Princeton University Press.

McPherson, James M. 1991. *Abraham Lincoln and the Second American Revolution*. New York: Oxford University Press.

Morton, W.L. 1967. "Clio in Canada: The Interpretation of Canadian History." In Carl Berger, ed., *Approaches to Canadian History*. Toronto: University of Toronto Press. 42–49.

Morton, F.L., and Rainer Knopff. 2000. *The Charter Revolution and the Court Party*. Peterborough: Broadview Press.

Nemni, Max, and Monique Nemni. 2006. *Young Trudeau: Son of Quebec, Father of Canada, 1919–1944*. Toronto: McClelland and Stewart.

Petter, Andrew. 1989. "Federalism and the Myth of the Spending Power." *Canadian Bar Review* 68: 448–79.

Rogers, Norman McL. 1933. "The Genesis of Provincial Rights." *Canadian Historical Review* 14: 9–23.

Smiley, Donald V. 1967. *The Canadian Political Nationality*. Toronto: Methuen.

Storing, Herbert J. 1981. *What the Anti-Federalists Were For*. Chicago: University of Chicago Press.

Supreme Court of Canada. 1998. *Reference re Secession of Quebec* 161 DLR. (4th) 385.

Sweeney, Alastair. 1976. *George-Etienne Cartier*. Toronto: McClelland and Stewart.

Taylor, Charles. 1993. *Reconciling the Solitudes: Essays on Canadian Federalism and Nationalism*. Montreal: McGill-Queen's University Press.

Trudeau, Pierre Elliott. 1968a. *Federalism and the French Canadians*. Toronto: Macmillan.

Trudeau, Pierre Elliott. 1968b. *A Canadian Charter of Human Rights*. Ottawa: Queen's Printer.

Trudeau, Pierre Elliott. 1972. *Conversation with Canadians*. Toronto: University of Toronto Press.

Trudeau, Pierre Elliott. 1985 [1971]. "Statement on Multiculturalism." In H.D. Forbes, ed., *Canadian Political Thought*. Toronto: Oxford University Press. 349–51.

Trudeau, Pierre Elliott. 1990. "The Values of a Just Society." In Thomas S. Axworthy and Pierre Elliott Trudeau, eds., *Towards a Just Society*. Markham: Viking. 357–85.

Trudeau, Pierre Elliott. 1992. *A Mess That Deserves a Big NO*. Toronto: Robert Davies.

Trudeau, Pierre Elliott. 1993. *Memoirs*. Toronto: McClelland and Stewart.

Waite, Peter. 1962. *The Life and Times of Confederation*. Toronto: University of Toronto Press.

Wills, Garry. 1992. *Lincoln at Gettysburg: The Words that Remade America*. New York: Simon & Schuster.

two

Citizenship, Communities, and Identity in Canada

WILL KYMLICKA

Much of the Canadian political system is founded on the premise that, in the words of the Supreme Court, the "accommodation of difference is the essence of true equality."[1] While Canadian history contains its share of intolerance, prejudice, and oppression, it also contains many attempts to find new and creative mechanisms for accommodating difference. As a result, Canada has developed a distinctive conception of the relationship between citizenship and identity.

As in all other liberal democracies, one of the major mechanisms for accommodating difference in Canada is the protection of the civil and political rights of individuals, such as those listed in sections 2–15 of the Canadian Charter of Rights and Freedoms. Freedom of association, religion, speech, mobility, and political organization enable individuals to form and maintain the various groups and associations that constitute civil society, to adapt these groups to changing circumstances, and to promote their views and interests to the wider population. The protection afforded by these common rights of citizenship is sufficient for many of the legitimate forms of diversity in society.

However, it is widely accepted in Canada that some forms of difference can only be accommodated through special legal measures, above and beyond the common rights of citizenship. Some forms of group difference can only be accommodated if their members have what Iris Marion Young calls "differentiated citizenship" (Young, 1989). These special measures for accommodating difference are the most distinctive, and also the most controversial, aspect of the Canadian conception of citizenship identity.

Forms of Group Difference in Canada

Historically, the major challenge in Canada has been the accommodation of ethnocultural difference. There are three forms of ethnocultural pluralism in Canada that need to be distinguished.

---

1. *Andrews v. Law Society of British Columbia* (1989) 10 C.H.R.R. D/5719 (S.C.C.).

First, Canada is a New World *settler* state — that is, it was constructed through the European colonization and settlement of territories historically occupied by Indigenous peoples. In this respect, it is like the other British settler states — Australia, New Zealand, and the United States — or the Spanish settler states of Latin America. Although the nature of European colonization and settlement varies enormously in these different countries, the rights of Indigenous peoples (and their relationship to the settler society built on their traditional territories) remains an issue in all of them, including questions about their land rights, treaty rights, customary law, and rights to self-government.[2]

Canada differs from these other European settler states, however, in that it was colonized and settled by two different European powers — Britain and France — who fought for supremacy over the territory of what is now Canada. While the British eventually won this struggle, and thereby incorporated "New France" into "British North America," the reality was that there were two distinct settler societies within Canada — one French, located primarily in Quebec, and one British — each with their own languages, laws, and institutions. As a result, when Canada became an independent state in 1867, it recognized "the French fact" through official bilingualism and through provincial autonomy for Quebec. In this respect, unlike other New World settler states, Canada is sometimes said to be a "bi-national" settler state, constructed through the joining together of its "two founding peoples" — the French and British settler societies.

Of course, to say that the French and British were "founding peoples" ignores the role of Indigenous peoples, on whose territory this new country was built and whose activities and agreements were vital to the building of Canada. They clearly are the "first peoples" of the country. As a result, it is more common today, and more accurate, to say that Canada is a *multination* state rather than a bi-national state. Its historical development has involved the federation of three distinct peoples or nations (British, French, and Aboriginal peoples).[3] These groups are "nations" in the sociological sense of being historical communities, institutionally complete, occupying a given territory or homeland, and sharing a distinct language and history. Since Canada contains more than one nation, it is not a nation-state but a multination state, and the

---

2. For Canada in comparative perspective with other settler states, see Pearson, 2001; Havemann, 1999.
3. It is misleading to describe Aboriginal peoples as a single nation, since the term "Aboriginal" covers three categories — Indian, Inuit, and Métis — and the term "Indian" itself is a legal fiction, behind which there are numerous distinct Aboriginal nations with their own histories and separate community identities.

Québécois[4] and Aboriginal communities form "substate nations" or "national minorities." The desire of these groups to be seen as "nations" is reflected in the names they have adopted. For example, the provincial legislature in Quebec is called the "National Assembly"; the major organization of Status Indians is known as the "Assembly of First Nations."[5]

The original incorporation of these national minorities into the Canadian political community was largely involuntary. Aboriginal homelands were overrun by French settlers, who were then conquered by the British. If a different balance of power had existed, it is possible that Aboriginal peoples and French Canadians would have retained their original sovereignty, rather than being incorporated into the larger Canadian federation. And it is still possible that Quebec will leave the federation. However, the historical preference of these national minorities has not been to secede but to renegotiate the terms of federation so as to increase their autonomy within it.

Many of the pivotal moments in Canadian political history have centred on these attempts to renegotiate the terms of federation between British, French, and Aboriginal peoples. The most recent effort at renegotiation ended in October 1992, when the Charlottetown Accord was defeated in both a pan-Canadian referendum and a separate Quebec referendum. This Accord (discussed below) would have entrenched an "inherent right of self-government" for Aboriginal peoples and accorded Quebec a special status as "the only society with a majority French language and culture in Canada and in North America."

In addition to being a multination state, Canada is also a *polyethnic* state. Canada, like the United States, accepts large numbers of individuals and families from other cultures as immigrants. They are expected to integrate into the public institutions of either the francophone or anglophone societies; for example, they must learn either French or English (Canada's two official languages) to acquire citizenship. Prior to the 1960s, they were also expected to shed their distinctive heritage and assimilate almost entirely to existing cultural norms. The ideal was that immigrants would become, over time, indistinguishable from native-born Canadians in their speech, dress, and lifestyle more generally. However, in the early 1970s, under pressure from immigrant groups, the Canadian government rejected the assimilationist

---

4. Throughout this paper, I use "Québécois" to refer to the French-speaking majority in the province of Quebec. There are francophones outside Quebec, and the French nation in Canada was not always identified so closely with the province of Quebec. For the change in self-identity from *la nation Canadienne-Française* to *Québécois*, see McRoberts, 1997.

5. On the adoption of the language of nationhood by Aboriginal groups, see Jenson, 1993 and Cairns, 2000.

model of immigration and adopted instead a more tolerant policy (known as the policy of "multiculturalism"), which allows and supports immigrants to maintain various aspects of their ethnic heritage. Immigrants are free to maintain some of their old customs regarding food, dress, recreation, and religion and to associate with each other to maintain these practices. This is no longer seen as unpatriotic or "un-Canadian."

But such groups are not "nations" and do not occupy homelands within Canada. Their distinctiveness is manifested primarily in their private and social lives and does not preclude their institutional integration. They still participate within either anglophone or francophone institutions, and they speak at least one of the official languages in public life. Because of extensive immigration of this sort, Canada has a number of "ethnic groups" as loosely aggregated subcultures within both the English- and French-speaking societies.

So Canada is both multinational (as a result of colonization, conquest, and confederation), and polyethnic (as a result of immigration). Those labels are less popular than the term "multicultural." But that term can be confusing, precisely because it is ambiguous between multinational and polyethnic. Indeed, this ambiguity has led to unwarranted criticism of Canada's "multiculturalism policy," the term the federal government uses for its post-1971 policy of promoting accommodation rather than assimilation for immigrants. Some Québécois have opposed the "multiculturalism" policy because they think it reduces their claims of nationhood to the level of immigrant ethnicity. Other people had the opposite fear: that the policy was intended to treat immigrant groups as nations and hence support the development of institutionally complete cultures alongside the francophone and anglophone societies. In fact, neither fear was justified, since "multiculturalism" is best understood as a policy of supporting accommodation within the national institutions of the anglophone and francophone societies. This is indeed explicit in the phrase "multiculturalism within a bilingual framework," which the government used when introducing the policy.

Three Forms of Group-Differentiated Citizenship

There are at least three forms of differentiated citizenship in Canada intended to accommodate these ethnic and national differences: (1) self-government rights; (2) accommodation rights; and (3) special representation rights.[6] I will say a few words about each.

---

6. For a more elaborate typology of forms of differentiated citizenship, see Levy, 1997.

1. Self-government Rights

As I noted, Aboriginal peoples and the Québécois view themselves as "peoples" or "nations" and, as such, as having the inherent right of self-determination. Both groups demand certain powers of self-government that they say were not relinquished by their (initially involuntary) federation into the larger Canadian state. They want to govern themselves in certain key matters to ensure the full and free development of their cultures and the best interests of their people.

This quest for self-government is not unique to Canada. National minorities in many other Western democracies make similar demands. Consider Puerto Rico in the United States, Catalonia and the Basque Country in Spain, Scotland and Wales in Britain, Flanders in Belgium, and Corsica in France. These are just a few of the many national minorities seeking greater self-government within Western democracies. Similarly, Indigenous peoples around the world are seeking greater autonomy, including the American Indians, the Maori in New Zealand, the Inuit in Greenland, and the Sami in Scandinavia.

One mechanism for recognizing claims to self-government is federalism. Where national minorities are regionally concentrated, the boundaries of federal subunits can be drawn so that the national minority forms a majority in one of the subunits. Under these circumstances, federalism can provide extensive self-government for a national minority, guaranteeing its ability to make decisions in certain areas without being outvoted by the larger society.

Federalism was adopted in Canada precisely for this reason. Under the federal division of powers, the province of Quebec has extensive jurisdiction over issues that are crucial to the survival of the francophone society, including control over education, language, and culture, as well as significant input into immigration policy. The other nine provinces also have these powers, but the major impetus behind the existing division of powers, and indeed behind the entire federal system, is the need to accommodate the Québécois. At the time when Canada was created in 1867, most English-Canadian leaders were in favour of a unitary state, like Britain, and agreed to a federal system primarily to accommodate French Canadians. Had Quebec not been guaranteed these substantial powers — and hence protected from the possibility of being outvoted on key issues by the larger anglophone population — it is certain that Quebec either would not have joined Canada in 1867 or would have seceded sometime thereafter.

While federalism has served to satisfy the desire for self-government to a certain extent, it is not a magic formula for resolving the claims of national minorities. Indeed, federalism has itself become a source of division in Canada.

The problem is that French- and English-speaking Canadians have adopted two very different conceptions of federalism, which we can call "multination" federalism and "territorial" federalism (Resnick, 1994). Whereas the former conception emphasizes the link between federalism and self-government for national minorities, the latter ignores or downplays this link. The public debates over the Meech Lake and Charlottetown Accords revealed that many of our constitutional dilemmas stem from these competing conceptions of federalism.

Purely "territorial" forms of federalism are not designed or adopted to enable a national minority to exercise self-government; they are simply intended to diffuse power within a single nation on a regional basis. The original and best-known example of such a "territorial" federalism is the United States; other examples include Germany, Australia, and Brazil. None of these federations have any federal subunits dominated by a national minority. As a result, they have no reason to give any of their subunits distinctive rights of national self-government.

In "multination" federations, by contrast, one or more subunits have been designed with the specific intention of enabling a national minority to form a local majority and to thereby exercise meaningful self-government. Historically, the most prominent examples of federalism being used in this way to accommodate national minorities are Canada and Switzerland. Since the Second World War, there has been a flood of new multination federations, including India, Belgium, Spain, Nigeria, Ethiopia, Iraq, Sudan, and Russia.[7]

The Canadian federation has many of the hallmarks of a genuinely multination federation. This is reflected in the fact that the 1867 Constitution not only united four separate provinces into one country, it also divided the largest province into two separate political units — English-speaking Ontario and French-speaking Quebec — to accommodate ethnocultural divisions. This decision to create (or, more accurately, to re-establish) a separate Quebec province within which the French formed a clear majority was the crucial first step towards accommodating national self-government within Canadian federalism.

However, many English-speaking Canadians have not fully accepted a multination model of federalism. Instead, they tend to view American-style territorial federalism as the model. This is reflected in demands for an American-style "Triple-E" Senate. It is also reflected in opposition to any form of "special status" for Quebec, whether in the form of asymmetrical powers or in the form of a "distinct society" clause. From the point of view

---

7. For a discussion of this trend, see Gagnon and Tully, 2001.

of multination federalism, the special status of Quebec is undeniable. It is the only province that is a vehicle for a self-governing national minority, while the nine other provinces reflect regional divisions within English-speaking Canada. Quebec, in other words, is a "nationality-based unit" — it embodies the desire of a national minority to remain as a culturally distinct and politically self-governing society — while the other provinces are "region-based units," which reflect the decision of a single national community to diffuse powers on a regional basis.

In a multination conception of federalism, since nationality-based units and region-based units serve different functions, there is no reason to assume that they should have the same powers or forms of recognition. Indeed, there is good reason to think that they will require some degree of differential treatment. Nationality-based units are likely to seek different and more extensive powers than region-based units, both because they may need greater powers to protect a vulnerable national language and culture and as a symbolic affirmation that they (unlike regional subdivisions within the majority) are "distinct nations." We see demands for asymmetry in most multination federations, including Spain, Britain, India, and Russia, as well as in Canada.

How we evaluate these demands for asymmetrical powers will depend on our conception of the nature and aims of political federation. For national minorities like the Québécois, federalism is, first and foremost, a federation of *peoples*, and decisions regarding the powers of federal subunits should recognize and affirm the equal status of the founding peoples. On this view, to grant the same powers to region-based units and nationality-based units is in fact to deny equality to the minority nation by reducing its status to that of a regional division within the majority nation. By contrast, for most English-speaking Canadians, federalism is, first and foremost, a federation of *regional communities*, and decisions regarding the division of powers should affirm and reflect the equality of the constituent units. On this view, to grant more expansive powers to nationality-based units is to treat some of the federated units as less important than others.

One of the fundamental questions facing Canada is whether we can reconcile these two competing conceptions of federalism. In the past, there was a sort of implicit compromise: English-speaking Canadians accepted a significant degree of *de facto* asymmetry in powers for Quebec but rejected attempts to formally recognize asymmetry in the Constitution (Gagnon and Garcea, 1988). For much of the 1980s and 1990s, this compromise position seemed to be coming unstuck: the Québécois were becoming more insistent on explicit constitutional recognition, and English-speaking Canadians were becoming more hostile to even *de facto* asymmetry. The Charlottetown Accord was an attempt to paper over the differences between these two conceptions.

It contained some provisions which seemed to endorse the multination model (e.g., the "distinct society" clause), while other provisions seemed to endorse the territorial model (e.g., the equality of provinces clause). The failure of the Accord suggests that there is no easy way to reconcile these two conceptions.

When the failure of the Accord was followed by the near-success of the 1995 referendum on secession in Quebec, many commentators argued that the opposing dynamics of public opinion within Quebec and the rest of Canada were inevitably pulling the country apart. Since 1995, however, there has been a noticeable pulling back from the precipice. One could argue, indeed, that the old historic compromise of *de facto* asymmetry without formal constitutional recognition has been successfully revived. This is reflected, for example, in House of Commons resolutions recognizing Quebec as a "distinct society" (1995) and as a "nation" (2006), in new intergovernmental agreements to expand Quebec's autonomy (e.g., the 2004 health care agreement), and in the Supreme Court's 1998 ruling that Quebec's distinctness must be taken into account when interpreting the Constitution.[8] Many people on both sides have come to recognize that this historic compromise was actually quite an accomplishment. It enabled both sides to work together to create a peaceful and prosperous country without insisting that either side renounce its fundamental beliefs about the nature of nationhood and statehood. The historic compromise allows the Québécois to think and act like a nation, while allowing English-speaking Canadians to think and act as if they live in a territorial rather than multination federation. The result may seem unsatisfactory for those who believe that states require a single unifying ideology or mythology, and of course the persistence of these opposing views makes federal-provincial relations an ongoing source of tension. But experience shows that these tensions can be managed, and potential conflicts sidestepped, so long as people put pragmatism over ideological purity.

The demands of Aboriginal peoples for recognition of their inherent right of self-government raise some of the same issues as Quebec's demand for asymmetry. In both cases, there is an insistence on national recognition, collective autonomy, distinctive rights and powers, and the equality of peoples. However, unlike the Québécois, traditional forms of federalism are unsuitable

---

8. For the Supreme Court discussion, see *Reference re Secession of Quebec*, [1998] 2 S.C.R. 217. For the *de facto* asymmetry in the 2004 health care agreement, see the special series on asymmetric federalism commissioned by the Institute for Intergovernmental Relations (http://www.queensu.ca/iigr/working/archive/Asymmetric.html). A new area of informal asymmetry concerns the role of provinces in international relations. Quebec has been much more active than other provinces in seeking representation and participation in international organizations, and in engaging in "substate diplomacy."

for Aboriginal peoples, since there is no way to redraw provincial boundaries to create a province with an Aboriginal majority.[9]

Instead, Aboriginal self-government has been primarily tied to the system of Status Indian reserves and the devolution of power from the federal government to the band councils that govern each reserve. Aboriginal bands have been acquiring increasing control over health, education, policing, criminal justice, and resource development. In some provinces, they have also negotiated self-government agreements with the provinces (e.g., the northern region of Nunavik in Quebec). In the future, it is widely expected that they will become a constitutionally recognized third order of government within or alongside the federal system, with a collection of powers carved out of both federal and provincial jurisdictions, as was proposed in the Charlottetown Accord (RCAP, 1996; Cairns, 2000). However, the administrative difficulties are forbidding — Indian bands differ enormously in the sorts of powers they desire and are capable of exercising. Moreover, they are territorially located within the provinces and must therefore coordinate their self-government with provincial agencies. And, just as many Canadians reject "special status" for Quebec, so too they are reluctant to provide any explicit recognition of national rights for Aboriginal peoples. In short, as with the Québécois, there is considerable *de facto* self-government for Aboriginal peoples, yet no explicit constitutional recognition of rights of self-government.

2. Accommodation Rights

Many immigrant groups and religious minorities have demanded various forms of public support and legal recognition of their cultural practices. These demands take a variety of forms, including recognition of Jewish religious holidays in school schedules; exemptions from official dress codes so that Sikh men can wear turbans; revision to the history and literature curricula in public schools to give greater recognition to the historical and cultural contribution of immigrant groups; greater representation of immigrant groups in the police; CRTC guidelines to avoid ethnic stereotyping in the media; anti-racism educational campaigns; cultural diversity training for the police, social workers, and health care professionals; workplace or school harassment codes prohibiting racist comments; funding of ethnic festivals and ethnic studies programs; and so on.

Most of these demands have been accepted as part of the policy of "multiculturalism," and a general commitment to such measures is reflected

---

9. There is one exception in the North, where the division of the Northwest Territories into two parts has created a new territory, Nunavut, with an Inuit-majority population.

in section 27 of the Canadian Charter of Rights and Freedoms, which says that "This Charter shall be interpreted in a manner consistent with the preservation and enhancement of the multicultural heritage of Canadians."

Unlike self-government rights, these accommodation rights are usually intended to promote integration into the larger society, not self-government.[10] None of the demands mentioned above involves the desire to establish a separate and self-governing society. On the contrary, they typically aim to reform *mainstream* institutions so as to make immigrant groups feel more at home within them. These measures are consistent with, and intended to promote, the integration of immigrants into the public institutions of the mainstream society. They seek to help ethnic groups and religious minorities express their cultural particularity and pride without hampering their success in the economic and political institutions of the dominant society.

Here again, Canada is not unique. We find similar developments in the other major immigration countries. While Canada was the first country to explicitly adopt an official "multiculturalism" policy, other countries quickly followed, including Australia, New Zealand, Britain, Netherlands, and Sweden (Kymlicka, 2007). We see many of the same developments occurring informally in the United States, even though that country does not have any official "multiculturalism" policy.

To be sure, these ideas are controversial, and some countries firmly resist any talk of multiculturalism (e.g., France). Moreover, some countries that initially embraced multiculturalism have since witnessed a clear backlash and retreat (e.g., Netherlands). In Canada, however, popular and elite support for multiculturalism remains high, in part because of evidence that it has indeed facilitated the integration of immigrants (Bloemraad, 2006). There was a lively debate in Quebec in 2007 about whether the "reasonable accommodation" of immigrants and religious minorities had "gone too far," and some people viewed this debate as a first sign that Canada too might witness the sort of growing resistance and backlash against multiculturalism found in Western Europe. However, a provincial government commission, co-chaired by Charles Taylor and Gerard Bouchard, found that the existing policy of accommodation was in fact working well and that there was no basis for a U-turn in policy; the issue has since died down.[11]

---

10. Some groups' demands take the form of withdrawal from the larger society. However, this is primarily true of ethno-religious sects rather than immigrant communities per se. For example, the Hutterites and Mennonites are allowed to pull their children out of school before the legal age of 16 and to put restrictions on the ability of group members to leave their community. This is not the result of Canada's multiculturalism policy, since the legal exemptions accorded these Christian sects long predate the multiculturalism policy.

11. For the Bouchard-Taylor report, see http://www.accommodements.qc.ca/index-en.html.

3. Special Representation Rights

While the traditional concern of national minorities and immigrant ethnic groups has been with either self-government or accommodation rights, there has been increasing interest by these groups, as well as other non-ethnic social groups, in the idea of special representation rights.

Many Canadians believe the political process is "unrepresentative" in the sense that it fails to reflect the diversity of the population. This was illustrated most vividly during the constitutional negotiations leading up to the Charlottetown Accord, in which the fundamental terms of Canadian political life were negotiated by 11 middle-class, able-bodied, white men (the prime minister and the premiers of the ten provinces). A more representative process, it was said, would have included women, members of ethnic and racial minorities, and people who are poor or disabled.

This has led to increasing interest in the idea that a certain number of seats in the Senate should be reserved for the members of disadvantaged or marginalized groups. During the debate over the Charlottetown Accord, for example, the National Action Committee on the Status of Women recommended that 50 per cent of Senate seats should be reserved for women and that proportionate representation of ethnic minorities also be guaranteed; others recommended that seats be reserved for the members of official language minorities or for Aboriginal peoples.

The recent demands for special representation by women and other disadvantaged groups are largely an extension of long-standing demands for increased Senate representation by disadvantaged *regions*. Canada currently has an unelected Senate, which is widely viewed as illegitimate and ineffective. Many Canadians would like to simply abolish it. But the outlying and less populated regions of English-speaking Canada — i.e., the Atlantic provinces and the Western provinces — want to reform the Senate and use it as a forum for increased regional representation at the federal level. They have demanded an American-style Senate in which each province would elect an equal number of senators regardless of its population. This is intended to ensure "effective representation" for smaller provinces that might be neglected in the House of Commons, where the majority of Members of Parliament (MPs) come from the two most populous provinces (Ontario and Quebec).

Some Canadians have begun to believe that if disadvantaged or marginalized regions need special representation, then so surely do disadvantaged or marginalized groups, such as women or the poor. Historical evidence suggests that these groups, even more than smaller provinces, are likely to be under-represented in Parliament and ignored in political decision-making. Here again, demands for group representation are not unique to Canada. We find very similar debates occurring in Britain, Scandinavia (Phillips, 1996), and the United States (Mansbridge, 2000; Williams, 1998).

In the end, the Charlottetown Accord rejected most proposals for the guaranteed representation of social groups and instead focused on increased regional representation. The one exception was a proposal for guaranteed Aboriginal seats. However, the Accord allowed each province to decide how its senators would be elected, and three of the ten provincial premiers said that they would pass provincial legislation requiring that 50 per cent of the Senate seats from their province be reserved for women (Ontario, British Columbia, and Nova Scotia). While the Accord was defeated, it is possible that any future proposal for Senate reform will have to address the issue of group representation as well as regional representation.

Group representation rights are often defended as a response to some systemic barrier in the political process that makes it impossible for the group's views and interests to be effectively represented. For example, Iris Marion Young, writing in the American context, argues that special representation rights should be extended to "oppressed groups" because they are at a disadvantage in the political process, and "the solution lies at least in part in providing institutionalized means for the explicit recognition and representation of oppressed groups" (Young, 1989: 259).

Insofar as these rights are seen as a response to oppression or systemic disadvantage, they are most plausibly seen as a temporary measure on the way to a society where the need for special representation no longer exists — a form of political "affirmative action." Society should seek to remove the oppression and disadvantage, thereby eliminating the need for these rights.

However, the issue of special representation rights is complicated in Canada because special representation is sometimes defended, not on grounds of oppression, but as a corollary of self-government for national minorities. The right to self-government in certain areas seems to entail the right to guaranteed representation on any bodies that can intrude on those areas. Hence, it is argued, a corollary of self-government is that the national minority be guaranteed representation on any body that can interpret or modify its powers of self-government (e.g., the Supreme Court)[12] or which can make decisions in areas of concurrent or conflicting jurisdiction.

On the other hand, insofar as self-government reduces the jurisdiction of the federal government over the national minority, self-government may

---

12. Quebec, with a civil law tradition that differs from the rest of Canada, is in fact guaranteed three seats (out of nine) on the Supreme Court, and the 1996 Royal Commission on Aboriginal Peoples recommended guaranteed Aboriginal representation on the Court (an idea endorsed by both the Assembly of First Nations and the Canadian Association of Law Teachers in 2004).

imply that the group should have *reduced* influence (at least on certain issues) at the federal level. For example, if self-government for the Québécois leads to the asymmetrical transfer of powers from Ottawa to Quebec, so that the federal government would be passing laws that would not apply to Quebec, some commentators argue that the Québécois should not have a vote on such legislation (particularly if they could cast the deciding vote).[13] In this context, it is worth noting that while Quebec has its own pension plan, separate from the Canada Pension Plan, federal ministers from Quebec have often been in charge of the latter. These are the three major forms of differentiated citizenship in Canada. As we've seen, they are not unique to this country, but are found in most Western democracies. Insofar as differentiated citizenship involves the adoption of one or more of these group-differentiated rights, then virtually every modern democracy recognizes some form of it.

While these forms of differentiated citizenship are common, they remain controversial. Many liberals have opposed these policies as inconsistent with liberal democratic principles of freedom and equality. I will discuss two standard liberal objections — the conflict between group rights and individual rights, and the bases of social unity.[14]

Individual and Group Rights

Recognizing groups in the Constitution is often perceived as an issue of "collective rights," and many liberals fear that collective rights are, by definition, inimical to individual rights. This view was popularized in Canada by former Prime Minister Pierre Trudeau, who explained his rejection of collective rights for Quebec by saying that he believed in "the primacy of the individual."

However, we need to distinguish two kinds of collective rights that a group might claim. The first involves the right of a group against its own members; the second involves the right of a group against the larger society. Both kinds of collective rights can be seen as protecting the stability of national, ethnic, or religious groups. However, they respond to different sources of instability. The first kind is intended to protect the group from the destabilizing impact of *internal* dissent (e.g., the decision of individual

---

13. This is one obstacle to asymmetrical federalism. There is no accepted model for determining the status of Quebec's MPs under a system of asymmetrical powers. How many MPs should Quebec have? What issues should they vote on? An analogous situation concerns the representation of Puerto Rico in the American federal government. Since Puerto Rico is generally self-governing, they have reduced representation in Congress compared to other American citizens.

14. I have discussed these objections more systematically in Kymlicka, 1995.

members not to follow traditional practices or customs), whereas the second protects the group from the impact of *external* pressures (e.g., the economic or political decisions of the larger society). To distinguish these two kinds of collective rights, I will call the first "internal restrictions" and the second "external protections." Internal restrictions involve *intra*-group relations; external protections regulate *inter*-group relations.

Internal restrictions are inconsistent with liberal-democratic values. Such collective rights are found in many parts of the world where groups seek the right to legally restrict the freedom of their own members in the name of group solidarity or cultural purity; this is especially common in theocratic and patriarchal cultures where women are oppressed and religious orthodoxy enforced. This type of collective right, then, raises the danger of individual oppression.

External protections, by contrast, do not raise problems of individual oppression. Here the aim is to protect a group's distinct identity not by restricting the freedom of individual members but by limiting the group's vulnerability to the political decisions and economic power of the larger society. For example, guaranteeing representation for a minority on advisory or legislative bodies can reduce the chance that the group will be outvoted on decisions that affect the community; financial subsidies can help provide goods and services to a minority that they could not afford in a market dominated by majority preferences; and revising dress codes and work schedules can help ensure that decisions originally made by and for the dominant group are sufficiently flexible to accommodate new ethnic groups.

These sorts of external protections are not inconsistent with liberal-democratic principles and may indeed promote justice. They may help put the different groups in a society on a more equal footing by reducing the extent to which minorities are vulnerable to the larger society.

Do the three kinds of differentiated citizenship in Canada involve internal restrictions or external protections? Primarily the latter. The Québécois, Aboriginal peoples, and ethnic minorities are primarily concerned with ensuring that the larger society does not deprive them of the conditions necessary for their survival. They are less concerned with controlling the extent to which their own members engage in untraditional or unorthodox practices. Special representation within the political institutions of the larger society, the devolution of self-government powers from the federal government to the minority, and the protection of cultural practices through accommodation rights all reduce the vulnerability of minority communities to the economic and political decisions of the larger society.

These various forms of external protections are, I believe, compatible with liberal values. One can imagine cases where external protections go too far in protecting a minority from a majority, to the point where the minority in fact is able to rule over the majority — apartheid in South Africa is a clear example where "minority rights" for whites were invoked to dispossess the majority. However, this does not seem to be a real danger for the particular external protections currently being claimed in Canada. The special veto powers demanded by the Québécois, or the land rights demanded by Aboriginal peoples, or the heritage language funding demanded by ethnic minorities will hardly put them in a position to dominate English Canadians. On the contrary, they can be seen as putting the various groups on a more equal footing, in terms of their relative power *vis-à-vis* each other.

Moreover, none of these external protections need conflict with individual rights, since they do not, by themselves, tell us anything about whether or how the ethnic or national group exercises power over its own members.

There are also some internal restrictions in Canada, although their scope is less clear. Both self-government rights and accommodation rights can, under some circumstances, be used to oppress certain members of the minority group. For example, some Québécois and Aboriginal leaders have sought qualification of, or exemption from, the Canadian Charter of Rights and Freedoms in the name of self-government. These limits on the Charter create the possibility that individuals or groups within Quebec or Aboriginal communities could be oppressed in the name of group solidarity or cultural authenticity.

Whether there is a real danger of intra-group oppression in Canada is a matter of debate. The most commonly discussed example concerns the potential for sexual discrimination in minority cultures.[15] Some women's groups (mostly from outside Quebec) worried that the Quebec government might use the "distinct society" clause to impose oppressive family policies on women (e.g., restricting access to birth control or abortion to maintain a high birth rate). Whether this was a realistic worry is dubious. Women's groups within Quebec were quick to reject the idea that enhanced or asymmetric autonomy for Quebec was a threat to their equality.

The concern has also been expressed that Aboriginal women might be discriminated against under certain systems of Aboriginal self-government if these are exempt from the Charter. This concern has been expressed by women's organizations both inside and outside Aboriginal communities. Indeed, the Native Women's Association of Canada has demanded that the decisions of Aboriginal governments be subject to the Canadian Charter (or a future Aboriginal Charter, if it also effectively protects sexual equality).

---

15. The potential conflict between multiculturalism and gender equality has been an issue, not just in Canada, but internationally (Okin, 1999; Deveaux, 2006; Eisenberg and Spinner-Halev, 2005).

On the other hand, many Aboriginal leaders insist that this fear of sexual oppression reflects misinformed or prejudiced stereotypes about Aboriginal cultures. They argue that Aboriginal self-government needs to be exempt from the Charter not in order to restrict the liberty of women within Aboriginal communities but to defend the *external* protections of Aboriginal peoples *vis-à-vis* the larger society. Their special rights to land or to guaranteed representation, which help reduce their vulnerability to the economic and political pressure of the larger society, could be struck down as discriminatory under the Charter. (For example, guaranteed representation for Aboriginal peoples could be seen as violating the equality rights of the Charter, as could restrictions on the mobility of non-Aboriginal peoples on Aboriginal lands). Also, Aboriginal leaders fear that non-Aboriginal judges may interpret certain rights (e.g., democratic rights) in ways that are culturally biased. Hence, many Aboriginal leaders seek exemption from the Charter but affirm their commitment to the basic human rights and freedoms that underlie the Charter.

Similar debates have occurred over accommodation rights. There are fears that some immigrant groups and religious minorities may use "multiculturalism" as a pretext for imposing traditional patriarchal practices on women and children. There are fears that some groups will demand the right to stop their children (particularly girls) from receiving a proper education so as to reduce the chances that the child will leave the community, or they will request the right to continue traditional customs such as clitoridectomy or forced arranged marriages. Such fears were often expressed in Quebec's recent debate about whether reasonable accommodation had gone too far.

Such internal restrictions clearly do have the potential to deny individual freedom, but these oppressive practices are not part of Canada's current multiculturalism policy, and there is little public support for allowing them, even within minority communities. Instead, most collective rights for ethnic and national groups are defended in terms of, and take the form of, external protections against the larger community.[16] There is widespread opposition to the idea that ethnic or national groups should be able to protect their historical customs by limiting the basic civil liberties of their members. For example, there is no public support for restricting freedom of religion in the name of protecting the religious customs of a community.

---

16. One case where internal restrictions and external protections are combined is the language laws in Quebec. For various views on how such language laws relate to liberal-democratic principles, see the essays in Kymlicka and Patten, 2003.

Social Unity and Differentiated Citizenship

Liberals are also concerned that differentiated citizenship will be a source of disunity and will inhibit the development of a sense of shared Canadian identity. It could lead to the dissolution of the country or, less drastically, to a reduced willingness to make the mutual sacrifices and accommodations necessary for a functioning democracy and effective welfare state. If groups are encouraged by the very terms of citizenship to turn inward and focus on their "difference" (whether racial, ethnic, religious, sexual, etc.), then citizenship cannot perform its vital integrative function. Nothing will bind the various groups in society together and prevent the spread of mutual mistrust or conflict.

This is a serious concern, reinforced by evidence from other countries, that there may be a negative correlation between diversity and solidarity.[17] In evaluating this, however, we need to keep in mind the distinction between the three forms of differentiated citizenship. Generally speaking, demands for both representation rights and accommodation rights are demands for *inclusion*. Groups that feel excluded want to be included in the larger society, and the recognition and accommodation of their "difference" is intended to facilitate this.

As I noted, the right to special representation can be seen as an extension of the familiar idea of guaranteeing special representation for underrepresented regions (e.g., an equal number of Senate seats for all states or provinces, whatever their population). This practice is widely seen as promoting both participation and fairness, and hence integration. Proponents of special representation simply extend this logic to non-territorial minorities, who may equally be in need of representation (e.g., ethnic and racial minorities, women, the disabled). There are practical obstacles to such a proposal (Phillips, 1995). For example, how do we decide which groups are entitled to such representation, and how do we ensure that their "representatives" are in fact accountable to the group? Nevertheless, the basic impulse underlying representation rights is integration, not separation.

Similarly, most demands for accommodation rights reflect a desire by members of ethnic minority groups to participate within the mainstream of

---

17. For two influential empirical studies of this apparent negative correlation, see Putnam, 2007 for the American case; Alesina, Baqir, and Easterly, 2001 for a global study. Within political theory, this is sometimes called the "recognition versus redistribution" debate: an identity-based politics focused on the recognition of cultural diversity is said to conflict with a class-based politics focused on the politics of redistribution (e.g., Fraser, 1997). For an overview of both the empirical and normative strands of this debate, see Banting and Kymlicka, 2006.

society. Consider the case of Sikhs who wanted to join the Royal Canadian Mounted Police, but, because of their religious requirement to wear a turban, could not do so unless they were exempted from the usual requirements regarding ceremonial headgear. Such an exemption was opposed by many Canadians, who viewed it as a sign of disrespect for one of Canada's "national symbols." But the fact that these men wanted to be a part of the RCMP, and to participate in one of Canada's national symbols, is evidence of their desire to participate in and contribute to the larger community.

Indeed, the evidence suggests that the adoption of the multiculturalism policy in 1971 has helped, rather than hindered, the integration process in Canada. Immigrants today are more likely to take out Canadian citizenship than immigrants who arrived before 1971. They are also more likely to vote, more likely to learn an official language, more likely to have friends (or spouses) from another ethnic group, more likely to participate in mainstream social organizations, and so on. On all of these criteria, ethnic groups in Canada are more integrated today than they were before the multiculturalism policy was adopted in 1971. Moreover, Canada does a better job of integrating immigrants on these criteria than countries that have rejected the idea of multiculturalism, like the United States or France.[18] Multiculturalism has been widely criticized for promoting ethnic separatism in Canada (Bissoondath, 1994), but in fact there is no evidence to suggest that multiculturalism has decreased the rate of integration of immigrants or increased the separatism or mutual hostility of ethnic groups. On the contrary, it seems that multiculturalism has succeeded in its basic aim: making immigrants and their children feel more at home within mainstream Canadian institutions.

Self-government rights, however, do raise problems for the integrative function of citizenship. While both representation and accommodation rights take the larger political community for granted, and seek greater inclusion in it, demands for self-government may reflect a desire to weaken the bonds with the larger community and may indeed question its very nature, authority, and permanence. If democracy is the rule of the people, group self-government raises the question of who "the people" really are. National minorities claim that they are distinct peoples, with inherent rights of self-determination that were not relinquished by their (often involuntary) federation into a larger country. Indeed, the retention of certain powers is often explicitly spelled out in the treaties or constitutional agreements that specified the terms of federation. Self-government rights, therefore, are the most complete case of differentiated citizenship, since they divide the people into

---

18. For the evidence, see Kymlicka, 1998; Adams, 2007; Bloemraad, 2006.

separate "peoples," each with its own historic rights, territories, and powers of self-government — and each, therefore with its own political community.

Can differentiated citizenship serve an integrative function in this context? If citizenship is membership in a political community, then self-government rights seem to give rise to a sort of dual citizenship and to conflicts about which community citizens identify with most deeply. Moreover, there seems to be no natural stopping point to the demands for increasing self-government. If limited autonomy is granted, this may simply fuel the ambitions of nationalist leaders who will be satisfied with nothing short of their own nation-state. Indeed, one of the defining features of nationalism, historically, has been the quest for an independent state. Even if not explicitly secessionist, nationalists typically insist that the nation is the primary locus of political loyalty and allegiance, so that participation in any supra-national political community is conditional, assessed on the basis of how well such participation serves the interest of the primary national community. Once the Québécois or Cree define themselves as a nation, therefore, it seems that their allegiance to Canada can only be derivative and conditional. Democratic multination states are, it would seem, inherently unstable for this reason.

It might seem tempting, therefore, to ignore the demands of national minorities, avoid any reference to such groups in the Constitution, and insist that citizenship is a common identity shared by all individuals, without regard to group membership. This is often described as the American strategy for dealing with cultural pluralism. But with a few exceptions — such as the (mostly outlying) Indian, Eskimo, Puerto Rican, and Native Hawaiian populations — the United States is not a multination state. It has faced the problem of assimilating voluntary immigrants and involuntary slaves, who arrived in America as individuals or families, rather than incorporating historically self-governing communities whose homeland has become part of the larger community. And where the "ethnicity-blind" strategy was applied to national minorities — e.g., American Indians — it has often been a spectacular failure. Hence, many of these national groups are now accorded self-government rights within the United States. Indeed, there are very few democratic multination states that follow the strict "common citizenship" strategy. This is not surprising, because refusing demands for self-government rights may simply aggravate alienation among these groups and increase the desire for secession.[19]

---

19. In any event, the state cannot avoid giving public recognition to particular group identities. It must decide which language(s) will serve as the official language(s) of the schools, courts, and legislatures. This shows that the "strict separation of state and ethnicity" view proclaimed by many American liberals is incoherent. See Kymlicka, 1995: chap. 6.

It might seem that we are caught between Scylla and Charybdis: granting self-government rights seems to encourage a nationalist project whose endpoint is independence; denying self-government seems to encourage alienation and withdrawal. It is not surprising, therefore, that many commentators have concluded that multination states are unlikely to be successful or stable.

And yet many multination federations have survived and, indeed, flourished. Countries like Switzerland, Belgium, Britain, and Canada have not only managed these conflicts in a peaceful and democratic way but also have secured prosperity and individual freedom for their citizens. It is a striking fact that no multination federation in the West has yet fallen apart. This is truly remarkable when one considers the immense power that nationalism has shown in this century. Nationalism has torn apart colonial empires and Communist dictatorships, redefined boundaries all over the world. Yet democratic multination federations have succeeded in taming the force of nationalism. No other form of political structure can make this claim.

This suggests that multination federations combine a rather weak sense of unity with surprising levels of resilience and stability. Weak bonds of social unity may nonetheless be enduring, and conditional allegiances may nonetheless be powerful. It remains a matter of debate what is the "glue" that provides this sort of resilience (Webber, 1994; Norman, 2006; Taylor, 1993; Gagnon and Tully, 2001). But the ideal of a stable and prosperous multination state, which recognizes the self-government rights of its national minorities while simultaneously promoting a common identity amongst all citizens, is neither a conceptual contradiction nor a practical impossibility. We do not yet have a theory about how such states are possible: we have no clear account of the basis of social unity in such a multination state. But we should not let the lack of a theory blind us to the reality that such states exist and prosper in the modern world.

Conclusion

Canada has a long history of accommodating group difference, particularly national and ethnic difference. It is difficult to say whether this history is a successful one. On the one hand, the continued existence of the country has often been in question and remains so today. On the other hand, Canada has enjoyed 140 years of peaceful co-existence between three national groups, and innumerable ethnic groups, with an almost total absence of political violence. While many groups continue to feel excluded, the political system has proven flexible enough to accommodate many demands for self-government, multicultural accommodations. and special representation. It is difficult to find a scale that allows us to add up these successes and disappointments to arrive at some overall judgements of the Canadian experiment in accommodating group difference. Indeed, perhaps the major lesson to be drawn from the Canadian experience is the sheer heterogeneity of group difference and of the mechanisms for accommodating them. The sorts of demands made by national, ethnic, and social groups differ greatly in their content and in their relation to traditional liberal democratic principles of equality, freedom, and democracy.

References and Suggested Readings

Adams, Michael. 2007. *Unlikely Utopia: The Surprising Triumph of Canadian Pluralism.* Toronto: Viking.

Alesina, Alberto, Reza Baqir, and William Easterly. 2001. *Public Goods and Ethnic Diversity.* NBER Working Paper No. 6069. Cambridge: NBER.

Banting, Keith, and Will Kymlicka, Eds. 2006. *Multiculturalism and the Welfare State: Recognition and Redistribution in Contemporary Democracies.* Oxford: Oxford University Press.

Beiner, Ronald. 1995. *Theorizing Citizenship.* Albany: State University of New York Press.

Bissoondath, Neil. 1994. *Selling Illusions: The Cult of Multiculturalism in Canada.* Toronto: Penguin.

Bloemraad, Irene. 2006. *Becoming a Citizen: Incorporating Immigrants and Refugees in the United States and Canada.* Berkeley: University of California Press.

Cairns, Alan. 2000. *Citizens Plus: Aboriginal Peoples and the Canadian State.* Vancouver: University of British Columbia Press.

Deveaux, Monique. 2006. *Gender and Justice in Multicultural Liberal States.* New York: Oxford University Press.

Eisenberg, Avigail, and Jeff Spinner-Halev, Eds. 2005. *Minorities within Minorities.* Cambridge: Cambridge University Press.

Fraser, Nancy. 1997. *Justice Interruptus: Critical Reflections on the "Postsocialist" Condition.* New York: Routledge.

Gagnon, Alain-G., and J. Garcea. 1988. "Quebec and the Pursuit of Special Status." In R.D. Olling and M. Westmacott, eds., *Perspectives on Canadian Federalism.* Scarborough: Prentice-Hall. 304–25.

Gagnon, Alain-G., and James Tully, Eds. 2001. *Multinational Democracies.* Cambridge: Cambridge University Press.

Havemann, Paul, Ed. 1999. *Indigenous Peoples' Rights in Australia, Canada, and New Zealand.* Oxford: Oxford University Press.

Jenson, Jane. 1993. "Naming Nations: Making Nationalist Claims in Canadian Public Discourse." *Canadian Review of Sociology and Anthropology* 30, 3: 337–58.

Kaplan, William. 1993. *Belonging: The Meaning and Future of Canadian Citizenship.* Montreal: McGill-Queen's University Press.

Kymlicka, Will. 1995. *Multicultural Citizenship.* Oxford: Oxford University Press.

Kymlicka, Will. 1998. *Finding Our Way: Rethinking Ethnocultural Relations in Canada.* Toronto: Oxford University Press.

Kymlicka, Will. 2007. *Multicultural Odysseys: Navigating the New International Politics of Diversity.* Oxford: Oxford University Press.

Kymlicka, Will, and Alan Patten, Eds. 2003. *Language Rights and Political Theory.* Oxford: Oxford University Press.

Levy, Jacob. 1997. "Classifying Cultural Rights." In Ian Shapiro and Will Kymlicka, eds., *Ethnicity and Group Rights*. New York: New York University Press. 22–66.

Mansbridge, Jane. 2000. "What Does a Representative Do?" In Will Kymlicka and Wayne Norman, eds., *Citizenship in Diverse Societies*. Oxford: Oxford University Press. 99–123.

McRoberts, Kenneth. 1997. *Misconceiving Canada: The Struggle for National Unity*. Toronto: Oxford University Press.

Norman, Wayne. 2006. *Negotiating Nationalism: Nation-Building, Federalism, and Secession in the Multinational State*. Oxford: Oxford University Press.

Okin, Susan. 1999. *Is Multiculturalism Bad for Women?* Princeton: Princeton University Press.

Pearson, David. 2001. *The Politics of Ethnicity in Settler Societies: States of Unease*. London: Macmillan.

Phillips, Anne. 1995. *The Politics of Presence*. Oxford: Oxford University Press.

Putnam, Robert. 2007. "E Pluribus Unum? Diversity and Community in the 21st Century." *Scandinavian Political Studies* 30, 2: 137–74.

Resnick, Philip. 1994. "Toward a Multination Federalism." In Leslie Seidle, ed., *Seeking a New Canadian Partnership: Asymmetrical and Confederal Options*. Montreal: Institute for Research on Public Policy, 71–90.

RCAP (Royal Commission on Aboriginal Peoples). 1996. *Report of the Royal Commission on Aboriginal Peoples*. Ottawa: Canada Communication Group Publishing.

Shachar, Ayelet. 2001. *Multicultural Jurisdictions: Preserving Cultural Differences and Women's Rights in a Liberal State*. Cambridge: Cambridge University Press.

Taylor, Charles. 1993. *Reconciling the Solitudes: Essays on Canadian Federalism and Nationalism*. Montreal: McGill-Queen's University Press.

Trudeau, Pierre Elliot. 1990. "The Values of a Just Society." In Thomas Axworthy and Pierre Trudeau, eds., *Towards a Just Society*. Toronto: Viking Press. 357–404.

Tully, James. 1995. *Strange Multiplicity: Constitutionalism in an Age of Diversity*. Cambridge: Cambridge University Press.

Webber, Jeremy. 1994. *Reimagining Canada: Language, Culture, Community, and the Canadian Constitution*. Montreal: McGill-Queen's University Press.

Williams, Melissa. 1998. *Voice, Trust, and Memory: Marginalized Groups and the Failings of Liberal Representation*. Princeton: Princeton University Press.

Young, Iris Marion. 1989. "Polity and Group Difference: A Critique of the Ideal of Universal Citizenship." *Ethics* 99, 2: 250–74.

three

Canadian Political Culture

STEPHEN BROOKS

Introduction

There is no more Canadian pastime than reflecting on what it means to be
a Canadian. Unlike the French, the English, the Chinese, the Russians, and
the Americans, to name a handful of other peoples, Canadians have long
obsessed over what it is in their values and beliefs that makes them distinctive,
that sets them apart from others. In fact, this long-standing and perennial
search for the cultural essence of the Canadian condition has most often
been about identifying and explaining the ways in which the values and
beliefs of Canadians are different from those of Americans. Various answers
have been given over the years. Until the latter half of the twentieth century, these answers more or less boiled down to this: Canadians believe in a
more orderly, less individualistic society than that of the United States, and
they expect the state to engage in activities that promote the welfare of
society and the development of an independent Canada. The affective tie
to Britain remained strong well into the middle of the century, and indeed
many Canadians thought of themselves as British and of their country as
more British than American in its institutions, values, and heritage.

This answer to the question of what it means to be a Canadian has
seemed less plausible as Canada has become less British over the last couple
of generations. Many still believe, however, that Canadian values continue
to be less individualistic and less hostile to government than in the United
States. Such words as "tolerant," "compassionate," and "caring" are often used
in comparisons between the two countries, always suggesting that Canadians
have more of these qualities than Americans. And it is not just Canadians
who make this claim. On the American left, Canada has for about a generation now served the function of a sort of "Nirvana to the north," a place that
shows what is possible in public policy and social relations and a model to be
emulated (Dunn, 2004). As the bonds joining Canada to the United States
economically and culturally have multiplied and deepened, the question of
what it means to be a Canadian continues to be a sort of national obsession.

This is not true, however, in French-speaking Canada, whose centre of
gravity is Quebec, home to over 90 per cent of Canadian francophones.
Insulated from American cultural influences by language and for much

of their history by the strongly Catholic character of their society, French Canadians have been much less likely than their English-speaking compatriots to define themselves and their history with reference to the United States. They have long worried about anglicizing influences on their language and culture, but they have tended to see the challenge as coming chiefly from within Canada, with its English-speaking majority, rather than from the United States. This perceived challenge has provided the basis for the rise of, first, French-Canadian nationalism and more recently of Quebec nationalism. In recent years, as non-traditional sources of immigration have become increasingly important in Quebec, the question of what it means to be Québécois has received greater attention. But in answering it, few French-speaking Canadians would think of using as a starting point the United States and what are believed to be American values and beliefs.

The Political Ideas of Canadians

What do Canadians believe about politics? Is it true that they value social order more, and individual freedom less, than their American counterparts? Does French Canada, and more particularly French-speaking Quebec, constitute a "distinct society" in terms of its values and beliefs? Is it reasonable to talk about the political ideas of English-speaking Canadians, or are the regional differences in political culture too great to warrant such an approach?

This chapter examines political culture in Canada under four themes: community, freedom, equality, and attitudes towards the state. These tap crucial dimensions of the core political values and beliefs of Canadians, while at the same time allowing us to explore important differences and similarities between French- and English-speaking Canadians, between different regions of the country, and between Canadians and Americans. The evidence we will use is drawn from history, survey research data on attitudes, and interpretations of the behaviour of individuals, groups, and governments from which values can be inferred.

Community

"Canadians," it is said, "are the only people who regularly pull themselves up by the roots to see whether they are still growing." This search for a national identity unites successive generations of Canadians. Indeed, as the above remark suggests, it may be that the obsessive and often insecure introspection of Canadians is itself one of the chief characteristics of the Canadian identity (in English Canada, at least).

The roots of this preoccupation with national identity go back to the Conquest and the American War of Independence. The Conquest laid the basis for a society in which two main ethnolinguistic communities would cohabit, communities whose values and aspirations would often be at cross-purposes. The American War of Independence was followed by the emigration of Loyalists from the United States to the British colonies that would become Canada. Founded by those who rejected the republican democracy to the south, English Canada would constantly compare itself to that society and seek to explain and justify its separate existence.

The term "political community" implies, quite simply, a shared sense of belonging to a country whose national integrity is worth preserving. This is something less than nationalism, which defines a community by its language, ethnic origins, traditions, or unique history. And it is not quite the same as patriotism, which one associates with a more fervent and demonstrative love of country and its symbols than is usually considered seemly in Canada. Political community is, rather, what historian W.L. Morton once described as "a community of political allegiance alone" (1965: 121). National identity, in such a community, is free from cultural and racial associations. Instead, national identity is essentially political — a sense of common citizenship in a country whose members have more in common with one another than with the citizens of neighbouring states and who believe that there are good reasons for continuing to live together as a single political nation. The term "political nationality" is used by Donald Smiley to refer to precisely this sort of non-ethnic, non-racial sense of political community.

Canada's sense of community has often seemed terribly fragile, threatened by French/English tensions, Western grievances against Ontario and Quebec, and, most recently, conflicts between the aspirations of Aboriginal Canadians and the policies of federal and provincial governments. This apparent fragility needs to be viewed alongside evidence that suggests that the country has been relatively successful in managing (repressing, critics would say) the tensions that have threatened it. The existing Constitution dates from 1867, making it one of the oldest and most durable in the world. Moreover, the territorial integrity of the country has (so far) remained unshaken by either civil war or secession. This is not to understate the importance of the rifts in Canada's sense of community. But the problems of Canadian unity and identity should be viewed from a broader perspective.

For most of Canada's history, relations between the francophone and anglophone communities have not posed a threat to the political community. The differences and tensions between Canada's two major language groups have been managed through political accommodations between their political elites. This practice arguably goes back to the Quebec Act of 1774.

Official protection was extended to the Catholic Church and Quebec's civil law system just when the British authorities were worried about the prospect of political rebellion in the American colonies spreading north. The tradition of deal-making between French and English Canada acquired a rather different twist in the couple of decades prior to Confederation, when the current provinces of Ontario and Quebec were united with a common legislature. The practice of dual ministries, with a leader from both Canada East (Quebec) and Canada West (Ontario), quickly developed, as did the convention that a bill needed to be passed by majorities from both East and West in order to become law. The federal division of powers that formed the basis of the 1867 Confederation continued this deal-making tradition. The assignment to the provinces of jurisdiction over education, property, civil rights, and local matters was shaped by Quebec politicians' insistence on control over those matters involving cultural differences.

This tradition of elitist deal-making has continued throughout Canada's history at two different levels. Nationally, the federal Cabinet and national political parties, particularly the Liberal Party of Canada, have been important forums where the interests of Quebec could be represented. But with the rise of a more aggressive Quebec-centred nationalism in the 1960s, the ability to represent the interests of French and English Canada within national institutions has become less important than whether compromises can be reached between the governments of Canada and Quebec.

The *modus vivendi* that for a couple of centuries prevented French/ English conflicts from exploding into challenges to the idea of a single Canada seemed to come unstitched during the 1960s. Quebec independence, which previously had been a marginal idea that surfaced only sporadically in the province's politics, became a serious proposition advocated by many French-speaking intellectuals and apparently supported by a sizeable minority of Québécois. The independence option spawned a number of organized political groups during the 1960s. In 1968, most of them threw their support behind the pro-independence Parti Québécois (PQ). Since then, the debate over whether the province should remain in Canada, and if so on what terms, has been one of the chief dimensions of Quebec political life.

According to public opinion polls, the level of popular support for Quebec independence has ranged between a low of about 20 per cent to a high of nearly 60 per cent over the last four decades. Without reading too much into the numbers, we may say that there appears to be a durable core of support for the idea of Quebec independence. The level of support varies over time and also depends on what sort of independence is envisaged by the pollster's question. Support always has been higher for "sovereignty-association" — a term generally understood to mean a politically sovereign

Quebec that would be linked to Canada through some sort of commercial union or free trade agreement — than for outright political and economic separation. It appears that a significant number of Québécois are conditional separatists. Indeed, even among PQ supporters there has always been much less enthusiasm for complete separation than for separation with economic association.

When the PQ was first elected to office in 1976, it was clear that Quebec voters were not casting their ballots for separatism. The PQ was committed to holding a referendum on Quebec independence, so that non-separatists and soft separatists were able to vote for the party without fear that a PQ government would necessarily mean Quebec independence. Indeed, a survey conducted during the 1976 campaign revealed that only about half of those intending to vote for the PQ actually favoured independence (McRoberts, 1988: 239). When the PQ sought re-election in 1981, it ran on its record in office rather than on its goal of Quebec independence. In fact, the party promised not to hold another referendum during its next term. As in 1976, the PQ's 1981 victory could not be interpreted as a vote for separatism. Similarly, in 1998 the PQ won re-election after a campaign in which such issues as unemployment and health care reform clearly overshadowed the issue of Quebec's future in or out of Canada. Premier Lucien Bouchard felt constrained to admit that the 43 per cent of votes cast for the PQ, versus 44 per cent for the Quebec Liberal Party, could in no way be viewed as a mandate for independence nor even for another referendum in the near term.

The first direct challenge to the Canadian political community came in May of 1980, when the PQ government held its promised referendum on sovereignty-association. The referendum was very carefully — opponents said trickily — worded. It stressed that what was being proposed was not a radical break from Canada, but a negotiated political independence for Quebec that would maintain economic ties to Canada. Despite the PQ's careful strategy, Quebec voters rejected the sovereignty-association option by a vote of 59.6 per cent ("Non") to 40.4 per cent ("Oui"). Even among francophones, a majority voted against Quebec independence (Lachapelle and Noiseux, 1980: 170). Advocates of Quebec separatism were quick to point out that sovereignty-association was more popular among younger than older voters. Time, they argued, would turn the tide in favour of independence. Others argued that the greater popularity of the "oui" option among those who entered adulthood in the nationalist 1960s and early 1970s — Quebec's "baby-boomers" — reflected the exceptional politically formative experiences of this generation and that subsequent generations, not raised in the intensely nationalist ferment that characterized the 1960s in Quebec, would find separatism less appealing.

Although support for Quebec independence has fluctuated over the years since the Quiet Revolution, later generations of Québécois have not been less attracted to this option than their predecessors. One of the politically significant ways in which this may be seen is in their weaker attachment to Canada, particularly among younger citizens. A 2006 survey found that only 19 per cent of francophones in Quebec between the ages of 18 and 30 said that they felt "very attached to Canada," compared to 71 per cent among anglophones and 45 per cent among allophones. Young francophones were also far less likely than anglophones to believe that Quebec's economic situation would be harmed by independence (29 per cent versus 72 per cent). It comes as no surprise, therefore, that young Québécois were found to be strongly in support of Quebec assuming the status of a country (59 per cent), while support was very weak among young anglophones (9 per cent) and allophones (30 per cent) (CRIC, 2006).

Freedom

"Live free or die" reads the motto on licence plates in the state of New Hampshire. Individual freedom is said to be part of the American political creed, symbolized in such icons as the Statue of Liberty, Philadelphia's Liberty Bell, the Bill of Rights, and the Declaration of Independence. Canadians, it is usually claimed, are more willing than Americans to limit individual freedom in pursuit of social order or group rights. Is this true?

The greater stress on individual freedom and suspicion of government control in the United States than in Canada is corroborated by many types of evidence. One of these is literature. Writers like Henry David Thoreau, Jack Kerouac, and Allan Ginsberg embody a powerfully individualistic current that runs through American culture. There is no Canadian equivalent to Thoreau, whose writings about civil disobedience and the need to resist the demands of society as the price to be paid for a life of virtue and freedom have had an important influence on the libertarian tradition in American politics. Individualism and freedom are also powerful themes in American popular culture. Hollywood's portrayal of the loner who is indifferent to social conventions and the law, whose virtue and attractiveness rest on these traits, has long been one of the most successful genres in popular film. Marlon Brando's brooding performance in *The Wild One* and Peter Fonda in *Easy Rider* maintained this tradition. Clint Eastwood, Sylvester Stallone, Charles Bronson, Harrison Ford, Bruce Willis, and Denzel Washington are among those actors whose film characters have embodied this against-the-grain individualism.

The individualistic ethos of Americans is linked to mistrust of the state. This mistrust is as old as the American War of Independence. It is woven into the American Constitution's systems of checks and balances; it was behind the adoption of a Bill of Rights scarcely before the ink had dried on that Constitution; and it was also part of the case for federalism, which, as James Madison argued in the famous *Federalist Papers* no. 51, was expected to help check the emergence of any political majority large enough to threaten individual and minority rights. In the American political culture, pride in their system of government and greater patriotism than in most other democracies have co-existed with a mistrust of government that has its roots in both the revolutionary experience and in the individualistic spirit of Americans. Thus, many Americans — and not just vitriolic conservative radio talk show hosts — accept as self-evident the argument that government may be the problem and the enemy and that citizens have a right to defend themselves and their property and should not have to rely on government to do it for them. Canadians are much less likely to share these views.

In Canada the state is viewed as more benign. As Seymour Martin Lipset (1989: 136) observes, "If [Canada] leans towards communitarianism — the public mobilization of resources to fulfill group objectives — the [United States] sees individualism — private endeavour — as the way an 'unseen hand' produces optimum, socially beneficial results." Canadian writer Pierre Berton (1982: 16) made the same point when he maintained that "We've always accepted more governmental control over our lives than ... [Americans] have — and fewer civil liberties."

Attitudinal data also provide a basis for generalizations about the value attached to freedom in the two societies. Using questions that require people to choose between the protection of individual liberty and the defence of social order, a survey conducted in the 1980s found that Americans consistently gave more freedom-oriented responses (Sniderman, 1988). This pattern of difference between Canadians and Americans has persisted over time. The 1991 World Values Survey found that Americans were considerably more likely than Canadians to say that, if required to choose, they would opt for liberty over equality (75 per cent versus 61 per cent). Unfortunately, this question was not asked of Americans and Canadians in the 2001 surveys.

Americans' greater stress on individual freedom is often credited to their individualist culture. Canadians, on the other hand, are often portrayed as less assertive about their rights as individuals and more concerned than Americans with social order. Attitudinal data provides some support for these claims. Some people object to this characterization of Americans as being more respectful of individual freedoms than Canadians on the grounds that Americans' understanding of "freedom" as "the absence of restraint, or individual behaviour" — what is sometimes called "negative freedom" — actually denies real freedom to many people. Canadians' greater willingness to permit government restrictions on individual behaviour does not mean that they value freedom less but that they are more likely than Americans to believe that real freedom often requires that government interfere with individual property rights and economic markets. Moreover, governments should guarantee to all citizens such things as public education and health care in order to help equalize the opportunities available both to the well-off and the less-privileged. Canadians, some argue, have what might be characterized as a positive conception of freedom, one that requires that governments act rather than get out of the way.

The somewhat weaker attachment of Canadians to what might be characterized as an individualistic notion of freedom is corroborated by the words and symbols that parties and candidates use in their attempt to win the support of voters. If we think of these words and symbols as being a sort of connective tissue between citizens and those who wish to represent them, it is clear that the key to electoral success lies in the use of ideas, images, words, and symbols that resonate positively with a large number of voters. A study of the campaign rhetoric of Canadian party leaders and the American presidential candidates in the 2000 elections held in their respective countries found that the core values and unifying themes expressed in the George W. Bush/Republican Party message were clearly more individualistic than that of any national leader and party in Canada (Brooks, 2006). This confirms the picture that emerges from attitudinal data and other evidence from which cultural values may be inferred: the defence of individual freedom can be a harder sell in Canada than in the United States. At the same time, however, Canadians tend to be more like Americans when it comes to individualism than they are to the French, Germans, British, and other Western European populations (see Figure 3.1).

In the wake of 9/11, both the American and Canadian governments passed laws that involved greater restrictions on individual rights and freedoms. Public opinion surveys showed that Canadians were considerably less likely than Americans to believe that such restrictions were necessary, but at the same time polls showed that Canadians were about as accepting of security measures that involved some loss of privacy safeguards as were Americans (Graves, 2005). In 2008 the CBC launched a prime time drama called *The Border*, which portrays Americans as more concerned with security and the protection of social order and Canadians as more vigilant in defending individual rights. A sort of role reversal has taken place, argue some, such that

Canada is now the society that cares more about freedom and the United States has become the country obsessed with threats to its security.

The evidence for this claim is less than clear. The post-9/11 spike in American support for measures that appeared to purchase security at the cost of reduced freedoms and rights for some has dissipated over time. Moreover, opposition to limitations on freedoms and rights existed in the United States from the moment the Patriot Act was passed in 2001, and this opposition gained strength and won victories in both Congress and the courts as time went on. Although it is arguable that 9/11 produced a short-term gap between Canadian and American attitudes concerning the security/freedom trade-off, it is not certain that the core beliefs of Americans became less freedom-oriented as a result.

Equality

If the Loyalists have left a Tory imprint on Canadian politics, we would expect to find that Canadians place a lower value on equality than do Americans. Tories, after all, believed that the organization of society along class lines was a natural and desirable state of affairs. They were apt to sneer at American democracy as "mobocracy." A long line of sociologists, political scientists, and historians, going back to Alexis de Tocqueville and other Europeans who visited North America in the nineteenth century, have generally agreed that American political culture is more egalitarian and Canada's more hierarchical.

Whatever the historical accuracy of this characterization might have been, it is no longer obviously true. As Figure 3.2 shows, Canadians appear to value equality *more* than do Americans. They are much more likely to support public policies, like a publicly funded health care system and a guaranteed minimum income, that are intended to narrow the gap between the poor and the well-off. A comparative study of the development of the welfare state in Canada and the United States corroborates this difference. Robert Kudrle and Theodore Marmor (1981: 110) argue that ideological differences between the two societies are the main reasons for the earlier enactment and more generous character of welfare state policies in Canada, observing that "In every policy area it appears that general public as well as elite opinion … [has been] more supportive of state action in Canada than in the United States."

At the same time some observers caution that too much is often attributed to cultural differences in explaining differences between social policies in these countries. Gerald Boychuk (2008) argues that the significance of race politics in the United States and territorial politics in Canada explains more

Figure 3.1 Individualism: A Cross-National Comparison

A. Individuals should take more responsibility for themselves

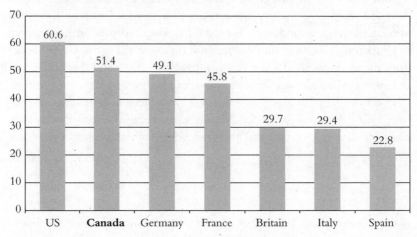

B. In the long run, hard work usually brings a better life

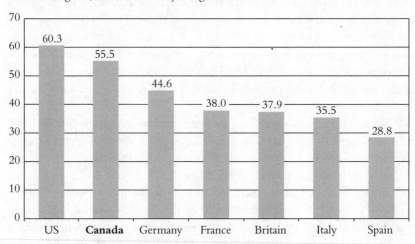

Source for Figures 3.1A, B, C, and E: World Values Survey, 2000.

Figure 3.1D is adapted from data in Nevitte, 1996: Tables 5-1 and 5-3, based on data from the 1990 World Values Survey. German data is for West Germany only.

Figure 3.1 (continued)

C. Some people feel they have completely free choice and control over their lives; while other people feel that they have no real effect on what happens to them. (Percentage expressing a great deal of freedom.)

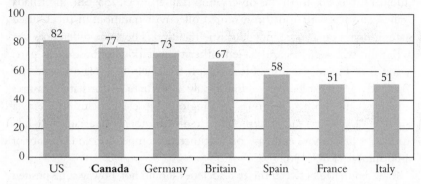

D. Why are there people who live in need?
(Percentage choosing "Because of laziness and lack of willpower" as their first choice.)

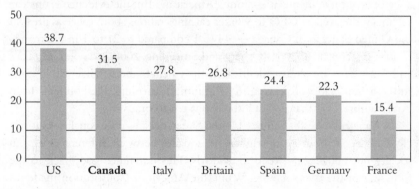

E. Competition is good. It stimulates people to work hard and develop new ideas. (Percentage agreeing.)

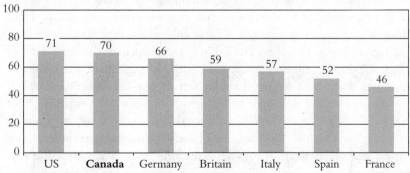

of the difference in the health policies of Canada and the United States than does political culture. Canadians are more likely than Americans to value equality of results, whereas Americans are more likely than their northern neighbours to value equality of opportunity. Numerous cross-national attitudinal surveys confirm this observation (Lipset, 1989: 155–58). In Canada egalitarianism has its roots in a more collectivist tradition, in the United States it draws on a more individualistic tradition. The value differences between the two societies are shaded rather than starkly contrasting, as parts A and B of Figure 3.2 show. Nevertheless, they help to explain Canadians' apparently greater tolerance — historically at any rate — for state measures targeted at disadvantaged groups and regions. Lipset's conclusion seems a fair one: "Canadians are committed to redistribution egalitarianism, while Americans place more emphasis on meritocratic competition and equality of opportunity" (1989: 156).

This difference between the two societies should not, however, be pushed too far. If Americans care more about equality of opportunity and Canadians about equality of condition, then we would expect to find greater acceptance of economic inequalities among Americans. But the evidence is unclear. Although the average CEO to worker earnings ratio is about twice as great in the United States as in Canada — 44 to 1 compared to 21 to 1 in the manufacturing sector, as of 2001 (Osberg and Smeeding, 2006: 461) — Canadians and Americans are almost identical in their beliefs about what would constitute a "fair" ratio of maximum to minimum earnings. Respondents from both countries say that it should be about ten to one.

In Canada, more than in the United States, debates over equality historically have been about group rights and equality between different groups in society, not equality between individuals. This difference goes back to the founding of the two societies. While the American Constitution made no distinction between groups of citizens, the Quebec Act of 1774 incorporated protection for religious rights and the British North America Act of 1867 provided protections for both religious and language rights.

A by-product of Canada's long tradition of recognizing group rights, many have argued, is greater tolerance of cultural diversity than one finds in the United States. This is the familiar, if exaggerated, theme of the Canadian "mosaic" versus the American "melting pot." Although there is considerable historical evidence to suggest that non-French, non-British groups have felt less pressure to abandon their language and customs in Canada than have non-English-speaking groups in the United States, rates of cultural assimilation have been high in both societies. Moreover, Canadian governments have shown themselves to be as capable as their American counterparts of discriminating against ethnic and religious communities. For example, in both

Figure 3.2 Dimensions of Equality in Canada and the United States

A. The Government has a responsibility to take care of the poor (percentage agreeing).

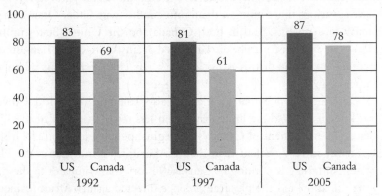

B. Both freedom and equality are important, but I would say that personal freedom is more important.

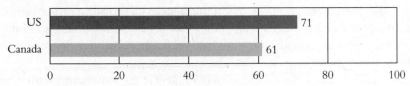

C. There are too many immigrants coming into this country who are not adopting Canadian/American values (percentage agreeing).

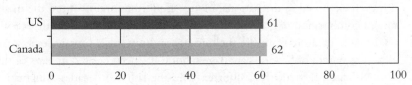

D. Do you approve of interracial marriages between Whites and Blacks? (percentage agreeing).

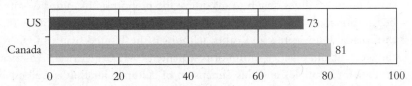

★ This is the percentage of white Americans who approve of interracial marriage. The figure for Canada includes people of all races.

countries many people of Japanese origin were deprived of their property and kept confined to camps during the Second World War. The religious practices of Doukhobors, Hutterites, Mennonites, and Jehovah's Witnesses have at various times brought them into conflict with either Ottawa or provincial governments. And in both Canada and the United States immigration policy has historically discriminated against non-white, non-European peoples — although this is no longer a fair characterization of policy in either country.

Despite evidence that, in Canada also, tolerance of cultural diversity has known limits, these limits have been less restrictive than in the United States. The treatment of Canada's Aboriginal peoples, for example, has been less harsh and less violent than that of Aboriginal minorities in the United States. And there is nothing in Canada's history that compares to the official discrimination and the physical violence directed against African Americans for much of that country's history. An official policy of multiculturalism has existed in Canada since 1971 and was entrenched in the Constitution in 1982. Moreover, Canada's Constitution appears to provide a firmer basis for affirmative action programs and other state activities that make legal distinctions between individuals on the basis of ethnicity, race, religion, and other group attributes.

The thesis of the Canadian mosaic versus the American melting pot should not be pushed too hard. Despite the fact that cultural assimilation seems historically to have been part of the American ethos, to the point that it is even expressed in the national motto "E pluribus unum" (from the many, one), a combination of government policies and court decisions in that country has steered away from the melting pot and towards a mosaic society. An extensive system of Spanish-language schools has been created in parts of the United States, particularly California, over the last two decades. Affirmative action policies, from university admission quotas to "minority set asides" (minority quotas in the allotment of government contracts) and congressional boundary lines drawn to maximize the proportion of minority voters, began earlier and arguably have been taken further in the United States than in Canada. Universities and other schools in the United States pioneered the concept and practice of minority-oriented curricula (African-American Studies, for example), and this dimension of cultural pluralism is well established there, even while some other aspects of multicultural policy appear to be under assault. Indeed, the very intensity of controversy over multiculturalism, affirmative action, and ascription-based policies in the United States is to some degree a reflection of just how successful the mosaic model has been in influencing public life in that society. The backlash attests to the inroads it has made. We should not imagine that the idea of multiculturalism and the programs and structures that seek to implement the mosaic model have gone unchallenged in Canada. Neil Bissoondath's best-selling book *Selling Illusions: The Cult of Multiculturalism in Canada* (1994) and Reginald Bibby's *Mosaic Madness: The Poverty and Potential of Life in Canada* (1990) are two of the salvoes launched against official multiculturalism (as opposed to tolerance of diversity and pluralism that is not sponsored and reinforced by the state).

In view of how deeply the Canadian mosaic versus American melting pot distinction is embedded in the collective psyche of Canadians, it seems surprising that there has been little effort to test empirically this article of faith. But perhaps this is not so surprising. After all, the thing about articles of *faith* is that they do not require proof. They are assumed to be so self-evidently true that a searching examination of the evidence on which they rest is considered a waste of time. Moreover, there may appear to be something sacrilegious in questioning a belief that is so central to Canadians' ideas of what distinguishes their society from that of the United States.

Raymond Breton and Jeffrey Reitz risk this sacrilege in what is the most ambitious and systematic attempt to test the proposition that Canadians are more tolerant of diversity than their allegedly more assimilationist neighbours to the south. In *The Illusion of Difference* (1994) they review existing studies of the mosaic versus melting pot thesis and examine a number of comparative surveys and census data from the two countries. They conclude that the differences between Canada and the United States are "more apparent than real." The Canadian style, they argue, "is more low-key than the American; moreover, Canadians have a conscious tradition of 'tolerance' that Americans do not have." These differences in the way multiculturalism and ethnic diversity have been thought of in the two societies "have not produced less pressure towards conformity in Canada, or less propensity to discriminate in employment or housing" (1994: 133). Comparing rates of language retention, ethnic group identification, participation in ethnically based social networks, and attitudes and behaviour towards racial minorities, Breton and Reitz make the case that there is almost no empirical basis for Canadians' cherished self-image of their society as being more tolerant and less assimilationist than that of the United States.

Gender equality is another dimension of group rights that has acquired prominence in recent decades. In both Canada and the United States attitudes concerning the appropriate roles and behaviour of men and women have changed sharply in the direction of greater equality. The visible signs of this change are everywhere, including laws on pay equity, easier access to abortion, affirmative action to increase the number of women employed in male-dominated professions, the ways in which females are portrayed by the media, and greater female participation in the political system. All of these are indirect measures of attitudes towards gender equality. Although they do not provide a direct indication of cultural values, we might reasonably infer these values from the actions of governments and private organizations. Comparing Canada to the United States using such measures, we come up with a mixed scorecard. The differences between the two societies tend not to be very large, Canada being "more equal" on some counts, and the United States on others. The percentage of female elected officials in each country's legislature is only marginally different (22 per cent in Canada's House of Commons versus 17 per cent in the United States House of Representatives). Public opinion regarding relations between the sexes and the roles appropriate to each are, according to the data collected by the World Values Survey, almost identical.

As in the case of the other dimensions of equality we have examined, there is no evidence to support the claim that Canadians value equality less than Americans do. Indeed, in terms of recognizing group rights, it is fair to say that Canadian governments have gone at least as far as their American counterparts. In one important respect, however, Canadians are unequivocally more committed to an egalitarian society than are Americans. This involves racial equality. Part D of Figure 3.2 suggests that racist sentiments are some-what more pervasive in the United States than in Canada. Although it is tempting to infer from the statistics on racial segregation, income differences associated with race, crime and sentencing data, and a host of other measures that Americans tend to be more racist than Canadians, such an inference may not be warranted.

To come at this a bit differently, should one infer from the fact that an African-American was elected president of the United States in 2008, while no black has ever been elected as the leader of a Canadian political party, or that the percentage of blacks holding public office in the United States is far greater than in Canada (although blacks have been appointed in Canada to the honourary positions of governor general and lieutenant-governor), or that the number of blacks among the CEOs of the largest 1,000 compan-ies in the United States is greater than for the largest 1,000 companies in Canada, that the United States, not Canada, is the more racially tolerant society? The answer, most would agree, is no. The enormous differences in the historical circumstances shaping race relations in the two societies and the much greater relative size of the black population in the United States will be cited by most as reasons for being wary of drawing such conclusions. The fact is that these two factors ensure that race and racism are far more central to American political life than to politics in Canada. But before jumping to conclusions about current attitudes towards race in the two societies, it is worth keeping in mind that the average incomes of black Canadians are about 80 per cent of those for white Canadians, roughly the same as in the United States, and that the likelihood of blacks and whites intermarrying is about the same (5 per cent) in both societies.

·Citizen Expectations for Government

Canadians, it has often been argued, are more likely than Americans to look to government to meet their needs. They are, moreover, more likely to accept state actions that they dislike, instead of mobilizing against such policies and the governments that institute them. Thomas Jefferson's declaration, "That government is best which governs least," has an oddly foreign tone to Canadians. The mistrust of government and implicit celebration of individualism that inspired Jefferson's aphorism are not sentiments that have resonated in Canada the way they have throughout American history.

This view of Canadians as both more demanding of the state and more passive towards it appears to be backed by a good deal of evidence. On the expectations side, Canadian governments do more than American ones to re-distribute wealth between individuals and regions of the country. They have been resistant to the expansion of a private presence in health care and post-secondary education. They own corporations whose activities range from producing electricity to television broadcasting, while American governments have generally been content to regulate privately owned businesses in these same industries. And they are much more actively involved in promoting particular cultural values, especially those associated with bilingualism and multiculturalism, than are most governments in the United States. In Canada the state accounts for a larger share of gross national expenditure than in the United States — and spends more on redistributive social programs and also takes a larger share of citizens' incomes in taxes. Overall, government appears to be more intrusive in Canadian society than in the United States.

What about the evidence for Canadians' alleged passivity in the face of government actions that they dislike? Is it true that Canadians are more defer-ential to authority, including political authority, than their American counter-parts? It was once fairly common to hear Canadian political experts intone that "freedom wears a crown," meaning that the more orderly society and the stability that Canadians experienced, compared to the rather chaotic "mobocracy" to the south, provided a sort of protective mantle under which citizens were better able to enjoy their democratic rights and freedoms. Although Pierre Berton, Canada's foremost popular historian, argued that Canadians accepted more government control and fewer civil liberties, he added, "the other side of the coin of liberty is license, sometimes anarchy. It seems to us that ... Americans have been more willing to suffer violence in ... [their] lives than we have for the sake of individual freedom" (1982: 16–17).

Canadians' apparent greater faith in government, compared to the more skeptical attitudes of Americans, owes a good deal to a collectivist ethos that sets Canadians and their history apart from the United States. It is this ethos that Canadian nationalists are invoking when they argue that Canada's public health care system and more generous social programs reflect the "soul" of this country and that their dismemberment would send Canadians down the allegedly mean-spirited path of American individualism. Some of Canada's most prominent thinkers, including George Grant and Charles Taylor, have argued that the collectivist ethos and greater willingness of Canadians than Americans to use the state to achieve community goals are central to the Canadian political tradition.

In *Lament for a Nation* (1970), Grant argued that the Canadian political tradition was marked by a communitarian spirit that rejected the individualism of American-style liberalism. He traced the roots of this spirit to the influence of conservative ideas and the British connection, which helped to keep alive a benign view of government as an agent for pursuing the common good. This distinctive national character was, Grant believed, doomed to be crushed by the steamroller of American liberalism and technology, which, he maintained in later works, would ultimately flatten national cultures throughout the capitalist world.

Grant's lament was in the key of what has been called "red Toryism." Red Tories are conservatives who believe that government has a responsibility to act as an agent for the collective good and that this responsibility goes far beyond maintaining law and order. Grant and others in this tradition are in favour of state support for culture as, for example, through the Canadian Broadcasting Corporation. Red Tories since Grant are comfortable with the welfare state and the principle that government *should* protect the poor and disadvantaged. Red Toryism involves, its critics would claim, a rather paternalistic philosophy of government and state-citizen relations. Defenders, however, maintain that it is compassionate and a true expression of a collectivist national ethos that distinguishes Canadians from their southern neighbours.

Charles Taylor is not a red Tory. Canada's most internationally acclaimed living philosopher is firmly on the left of the political spectrum. He agrees with Grant about the importance of collectivism in Canada's political tradition. Taylor has always been extremely critical of what he calls the "atomism" of American liberalism, a value system that he believes cuts people off from the communal relations that nurture human dignity. Like most Canadian nationalists, he believes implicitly in the moral superiority of Canada's collectivist political tradition.

Taylor is one of the leading thinkers in the contemporary movement known as communitarianism. This is based on the belief that real human freedom and dignity are possible only in the context of communal relations that allow for the public recognition of group identities and that are based on equal respect for these different identity groups. Taylor argues that the key to Canadian unity lies in finding constitutional arrangements that enable different groups of Canadians to feel that they belong to Canada and are recognized as constituent elements of Canadian society. "Nations ... which have a strong sense of their own identity," says Taylor, "and hence a desire to direct in some ways their common affairs, can only be induced to take part willingly in multinational states if they are in some ways recognized within them." He calls this the recognition of "deep diversity" (Taylor, n.d.). The realization of deep diversity would require, at a minimum, official recognition of Quebec as a distinct society and probably constitutional acknowledgement of an Aboriginal right to self-government. To some this might sound like a recipe for dismantling whatever fragile sense of Canadian community already exists. Taylor insists, however, that one-size-fits-all notions of community do not work in the modern world.

The characterization of Canada as a deferential society, or at least one where citizens are less likely to question political and other sources of established authority than in the United States, has been challenged in recent years.

In *The Decline of Deference* (1996), Neil Nevitte agrees that Canadians are less deferential today than in the past. He attributes this to the post-materialist values of those born in the post-Second World War era. Post-materialism attaches comparatively greater importance to human needs for belonging, self-esteem, and personal fulfillment than does materialism, which places greater stress on economic security and material well-being. Such issues as employment and incomes matter most to materialists, whereas post-materialists are likely to place higher value on so-called quality-of-life issues such as the environment, human rights, and group equality. Materialists are less likely than post-materialists to have confidence in public institutions and to trust in the judgements of elites.

Nevitte shows that Canadians' confidence in government institutions, a category that includes the armed forces, police, Parliament, and the public service, declined during the 1980s and that high levels of confidence are much less likely to be expressed by those between the ages of 25–54 than among older citizens. He also finds that Canadians are, if anything, slightly more skeptical of government institutions than are Americans — not what one would expect to find if the traditional stereotype of deferential Canadians versus defiant Americans holds true.

We should not be too quick to conclude, however, that the old characterization of Canadians as being more deferential towards political authority and trusting of government than Americans is no longer accurate. What Nevitte and others call post-materialism may be more pervasive in Canada than in the United States. But the differences between these two societies, as measured by both the 1990 and 2000 waves of the World Values Survey, is marginal. Only with respect to the armed forces do Americans express much more confidence than Canadians. Levels of confidence in the police, Parliament/Congress, the public service, and government are about the same in the two countries.

Asking people how much confidence they have in state institutions is one possible measure of deference. But another involves behaviour that requires people to act in a defiant manner towards authority. When Canadians and Americans are asked whether they have or might attend a lawful demonstration, join an unofficial strike, or occupy a building or factory, Canadians are somewhat less likely to say that they have done or might do this (World Values Survey). The differences between the two populations are not great — and they were even smaller when this survey was done ten years earlier — but this piece of evidence certainly does not support the revisionist claim that Canadians, emboldened by the experience of life under the Charter, have become less deferential than Americans.

Another angle on citizen expectations for government is provided by what political scientists call *social capital*. This involves the fabric of connections between members of a community. It is made up both of norms, such as trust in one's neighbours, and of behaviours, such as voting and participating in community organizations. The roots of this concept can be found in Alexis de Tocqueville's observations on the propensity of mid-nineteenth-century Americans to join together in voluntary associations in order to achieve communal goals. Tocqueville believed that these voluntary associations were the connective tissue of American democracy. They reminded citizens in immediate and practical ways of the fact that they belonged to a community and depended on one another.

Many commentators on American society argue that social capital in that country has been in serious decline for years. The evidence for this claim is not, however, rock solid. What is clear is that Americans continue to be more likely than Canadians and the citizens of other rich democracies to belong to voluntary associations and to participate in their activities. Figure 3.3 shows that a much larger share of the American population devotes some of their time to unpaid work for religious, youth, sports and recreation, educational, and cultural groups. These are activities that, in Canada, are more likely to be the responsibility of state agencies and financed by public revenues. One

Figure 3.3 Social Capital in Canada and the United States

(Percentage of the population claiming to do unpaid voluntary work for the following groups.)

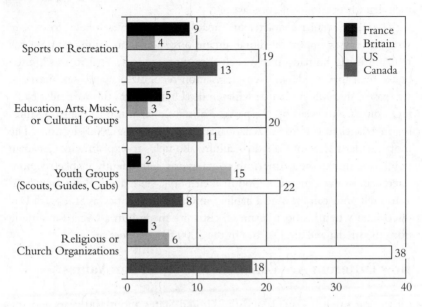

might conclude from this difference that Americans are more likely than Canadians to believe that private citizens and the voluntary associations they create — not the state — should be responsible for meeting many of society's needs. Canadians are more likely to see these activities as the responsibility of government.

Some significant part of the civic and communal engagement of Americans is due to the far greater strength of traditional religious values in the United States compared to Canada. Canada is, quite simply, a more secular society than the United States, though not nearly as secular as some Western European democracies. Secularization involves a decline in the belief that religion and religious authorities should be looked to for guidance about how to behave and how to evaluate behaviour, and an increase in the social, cultural, and political influence of elites whose expertise is not based on religious faith.

For most of their respective histories, Canada, and especially French-speaking Canada, were generally thought of as being more traditionally religious than the United States. Religious elites certainly appeared to have more influence in Canada, at least until the 1960s. Since then, the process of secularization has advanced more rapidly in Canada and other Western democracies than in the United States. Figure 3.4 shows that on a range of measures, Americans tend to be more traditionally religious than Canadians. France and Britain, the two European countries that colonized Canada, are included for purposes of comparison.

The more secular character of Canada's political culture helps to explain why issues with important moral dimensions, such as abortion and stem cell research using human embryo cells, are more controversial in the United States than in Canada and why legislation recognizing same-sex marriage was passed in 2005 in Canada while in the United States this particular battle rages on, as witnessed by the passage of state constitutional bans on same-sex marriages in California, Arizona, and Florida in the 2008 elections. The more secular nature of Canadian culture also helps to explain why Canadian politicians, unlike their American counterparts, infrequently invoke religious references or even mention God in their public statements. Being perceived as too religious can even be a liability in Canadian politics, as Stockwell Day discovered when his born-again Christianity made him a target for sniping from the media and rival parties in the 2000 federal election.

How Different Are Canadian and American Values?

Observing English Canada and the United States about 100 years ago, the French sociologist André Siegfried (1907) argued that the differences between them were relatively small and certainly insignificant by European standards. Siegfried was one of the first to weigh in on a question that has been at the centre of the comparative study of political culture in Canada and the United States: which are politically more significant, the similarities or differences in the values and beliefs of these two societies?

One hundred years after Siegfried, Michael Adams (2003) and Philip Resnick (2005) are among those who argue that these value differences are significant and growing. Adams goes so far as to conclude that Canada and the United States are fundamentally different and maintains that this has always been the case. Resnick is more cautious. He acknowledges the undeniable similarity between Canadian and American culture but argues that, in many important ways, Canadians have more in common with Western Europeans, such as the French, than they do with Americans. Moreover, Resnick believes that this affinity with Europeans and the gap between Canadians and Americans have been growing in recent years.

Drawing on data from the three rounds of the World Values Survey (1981, 1990, and 2000), Christian Boucher tests the Adams-Resnick hypothesis. Based on 28 measures that have been included in all three waves of the survey, Boucher arrives at the following conclusions:

Figure 3.4 The Strength of Traditional Religious Values: Canada, the United States, France, and Britain, 2000

A. "Religion is very important in my life." (Percentage agreeing.)

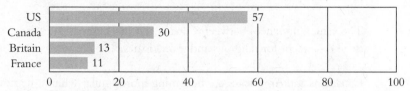

B. "I do unpaid voluntary work for a religious or church organization." (Percentage agreeing.)

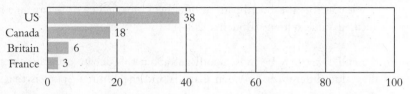

C. "I agree that marriage is an out-dated institution."

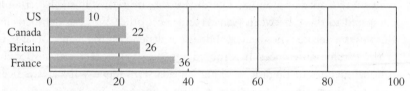

D. "It would be better for the country if more people with strong religious beliefs held public office." (Percentage disagreeing.)

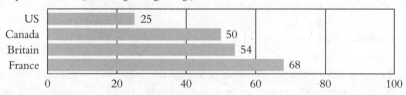

E. "There are absolutely clear guidelines about what is good and evil." (Percentage agreeing.)

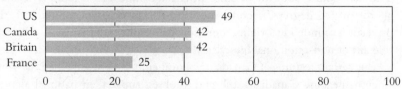

F. "I believe in sin." (Percentage agreeing.)

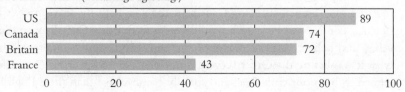

Both Canada and the United States have undergone substantial value change over the last two decades, both becoming more "progressive and secular regarding some aspects of economic, social, political and moral issues."

The value differences between Canada and the United States are small — except for religious and moral issues.

Canadians and Americans are becoming more similar when it comes to some values and more different in regard to others. There is no clear, across-the-board pattern of either convergence or divergence in their value systems (Boucher, 2004).

In the end, what may be most significant about this debate over the extent of the value differences between Canada and the United States is that it has gone on so long and continues to generate controversy among those who study Canadian politics. The differences are relatively small, certainly, compared to those between Canada and most other Western democracies. But this is a debate whose survival does not depend on the reality of large or growing value differences. It is rooted, instead, in the precariousness of the national identity of English-speaking Canada. This identity has always been based on the premise of significant value differences between Canada and the United States, a premise used to explain why these two countries are not united under one constitution and *should not* be so united.

Conclusion

The political attitudes and beliefs of Canadians today are quite different from what they were a century ago and even, in important ways, a generation ago. This is, of course, also true of other advanced democratic societies. They have all, to varying degrees, become more secular, more preoccupied with the protection of individual rights, more supportive of gender equality, and more tolerant of non-traditional lifestyles.

But certain features of Canadian political culture have remained the same. English-speaking Canadians still tend to obsess about their national identity and, more particularly, how their values and beliefs are different from those of Americans. French-speaking Canadians, the vast majority of whom live in Quebec, continue to be significantly different from other Canadians in their values and beliefs. But the nature of this gap is today quite different from what it was before the Quiet Revolution, when French-speaking Canadians tended to be more traditional and socially conservative than their English-speaking counterparts. Today, the Québécois tend to be more collectivist, more pacifistic, and more open to non-traditional lifestyles than other Canadians.

The old stereotype of Canadians as less egalitarian, more conservative, and more deferential to political authority than Americans no longer seems plausible. But whether Canadians or Americans are the more egalitarian, rights-oriented, or civically engaged population is perhaps less important than the fact that the differences between their core values are not very large. Seymour Martin Lipset's observation that "the two [political cultures] resemble each other more than either resembles any other nation" (1989: 212) surely remains true. This is not to say that their value differences are inconsequential but only that the preoccupation with identifying and explaining difference has often obscured this rather obvious reality.

References and Suggested Readings

Adams, Michael. 2003. *Fire and Ice: The United States, Canada, and the Myth of Converging Values*. Toronto: Penguin.

Bell, David. 1992. *The Roots of Disunity*, rev. ed. Toronto: Oxford University Press.

Berton, Pierre. 1982. *Why We Act Like Canadians*. Toronto: McClelland and Stewart.

Bibby, Reginald. 1990. *Mosaic Madness: The Poverty and Potential of Life in Canada*. Toronto: Stoddart.

Bissoondath, Neil. 1994. *Selling Illusions: The Cult of Multiculturalism in Canada*. Toronto: Penguin Books.

Boucher, Christian. 2004. "Canada-U.S. Values: Distinct, Inevitably Carbon Copy, or Narcissism of Small Differences?" *Horizons* 7, 1: 42–47.

Boychuk, Gerald. 2008. "National Health Insurance in Canada and the United States: Race, Territorial Integration, and the Roots of Difference." Paper presented at the annual meeting of Canadian Political Science Association, Vancouver, June.

Breton, Raymond, and Jeffrey Reitz. 1994. *The Illusion of Difference*. Toronto: C.D. Howe Institute.

Brooks, Stephen. 2006. "A Tale of Two Elections: What the Leaders' Rhetoric in the 2000 Elections Tells Us about Canada-US Differences." In Rick Farmer *et al.*, eds., *The Elections of 2000: Politics, Culture, and Economics in North America*. Akron: University of Akron Press. 136–66.

Centre for Research and Information on Canada. 2006. "Quebec Youth Survey."

Dunn, Katherine. 2004. "In Search of the Canadian Dream." *The Atlantic* (December). http://www.theatlantic.com/doc/200412u/fb2004-12-28.

Grant, George. 1970. *Lament for a Nation: The Defeat of Canadian Nationalism*. Toronto: McClelland and Stewart.

Graves, Frank. 2005. "The Shifting Public Outlook on Risk and Security." *One Issue, Two Voices*. Washington, DC: Canada Institute, Woodrow Wilson Center (October): 10–15.

Kudrle, Robert, and Theodore Marmor. 1981. "The Development of Welfare States in North America." In Peter Flora and Arnold J. Heidersheimer, eds., *The Development of Welfare States in Europe and America*. New Brunswick, NJ: Transaction Books. 81–121.

LaChapelle, Guy, and Jean Noiseux. 1980. "La Presse Quotidienne." In Édouard Cloutier, ed., *Québec un pays incertain. Réflexions sur le Québec post-référendaire*. Montréal: Québec Amérique. 135–55.

Lipset, Seymour Martin. 1989. *Continental Divide: The Values and Institutions of the United States and Canada*. Toronto: C.D. Howe Institute.

McRoberts, Kenneth. 1988. *Quebec: Social Change and Political Crisis*, 3rd ed. Toronto: McClelland and Stewart.

Morton, W.L. 1965. "The Dualism of Culture and the Federalism of Power." In Richard Abbott, ed., *A New Concept of Confederation*. Ottawa: Proceedings of the Seventh Seminar of the Canadian Union of Students. 121–38.

Nevitte, Neil. 1996. *The Decline of Deference: Canadian Value Change in Cross-National Perspective*. Peterborough: Broadview Press.

Osberg, Lars, and Timothy Smeeding. 2006. "'Fair' Inequality? Attitudes to Pay Differentials: The United States in Comparative Perspective." *American Sociological Review* 71 (June): 450–73.

Resnick, Philip. 2005. *The European Roots of Canadian Identity*. Peterborough: Broadview Press.

Siegfried, André. 1907. *The Race Question in Canada*. London: Nash.

Smiley, Donald. 1967. *The Canadian Political Nationality*. Toronto: Methuen.

Sniderman, Paul M. *et al.* 1988. "Liberty, Authority, and Community: Civil Liberties and the Canadian Political Culture." Berkeley: Survey Research Center, University of California.

Taylor, Charles. n.d. "Deep Diversity and the Future of Canada." http://www.uni.ca/taylor.html.

Thomas, David, and Barbara Boyle Torrey, Eds. 2008. *Canada and the United States: Differences That Count*, 3rd ed. Peterborough: Broadview Press.

Wiseman, Nelson. 2007. *In Search of Canadian Political Culture*. Vancouver: University of British Columbia Press.

four

Regions and Regionalism[1]

JAMES BICKERTON & ALAIN-G. GAGNON

Introduction

What is a region? It is a unit of geographical or territorial space. But beyond that there are many meanings attached to it, and many approaches used to understand it. It has been called "a multiple abstraction, and a slippery idea for those who use it as a conceptual tool" (Rasporich, 1997: 322). It may relate to an identity and it often has a cultural element; it may refer to an economic space or a unit of government and administration; it may even sustain a wide range of social institutions and a distinct society. And all these meanings may coincide, to a greater or lesser degree (Keating, 2004: xi).

The idea of region is both simple and highly ambiguous. Spatially, it exists between the national and the local and is liable to attract the attention and sometimes intervention of political, economic, and social actors from all levels: local, regional, national, and even supranational. Functionally, it can be conceived as a space in which different types of agency interact and, since it is often weakly institutionalized itself, a sort of "terrain of competition" among them (Keating, 1997: 17). Sometimes used when referring to intermediate levels of political representation or governance (provinces, states, counties, metropolitan areas), region also has been employed to refer to a spatial area within a nation-state encompassing more than one political unit (New England, the Maritimes) or even an area stretching across national boundaries (the Great Lakes region, the Cascadia region). Indeed, it may not be demarcated by political boundaries at all but by particular cultural or economic characteristics (Acadia, Silicon Valley). When used in this latter sense, the term denotes "a territorial entity having some natural and organic unity or community of interest that is independent of political and administrative boundaries" (Stevenson, 1980: 17).

Not surprisingly, then, historians, geographers, economists, sociologists, and political scientists all define region using different criteria, leading Simeon to argue that "regions are simply containers ... and how we draw the boundaries around them depends entirely on what our purposes are: it is an *a priori* question, determined by theoretical needs or political purposes" (1977: 293).

---

1. This chapter is based on arguments first presented in Bickerton and Gagnon, 2008.

With such a malleable nature, "political entrepreneurs themselves seek to shape the definition of region to reflect their values and interests" (Keating, 1997: 17). So while the concept of region continues to be associated with territorial space (as it traditionally has been), it also should be understood as a social, economic, and political construction, that is, the historical work of human actors and actions. Regions and regionalism are not static and unchanging, then, or simply geographically determined; they are the continuous creation of human history, the product of complex interactions between the region's external environment and its internal life. This makes the task of delineating regions — their number, shape and character, and the identities associated with them — dependent upon a host of factors.

That regions and regionalism exist politically is an irrefutable fact of political life in almost all states. Therefore, their study is an important part of the collective effort to understand politics in all its complexity. In Europe, North America, and other areas of the world, regions have influenced the size and character of political party systems; set political agendas; shaped constitutions, legislatures, and government structures; fuelled the contestation of national identities; and been the stimulus for a wide range of public policies. In short, its impact on government structures and political processes has been significant. Yet its multiple and overlapping meanings, its pervasive character, and often its intangibility — both as a concept and a political phenomenon — make its study a challenging and imprecise exercise. Nonetheless, the various manifestations of region, and the complicated dynamics of regionalism, are as important an aspect of politics today as they have ever been.

Theories and Approaches

The Modernization Paradigm

Until the 1960s, the study of regions in social science was dominated by the modernization paradigm and development theory. Industrialization, bureaucratization, and the consolidation of the nation-state as the dominant form of political organization generated a scholarly focus on functional and national integration as the hallmarks of modern societies. Regions and regionalism were seen as remnants of pre-industrial, pre-modern societies, fated to be eclipsed by the inexorable march of progress in the form of the increasingly homogeneous, functionally organized, nationally integrated nation-state. This view of regions fit well with the models of neo-classical economists who held that the establishment of free markets would lead eventually to a situation of spatial equilibrium where levels of economic growth and development would differ little from region to region.

For modernization theorists such as Shils, cultural homogenization is a key process in the inevitable decline of regionalism and territorially based conflict. Regional peripheries are seen as isolated, distant from the centre, and oppressively traditional in their cultural values. The challenge for modernizing elites is to diffuse their values to these backward peripheries, thereby securing adherence to a single centralized value system. Governance in this model consists of the universalization within society of the values and the rules inherent in the functional ordering of modern societies (Shils, 1975; Tarrow, 1977: 20).

In conjunction with this functionalist approach, a behaviouralist regional science emerged that increasingly emptied region of its historical and social content, substituting criteria such as population density or income as its delineators. This allowed economists to apply microeconomic models to these regional units unfettered by concerns such as regional history, culture, or social conflict. Reconfigured as purely economic development units, regions could be subjected to technocratic forms of planning. Out of this grew such notions as "stepping down" the economic dynamism of the metropolitan core to other regions, leading to the spread of growth centre strategies as the leitmotiv of regional planning in the 1960s and 1970s (Perroux, 1950; Myrdal, 1957). Despite its rather immodest attempts at scientific precision and its shunning of the insights of other disciplines, this new regional science was innovative in conceptualizing regional space, particularly the insight that "the proximity or remoteness of economic agents to each another ... is a central feature of regional life" (Markusen, 1987: 253–55).

If the pervasive influence of the modernization paradigm led to the neglect of regions, or their reduction to mere spatial economic units, interest in regions and regionalism was reinvigorated by social scientists who began to challenge the notion that territorial cleavages were of declining significance and relevance in the modern world. They did this by demonstrating the persistence of earlier territorial cleavages into modern times. Indeed, the 1970s and 1980s were marked by regional protest movements and territorial concentrations of economic and cultural opposition to centralizing elites. Seeking more autonomy, self-determination, and special recognition, these movements were often successful in stimulating decentralizing strategies of accommodation in response (Rokkan, 1980). Indeed, as noted by Maiz and Requejo, this is now part of a worldwide tendency: "many groups and communities tend increasingly to regard themselves as nations in order to strengthen their demands for self-government and cultural autonomy" (2005: 5).

Cultural Approaches

One way scholars have attempted to understand the persistence of regionalism, contrary to the expectations of the modernization paradigm, has been to view it from a cultural perspective. A distinct regional culture can sustain a sense of regional community and provide the basis for a set of values and policy preferences that differs from other regions or the larger national community. This cultural approach has long informed the historical treatment of regions and the phenomenon of regionalism. For instance, Frederick Jackson Turner's provocative essay, "The Significance of the Frontier in American History" (1894), provided an explanation for regional dissent in the American West that emphasized the unique conditions and experience of the frontier. This encouraged distinctive cultural values such as self-reliance, ingenuity, and participatory democracy that in turn fed a sense of political alienation towards what was perceived to be an old-world, corrupt, and domineering East. In more recent times, the same type of cultural argument has been deployed to help explain the persistence of Western regionalism in Canada (Gibbins and Berdahl, 2003).

Almond and Verba (1965), Hartz (1955; 1964), Lipset (1990), Nevitte (1996), and others have used a cultural approach to explain cross-national variations in political life based on differences in national values. Widely shared identities and values are thought to structure a society's political behaviour. Used to explain regionalism within countries, different regional political cultures or the lingering cultural effects of different initial settlement patterns (what Hartz called "founding fragments") are said to have produced regionally distinct value systems capable of supporting different political outlooks and policy preferences (McRae, 1964; Elkins and Simeon, 1974; Wiseman, 1981).

Regions as cultural spaces, however, are notoriously difficult to locate within, or isolate to, a single specific spatial context. Instead, such sensibilities, outlooks, or identities often exist within a number of different spatial contexts simultaneously, nested in such factors as physical geography, economy, institutions, and social characteristics such as class, religion, language, ethnicity, and community heritage (Soja, 1989). Still, complex though they may be, such regional identities do exist and therefore are available to be mobilized politically, given the right conditions and the availability of the means and resources to give them voice. In this way, the histories, mythologies, and culturally linked symbols of regional communities become discursive and ideological resources that can be tapped and deployed by political actors.

Sometimes, the role of culture in shaping the distinctiveness, if not the singularity, of the regional experience is magnified by the presence of an

74

ethnic or linguistic minority with claims to historic nation status. In such circumstances, the myth of the nation-state has been countered by the assertion of an alternate national identity that is similar in its all-encompassing character. This contradicts assumptions and expectations about the eventual assimilation of all such minorities. Certainly minority nationalism tends to differ qualitatively from other forms of regional identity, which tend to make more modest claims towards state authorities. Not surprisingly, then, regions that are also home to minority nations — such as the case with the Québécois in Canada, Scots in Britain, or Catalans in Spain — are where the most persistent and politically potent forms of regionalism can be found (Gagnon and Tully, 2001).

Interestingly, that cultural differences *per se* may be diminishing over time does not seem to herald any similar decline in the salience of regional identities. In Canada, Québécois and Western Canadian identities actually became more politicized precisely at a time when inter-regional and inter-group cultural differences were much less significant than they had been historically (Gibbins, 1980; Cairns, 2004). The same could be said about the recent upwelling of various regionalisms in Europe. Still, with the appropriate arrangements in place, cultural convergence can expand the basis for people with distinct identities to share common political institutions; it can increase their potential for living together and living apart at the same time.

Marxist Theories

Marxism has provided yet another theoretical jumping-off point for the study of regions, one critical of both the modernization paradigm and cultural approaches. A variety of class and dependency theorists share in common the premise that the free market system associated with capitalism does not operate in a spatially impartial way and that political power has been a key factor in structuring unequal relations in the marketplace. Certainly the national and global market within which regional industries and workers must compete has always been a political creation, the parameters and rules of which are continually reshaped through the exercise of political power. Though initially developed to explain persistent conditions of underdevelopment in the Third World, Marxist-inspired regional theories also have been applied to explain the situation of less-developed regions within industrialized countries. Generally, the argument has been that regions cannot be studied in isolation from their larger national and world settings, in particular the dynamics inherent within capitalist development and global capitalism.

There are a number of contending approaches to regions within the Marxist tradition. What might be termed the "logic of accumulation" approach sees the causes of regional underdevelopment as structural, one of several forms of uneven development under capitalism, and a necessary condition of accelerated capital accumulation. In other words, development and underdevelopment are two sides of the same coin: just as capitalism produces a global system of metropolitan domination and periphery subordination that victimizes Third World countries, so too does it produce regional disparities and inequalities within developed countries (Carney, 1980; Clark, 1980). Other scholars offer variations on this approach by stressing the existence of older, slower developing modes of production that either act as barriers to regional development under capitalism (Brenner, 1977) or make regions vulnerable to imperialist exploitation by advanced capitalist countries (Wallerstein, 1979).[2] Finally, there are scholars who reject this type of mechanistic explanation and instead advocate detailed historical case studies into the set of forces shaping capitalist development within each specific region (Vilar, 1977).

This disagreement over regions and regionalism to some extent reflects Marxism's theoretical difficulties with the concepts of nation and nationalism. A famous debate on the left over the meaning of minority nationalist movements is instructive here. Hobsbawm (1977) links such movements to the gradual disintegration of national economies within global capitalism, which he sees as a negative process for the small, vulnerable states that are the probable outcome of movements is pursuing separatist agendas. Nairn (1977), while agreeing with Hobsbawm that the political fragmentation set into motion by minority nationalist movements is a response to the uneven development of capitalism in the modern era, views the prospect as both positive and inevitable.

Certainly these Marxist debates illustrate the benefits of historical specificity for students of regionalism, as well as how a theory of the economy can inform the study of regional movements (Markusen, 1987).

Institutionalism

Despite such prognostications of political fragmentation due to uneven development, Urwin has shown the limited success of political mobilization of regions or minority nations within liberal democratic states. There are instances where greater regional autonomy has been won, such as Belgium,

---

2. Hechter's study (1975) of the Celtic fringe in Britain applies some of these concepts, including notions of unequal exchange between the metropolitan centre and peripheral regions, to describe how military, political, and economic coercion, as well as cultural and ideological symbols, are used to create, enforce, and legitimate cases of internal colonialism.

Spain, and the United Kingdom; and Quebec's impact clearly has altered the Canadian political agenda and federalism practices. Yet no liberal democratic state has been dismembered or come to an end, and over time some regional movements actually have become less dynamic and threatening to these states (Urwin, 1998). That regionalist and minority nationalist sentiment has been contained is explained both by institutional inertia and a willingness on the part of liberal democratic states to bend if necessary "to accommodate either symbolically or in limited ways the demands of regional minorities, though not necessarily admitting the need for institutional change or territorial adjustment" (Urwin, 1998: 226). What Urwin claims this experience shows is that the interplay of state, territory, and identity is constrained by some basic facts about liberal democratic societies: "powerful and influential structures and institutions; broad and positive acceptance of pluralism and difference; tolerance as an integral element of democratic practice; and the ability of many people to live reasonably comfortably with dual identities" (1998: 240).

These observations about states like Canada suggest the need for a corrective to the societal focus of various cultural and economic approaches to the study of regions. This is supplied in the form of institutional approaches, in particular neo-institutional and new institutional theorists who conduct political analysis through a focus on institutions. Institutionalists proclaim the central importance of a range of institutions — constitutions, bureaucratic and governance structures, courts, party and electoral systems — not only for providing the basic framework for regions but for explaining the extent and form of regionalism in a society. In short, institutional design can entrench and strengthen territorial politics and regional identities in a society or weaken this basis of identity.

Institutionalist approaches are now used to explain human action, behaviour, and outcomes within a wide range of political and economic contexts and can be found in three distinct varieties. Historical institutionalism (located within the political science tradition) can be associated with the idea of path dependency, "which is the idea that once institutions are formed, they take on a life of their own and drive political processes" (Lecours, 2005: 9). Rational choice institutionalism (from rational choice theory) emphasizes the importance of institutions — seen as the rules that govern the game — in the strategic calculations of political actors. Sociological institutionalism defines institutions in terms of norms, values, culture, and ideas; it sees institutions as shaping the perceptions of actors, leading to behaviour that reinforces and reproduces those very same institutions (Lecours, 2005: 16–17). What each of these varieties of institutionalism shares in common is their attribution to institutions of an independent causal effect on the political behaviour of individuals and communities, whether local, regional, or national.

Regional Cultures and Identities

While feeling some attachment to a particular place or territory is a nearly universal phenomenon, this takes different forms and is embedded in different social, cultural, and historical experiences. How and why these identities become politicized and mobilized can be explained only by reference to the particular circumstances of each region.

Studies proclaiming the existence of regional political cultures have received much coverage in Canada. Researchers have been interested in describing those cultures and explaining how they emerged and evolved through time. Naturally, these studies have been produced at a given moment and tend to reflect the dominant interpretative biases in the literature at that time. As a result, such accounts are not culturally or methodologically neutral, though they do constitute an important contribution to our understanding of political realities.

The aspects of a culture most directly relevant to politics — "political culture" — can be defined as "the pattern of orientations, beliefs, values, feelings, assumptions, and understandings about political phenomena that exist in any given collectivity" (Stewart, 1990: 89). One way of understanding Canada's political culture has been the historical approach commonly referred to as Hartzian fragment theory. First developed by historian Louis Hartz (1955), this approach has been applied to Canada by a number of scholars, but two in particular are notable for their identification of a regional dimension in Canadian political culture.

Ken McRae (1964) has argued that English Canada's political culture has the same historical origins, and the same pattern of values and attitudes, as the United States. This shared political culture can be traced to the United Empire Loyalists who flocked to Upper Canada and the Maritimes from the American colonies immediately after the American War of Independence. They did so in such numbers, and came into such a relatively empty land, that they formed English Canada's founding cultural fragment. The political culture borne by these American emigrants was liberalism. Quebec, on the other hand, had feudal or absolutist origins, dating from France's pre-revolutionary *ancien régime*. This "dual fragment" at the roots of Canada's origins is the key, McRae argues, to understanding the subsequent political development of the country.[3]

---

3. This fundamental cultural duality was characterized by one eminent social scientist early in the twentieth century as "two nations warring within the bosom of a single state" (Siegfried, 1966), and sometime later by an equally eminent Canadian writer as Canada's "two solitudes" (MacLennan, 1945). Another well-known Canadian interpretation of the Hartzian approach, that of political scientist Gad Horowitz, did not

Nelson Wiseman extended this analysis westward to the Prairie region. Only the political culture of Manitoba, he argues, is similar to that of eastern English Canada. This is because Manitoba's "founding fragment" was a wave of settlers from Ontario who brought their political culture with them. Saskatchewan and Alberta, later entrants into Confederation, had different ideological origins, the former shaped by early twentieth-century British immigration and the latter by American settlers who brought with them the populist and radical liberal views of the American plains. According to Wiseman, these different founding fragments help to account for the dramatically different political histories of what were otherwise quite similar provinces (Wiseman, 1981).

Another American-exported model — the civic culture approach — produced a spate of political culture studies of Canadian regionalism in the 1970s, using the behaviouralist method of survey data to "measure" and "quantify" individual beliefs, attitudes, and feelings on three political dimensions: political efficacy, political trust, and political involvement (see Almond and Verba, 1965). An important study of this type was Elkins and Simeon's "Regional Political Cultures in Canada" (1974), which identified regional differences in popular levels of efficacy and trust that were sufficient to declare the existence of distinct regional political cultures in Canada.[4] While widely cited, neither Elkins and Simeon nor other studies in this genre were without problems. Their approach is primarily descriptive rather than theoretical: "the linkage forward (what are the consequences of the civic culture?) was riddled with ambiguities, while the linkage backward (what are the origins of the civic culture?) was all but ignored" (Stewart, 1990: 91). The durability of the survey findings is also highly suspect. Elkins and Simeon's findings have been contradicted by new survey data gathered since that time (for example, see Ornstein, 1986; Adams, 2003).

Other more recent studies have made use of more refined notions of region and more sophisticated methodological techniques (MacDermid,

---

contest McRae's "dual fragment" notion of Canada's historical origins, but differed in its understanding of English Canada's political culture, arguing that a significant portion of Canada's early settlers were "unreconstructed tories" rather than liberals, and this "tory touch" created a political dialectic in this country that established the ideological space and legitimacy for a distinctive Canadian socialism, as represented by the CCF–NDP (Horowitz, 1968).

4. By using survey responses to questions formulated to measure efficacy, trust, and involvement, Elkins and Simeon (1974) were able to identify different "citizen types": supporter, critic, deferential, or disaffected. Different regions were found to have different proportions of each citizen type (e.g., disaffected in Atlantic Canada, supporters in Ontario), thereby giving a distinctive character to each regional political culture.

1990), or have focused on the relationships between region, religion, class, and voting (Johnston,1985; Gidengil, 1989). Still, the character and content of regional political cultures is rather vague, and the relationship between political culture and power is not well understood. Clearly, mass political culture should not be thought of as a direct determining factor in politics. Rather, its influence seems to be that of a broad parameter on the distribution and exercise of power within society, a conditioning or constraining factor that affects the range of political choices or types of political actions deemed possible or appropriate.

So, in pondering whether the existence of political regionalism depends upon the presence of regional political cultures, the short answer is no; regionalism may be more salient to political elites than to the mass public. It may affect elite behaviour more than mass political behaviour, and regional conceptions of Canada championed by provincial politicians may not be completely shared by their electorates. But regionalism becomes a truly potent political force when self-conscious regional identifications are linked to broadly shared perceptions of regional injustice. This accounts for the considerable political impact in Canada of various historic episodes of Western alienation, Maritime disaffection, Newfoundland neo-nationalism, and last but certainly not least, Quebec nationalism.

How have national elites responded to regionalism in Canada? It seems they have generally adopted one of two postures: either they have championed the idea of a national interest and national identity that supercedes that of region, or they have used regionalist appeals themselves in order to court regional support. Prior to the Second World War, the glue that national elites repeatedly used to bind English Canadians together was an appeal to their common British heritage and allegiance. Unfortunately, the unifying effect of ethnicity and culture within English Canada had a corresponding dis-unifying effect with regard to French Canada by providing the context and justification for policies that reduced the safe haven for French language and culture to "fortress Quebec." Having had this political reality repeatedly impressed upon them, French Canadians who controlled their own provincial jurisdiction eventually would abandon their ancient identity — that of French Canadian — for the more secure, secular, and regional identity of "Québécois." From this perspective, English-Canadian unity and national identity was secured at the cost of contributing to the rise in Quebec of a regional nationalism.

One way of illustrating this is to measure the extent to which citizens in Quebec express a dual political identity. Such dual identities are not uncommon in the context of states with significant ethno-territorial minorities. Sometimes the state identity prevails, while at other times the ethno-

Table 4.1 Dual Identity in Catalonia, Scotland, and Quebec (1997–2005)

	Catalonia		Quebec		Scotland	
	1998	2005	1998	2005	1997	2005
Only ★	11.5	14.5	12.0	19.0	23.0	32.0
More ★ than ✪	23.4	23.4	31.0	32.0	38.0	32.0
As ★ as ✪	43.1	44.8	32.0	35.0	27.0	22.0
More ✪ than ★	7.6	8.2	17.0	7.0	4.0	4.0
Only ✪	13.0	7.7	5.0	6.0	4.0	5.0
Do not know or refuse to answer	1.4	1.6	3.0	2.0	4.0	5.0

★ = Catalan, Québécois, Scots   ✪ = Spanish, Canadian, British

Source: Luis Moreno, Ana Arriba, and Araceli Serrano, *Multiple Identities in Decentralized Spain: The Case of Catalonia*, Madrid, Instituto de Estudios Sociales Avanzados (CSIC), Working Paper 97-06; Spanish Center for Sociological Research (CSI Studies nos. 1523, 2286 et 2455); Paul Wells, "Quebecers? Canadians? We're Proud to be Both," *The Gazette*, 4 April 1998. Data came from a poll conducted by CROP on behalf of *The Gazette* between 27 March and 1 April 1998; Sondage Léger Marketing, *The Globe and Mail, Le Devoir, Sondage Québécois,* Press release available at: http://legermarketing.com/documents/spclm/050427fr.pdf; Scottish Social Attitudes Surveys (National Centre for Social Research: http://www.natcen.ac.uk/natcen/pages/or_socialattitudes.htm#ssa.

territorial dominates. Maintaining a balance between these two allegiances is an important variable in the stability of such states. The above table documents the tensions that exist between ethno-territorial and state identities in the regions of Quebec, Catalonia, and Scotland (see Table 4.1).

Since the 1960s, an appeal has been made to all Canadians to identify with a new set of national symbols, values, and institutions. A distinctive Canadian flag, official bilingualism, national social programs, support for multiculturalism, and a Charter of Rights and Freedoms are all elements of this new national identity that all Canadians are expected to embrace. And, indeed, for the most part they have done so, but not without some reservations, as demonstrated by continuing tensions over bilingualism, multiculturalism, the Charter, and social programs, not to mention the rise of Aboriginal nationalism and the sovereigntist movement in Quebec.

Regional Parties

Regional parties have demonstrated their relevance in different ways over the years. They have addressed issues of representation in the case of fragmented societies. They have influenced the policy process, making governing parties accountable to a larger population by forcing them to address issues of regional redistribution. The emergence and strengthening of regional parties can be connected with the mobilization of ethnic and nationalist movements or to the sense of alienation within regional electorates that have perceived themselves to be poorly represented by traditional political elites in national parties. In short, the prevalence and role of regional parties constitutes an important phenomenon that requires an analysis of party system dynamics to account for the emergence and continuing salience of this regionalist trend. Region has been a central feature of Canadian life for as long as the country has existed, and its incorporation and representation by political parties has been a constant of national politics. Certainly it is true that "Regional politics flows from regional parties" (Carty *et al.*, 2000-01: 29), but this begs the question of what gives rise to regional parties in the first instance. As well, is it only regional parties that practice regional politics? Or is this a more or less inevitable and "normal" feature of party politics in Canada, with or without the presence of regional parties?

The emergence of a regionalist party in Quebec has been the result of forceful demands for autonomy fed by a strong sentiment of shared identity and culture. It should be stressed, however, as pointed out by Lancaster and Lewis-Beck, that "regional parties should not be equated with extremist, violent, or anti-system sentiment. Nor should regional parties always be viewed from the dominant centrist perspective, as an impediment to national political integration" (1989: 31, 33). For instance, it is worth noting that although the Bloc Québécois has as its principal goal the secession of Quebec from Canada, other federal parties have not contested the legitimacy of their elected representatives within the House of Commons. And since 1993 Bloc Québécois MPs have shown that it is possible for a regionalist party to promote an *indépendentist* stance while also making a continuous contribution to the overall performance of national political institutions in their day-to-day work (Gagnon and Hérivault, 2007).

Beyond the minority nationalism that so marks politics in Quebec, regionalism more generally has played a key role in the construction of political identities in the rest of Canada, where distinct regional patterns of voting behaviour are a long-standing political phenomenon.[5] The classic works of Lipset (1968 [1950]) and Macpherson (1953) on the emergence of regional parties in the Canadian West during the first half of the twentieth century

---

5. This is illustrated by support obtained in federal elections by the Western-based Progressives, Social Credit, and Co-operative Commonwealth Federation parties from the 1920s to the 1950s, the Reform Party in the 1990s, and the Bloc Québécois during the last 15 years (Bickerton, Gagnon, and Smith, 1999).

were influential in accounting for the sources and impact of regionalism on Canadian politics. Their conclusions were that regional class structure and economic conditions were central to the emergence and persistence of right-wing and left-wing agrarian parties in Alberta and Saskatchewan, respectively. These initial studies have since been joined by many others (Simeon, 1977; Forbes, 1979; Brym, 1986; Bickerton, 1990; Young and Archer, 2002), all of which highlight the continuing importance of regionalism in Canadian politics.

In federal countries, political parties are involved at multiple levels of governance, and electoral success at one level is not necessarily replicated at the other level; in fact, parties may compete exclusively at one level or the other. During the last two decades, the Bloc Québécois and the Reform/Canadian Alliance Party are two regionalist parties that achieved electoral success at the federal level by stressing regional issues, interests, and identities, whereas the previous period of electoral competition had been marked by the absence of such parties (Bickerton, 2007: 412).

This tension and periodic oscillation between centralist and regionalist parties has often been neglected by students of party politics in Canada and elsewhere.[6] As argued by Richard Johnston, the most recent rise of regional parties in Canada is consistent with the unfolding of a recurring and long-term cycle of protest that results in the regional fragmentation of the party system, to be followed by a period of reconsolidation and nationalization, but seemingly at a higher level of party system fragmentation than existed previously (Johnston, 2005). In other words, individual political parties — as well as the party system as a whole — have exhibited a diminishing capacity over time to shoulder the burden of national political integration imposed by Canada's regional diversity. This feature of Canada's party system has necessitated reliance upon mechanisms of regional representation other than parties, some of which are clearly no longer viable, while others have proven inadequate to the task as well as having negative effects for the political system as a whole.

To what extent can the declining integrative capacity of the national party system be blamed on the parties themselves as opposed to the workings of the broader political system within which they have operated? Perhaps

---

6. Recently, there has been some added interest, perhaps due to a desire by nation-states to play a stronger role in the globalizing world. Pierre Trudeau, Canada's Liberal prime minister for virtually the whole period from 1968 to 1984, was fond of saying that Canada was more than the sum of its parts. This stance contributed to intense political clashes with Quebec-centred parties, whether federal parties such as Ralliement créditistes and the Bloc Québécois, or provincial parties such as the Union Nationale, Parti Libéral, or Parti Québécois (Bickerton, Gagnon, and Smith, 1999: 164–92).

national parties have been frustrated in their attempts to be effective vehicles of regional representation, leading to the aforementioned deteriorating cycle of fragmentation-reconsolidation of the party system that both contributes to and helps to sustain Canada's already prominent regionalism.

Federalism, the Electoral System, and the Senate

Canadian political scientists have long suspected that certain institutional features of the Canadian political system have been primary factors in the persistence and intensity of regionalism in Canada. To illustrate this, compare the United States and Canada. Both are geographically large, diverse federations on the North American continent. In federations, regions are constituted as autonomous political entities with constitutionally protected powers and the right to participate in national politics through a second legislative chamber at the national level or through mechanisms of intergovernmental cooperation and negotiation. When compared to American states, it becomes clear that Canadian provinces can exercise a more extensive array of powers — including a strong capacity to raise revenues to cover their own expenditures (Watts, 1999: 119). This has given provincial political and bureaucratic elites the ability to shape their regional societies and engage in province-building strategies that have often spurred conflict with their nation-building federal counterparts (Cairns, 1977).

Canada, then, is a country in which regionalism is both strong and pervasive, whereas its existence in American politics is muted at best. These differences can be traced in part to the two countries' constitutional frameworks and party systems. The American Constitution fragments its geographic regions into a multitude of states, and aside from the Civil War, "no constitutional or institutional attempt has been made to put the potential regional Humpty Dumpties back together again" (Gibbins, 2004b: 40). Regional communities such as the South or Midwest exist conceptually but have little or no institutional structure. In Canada the federal division of the country has been into fewer and larger provinces and territories with (as previously noted) significantly more powers than their American counterparts. Indeed, the large provinces of Ontario, Quebec, and British Columbia constitute their own regions, a fact recognized by legislative revisions to Canada's constitutional amendment formula (Gibbins, 2004a).

More important than this, however, is that "the Canadian constitutional order *inadvertently* encourages regionalism through the impairment of territorial representation, whereas the opposite is true for the United States" (Gibbins, 2004b: 42). This is because in the United States *intrastate* federalism — the representation of territorial interests within national parliamentary institutions by national politicians — is strong, while in Canada this function is sacrificed for responsible government that comes with Cabinet solidarity, tight party discipline, and *de facto* unicameralism (since the regionally constituted Canadian Senate is an empty shell in terms of power and effectiveness). As a result, Canadian federalism is of the *interstate* variety, where regional conflict is externalized to the realm of intergovernmental relations, with provinces assuming the role of defenders of the regional interest.

The regionalizing effect of Canada's interstate federalism is reinforced by its single member, simple plurality electoral system, which punishes smaller parties enjoying diffuse national support while simultaneously rewarding parties with regionally concentrated support (Cairns, 1968; Gibbins, 2005). This has adverse consequences for national unity by hindering the capacity of the party system "to act as a unifying agency in a country where sectional [regional] cleavages are significant" (Gibbins, 2005: 40).

In a review and update of the early work of Alan Cairns on the relationship between the electoral system and party system, Roger Gibbins notes the same electoral system effects at work that Cairns noted 40 years earlier: it continued to favour minor parties with regional strongholds and turned national parties with some regional bias in their support base (such as Reform/Canadian Alliance) into almost purely regional parties that were perceived and attacked as such. With the natural partisan heterogeneity within regions artificially reduced through this electoral system effect, diverse regional electorates have tended to be simplistically and misleadingly compressed into a single partisan voice (Gibbins, 2005: 43–46). In effect, regions have been both under- and over-represented within party caucuses, distorting their ability to fairly and effectively represent the diversity of interests and identities present in all regions and, just as important, to present themselves to the electorate as such.

If the electoral system has let the parties down in terms of facilitating their role in the national integration of regions, so too has the Canadian Senate. Unelected and unaccountable, the Senate lacks the most basic democratic legitimacy and is therefore deprived of a mandate for representing regional interests. This places a severe and ultimately unsustainable burden on the lower house to perform a function for which it is poorly designed. In other federal countries, elected Senates balance lower houses elected according to "representation-by-population" with a powerful upper house constituted on the basis of equal or equitable representation for each state or region. In this way, the Senate becomes a key institution for defending diverse regional interests in each country by providing the institutional means for continuous, systematic, and accountable representation of regions. The national legislature becomes the primary site for resolving regional grievances and undertaking inter-regional bargaining and compromises. National integration is reinforced and tendencies to regional fragmentation moderated. This demonstrably has not been the case in Canada.

Political Economy of Regions

A central theme in the study of the political economy of regions is the degree to which regional inequalities have been internally determined — related to some characteristic of regions or their peoples — or, alternatively, have been ordained by structures and conditions that have been externally imposed on those regions that are less economically advantaged.

From the mid-nineteenth to the mid-twentieth centuries, Canada, like many countries, was transformed by processes of political, social, and economic integration associated with its consolidation as a state, bureaucratic modernization, and development of what was for the most part a protected national economy. Canada's diverse regions were incorporated into this emergent national political economy, though not on equal terms. Location, initial resource endowments, population base, transportation links, and various other forms of infrastructure were all relevant factors in determining the advantages or disadvantages accruing to each of its regions in successive phases of growth and development. The migration of labour to growing urban and industrial centres, and the stimulus this gave to new rounds of investment, produced "agglomeration effects" that reinforced the initial advantages of some regions while draining capital and human resources from others, leading to their further differentiation (Massey, 1998).

The role that politics and state policy played in all this was not negligible. It was national politicians who initiated, planned, and supervised the incorporation into Canada of far-flung lands and peoples; it was through politics that the policy frameworks that supported and directed national development were created, installed, and maintained. In Canada's case, the National Policy, which began in 1879 and prevailed until the 1930s, provided the framework for national integration and economic development to the benefit of some regions (central Canada) and the detriment of others (the Maritimes and to a lesser extent the West) (Brodie, 1990). Such state and nation-building projects are sustained and legitimized with nationalist visions, symbols, and rhetoric, and the political promise of security and economic prosperity. Regionalist resistance to this process in Canada was only occasionally violent and dramatic (as with the Métis-led rebellions in the West); more often it was limited to periodic episodes of political contestation through social movements or regional political parties (see the discussion of regional movements and parties above).

In the postwar era of economic expansion (1945–75), regional concerns about inequality and fair representation tended to be subsumed under the politics associated with the construction of the welfare state. But regional disparities in economic growth, per capita income, and unemployment rates were not eliminated, and in the 1960s and early 1970s greater attention was given to the development of growth centres in peripheral regions. These initiatives were meant to foster industrial growth to address regional disparities. In Canada a spate of development agencies and programs were consolidated in a new Department of Regional Economic Expansion, focused initially on reducing economic disparities between the Atlantic region (inclusive of eastern Quebec) and the rest of Canada (Savoie, 1986).

The economic logic of regional development policies was to make regions self-sustaining, whereupon active regional policy would no longer be necessary and regions could positively contribute to national economic growth. But there also were separate political and social logics at work in the creation of these policies. The political weight of poorer regions was used by regional elites to counter their economic weakness, and regional demands to bring work to the workers rather than vice versa could not be easily ignored, especially when their political importance to national governing coalitions was significant, or they harboured the potential for political disruption or even separatism. As well, in advanced industrial countries such as Canada, citizenship was increasingly undergoing a "thickening" process, with the state assuming responsibility for the social integration of all its citizens by equalizing opportunities and living standards (Keating, 1997: 18–20).

Regional policy went into decline with the widespread onset of stagflation (low growth with simultaneously rising unemployment and inflation) and growing international competitive pressures from the mid-1970s onward. As the federal government began to shift its attention and concern to shoring up Canada's national competitiveness, which was dependent upon the economic health and vitality of core industrial areas and sectors, reducing regional disparities became much less of a priority.

As Keating has noted, into this growing policy and political vacuum three types of regionalist politics emerged: first, a *defensive regionalism* resisting change that was tied to traditional economic sectors and the threatened communities that depended on them; second, an integrating or *modernizing regionalism* aimed at adapting to change and re-inserting the region into the national economy; third, an *autonomist regionalism*, particularly in regions with historic claims to nation status, seeking a distinctive path to modernization by combining autonomy, cultural promotion, and economic modernization (1997: 24). Since the 1970s these modes of regionalism have co-existed within many countries, including Canada, often disharmoniously due to the basic contradictions between them at the level of politics and policy.

There is today a new international context for regions, creating for them opportunities but also dangers and providing the conditions for the incubation of a new regionalism. A number of interrelated changes have contributed to this altered context: falling international trade barriers; the adoption of a neoliberal policy framework with its agenda of deregulation and free markets; the creation of free trade and economic union agreements (for example, the North American Free Trade Agreement and the European Union); and in general the sweeping economic, technological, political, and cultural changes associated with globalization. In many ways these changes have undermined or threatened to destroy the traditional employment base of regions, as well as the established program supports for these regions.

Another consequence of these changes for regions, however, is that it has opened up new possibilities and potentials that were not previously available. This has occurred because of the changing character of international economic competition, itself a function of changes in technology, production methods, and the removal of restrictions on international trade and investment. This has made accessible to regions global markets that absorb an increasingly diverse range of products and services. As a result, the determinants of regional competitiveness in the global economy have shifted. Traditional factors of comparative advantage, such as economies of scale and plentiful supplies of labour, may still matter, but these are now joined and often superseded by entrepreneurial, technological, social, and cultural factors (Piore and Sabel, 1984; Porter, 1990).

In response to these changes, regional policies in many countries have been revamped. To be more specific, governments have recognized that the changes associated with globalization have altered the basis of regional development, such that the competitive imperative is now different in terms of the factors and resources that are directly relevant to long-term regional success. This means that governments have found it necessary to adapt to the new context by supporting new forms of regionalization, involving partnerships between various levels of government (supranational, national, provincial/regional, local), as well as the private sector and key actors in civil society, in order to create collaborative regional policy frameworks. And much greater significance is now being accorded to so-called *endogenous* factors based on the character and quality of a region's human, social, and cultural capital, what some have called a socially embedded growth model (Amin, 1999; Florida, 2003; Savoie, 2006).

In summary, the new understanding of regional development is to involve a broader range of actors and policies than previously and to create more region-specific strategies tailored to local needs, circumstances, and potentials. This in turn requires a high degree of decentralization and regionalization of governance, involving extensive cooperation at the regional/local level between all levels of government, as well as private sector and civil society actors. Creating this new institutional and fiscal nexus for regional development requires all levels of government to acknowledge that the policies and decisions most likely to nurture sustainable regions will emerge from a strong network of regional actors brought together on the basis of a shared territorial and cultural identity and a direct interest in the economic fate of the community and its residents. If regions can cohere socially and culturally, and if they are actively supported by government, they will be more capable of meeting the new economic challenges with which they are faced.

Conclusion

Region as a concept for political scientists can be malleable and abstract, as well as mundane. Its pliability and amorphous character is due to its multiple potential meanings. Political actors will define it to reflect their values and their particular interests and needs. In this sense, though region may be tied to geographic space, it is very much a product of human construction.

There are a number of different theories and approaches that have been used to describe and inquire into the meaning of regions as economic, social, cultural, and political phenomena. Mainstream modernization and development theory ascribed diminishing significance to regions, since the differences they represented were inevitably fated to fade as the integration processes linked to modernity and capitalism proceeded apace. Other approaches and perspectives remained skeptical of this outcome. Culturalists described the persistence of spatially distinct value systems and identities that continued to define regions as cultural spaces, a persistence that was especially notable for regions populated by minority nations. In these cases, individuals frequently espouse multiple political identities, which continue to be available to political elites for mobilization purposes despite a trend over time towards cultural convergence. Marxists, too, are less sanguine than modernization theorists about the convergence of regions undergoing development within a global capitalist system, though there remains some disagreement on this point. What is shared within this approach is certainty about the necessity to understand the past, present, and future of regions in terms of the economic forces acting on and within them. Institutional theorists of various persuasions bring to the study of regions their insights into the independent shaping effect on regions and regionalism exerted by the design and workings of political and social institutions.

The degree of institutionalization of regions, and the extent of their autonomy from central governments, is directly related to two factors: (1) whether the country in question is a federal state with a constitutionally protected division of powers between central and regional governments and autonomous, democratically elected representative assemblies; and (2) whether the state in question is a multinational one, in the sense of having one or more clearly defined ethno-territorial minorities with claims to historic nation status. In the case of Canada, both of these conditions exist, virtually ensuring the ongoing development of power-sharing arrangements as political elites seek to accommodate regionalist movements and sentiment.[7]

Finally, the regional differentiation produced by the processes associated with economic development is linked to the timing and forms of regionalism that subsequently emerged. Changes in regional development policy can be related to changes in Canada's political economy, most recently the changes associated with globalization. As the determinants of regional economic success have come to rely more on the social, cultural, and technological strengths of regions that must now compete within a global marketplace, a more complex understanding of regional development has taken shape, initiating some movement towards more regionalized forms of governance.

References and Suggested Readings

Adams, Michael. 2003. *Fire and Ice: Canada, the United States, and the Myth of Converging Values*. Toronto: Penguin.

Almond, G., and S. Verba. 1965. *The Civic Culture*. Boston: Little, Brown.

Amin, A. 1999. "An Institutionalist Perspective on Regional Economic Development." *International Journal of Urban and Regional Research* 23, 2: 365–78.

Aucoin, Peter. 1985. "Regionalism, Party, and National Government." In P. Aucoin, research coordinator, *Party Government and Regional Representation in Canada*, Vol. 36, Research Studies: Royal Commission on the Economic Union and Development Prospects for Canada. Toronto: University of Toronto Press. 137–60.

Bickerton, J. 1990. *Nova Scotia, Ottawa, and the Politics of Regional Development*. Toronto: University of Toronto Press.

Bickerton, J. 1999. "Regionalism in Canada." In J. Bickerton and Alain-G. Gagnon, eds., *Canadian Politics*, 3rd ed. Peterborough: Broadview Press. 209–38.

Bickerton, J. 2007. "Between Integration and Fragmentation: Political Parties and the Representation of Regions." In Alain-G. Gagnon and B. Tanguay, eds., *Canadian Parties in Transition*, 3rd ed. Peterborough: Broadview Press. 411–35.

Bickerton, J., and Alain-G. Gagnon. 2008. "Regions." In D. Caramani, ed., *Comparative Politics*. Oxford: Oxford University Press. 367–391.

Bickerton, J., Alain-G. Gagnon, and P. Smith. 1999. *Ties That Bind: Parties and Voters in Canada*. Toronto: Oxford University Press.

---

7. As evidenced by Quebec within Canada, where minority nationalist movements are present, the tendency will be for this regional accommodation to evolve in the direction of asymmetrical arrangements.

Brenner, R. 1977. "The Origin of Capitalist Development: A Critique of Neo-Smithian Marxism." *New Left Review* 104 (July–August): 25–92.

Brodie, J. 1990. *The Political Economy of Canadian Regionalism.* Toronto: Harcourt, Brace, Jovanovitch.

Brym, R., Ed. 1986. *Regionalism in Canada.* Richmond Hill: Irwin.

Cairns, A. 1968. "The Electoral System and the Party System in Canada, 1921–1965." *Canadian Journal of Political Science* 1, 1: 55–80.

Cairns, A. 1977. "The Governments and Societies of Canadian Federalism." *Canadian Journal of Political Science* 10, 4: 695–725.

Cairns, A. 2004. "First Nations and the Canadian Nation: Colonization and Constitutional Alienation." In J. Bickerton and Alain-G. Gagnon, eds., *Canadian Politics*, 4th ed. Peterborough: Broadview Press. 349–67.

Carney, J. 1980. "Regions in Crisis: Accumulation, Regional Problems, and Crisis Formation." In J. Carney, R. Hudson, and J. Lewis, eds., *Regions in Crisis: New Perspectives in European Regional Theory.* London: Croom Helm. 28–59.

Carty, R. Kenneth, William Cross, and Lisa Young. 2000-01. "Canadian Party Politics in the New Century." *Journal of Canadian Studies* 35, 4: 23–39.

Clark, G. 1980. "Capitalism and Regional Disparities." *Annals of the American Association of Geographers* 70, 2: 521–32.

Elkins, D., and R. Simeon. 1974. "Regional Political Cultures in Canada." *Canadian Journal of Political Science* 6, 3: 397–437.

Elkins, D., and R. Simeon, Eds. 1980. *Small Worlds: Provinces and Parties in Canadian Political Life.* Agincourt: Methuen.

Florida, R. 2003. *The Rise of the Creative Class.* New York: Basic Books.

Forbes, E. 1979. *The Maritime Rights Movement, 1919–1927: A Study in Canadian Regionalism.* Montreal: McGill-Queen's University Press.

Gagnon, Alain-G., and J. Tully, Eds. 2001. *Multinational Democracies.* Cambridge: Cambridge University Press.

Gagnon, Alain-G., and J. Hérivault. 2007. "The Bloc Québécois: Charting New Territories?" In Alain-G. Gagnon and B. Tanguay, eds., *Canadian Parties in Transition*, 3rd ed. Peterborough: Broadview Press. 111–36.

Gagnon, Alain-G., and R. Iacovino. 2007. *Federalism, Citizenship, and Quebec: Debating Multinationalism.* Toronto: University of Toronto Press.

Gibbins, R. 1980. *Prairie Politics and Society: Regionalism in Decline.* Toronto: Butterworths.

Gibbins, R. 2004a. "Constitutional Politics." In J. Bickerton and Alain-G. Gagnon, eds., *Canadian Politics,* 4th ed. Peterborough: Broadview Press. 127–44.

Gibbins, R. 2004b. "Regional Integration and National Contexts: Constraints and Opportunities." In S. Tomblin and C. Colgan, eds., *Regionalism in a Global Society: Persistence and Change in Atlantic Canada and New England.* Peterborough: Broadview Press. 37–56.

Gibbins, R. 2005. "Early Warning, No Response: Alan Cairns and Electoral Reform." In G. Kernerman and P. Resnick, eds., *Insiders and Outsiders: Alan Cairns and the Reshaping of Canadian Citizenship.* Vancouver: University of British Columbia Press. 39–50.

Gibbins, R., and L. Berdahl. 2003. *Western Visions, Western Futures: Perspectives on the West in Canada*, 2nd ed. Peterborough: Broadview Press.

Gidengil, E. 1989. "Class and Region in Canadian Voting: A Dependency Interpretation." *Canadian Journal of Political Science* 22: 563–88.

Hartz, L. 1955. *The Liberal Tradition in America.* New York: Harcourt, Brace and World.

Hartz, L., Ed. 1964. *The Founding of New Societies.* New York: Harcourt, Brace and World.

Hechter, M. 1975. *Internal Colonialism: The Celtic Fringe in British National Development, 1536–1966*. Berkeley: University of California Press.

Hobsbawm, E. 1977. "Some Reflections on 'The Breakup of Britain.'" *New Left Review* 105: 3–23.

Horowitz, G. 1968. *Canadian Labour in Politics*. Toronto: University of Toronto Press.

Johnston, R. 1985. "The Reproduction of the Religious Cleavage in Canadian Elections." *Canadian Journal of Political Science* 18: 99–114.

Johnston, R. 2005. "The Electoral System and the Party System Revisited." In G. Kernerman and P. Resnick, eds., *Insiders and Outsiders: Alan Cairns and the Reshaping of Canadian Citizenship*. Vancouver: University of British Columbia Press. 51–64.

Keating, M. 1997. "The Political Economy of Regionalism." In M. Keating and J. Loughlin, eds., *The Political Economy of Regionalism*. London: Frank Cass. 17–40.

Keating, M. 2004. "Introduction." In M. Keating, ed., *Regions and Regionalism in Europe*. Cheltenham: Edward Elgar. xi–xv.

Lancaster, T., and M. Lewis-Beck. 1989. "Regional Vote Support: The Spanish Case." *International Studies Quarterly* 33, 1: 29–43.

Lecours, A. 2005. "New Institutionalism: Issues and Questions." In A. Lecours, ed., *New Institutionalism: Theory and Analysis*. Toronto: University of Toronto Press. 3–26.

Lipset, S. 1968 [1950]. *Agrarian Socialism: The Cooperative Commonwealth Federation of Saskatchewan: A Study in Political Sociology*. Garden City: Doubleday.

Lipset, S. 1990. *Continental Divide: The Values and Institutions of the United States and Canada*. New York: Routledge.

MacDermid, R. 1990. "Regionalism in Ontario." In Alain-G. Gagnon and James Bickerton, eds., *Canadian Politics: An Introduction to the Discipline*. Peterborough: Broadview Press. 360–90.

MacLennan, H. 1945. *Two Solitudes*. Toronto: MacMillan.

Macpherson, C. 1953. *Democracy in Alberta: The Theory and Practice of a Quasi-Party System*. Toronto: University of Toronto Press.

Maiz, R., and F. Requejo. *Democracy, Nationalism, and Multiculturalism*. London: Routledge.

Markusen, A. 1987. *Regions: The Economics and Politics of Territory*. Totowa: Rowman and Littlefield.

McRae, K. 1964. "The Structure of Canadian History." In L. Hartz, ed., *The Founding of New Societies*. New York: Harcourt, Brace and World. 219–74.

Myrdal, G. 1957. *Economic Theory and Underdeveloped Regions*. London: Gerald Duckworth.

Nairn, T. 1977. *The Break-up of Britain: Crisis and Neo-nationalism*. London: New Left Books.

Nevitte, N. 1996. *The Decline of Deference: Canadian Value Change in Cross-National Perspective*. Peterborough: Broadview Press.

Ornstein, M. 1986. "Regionalism and Canadian Political Ideology." In Robert Brym, ed., *Regionalism in Canada*. Toronto, ON: Irwin. 47–88.

Perroux, F. 1950. "Economic Space: Theory and Applications." *Quarterly Journal of Economics* 64: 89–104.

Piore, M., and C. Sabel. 1984. *The Second Industrial Divide: Possibilities for Prosperity*. New York: Basic Books.

Porter, M. 1990. *The Competitive Advantage of Nations*. New York: Free Press.

Putnam, R. 1993. *Making Democracy Work: Civic Traditions in Modern Italy*. Princeton: Princeton University Press.

Rasporich, B. 1997. "Regional Identities: Introduction." In D. Taras and B. Rasporich, eds., *A Passion for Identity: An Introduction to Canadian Studies*, 3rd ed. Toronto: Nelson.

Rokkan, S. 1980. "Territories, Centres, and Peripheries: Toward a Geoethnic, Geo-economic, Geopolitical Model of Differentiation within Western Europe." In J. Gottman, ed., *Centre and Periphery: Spatial Variation in Politics.* Beverly Hills and London: Sage Publications. 163–204.

Savoie, D. 2006. *Visiting Grandchildren: Economic Development in the Maritimes.* Toronto: University of Toronto Press.

Shils, E. 1975. *Center and Periphery: Essays in Macrosociology.* Chicago: University of Chicago Press.

Siegfried, A. 1966. *The Race Question in Canada.* Toronto: MacMillan.

Simeon, R. 1977. "Regionalism and Canadian Political Institutions." In J. Meekison, ed., *Canadian Federalism: Myth or Reality?* Toronto: Methuen. 292–301.

Smiley, Donald, and Ronald L. Watts. 1986. *Intrastate Federalism in Canada.* Vol. 39, Research Studies: Royal Commission on the Economic Union and Development Prospects for Canada. Toronto: University of Toronto Press.

Soja, E. 1989. *Postmodern Geographies: The Reassertion of Space in Critical Social Theory.* New York: Verso.

Stevenson, G. 1980. "Canadian Regionalism in Continental Perspective." *Journal of Canadian Studies* 15, 2: 16–27.

Stewart, I. 1990. "Putting Humpty Dumpty Together: The Study of Canadian Political Culture." In Alain-G. Gagnon and James Bickerton, eds., *Canadian Politics: An Introduction to the Discipline.* Peterborough: Broadview Press. 89–105.

Stohr, W., Ed. 1990. *Global Challenge and Local Response: Initiatives for Economic Regeneration in Contemporary Europe.* London and New York: The United Nations University and Mansell Publishing.

Storper, M. 1995. "The Resurgence of Regional Economies, Ten Years Later: The Region as a Nexus of Untraded Interdependencies." *European Urban and Regional Studies* 2, 3: 191–221.

Tarrow, S. 1977. *Between Center and Periphery: Grassroots Politicians in Italy and France.* New York: Yale University Press.

Turner, F. 1894. "The Significance of the Frontier in American History." *Annual Report for 1893.* Washington, DC: American Historical Association. 199–277.

Urwin, D. 1998. "Modern Democratic Experiences of Territorial Management: Single Houses, But Many Mansions." *Regional and Federal Studies* 8, 2: 81–110.

Vilar, P. 1977. *Catalunya en la Espana moderna.* Barcelona: Editorial Critica.

Wallerstein. 1979. *The Capitalist World Economy.* Cambridge: Cambridge University Press.

Watts, R. 1999. *Comparing Federal Systems,* 2nd ed. Kingston: Institute of Intergovernmental Relations.

Wiseman, N. 1981. "The Pattern of Prairie Politics." *Queen's Quarterly* 88: 298–315.

Young, L., and K. Archer, Eds. 2002. *Regionalism and Party Politics in Canada.* Don Mills: Oxford University Press.

PART II

Institutions

five

Constitutional Politics

ROGER GIBBINS

Given the pervasive nature of constitutional discourse in Canada, it may come as a surprise that our political life has not always been wracked by constitutional debate. In fact, constitutional politics played little role in the first 100 years following Confederation in 1867. True, the political institutions put into place by the 1867 Constitution Act shaped political life, as did principles implicitly embedded in the Constitution, such as responsible government and party discipline. However, the constitutional order itself received little attention. The great clashes of Canadian politics were not fought on the constitutional plain, nor did the Constitution provide many of the rhetorical weapons of political combat. The constitutionalization of political life is a recent event, albeit one that taps political cleavages generations old.

The objective of this chapter is to map out the evolution of constitutionalization. The first section will examine the 1867 constitutional settlement, the second the relatively static constitutional landscape from 1867 to 1960, and the third the more turbulent period stretching from 1960 to the 1995 Quebec referendum on sovereignty-association. This historical treatment provides the essential context within which contemporary constitutional politics must be viewed; as we will see, the constitutional politics of any one era largely reflect the unresolved constitutional issues of preceding eras. Throughout, the primary although not exclusive focus will be on the formal Constitution as embodied in such documents as the Constitution Act, 1867 (formerly known as the British North America Act, 1867) and the Constitution Act, 1982, which includes the Charter of Rights and Freedoms. Less attention will be paid to the constitutional conventions, such as those structuring party discipline and ministerial responsibility, conventions rooted in the formal constitution but lacking textual status. They are the "rules of the game" that can only be broken or set aside at considerable risk. Although these latter elements are important components of the larger constitutional order, they have not had as high a profile in recent debate as has the formal text of the Constitution.

The Confederation Settlement of 1867

When our founding fathers met in Charlottetown, Quebec City, and London, England, during the mid-1860s to draft a new constitution, they were not writing on a blank slate. Documents such as the 1763 Royal Proclamation and the 1774 Quebec Act were part of the frame within which they worked, as was the long history of British constitutional evolution dating back to the Magna Carta in 1215. Nor, for that matter, was the political agenda all that new: fending off military threats from the United States, overcoming deadlock in the colonial legislatures, providing a financial foundation for western expansion, and bridging both linguistic and religious conflicts between English Canada and French Canada were ongoing tasks. Nonetheless, the immediate constitutional problems the founding fathers faced were new: (1) how to design a national government encompassing the existing colonies of Canada, New Brunswick, and Nova Scotia while allowing for the future entry of new provinces; (2) how to forge a *federal* system linking this national government to new provincial governments; and (3) how to create a new imperial relationship between Canada and the British Crown.

All of these tasks were accomplished through the 1867 Constitution Act. A Canadian Parliament was created with two legislative chambers, the elected House of Commons and the appointed Senate. The governor general, whose consent was needed before any bill passed by the two chambers became law, provided a link to the British Crown and, for some time, to the British government. Legislative assemblies were created for the new provinces of Ontario and Quebec, the existing legislative assemblies in Nova Scotia and New Brunswick were incorporated, and all four were linked by their lieutenant-governors to the government of Canada. A national judiciary was created, and the legislative powers of the new Canadian state were divided between the federal and provincial orders of government. The federal government was assigned the principal economic and taxation powers of the day while the provincial jurisdiction encompassed matters of more local concern, including schools, hospitals, municipal institutions, the management of public lands, and property and civil rights.

The Act also declared that Canada should have a system of government "similar in Principle to that of the United Kingdom." It was through this clause that we imported the British conventions of responsible government and party discipline, and consolidated existing Canadian practice in these respects. The conventions included the assumption that governments will tender their resignation if they are unable to command a majority vote in the House of Commons for major legislative initiatives and thus established the dominating role that party discipline plays to this day in legislative politics in both Ottawa and the provincial capitals. Despite the lack of a more explicit constitutional definition than "similar in principle to," Canadians were to hold fast to these conventions long after they had come under creative reform in the home Parliament. Oddly enough, Canadians have been more faithful than the British to the strict application of party discipline, even though it can be argued that our far-flung, regionally diverse federal system is not well served by rigid party discipline in the national legislature.

Much was accomplished by the 1867 Constitution Act. However, when Canadians think of the Act, it is the *federal elements* of the Act that come to the fore. Indeed, for most people the division of powers in Sections 91 and 92 between the national and provincial legislatures is about all that comes to mind. This perception captures an important feature of the 1867 Act — its almost unbroken silence with regard to a host of fundamental issues.

1. Apart from the establishment of both English and French as languages of record and debate in the federal Parliament and Quebec National Assembly, the 1867 Act is silent on the place of the francophone community in the new Canadian nation and state. Quebec is present, to be sure, but in most respects it is present as a province like the others; there is no hint of a special constitutional status as a *distinct society*. Nor does *French Canada* figure in the Act, even though it was one of the most important realities with which the founding fathers wrestled.

2. The 1867 Act says nothing about the position of Aboriginal peoples in the new federal state other than the sparse Section 91, clause 24 assignment of "Indians, and Lands reserved for Indians" to the jurisdictional domain of the national Parliament. Certainly there is nothing to suggest that Aboriginal peoples should be recognized as founding peoples or that they might have some special relationship with the settler communities to come. The nation-to-nation underpinnings of the 1763 Royal Proclamation were not explicitly imported into the 1867 Act, although it can be argued that the eventual Canadianization of the Crown had this effect. Thus, when references to the Crown gradually came to mean "the Crown in Canada" rather than "the Crown in Britain," Aboriginal peoples could assert a new nation-to-nation relationship within the Canadian state.

3. There is no recognition of popular sovereignty; the American notion of "We the People" is completely absent. Popular consent for the Act was not sought and might not have been found had it been sought.

4. There are no references in the Act to the rights of citizens. Whereas the French Revolution produced the 1789 Declaration of the Rights

of Man and Citizen, and the even earlier 1776 American Declaration of Independence referred to universal rights — "We hold these truths to be self-evident that all men are created equal" — the 1867 Act refers only to the powers of the Crown and the distribution of legislative responsibilities between the national and provincial governments. As a consequence, the Act has never served as a vehicle for civic education; schoolchildren have been spared the task of memorizing its dry and often arcane passages.

5. There was no declaration of independence from Britain embedded in the Act, or even the suggestion that this might come. Moreover, because the Act was an act of the British Parliament, it could only be amended by that Parliament. Unlike the earlier American Constitution (1791) or the later Australian Constitution (1901), the Constitution Act did not contain an amending formula; it could not be amended directly by Canadian legislatures until 1982.

There is one additional silence that warrants more detailed comment, and that is the matter of intergovernmental relations. Although we can read a form of national control of provincial legislatures into the role of the lieutenant-governors, and into the authority of the federal Parliament to disallow acts of provincial legislation even when these are passed within the legislative domain of the provinces, there is no hint of the vast network of intergovernmental relations that has come to characterize the contemporary federal state. This omission is not surprising. Both the national and provincial governments were new, minute in comparison with their contemporary counterparts, and were neither prepared nor inclined to fully occupy their own policy spheres, much less encroach on one another. Nonetheless, it is important to note that the contemporary intergovernmental infrastructure is not anchored to the 1867 Constitution, although it is connected to the governments created by that constitution and to the concentration of power within those governments brought about by the conventions of responsible government.[1]

When the many silences or abeyances in the 1867 Constitution Act are considered, we might have expected that the decades following

---

1. Canadian governments are able to negotiate with one another because they are not faced with the uncertainty of legislative ratification for any deals that might be struck. Because governments dominate their own legislative processes, they can be confident that any deal brought before their legislatures will be ratified. The only exception to this rule, and it is a big exception, is on the constitutional front where provincial governments can no longer be confident of their ability to control the legislative and public consultation dynamics of constitutional amendment.

Confederation would have been chock full of debate as Canadians sought to flesh out their skeletal constitutional blueprint. This is particularly the case given that the "national question" — the principled relationship between English and French Canada — was scarcely addressed, much less resolved, in 1867. However, this expectation was not met. Although many political conflicts were to come, the Constitution itself was seldom the target or arena of debate. It would take almost 100 years before Canadians began to address the gaps in the 1867 Act.

The Next Hundred Years

It is difficult to reconstruct in a few short pages the nearly 100 years of rich and complex Canadian political history stretching from Confederation to Quebec's Quiet Revolution in the early 1960s. Nevertheless, it is possible to offer a few broad observations.

The first and perhaps most important observation, and certainly the most surprising, is that the lack of specification for the relationship between French and English Canada produced very little constitutional agitation in Quebec and *no* agitation outside Quebec. There was no sustained campaign to change the constitutional framework. Rather, the primary effort of Quebec politicians was to protect the framework put in place in 1867. Admittedly, there was unease and even dismay when the settlement of the Canadian West departed so radically from the bicultural and bilingual format of central Canada and when the constitutional guarantees for linguistic minorities embedded in the legislative frameworks of the new prairie provinces were ignored. However, when conflicts arose, Quebec opted not to risk its own autonomy by encouraging federal intervention in the internal affairs of other provinces. Quebec nationalism, therefore, was defensive in character, seeking to maintain rather than to change the status quo.

This strategy was put to the test in the 15 years following the end of the Second World War when the federal government began to flex its spending power to encroach on provincial fields of jurisdiction. The creation of conditional grant programs and the consequent infusion of federal funds with respect to health care, social assistance, highways, and post-secondary education raised little concern outside Quebec, in large part because they came at a time of exploding demand that provincial tax revenues were simply unable to meet. However, they were challenged by the Quebec government as an assault on the original federal pact. Again, Quebec's strategy was defensive: to protect the existing constitutional division of powers from intrusions by the federal government even when those programs came with funds attached.

The potential for constitutional discontent simmered in the Canadian West. The regional agricultural community railed against freight rates, tariffs, bottlenecks in the transportation of grain, and inequities in the marketing of grain. At times, this regional discontent verged on challenges to the constitutional status quo. However, and with the important exception of agitation leading to the 1930 Natural Resources Transfer Act, which put Crown lands in the West on an equal footing with Crown lands elsewhere in the country, regional discontent was channelled into partisan outlets and attacks on the party system. Western Canadians sought a reduction in partisan constraints on political representation and, when that failed, launched a series of new political parties and movements to take the region's case to Ottawa. What was absent was any serious questioning of federal institutions or the federal division of powers. What was sought was a more effective voice within the national Parliament rather than the devolution of powers from Ottawa to provincial legislatures. This Western strategy stemmed from a simple reality: the legislative powers that really counted for Western Canadians — tariffs, international trade, interprovincial transportation, bank rates, and so forth — belonged logically to the national government; they could not be devolved to the provinces without breaking the country apart, and this Western Canadians had no desire to do.[2] As the Reform Party was to frame the issue in the late 1980s, "The West wants in." Thus, in the decades leading up to Quebec's Quiet Revolution, regional discontent seldom found expression in *constitutional* politics.

Other potential drivers of constitutional politics in this period were not factors in the first six decades of the twentieth century. After the suffragists won a monumental victory by securing the vote for women in the second decade of the century, feminism waned as a public policy issue until the early 1960s. There was no concerted effort to address the social, economic, and political aspirations of women through constitutional channels or constitutional reform. Aboriginal peoples, who were not given an unconstrained right to vote until 1961, were very much at the margins of Canadian political discourse and lacked sufficient political voice to drive constitutional reform even had they been interested in doing so. The Maritime Rights Movement in the early 1920s had challenged the fairness of the Canadian federal state, but the grievances it articulated came to be addressed through federal programs rather than through proposals for constitutional reform. Those who sought a more powerful central government capable of delivering univer-

---

2. These economic powers could, however, be devolved to the market. This happened through the Canada–US Free Trade Agreement and the North American Free Trade Agreement (NAFTA).

sal social programs found that any constitutional constraints wilted before Ottawa's expanding revenues and unbridled use of the spending power.

Therefore, for almost 100 years after Confederation it appeared that the 1867 constitutional agreement was holding fast, that the founding fathers had constructed a durable constitutional framework for a country marked by great regional, ethnic, and linguistic diversity. This belief was quickly dispelled when Quebec's Quiet Revolution began in the early 1960s.

From the Quiet Revolution to 1982

Although the onset of the Quiet Revolution is identified with the 1960 election of the Quebec Liberal Party, it is best seen as an accumulation of social and economic change that began before 1960 and carried through into the following decades. Quebec was transformed from a society in which religious institutions and norms played a dominant role to one of the most secular provinces in Canada. Economic activity shifted from the rural countryside to the urban heartland, and the public philosophy of government changed from narrow conservatism, both social and economic, to expansive state intervention in the social and economic orders. The Quebec birth rate dropped from the highest in Canada to the lowest within a period of little more than two decades. The French language enjoyed a strong renaissance, becoming the language not only of culture in the province but also of business. In short, Quebec rapidly emerged as a very different kind of province.

The political effects of the Quiet Revolution were somewhat unexpected, for although Quebec moved closer to the Canadian social and economic mainstreams, increased similarity did not moderate political differences between Quebec and the rest of Canada. The differences, in fact, intensified as a strong nationalist movement developed in Quebec. Its slogan — "*Maîtres chez nous*," or "masters in our own house" — captured a fundamental challenge to the constitutional status quo as a series of Quebec governments demanded, at the very least, the roll-back of federal intrusions into provincial fields of jurisdiction and the expansion of those fields. More broadly, the nationalist movement advanced the argument that Quebec was not a province like the others, that it alone was home to a national community. This meant, in turn, that Quebec should have a unique constitutional status as a distinct society. More extreme manifestations of the same argument, and they were many, maintained that Quebec should become a sovereign state with full control over its own destiny.

Given the transformation of Quebec society and that Quebec voters made up more than 25 per cent of the national electorate, there is no question that the Quiet Revolution would have caused waves within the federal system.

However, those waves were greatly amplified by the threat of separation and the possible destruction of Canada as we had come to know it. It was the existence of sovereigntists intent upon the creation of an independent Quebec that gave a sense of urgency for reform of the federal system. Now that Quebec had dropped its defence of the constitutional status quo, the rest of the country did the same and embarked on an extensive search for reform proposals to counter the arguments of Quebec sovereigntists. This process was intensified and complicated by the emergence of other sources of political unrest. Economic prosperity in the West coupled with the lack of effective regional representation in the House of Commons, the radicalization of Aboriginal peoples, and the growing political clout of new social movements such as feminism and environmentalism all added to the constitutional ferment.

Constitutional politics came to a boil in 1976 when Quebec voters elected a Parti Québécois (PQ) government committed to holding a referendum on sovereignty (or sovereignty-association) before the end of its term. From the election of the PQ through to the referendum in the spring of 1980, the country went through an intense period of constitutional debate, proposals, and counter-proposals. The tension rose after February 1980, when Pierre Trudeau and his Liberal government returned to power in Ottawa after the short-lived Progressive Conservative government of Joe Clark. The 1980 federal election placed Trudeau and Quebec Premier René Lévesque toe-to-toe in the Quebec referendum campaign as the respective champions of federalism and sovereignty. In that campaign, Trudeau promised the Québécois specifically and Canadians more generally a "renewed federalism" should Quebec reject the ballot proposal for sovereignty-association between Quebec and Canada. When it was defeated by a 40/60 margin, Canadian governments turned again to constitutional negotiations.

Reform, it seemed, was inescapable, for although the Quebec sovereigntists had lost the referendum, they had not been driven from the field. Held at bay in the referendum by the promise of constitutional reform, the PQ nonetheless won the subsequent provincial election. It was assumed, therefore, that any reform would address explicitly the place of Quebec in Canada. The Québécois may have rejected sovereignty-association, but the separatist threat was still very much alive. Something had to give.

The Constitution Act, 1982

There is no question that the proclamation of the Constitution Act on April 17, 1982, by Her Majesty Queen Elizabeth II at a rain-swept ceremony on Parliament Hill was a momentous event in Canada's constitutional history and evolution. The Act patriated Canada's founding constitutional document (the Constitution Act of 1867) and established a set of amending formulae that would require only the consent of Canadian legislative assemblies and not the British Parliament.[3] It provided the first explicit constitutional acknowledgement of Aboriginal rights; a limited form of provincial equality; and constitutional recognition of multiculturalism, gender equality, regional equalization, and intergovernmental relations (through its mention of First Ministers' Conferences). The Act incorporated the Canadian Charter of Rights and Freedoms, and thus, for the first time, the courts could strike down federal or provincial legislation on grounds other than a violation of the federal-provincial division of powers. The courts were thereby catapulted into the centre of Canadian political life, although their power was counterbalanced by Section 1 ("The Canadian Charter of Rights and Freedoms guarantees the rights and freedoms set out in it subject only to such reasonable limits prescribed by law as can be demonstrably justified in a free and democratic society") and, less effectively, by the notwithstanding provision in Section 33.[4] It is difficult, therefore, to overestimate the impact of the 1982 Act.

However, and like the 1867 Act before it, the 1982 Act is also notable for what it did *not* do. Apart from providing some additional protection for the provincial ownership of natural resources, it did not modify the existing federal division of powers, despite the fact that that division had been the focus of 15 years of constitutional debate. The Act, like its predecessor, did not embody any expression of popular sovereignty; the assent of the Canadian people was required neither for its passage in 1982 nor for its subsequent amendment.[5] Although the amending formulae do require legislative consent and not just the signatures of the first ministers, direct popular consent is not needed. Parliamentary institutions, including the appointed and widely scorned Senate, were left untouched. The most outstanding omission, however, was the Act's silence on the national question or, more specifically, on the place of French Canada and Quebec in the national fabric. The Act did constitutionalize the official status of the English and French languages, but it did not address Quebec's role as a founding partner. It did not provide any special role for

---

3. The amending formulae are set out in Sections 38 to 49 of the Constitution. The basic formula calls for the consent of Parliament plus the legislatures of at least two-thirds (seven) of the provinces, which, among them, contain at least 50 per cent of the Canadian population.

4. The "notwithstanding" clause allows legislatures to override Sections 2 or 7 through 15 of the Charter for a period of up to five years (renewable) provided that they explicitly do so by invoking the notwithstanding clause.

5. For a still insightful look at the very tentative fashion in which Canadian constitutional politics has embraced popular sovereignty and democratic principles, see Whitaker, 1983.

Quebec in the amending formulae, nor did it address long-standing Quebec aspirations for a larger share in the federal division of powers.

The Act's silence on these issues provided a critically important *implicit* statement. Silence implied that Quebec had no special role, that the terminology of "founding peoples" had been rejected, that the Constitution could be amended in many respects without Quebec's consent, that Quebec provincial legislation would be subject to the Charter and to interpretation by a Supreme Court that Quebec played no role in appointing, and that the Quebec National Assembly would exercise (at least formally) the same powers as other provincial legislatures. In short, Quebec within the 1982 Act was a province like the others. This message was driven home when the new Constitution took effect even though it had not been signed by Quebec Premier René Lévesque and had been rejected by an all-party resolution passed in the Quebec National Assembly.

Here was a fascinating paradox: nearly two decades of constitutional debate, driven largely by the nationalist movement in Quebec, finally gave birth to a new constitutional order that failed to address (except by silence) the central concerns of the nationalist movement and was rejected by Quebec.[6] Indeed, it can be argued that with the possible exception of the constitutionalization of official bilingualism, the 1982 Act could well have been written by the rest of Canada without any reference to Quebec. Thus, the new constitutional order initiated by the desire to quell the sovereigntist movement soon led to a reinvigorated national unity crisis. Donald Smiley's 1983 description of the Act as a "dangerous deed" was prophetic.

The Legacy of 1982

The proclamation of the Constitution Act in 1982 left Canada an awkward legacy: a constitutional process designed to assuage nationalist sentiment in Quebec had instead rendered the province a constitutional outsider, bitter and angry that a new constitution had been "imposed" without its consent. Although the 1982 Act, and particularly the Charter, had been well received in the rest of Canada, Quebec political elites proved an exception. (Quebec elites did not oppose the liberal values embedded in the Charter but rather the constraints of Canada-wide jurisprudence on Quebec legislation.) It was

---

6. Perceptions outside Quebec of Quebec's rejection were blunted by the close association between Pierre Trudeau and the Constitution Act. The fact that Trudeau's Liberals held 74 of the 75 seats in Quebec made it possible to argue that although the government of Quebec rejected the new Constitution, the people of Quebec did not. Whether the people of Quebec sided in this matter with their provincial or federal representatives was not put to the test.

inevitable, therefore, that someone would try to address this legacy and bring Quebec back into the "constitutional family." The man who stepped into this breech was Prime Minister Brian Mulroney who, during his term of office stretching from 1984 to 1993, enjoyed strong electoral support in Quebec.

Mulroney made two attempts to bring constitutional peace to the land: the Meech Lake Accord, drafted by the 11 first ministers in the early spring of 1987, and the Charlottetown Accord, put together through a much more elaborate process extending from the summer of 1991 to the late fall of 1992. Although both ended in failure, leaving the formal constitutional text unchanged, they had a lasting impact on constitutional conventions and the process of constitutional reform. Both, moreover, encapsulated a particular vision of the Canadian federal state, and it is the defeat of this vision that forms our new constitutional legacy for the twenty-first century.

There is insufficient space here to describe in detail the content of the two accords or the political dynamics in which they became enmeshed. It should be stressed, however, that both were built around the core principle that Quebec should be recognized as having a constitutional status in some way distinct from that of other provinces. The Meech Lake Accord, put together in a private meeting of the 11 first ministers and with virtually no public anticipation, embraced little more than this principle. Quebec was to be recognized as a distinct society, and in light of this recognition, additional constitutional amendments were proposed relating to Quebec's role in immigration, constitutional amendment, the appointment of Supreme Court judges, and opting out of national social programs without financial penalty. Meech Lake was conceived and described as the "Quebec round" in an ongoing process of constitutional reform; other issues were delayed until the hypothetical rounds to follow. Issues such as Senate reform or the constitutional recognition of Aboriginal self-government, it was argued, could only be addressed once Quebec's aspirations had been satisfied and the Quebec National Assembly had retroactively endorsed the 1982 Constitution Act.

The Meech Lake Accord, even though it came within a whisker of ratification, is now remembered as a major failure and serious miscalculation by the Mulroney government. Failure came not on the heels of public outcry but rather through a series of miscues in New Brunswick, Manitoba, and Newfoundland. True, when the Accord finally died in the late spring of 1990, public support had waned considerably, but there was no reason to conclude that Canadians had rejected the Accord's principled core. However, there was a broad political consensus on two important conclusions. First, any future attempt at constitutional reform would have to entail a much broader process of public consultation; reform could no longer be entrusted to "11 white men" meeting behind closed doors. An inevitable consequence of broader consultation would be an expanded reform agenda, and hence the second conclusion: Quebec's constitutional aspirations could no longer be addressed first or in isolation. The "Quebec round" in 1987 therefore became the "Canada round" in 1992 when Quebec's concerns were addressed in conjunction with the constitutional aspirations of Senate reformers, Aboriginal peoples, social democrats, feminists, environmentalists, and whatever other group or interest was able to shoulder its way to the increasingly crowded constitutional table.

There is little question in my mind that both conclusions were sound and seemingly inescapable, yet they also led to a constitutional process in 1991–92 that was unworkable. Too many competing demands hatched too many compromises, and the diluted final product satisfied no one. Senate reform was proposed — but not in a form that appealed to true believers in the West. Quebec's specificity was addressed — but not to the satisfaction of even "soft nationalists" in that province. Perhaps the only ones whose concerns were fully, even exceptionally, addressed were Aboriginal peoples, whose interests were woven into virtually every clause of the 1992 Charlottetown Accord. (Even then, Aboriginal people in the end did not support the Accord.) When it became clear that Quebec, Alberta, and British Columbia would hold referendums prior to ratification, the federal government reluctantly agreed to hold a rest-of-Canada referendum in conjunction with the Quebec vote. Despite endorsement from all federal parties except the Reform Party of Canada, and from all provincial governments and the business community, the Canadian electorate was not impressed. On October 26, 1992, the Accord went down to national defeat. Only voters in Newfoundland, Prince Edward Island, New Brunswick, and, by the narrowest of margins, Ontario approved the Accord. Across the country, 45.7 per cent voted "yes" and 54.3 per cent "no," virtually identical to the 43.3/56.7 per cent split in Quebec alone.

The referendum defeat brought the reform process to a shuddering halt. Intergovernmental negotiations stopped, and public consultation was avoided like the plague. If countries can "burn out," then Canada had. Thus, when the PQ government held a referendum on sovereignty (with an economic partnership) in October 1995, the rest of the country could do little more than hold its collective breath. When the referendum was defeated by a very narrow margin — approximately 50,000 votes province-wide — the federal Liberal government rushed legislation through Parliament recognizing Quebec as a distinct society within the operations of the federal government and "lending" Parliament's veto to Quebec, thereby ensuring that Parliament could not pursue constitutional amendments without the prior consent of the Quebec National Assembly. (In effect, Parliament unilaterally overrode the 1982 amending formula by granting Quebec a *de facto* veto.) Still, the formal text of the Constitution was left unchanged, and there is little evidence that electoral support for independence was significantly eroded by the jerry-rigged amending formula and parliamentary recognition of an established fact of Canadian political life, that Quebec's concerns were to be treated with special sensitivity within the federal government.

In the wake of the 1995 Quebec referendum, the nine premiers from outside Quebec met in Calgary to consider a non-constitutional offer to the people of Quebec, an offer couched for the most part in general principles that might be acceptable across the country. Quebec would be recognized as a distinct society, but within a framework of individual *and provincial* equality, in more limited terms than in either the 1987 or 1992 accords, and through acts of provincial legislatures rather than in the formal text of the Constitution. The Calgary Declaration escaped the assumed prohibition on another "Quebec-only" round by appealing to general principles and characteristics of Canada, and by sidestepping the formalities of constitutional reform altogether. The Declaration was presented as an alternative to constitutional reform, although it is hard to escape the suspicion that the drafters saw it as much as a precursor as they did an alternative. Certainly the federal government, which had served as the behind-the-scenes midwife for the Declaration, did little to promote it as a constitutional initiative once mixed reviews came in from the Quebec electorate. The assumed need for public consultation was met by post hoc public consultations that differed from province to province, but in all cases stopped short of referendums.

The Calgary Declaration may have provided a modicum of constitutional relief. However, when the PQ government went to the people in a 1998 provincial election, the Declaration did little to arm federalists within the province and was soon abandoned even outside Quebec as a useful initiative. Francophone support for the sovereigntists held firm, and the arrival of former federal Progressive Conservative leader Jean Charest to lead the provincial Liberals had little immediate effect. The PQ was re-elected and promised to hold another referendum as soon as the "winning conditions" could be ensured. Canada's uneasy perch on the knife-edge of uncertainty continued.

The federal government's response to this uncertainty was the 1999 Clarity Act which gave the national Parliament the right to determine whether any future referendum question met the Supreme Court's reference case requirements for a "clear majority" on a "clear question." In the words of the Act, the House of Commons and not provincial governments would determine if a referendum question on secession was sufficiently clear to provide "a clear expression of the will of the population of a province on whether the province should cease to be part of Canada and become an independent state." The

Clarity Act, however, does not define a clear majority, although it is assumed that 50 per cent plus one would fall short. The Quebec National Assembly responded in turn with Bill 99, which rejected the application of either the Supreme Court reference case or the Clarity Act to Quebec, deeming both unacceptable limitations on the democratic will of the Quebec people. While there is no question that, through the Clarity Act, the federal government holds the upper hand in a legal sense, the political dynamics should another sovereignty referendum be held are by no means clear.

Looking Ahead

What, then, can be said of constitutional politics in the first decade of the twenty-first century? Certainly there is an emphatic consensus among political elites that Canadians are both wary and weary of constitutional debate. At the very least, mega-constitutional packages of the type exemplified by the 1992 Charlottetown Accord are not on the horizon, and even more limited constitutional initiatives such as Senate reform are argued to be impossible because they would require "opening up the Constitution." Canadians, it is assumed and asserted, would much prefer to make do with political institutions poorly designed for the nineteenth century rather than engage in constitutional reform. We are, in this sense, an extraordinarily conservative country.

The failure to ratify the 1992 Accord has been taken to heart, and it will take an extraordinary set of circumstances to embolden political leaders to embark again on formal constitutional change. The existing amending formula, coupled with the commitment to public ratification found in Alberta, British Columbia, and Quebec, has rendered formal change difficult in the extreme. When the 1996 parliamentary amendments to the formula are taken into account — those that require regional acceptance before parliamentary action can even be initiated — the task seems virtually impossible. The constitutional status quo, for better or for worse, is assumed to be the legacy for our children and their children.

But what about the drivers of constitutional reform in the past? Will their pressure cease? Here the major player is still Quebec, and it is unlikely that the sovereigntist threat will disappear, despite the respite provided by the federalist Charest government. However, an effective constitutional response by the rest of Canada to that threat, should it re-emerge, looks less and less likely. There is no constitutional middle ground beyond the status quo that will appease significant numbers of sovereigntists and at the same time be acceptable to the rest of the country. Three decades of effort have dispelled any illusion that a compromise can be found.[7] Instead, we may be locked into a perpetual game of "constitutional chicken" between the status quo and an independent Quebec, a game in which one side or the other (or both) swerves at the last second, but does so only to race again. While this may seem a form of collective madness, it is one that maximizes both Quebec's leverage on the national political scene and the electoral prospects of the federal Liberal Party, positioned as it is as the single party spanning Canada's linguistic cleavage. In short, there are no strong incentives to disengage from this constitutional war of nerves. Mega-constitutional change is more likely to occur in the wake of Quebec's departure than it is to occur as a way to prevent that departure.

Other drivers of constitutional change have included the West and Aboriginal peoples, but neither has the political weight alone to move the constitutional process. They can act only in conjunction with a crisis generated by Quebec, and then only if their constitutional aspirations coincide with federalist visions for Quebec. Thus, while Western Canadians may continue to agitate for Senate reform, such agitation will continue to fall on deaf ears in Ottawa. Given that Ottawa's impact on the Western Canadian economy and social programs continues to decline, there is also less and less reason to get "in," and the interest in institutional reform may fade to indifference. Aboriginal peoples face a similar dilemma; they lack the political weight to move the process along and therefore will work through the courts. There may be an exception if the general electorate is able to force popular ratification of future land claim settlements that entail Aboriginal self-government and substantial cash settlements. However, the emphatic reluctance of both the federal and British Columbia governments to submit the Nisga'a settlement to public ratification suggests that the future settlement of claims is unlikely to engage formal constitutional amendment.

All of this, of course, does not mean that the Constitution writ large will be static in the years to come. It means only that the formal text is unlikely to change, and the Canadian electorate is unlikely to become embroiled in constitutional politics. However, in many other ways constitutional change will still occur. As noted above, in 1996 the federal Parliament unilaterally altered the constitutional amending formula by "lending" its constitutional veto to Quebec, thus demonstrating that even the amending formula is not immune to unilateral amendment. The Nisga'a settlement shows that a constitutionally entrenched third order of government can be created without modifying the text of the Constitution Acts of 1867 and 1982. Although

---

7. It is pessimism in this regard that led Guy Laforest and I to propose a new Canada-Quebec partnership. See Gibbins, 1998.

the macro-constitutional reforms articulated in the final report of the Royal Commission on Aboriginal Peoples, including a parallel Aboriginal Parliament, are dead in the water, smaller scale *de facto* constitutional change can still be pursued through tripartite negotiations among the First Nations, provincial, and federal governments. By retaining linkages to existing treaty obligations, or in the case of British Columbia to the lack of such obligations, tripartite agreements can be effectively entrenched.

Much of the democratic reform impulse in Canada is being directed to targets that would not require formal constitutional change, at least in the short run. For example, there is a growing interest in electoral reform, albeit an interest that is much stronger in the provinces than it is among federal parties or leaders. Paul Martin's Liberal government was committed to parliamentary reform that would modestly increase the power of backbench MPs and parliamentary committees while leaving the archaic Senate untouched. Even the proponents of Senate reform themselves are arguing that constitutional change is not required, at least not yet. The Alberta government and the Canada West Foundation, for instance, argue that future Senate appointments be made from lists submitted by provincial governments, a change that would require nothing more than prime ministerial will. Stephen Harper's Conservative government attempted to implement this strategy by placing a moratorium on new Senate appointments until provincially run elections were held to fill any vacant position, but this strategy was abandoned when Harper appointed 18 new senators in December 2008, at a point when the survival of this minority government was in doubt (Fitzpatrick, 2008).

The courts will continue to rewrite and expand existing constitutional provisions. Indeed, and as the American experience has shown, the political rigidity of the formal amending formula gives the courts greater rein to pursue constitutional change through judicial interpretation, and certainly Canadian courts have shown little reticence in this respect. International agreements may impose constraints on Canadian governments that will have constitutional force even though they may not be formally incorporated into Canada's constitutional order.

Finally, it is important to note the capacity of intergovernmental relations to rewrite the federal script in Canada without the necessity of constitutional change. Although the Social Union Framework Agreement has left a relatively light impression on the federal system (and no impression whatsoever on the Canadian public), the recently created Council of the Federation has much greater potential. For Quebec, it provides a forum for the nation-to-nation interaction implicit in notions of sovereignty-association. New federal institutions such as the Health Council are tailored for Quebec exceptionalism or special status; the fact that Quebec is not a member is treated as a simple reflection of the new federal order, whereas Alberta's reluctance to join is decried and ridiculed. For all provincial governments, the Council of the Federation dampens the appeal and urgency of parliamentary reform, with its concomitant risks of constitutional change. Strengthened intergovernmentalism becomes the preferred alternative to democratic reform, although it remains to be seen if Canadian citizens will be happy with the alternative.

The future, then, will not be devoid of constitutional politics, broadly defined. The action, however, will not be directed to changes in the written text of the Constitution. (Court action is always directed to constitutional interpretation, to "reading in" new meaning, and not to changes in the formal text.) Moreover, constitutional politics will take place well away from the arenas of public participation, ratification, or consent. It might be argued, therefore, that it was not an oversight in the 1860s when the founding fathers failed to incorporate any notion of popular consent or sovereignty into Canada's constitutional framework. They may have had greater foresight than we often realize.

References and Suggested Readings

Boyer, Patrick. 1998. "'Whose Constitution is it, Anyway?' Democratic Participation and the Canadian Constitution." In Martin Westmacott and Hugh Mellon, eds., *Challenges to Canadian Federalism*. Scarborough: Prentice-Hall. 79–99.

Cairns, Alan C. 1995. "The Constitutional World We Have Lost." In A.C. Cairns, *Reconfigurations: Canadian Citizenship and Constitutional Change*. Toronto: McClelland and Stewart. 97–118.

Fitzpatrick, Meagan. 2008. "Harper appoints 18 senators." *Ottawa Citizen*, 22 December 2008.

Gibbins, Roger. 1997. "Quebec and the West." *Québec Studies* 24 (Fall): 34–45.

Gibbins, Roger, and Guy Laforest, Eds. 1998. *Beyond the Impasse: Toward Reconciliation*. Montreal: Institute for Research on Public Policy.

LaSelva, Samuel V. 1996. *The Moral Foundations of Canadian Federalism: Paradoxes, Achievements, and Tragedies of Nationhood*. Montreal: McGill-Queen's University Press.

McRoberts, Kenneth, Ed. 1995. *Beyond Quebec: Taking Stock of Canada*. Toronto: Oxford University Press.

McRoberts, Kenneth, and Patrick Monahan, Eds. 1993. *The Charlottetown Accord, the Referendum, and the Future of Canada*. Toronto: University of Toronto Press.

Russell, Peter H. 1993. *Constitutional Odyssey: Can Canadians Become a Sovereign People?* 2nd ed. Toronto: University of Toronto Press.

Smiley, Donald. 1983. "A Dangerous Deed: The Constitution Act, 1982." In Keith Banting and Richard Simeon, eds., *And No One Cheered: Federalism, Democracy, and the Constitution Act*. Toronto: Methuen. 74–95.

Taylor, Charles. 1993. *Reconciling the Solitudes: Essays on Canadian Federalism and Nationalism*. Montreal: McGill-Queen's University Press.

Thomas, David M. 1997. *Whistling Past the Graveyard: Constitutional Abeyances, Quebec, and the Future of Canada*. Toronto: Oxford University Press.

Whitaker, Reg. 1983. "Democracy and the Canadian Constitution." In Keith Banting and Richard Simeon, eds., *And No One Cheered: Federalism, Democracy, and the Constitution Act*. Toronto: Methuen. 240–60.

six

Power at the Apex:
Executive Dominance

DONALD J. SAVOIE

The executive has long held a dominant position in a Westminster-style parliamentary government. In formal constitutional terms, power is concentrated
in the hands of the prime minister and Cabinet. Recent developments in
Canada, however, suggest that the hand of the prime minister has been considerably strengthened. Indeed, when it comes to the political power inherent
in their office, Canadian prime ministers now have few equals in the West.

Gordon Robertson, former secretary to Cabinet and once described as
the gold standard for the position of Clerk of the Privy Council, wrote 30
years ago that in our system "ministers are responsible. It is their government"
(Robertson, 1971: 497). The Privy Council Office (PCO) argued in its 1993
publication on the machinery of government that "we operate under the
theory of a confederal nature of decision-making where power flows from
ministers" (Canada, 1993). I maintain, to the contrary, that power no longer
flows from ministers, but from the prime minister, and unevenly at that.

The above speaks to the evolution of how policies are struck and decisions
are made in Ottawa. J.S. Dupré argued that an "institutionalized" Cabinet
replaced the "departmentalized" Cabinet in the late 1960s and early 1970s.
Individual ministers and their departments lost a great deal of autonomy
to full Cabinet, as well as shared knowledge and collegial decision-making
(Dupré, 1987: 238–39). But, I argue, this era did not last very long before
court government started to take root. To be sure, information was gathered
at the centre. However, it was gathered for the benefit of the prime minister and a handful of senior advisors operating in the PCO and the Prime
Minister's Office (PMO), not for collegial decision-making. Court government took root in Ottawa under Trudeau, and, if anything, it has grown
stronger under Mulroney, Chrétien, Martin, and Harper. It will be recalled
that Paul Martin said in his leadership campaign that under his predecessor, Jean Chrétien, the key to getting things done was the PMO. He made
the point that "Who you know in the PMO" has become what matters in
Ottawa. However, according to observers, once in power his government was
"more centralized than anything seen in the Chrétien era" (Simpson, 2005:
A15). Stephen Harper has continued in the tradition of centralizing power
in his office. It will be recalled that he tabled a motion in Parliament in 2006

that read "This House recognizes that the Québécois form a nation within a united Canada" after consulting only a handful of his closest advisers. Cabinet was left outside the loop. Even the minister responsible for intergovernmental affairs was not informed, let alone consulted, before the decision was made and before full caucus was told (*Globe and Mail*, 2006: A1, A4).

This chapter reports on the forces that have strengthened the hand of the prime minister in government. It then reviews the levers of power available to the prime minister and new developments that have made his or her office and central agencies the dominant actors within the federal government — in short, the arrival of court government.

The Forces

An important development that gave rise to court government in Ottawa was the 1976 election to office of the Parti Québécois (PQ), a provincial party committed to taking Quebec out of Canada. The impact was felt in every government building in Ottawa, but nowhere was it more strongly felt than in the Langevin Building, home to both the PMO and the PCO.

One's place in history matters a great deal to prime ministers. No Canadian prime minister wants the country to break up under his or her watch. Thus, the main task at hand is keeping the country united. No other politician in Canada feels so directly responsible for Canadian unity as does the prime minister. Indeed, should Canada break up, the prime minister will be the first to be held to account.

In any event, briefing material prepared by the PCO for new ministers makes it clear that "the Prime Minister has direct responsibility for the conduct of federal-provincial relations."[1] Federal-provincial relations now cover virtually every aspect of the federal government's decision-making process. Prime ministers invariably believe that provincial governments are much better at understanding this and applying it in their decision-making process than is the federal government.

The preoccupation with national unity tends to recast substantive policy issues into the question of their impact on Quebec and the likelihood of securing federal-provincial agreements. There are plenty of examples. Andrew Cooper, for example, in his comparative study of Canadian and Australian foreign affairs, writes, "a tell-tale sign of how Canada's economic and diplomatic strategy was subordinated to political tactics in agricultural trade was the routing of all important decisions in this area ... through the central agencies of the Prime Minister's Office and the Privy Council Office. The

---

1. Based on material provided to me by a former senior official with the Federal-Provincial Relations Office, Ottawa, January 1993.

decisive impact of the constitutional issue in this matter inevitably stymied the government's ability to perform effectively in the concluding phase of the Uruguay Round" (Cooper, 1997: 217). The participants directly involved in recasting or rerouting the issues are for the most part political strategists or generalists operating at the centre and are not usually specialists in health care, social or economic development policy, and so on (Cameron and Simeon, 2000: 58–118). They are also often directly tied to the prime minister and his office in one fashion or another.

What kind of federal-provincial issue can involve the centre of government and even the prime minister? The short answer is anything, everything, and it depends. There are no set rules. All major federal-provincial issues qualify, of course, but some minor ones can too, and on a moment's notice. The level of funding for a specific program or whether a federal program applies in one region but not in Quebec (or vice versa) can appear on the prime minister's radar screen. It will make it to his radar screen if it gains media visibility.

The prime minister, it will also be recalled, was firmly in charge of the failed Meech Lake and Charlottetown constitutional accords. Neither initiative was born out of Cabinet's collective decision-making. Similarly, Chrétien's Verdun speech on national unity, where firm commitments were made to Quebeckers, was drafted by his advisors and others at the centre. Cabinet was not consulted on its contents, let alone asked to make a contribution (Savoie, 1999: 152).

Provincial premiers have direct access to the prime minister and do not hesitate to pursue an issue with him. If the prime minister decides to support the premier, then the issue is brought to the centre of government in Ottawa for resolution. Commitments are made between two first ministers for whatever reasons, and the prime minister cannot take the risk of seeing the system or the process not producing the right decision. As a result, someone at the centre will monitor the decision until it is fully implemented. When that happens, ministers and their departments inevitably lose some of their power to the prime minister and his advisors.

The program review exercise of the mid-1990s brought home the point that Cabinet is not able to make spending decisions and that the decision-making power had to be concentrated in the hands of a few individuals, notably the prime minister and the minister of finance. It became accepted wisdom in Ottawa that the reason the federal government lost control of its expenditure budget was that ministers in Cabinet were unwilling to say no to the proposed spending plans of colleagues, knowing full well that the time would come when they too would come forward with their own spending proposals (Savoie, 1990). One can hardly overstate the importance of the expenditure budget to public policy and government operations. It steals the stage. When the prime minister and his or her courtiers decide to bring both fiscal policy and key spending decisions to the centre of government, they are in fact bringing the key policy-making levers.

The Media

All important files have the potential of bringing the centre of government into play. But what makes a file important is not at all clear. Again, it depends on the circumstances. And again, media attention can, on very short notice, turn an issue, however trivial, into an important file. When this happens, there is no distinction made between policy and administration. A file that receives media attention becomes political and at that point the prime minister and his advisors will want to oversee its development. Without putting too fine a point on it, the front page of the *Globe and Mail* or a CBC or CTV news report can make a file important, no matter its scope or nature. Today, the media, much like society itself, are far less deferential to political leaders and political institutions. Nothing is off limits anymore, and political leaders and government officials must continually be cautious of letting their guard down when meeting the press.

The media will also focus on party leaders at election time rather than on selected party candidates, even those enjoying a high profile. Journalists buy seats on the chartered aircraft of party leaders and follow them everywhere. In Canada, at least, the media and, by extension, the public, focus on the clash of party leaders. For one thing, there are the leaders' debates on national television, in both English and French. How well a leader does in the debates can have an important impact, or at least be perceived to have an important impact, on the election campaign, if not the election itself. It is now widely accepted in the literature, however, that "debates are more about accidents and mistakes than about enlightenment on the capabilities of candidates to govern" (Polsby and Wildavsky, 1991: 246).

Since Trudeau, Canadian prime ministers have made themselves into television personalities. The same cannot be said for Cabinet ministers. A Gallup poll conducted in 1988 is very revealing on this point. It reported that only 31 per cent of respondents could name a *single* Cabinet minister four years after the Mulroney government had come to power.

Increasingly, Canadian political leaders would appear to be the only substantial candidates in the election race. In the past, Canada had powerful Cabinet ministers with deep roots in the party or strong regional identification and support. One can think of Jimmy Gardiner, Chubby Power, Jack Pickersgill, Ernest Lapointe, Louis Saint-Laurent, Don Jamieson, and Allan

MacEachen. We no longer seem to have powerful regional or party figures who can carry candidates to victory on their coattails or speak to the prime minister from an independent power base in the party.

In Canada winning candidates on the government side are aware that their party leader's performance in the election campaign explains in large measure why they themselves were successful. The objective of national political parties at election time is more to sell their leaders to the Canadian electorate than it is to sell their ideas or their policies. Canadian elections invariably turn on the question of who — which individual — will form the government (Johnson, 1992: 168). It should come as no surprise then that if the leader is able to secure a majority mandate, the party is in his debt, and not the other way around.

National political parties, at least the Canadian variety, are not much more than election-day organizations, providing the fund-raising and poll workers needed to fight an election campaign. They are hardly effective vehicles for generating public policy debates, for staking out policy positions, or for providing a capacity to ensure their own party's competence once in office. Robert Young argues that "the Pulp and Paper Association has more capacity to do strategic analytical work than the Liberal and Conservative parties combined" (Sutherland, 1996: 5). Regional cleavages in Canada, as is well known, dominate the national public policy agenda, and national political parties shy away from attacking regional issues head on for fear they will split the party along regional lines and hurt its chances at election time. The thinking goes, again at least in the parties that have held power in Ottawa, that the regional issue is so sensitive and so politically explosive that it is better left in the hands of party leaders and a handful of advisors.

The Centre of Government

The centre of government has remained largely intact, despite a management delayering exercise in the early 1990s, a massive government restructuring introduced in 1993, and the program review exercise launched in 1994. It has remained intact even though the workload of central agencies should have decreased substantially, given that the PCO has far fewer Cabinet committees to service than was the case in the 1970s and 1980s.

One might well ask, then, what do officials at the centre do? When Trudeau decided to enlarge the size and scope of the PMO in the late 1960s, his first principal secretary sought to reassure critics and Cabinet ministers that the office would remain essentially a service-oriented organization. He explained that it existed to "serve the prime minister personally, that its purpose is not primarily advisory but functional and the PMO is not a mini-Cabinet; it is not directly or indirectly a decision-making body and it is not, in fact, a body at all" (quoted in Sutherland, 1996: 520). It is, of course, not possible to distinguish between a service function and a policy advisory function in this context. Drafting a letter or preparing a speech for the prime minister can constitute policy-making, and many times it does. There is also no doubt that several senior officials in the PMO do provide policy advice to the prime minister, and if some in Trudeau's early PMO denied this, present-day advisors and assistants certainly do not (Savoie, 2008).

PMO staffers have the prime minister's ear on all issues they wish to raise, be it political, policy, administrative, or the appointment of a minister or deputy minister. They can also work hand in hand with a minister to initiate a proposal, and the minister will feel more secure, knowing that someone close to the prime minister is supportive of the proposal. They can also, however, undercut a proposal when briefing the prime minister. In short, senior PMO staff members do not consider themselves simply a court of second opinion. They are in the thick of it and do not hesitate to offer policy advice or to challenge a Cabinet minister.

The role of the PCO has also changed in recent years. Arnold Heeney, the architect of the modern Cabinet office in Ottawa, wrote after his retirement that he had successfully resisted Mackenzie King's desire to make the secretary to the Cabinet "a kind of deputy minister to the Prime Minister" or "the personal staff officer to the Prime Minister" (Heeney, 1968: 367). It is interesting to note, however, that no secretaries to the Cabinet since Gordon Robertson have described their main job as secretary to the Cabinet. In 1997, the PCO produced a document on its role and structure whose very first page makes it clear that the secretary's first responsibility is to the prime minister. It states that the "Clerk of the Privy Council and Secretary to the Cabinet" has three primary responsibilities:

1. As the Prime Minister's Deputy Minister, provides advice and support to the Prime Minister on a full range of responsibilities as head of government, including management of the federation.
2. As the Secretary to the Cabinet, provides support and advice to the Ministry as a whole and oversees the provision of policy and secretariat support to Cabinet and Cabinet committee.
3. As Head of the Public Service, is responsible for the quality of expert, professional and non-partisan advice and service provided by the Public Service to the Prime Minister, the Ministry and to all Canadians (Canada, 1997: 1).

It is also important to recognize that the prime minister no longer needs to rely on regional ministers for an understanding of how government policies are being received. Public opinion surveys are more reliable, more objective, less regionally biased, more to the point, and easier to cope with than are ministers. They can also be used to deal with any public policy issue. All prime ministers, again since Trudeau, have had their own pollsters in court interpreting events and providing advice. Trudeau had Martin Goldfarb, Mulroney had Allan Gregg, Chrétien had Michael Marzolini, Paul Martin had David Herle, while Stephen Harper has relied on Ottawa-based Praxicus Public Strategies. Surveys can enable prime ministers and their advisors to challenge the views of ministers. After all, how can even the most senior ministers dispute what the polls say?

Pollsters, again better than ministers, can assist prime ministers in deciding what is important to Canadians and what is not, what is politically sensible and what is not. A pollster in court always at the ready with data can be particularly helpful in dealing with the problem of political overload. "Political overload" refers to a pervasive sense of urgency and an accompanying feeling of being overwhelmed both by events and the number of matters needing attention. A pollster can also advise the prime minister on "hot button" issues.

Prime ministers, at least since Trudeau, have decided that the best way to deal with the overload problem is to focus on a handful of policy issues and to rely on central agencies to manage the rest. All of the major policy initiatives in Trudeau's last mandate (1980–84), including the national energy program, the Constitution, and the "six and five" wage restraint initiative, were organized outside of the government's formal decision-making process (*Globe and Mail*, 1997: A1). Similarly, Mulroney sidestepped Cabinet in pursuing constitutional reform, the Canada-US Free Trade Agreement, and the establishment of regional agencies. At a considerable cost to the Treasury, Chrétien paid no attention to the formal decision-making process when he decided to introduce the millennium scholarship fund for low-to-moderate income students. The Cabinet was not consulted before the fund was unveiled, even though Chrétien called it "the government's most significant millennium project" (Savoie, 1999: 297). Chrétien, like Mulroney and Trudeau before him, also did not consult Cabinet before striking a number of important bilateral deals with provincial premiers. Martin negotiated a costly health care agreement with the provinces without consulting Cabinet, and Harper, as already noted, decided to recognize Quebec as a nation within Canada without consulting Cabinet.

So, what actually goes on in Cabinet meetings? The first item is "General Discussion," which the prime minister opens and leads. He can raise any matter he chooses, ranging from a letter he may have received from a premier, to a purely partisan matter, to diplomacy. The PCO prepares a briefing note of possible talking points for the prime minister to speak from. But he can, of course, completely ignore it. However, the "General Discussion" can be particularly useful to prime ministers as a cover to make it appear that Cabinet has indeed considered an important issue that could be, for example, life-threatening or require military intervention. Mulroney, for instance, agreed to participate in the first Gulf War in a discussion with President George H. Bush, but raised the matter in Cabinet so that he could report that Cabinet had indeed reviewed the situation.

The second item on the Cabinet agenda is called "Presentations." Ministers, accompanied by their deputy ministers, are on occasion invited to give briefing sessions on various issues. The minister of finance and his deputy minister might present a "deck" on the government's fiscal position. Or the minister of industry and his deputy might make a presentation on Canada's productivity in relation to the United States. At the end of the presentation, ministers are free to raise any question or to ask for further clarification or explanation. But actual decisions rarely, if ever, flow out of these discussions. The purpose is to brief Cabinet, not to secure decisions.

The third item is "Nominations." Government appointments, ranging from a Supreme Court judge, to a senator, to a deputy minister, to a member of the board of a Crown corporation, all require an order-in-council. There is always a list of appointments to be confirmed at every Cabinet meeting. However, the nominations have all been sorted out well in advance of the meeting. The PMO and the PCO manage the appointment process, and they consult with others only to the extent they want to.

To be sure, prime ministers do not seek Cabinet consensus when appointing Supreme Court judges or even senators. Suffice to note that the Ottawa *Citizen* had it right when it wrote that "Mulroney's Supreme Court may soon become Jean Chrétien's court" because of "an unusual confluence of expected retirements" (*Citizen*, 1997: A7). It did, and Chrétien's court is poised to become Harper's court. Nor do prime ministers seek Cabinet consensus when appointing deputy ministers or the administrative heads of government departments. Frequently, they do not even consult the relevant minister when appointing his or her deputy. I asked a former senior PCO official why it was that Jean Chrétien when minister of, say, justice or energy in Trudeau's government could not be trusted to appoint his own deputy minister, but that the moment he became prime minister he could be trusted to appoint all the deputy ministers? His response was simply: "Because he became king" (Savoie, 1999: 283).

The fourth item is "Cabinet committee decisions," presented as appendices on the agenda. In overhauling the Cabinet decision-making process,

Trudeau made it clear that all decisions taken in Cabinet committee could be reopened for discussion in Cabinet. A former Trudeau minister reports that in his early years in office Trudeau was quite willing to let ministers reopen a Cabinet committee decision in full Cabinet. In time, however, he became annoyed with the practice and did not hesitate to show his displeasure whenever a minister sought to review an appendix item. Cabinet, he felt, simply did not have time available to discuss Cabinet committee decisions. In any event, by the late 1970s and early 1980s, Trudeau automatically sent a Cabinet committee decision back to the committee for review whenever a minister raised questions about it in full Cabinet. Mulroney did much the same or relied on the operations committee of Cabinet, chaired by Don Mazankowski, to sort out problems with Cabinet committee decisions. Chrétien did not react well when a Cabinet committee decision was challenged, and, like Trudeau in his later years, he automatically referred it back to the Cabinet committee without any discussion in full Cabinet. Harper is much like Chrétien. The result is that Cabinet committee decisions are now very rarely challenged in full Cabinet.

Mulroney, we now know, had little patience for the Cabinet process and at one point said that he "favoured any decision-making system that minimized the time he spent in cabinet" (Kroeger, 1998: 10). He preferred to deal with big issues outside of Cabinet. The telephone and face-to-face conversation were his "stock in trade." Indeed, we are now informed that "under Mulroney, important matters such as energy mega-projects were often decided without benefit of any Cabinet documents at all" (Kroeger, 1998: 10). The point is that Trudeau, Mulroney, Chrétien, Martin, and now Harper have all preferred to deal with major issues outside of the constraints imposed by the system. The result is that we now have policy-making by announcement. That is, the prime minister makes a major policy announcement, for example, as Chrétien did in the case of the Kyoto Accord, and the system scrambles to implement it.

On the heels of his 2008 re-election, Harper sent a directive to his minister of finance to scrap the $28 million in public subsidies that political parties receive for each vote they garner in a federal election. Word soon circulated around Ottawa and in the media that the decision was Harper's alone. His Cabinet was not consulted, nor obviously his caucus. He simply sent, at the last minute, a directive to the minister of finance to include it in his economic update statement "without ministers or deputy ministers knowing." This, in turn, the media argued, demonstrated that he was a "ferociously partisan leader" with a profound desire to centralize "everything in his own hands" (Simpson, 2008).

To be sure, prime ministers do not always bypass their Cabinets or only consult them after the fact. They pick and choose issues they want to direct and, in some circumstances may decide to let the Cabinet's collective decision-making process run its course. They may also even let the government caucus have its day from time to time and permit a government proposal or legislation to be pulled back and reworked to accommodate the views of caucus members. These are issues on which a prime minister may hold no firm view and so may decide that it is best to keep one's political capital in reserve for another day and another issue.

Trudeau's reforms to Cabinet and central agencies, which have in essence lasted to this day, ostensibly were designed to remove power from strong ministers and their mandarins and bring it to the centre to strengthen the hand of Cabinet ministers acting as a collectivity. In hindsight, it is now clear that the results have fallen far short of the mark. In explaining the Trudeau reforms, Gordon Robertson wrote that "ministers now, in many cases, have to give up some share of their authority and control to other ministers if the totality of policies is to be coordinated ... ministers have less chance to appear in roles of clear and firm decision" (Robertson, 1971: 500). There is no doubt that beginning with Trudeau, and continuing to this day, power has not shifted to Cabinet, as might have been initially hoped. Rather, it has increasingly gone to the prime minister and central agencies.

Globalization

"Globalization," a word that suffers greatly from overuse, has also served to strengthen the hand of the prime minister. In hindsight, we may well have overstated the probability that globalization would spell gloom and doom for nation-states (Savoie, 1995). Many national governments are discovering that the international environment can actually enhance their own power.

In any event, Canadian prime ministers belong to a series of international clubs of heads of government, from the G8 to Asia Pacific Economic Cooperation (APEC) and *la francophonie*. Deals, even bilateral ones, between heads of governments are struck at these meetings. The globalization of the world economy means that many more issues or files are placed in the prime minister's in-basket. Everything in a government department now seems to connect to other departments and other governments, whether at the provincial level or internationally. In Canada, prime ministers and premiers sit at the centre of public policy issues, and when they decide to focus on one, they can very easily make it their own.

National governments, precisely because of global economic forces, now need to work increasingly with each other and with regional and international trade agreements. They also need a capacity to move quickly to strike new deals when the time is right or to change course because of emerging political and economic circumstances and opportunities. The focus will be on the heads of national governments. It is they, not their ministers, who lead the discussions at G8, at Commonwealth meetings, at *la francophonie*, and at the APEC conference.

The Canadian prime minister, unlike the American president, who has to deal with Congress, or the Australian prime minister, who has to deal with a powerful and elected Senate, has a free hand to negotiate for his government and to make firm deals with foreign heads of government. The final hours of negotiations on NAFTA between Prime Minister-elect Chrétien and the American President, through his ambassador to Canada, are telling. At one point, the American ambassador wondered about Chrétien's political authority to agree to a final deal, given that he had yet to appoint his Cabinet. The ambassador put the question to Chrétien: "What happens if we work all this out and then your new trade minister doesn't agree?" Chrétien replied, "Then I will have a new trade minister the following morning" (Greenspon and Wilson-Smith, 1996: 48). It is hardly possible to overemphasize the fact that the Canadian prime minister has few limits defining his political authority within the government.

The Working of Court Government

Canadian prime ministers have in their hands all the important levers of power. Indeed, all major national public policy roads lead one way or another to their doorstep. They are elected leader of their party by party members; they chair Cabinet meetings, establish Cabinet processes and procedures, set the Cabinet agenda, and establish the consensus for Cabinet decisions; they appoint and fire ministers and deputy ministers, establish Cabinet committees, and decide on their membership; they exercise virtually all the powers of patronage and act as personnel manager for thousands of government and patronage jobs; they articulate the government's strategic direction as outlined in the Speech from the Throne; they dictate the pace of change and are the main salespersons promoting the achievements of their government; they have a direct hand in establishing the government's fiscal framework; they represent Canada abroad; they establish the proper mandate of individual ministers and decide all machinery of government issues; and they are the final arbiter in interdepartmental conflicts. The prime minister is the only politician with a national constituency, and unlike MPs and even Cabinet ministers, he does not need to search out publicity or national media attention, since attention is invariably focused on his office and his residence, 24 Sussex Drive. Each of these levers of power taken separately is a formidable instrument in its own right, but when you add them all up and place them in the hands of one individual, they constitute an unassailable advantage.

There is nothing new about this; Canadian prime ministers have enjoyed these avenues of power for some time. However, there have been other developments lately that have served to consolidate the position of the prime minister and his advisors even further. Indeed, this is now evident even before they and their party assume office. Transition planning has become a very important event, designed to prepare a new government to assume power. Transition planning also strengthens the hand of court government, given that by definition it is designed to serve the prime minister. It is the PCO, however, that leads the process, and it is clear that "transition services are for the incoming prime minister" (Savoie, 1993: 8). Indeed, the focus of the PCO transition planning process is entirely on party leaders or would-be prime ministers. In any event, it would be difficult for it to be otherwise, since in the crucial days between the election victory and formally taking power, the only known member of the incoming Cabinet is the prime minister-elect. For other potential Cabinet ministers, it is a "moment of high anxiety," waiting to see if they will be invited to sit in Cabinet, and if so, in what portfolio (Savoie, 1993: 8).

The central purpose of transition planning is to equip the incoming prime minister to make his mark during the government's first few weeks in office. It is now widely recognized that these early weeks can be critical in setting the tone for how the new government will govern. It is also the period when the prime minister, as recent history shows, will make important decisions on the machinery of government and decide which major policy issues his government will tackle during its mandate. These and such key decisions as whether to try to amend the Constitution or fight the deficit are taken or set in motion during the transition period.

In the late 1970s, the PCO began the practice of preparing mandate letters for delivery to ministers on the day of their appointments. It has since become an integrated part of the Cabinet-making process. Mandate letters are also now handed to all ministers when they are assigned to a new portfolio. All ministers in the Chrétien government, for example, were given a mandate letter at the time he formed the government in 1993, again when his second mandate began in 1997, and yet again in his third mandate in 2000.

What are the contents of these mandate letters? In most cases, they are brief, only about two to three pages in length. They are also tailored to the recipient. That is, a mandate letter to a newly appointed minister will be different from one to a veteran minister. In the first instance, it will outline basic information about becoming a Cabinet minister, including conflict-of-interest guidelines and the need to respect the collective nature of Cabinet decisions. In all cases, the letters will delineate issues the minister should attend to and identify priority areas, if any, to be pursued. Here, again, there are two basic mandate letters. One states, in effect, "Don't call us, we'll call you." That is, the prime minister has decided that the department in question should not come up with a new policy agenda or legislative program. In these cases, the message is essentially: keep things going, do not cause any ripples, and keep out of trouble (Savoie, 1999: 138). In other instances, the letter will refer to particular policy objectives and major challenges. In these cases, they can be quite specific, singling out proposed legislation, a special concern that needs attending to, or a program that needs to be overhauled. Mandate letters are now also prepared for newly appointed deputy ministers. Here again the purpose is to outline the main challenges the new deputy ministers will be confronting and the priorities they will be expected to follow.

Are mandate letters taken seriously? The answer is yes. Indeed, ministers consulted said that it is the very first thing that they read after leaving the swearing-in ceremony at Rideau Hall and that they take their contents quite seriously. They know, as one observed, that "the prime minister can always dig out his copy and ask about the status of a particular point" (personal communication). More importantly, the letters reveal what the prime minister expects from them during their stay in their departments. Both present and former PMO and PCO officials report that all prime ministers, from Trudeau to Harper, take the mandate letters seriously and that they spend the required time to ensure that each says what they wish it to say.

It is a rare occurrence for a minister to resign over a policy issue. In looking at the causes of ministerial resignations from Confederation to 1990, one observer of Canadian politics found that "solidarity" problems were responsible for only 19 per cent (or 28 cases) of all resignations. By "solidarity" problems she means ministers unable or unwilling to agree with Cabinet colleagues or "with the Prime Minister in particular" (Sutherland, 1991: 101). In more recent years, resignations from the Diefenbaker government comprised the following: Douglas Harkness, Pierre Sévigny, and George Hees (1963); from the Trudeau government: Judy LaMarsh (1968), Eric Kierans (1971), Jean Marchand (1976), and James Richardson (1976); from the Mulroney government: Suzanne Blais-Grenier (1985 — here, however, former PMO officials report that she jumped just before she was going to be dropped from Cabinet), Lucien Bouchard (1990); from the Harper government: Michael Chong (2006). It is interesting to note that, in contrast, 41 per cent of ministers who left Cabinet did so to accept a political appointment offered by the prime minister. It is also interesting to note that, since 1976, all ministers who resigned did so over the language issue or the national unity question.

The budget has become the government's major policy statement and defines in very specific terms what the government will do in the coming months and where it will be spending new money. Traditionally, the government's budget process pitted guardians (e.g., the prime minister and minister of finance) against spenders (ministers of line departments and regional ministers) (Savoie, 1990). Efforts were made under Trudeau and Mulroney to establish various systems to allocate the spending of "new" money, but they all fell far short of the mark.

The prime minister, the minister of finance, and their advisors have, for some time now, combined the guardian and spender roles. The budget exercise is no longer strictly concerned with the country's broad economic picture, projecting economic growth, establishing the fiscal framework, and deciding which taxes ought to be introduced, increased, or decreased. It now deals with both "big" and "small" decisions, "revenue" projections, and spending decisions. For example, when senior military officials in Canada sought to replace their armoured vehicles, they bypassed Cabinet to appeal directly to the prime minister. Lieutenant-General Andrew Leslie told the media that he hoped "Stephen Harper will replace the old tanks," adding that he expected "the Prime Minister's decision within about a week" (*Globe and Mail*, 2007: A1).

In addition, when the centre decides to sponsor new initiatives, it will much more often than not secure the required funding outside of the Cabinet process. Examples abound and include both large and small expenditures, ranging from the millennium scholarship fund (Chrétien), to the establishment of two new regional development agencies (Mulroney), to the Canada Foundation for Innovation (Martin). This also applies to less costly initiatives. Indeed, some ministers became openly critical of Paul Martin, the minister of finance, when he announced a cut in what was then called the "UI tax cut" without discussing it in Cabinet. Another minister told the media that it "was not necessarily what Canadians are asking for" (*Globe and Mail*, 1997: A1). A finance official replied, however, that Paul Martin had not made the UI tax cut unilaterally, but had done so "with the approval of Prime Minister Chrétien."

The role of the Clerk of the Privy Council and secretary to the Cabinet has changed a great deal in recent years, and the clerk's influence in Ottawa is readily apparent to everyone inside the system. Outsiders, however, know very little about the clerk's role and responsibilities. One of the main challenges confronting a clerk is to establish a proper balance between representing the public service as an institution to the prime minister and Cabinet and representing the prime minister to the public service. The balance appears to have shifted to the latter with the appointment of 37-year-old Michael Pitfield as clerk-secretary in 1975 by Trudeau. The balance may well have shifted even further in favour of the prime minister when Paul Tellier decided, as clerk-secretary under Mulroney, to add the title of the prime minister's deputy minister to his job.

Tellier's decision, however, probably simply reflected the reality of his day-to-day work. Indeed, the clerk-secretary is accountable to the prime minister, not to Cabinet, and the great majority of his daily activities are now designed to support the prime minister, not Cabinet. The prime minister, not Cabinet, appoints the clerk; the prime minister, not Cabinet, evaluates his performance; and the prime minister, not Cabinet, will decide if he stays or if he should be replaced. All this is to say that not only does the secretary to Cabinet wear the hat of deputy minister to the prime minister, it is without doubt the hat that fits best and the one he wears nearly all the time. A former senior PCO official observed that "all clerks since Pitfield have done an excellent job at being deputy minister to the prime minister. As far as secretary to the Cabinet, the performance has been spotty."[2]

The way to govern in Ottawa — at least since Trudeau — is for prime ministers to focus on three or four priority issues, while also always keeping an eye on Quebec and national unity concerns. Tom Axworthy, former principal secretary to Pierre Trudeau, in his appropriately titled article, "Of Secretaries to Princes," wrote that "only with maximum prime ministerial involvement could the host of obstacles that stand in the way of reform be overcome ... the prime minister must choose relatively few central themes, not only because of the time demands on the prime minister, but also because it takes a herculean effort to coordinate the government machine" (Axworthy, 1998: 247). To perform a herculean effort, a prime minister needs carefully selected individuals in key positions to push his agenda. Cabinet, the public service as an institution, or even government departments are not always helpful.

The result is that important decisions are no longer made in Cabinet. They are now made in federal-provincial meetings of first ministers, in the PMO, in the PCO, in the Department of Finance, in international organizations, and at international summits. There is no indication that the one person who holds all the cards, the prime minister, and the central agencies that enable him to bring effective political authority to the centre, are about to change things. The Canadian prime minister has little in the way of internal institutional checks to inhibit his ability to have his way.

In Canada national unity concerns, the nature of federal-provincial relations and the role of the media tend, in a perverse fashion, to favour the

---

2. Consultation with a former senior PCO official, Ottawa, November 1997.

centre of government in Ottawa. The prime minister's court dominates the policy agenda and permeates government decision-making to such an extent that it is only willing to trust itself to overseeing the management of important issues. In a sense, the centre of government has come to fear ministerial and line department independence more than it deplores line department paralysis. As a result, court government is probably better suited to managing the political agenda than is Cabinet government. The prime minister, like the European monarchs of yesterday, decides, at least within the federal government, who has standing at court. Prime Minister Chrétien left little doubt that Canada had made the transition to court government when he observed that "The Prime Minister is the Prime Minister and he has the cabinet to advise him. At the end of the day, it is the Prime Minister who says 'yes' or 'no' " (*Globe and Mail*, 2000: A4).

Advisors, much like courtiers of old, have influence, not power. Jean Chrétien made his view clear that ministers have influence, not power in Cabinet when he wrote: "ministers may have great authority within his department, but within Cabinet he is merely part of a collectivity, just another advisor to the prime minister. He can be told what to do and on important matters his only choice is to do or resign" (Chrétien, 1985: 85). One of Chrétien's former senior policy advisers unwittingly described court government well when he wrote that "Everything a prime minister says is unfortunately taken by some as coming from the fount of all wisdom. Often the prime minister is just throwing out an idea or suggestion for debate and discussion — it is solemnly transcribed as if it were one of the Ten Commandments" (Goldenberg, 2006: 83). He was referring to both elected politicians and senior civil servants. Kings Henry II and Henry VIII would have expected nothing less from their courtiers.

References and Suggested Readings

Axworthy, Thomas S. 1998. "Of Secretaries to Princes." *Canadian Public Administration* 31, 2: 247–64.

Cameron, David, and Richard Simeon. 2000. "Intergovernmental Relations and Democratic Citizenship." In B. Guy Peters and Donald J. Savoie, eds., *Revitalizing the Public Service: A Governance Vision for the XXIst Century*. Montreal: McGill Queen's University Press. 58–118.

Canada, Privy Council Office. 1993. *Responsibility in the Constitution*. Ottawa.

Canada, Privy Council Office. 1997. *The Role and Structure of the Privy Council Office*. Ottawa.

Chrétien, Jean. 1985. *Straight from the Heart*. Toronto: Key Porter Books.

Citizen. 1997. "Chrétien set to remake top court," 14 December: A7.

Cooper, Andrew F. 1997. *In Between Countries: Australia, Canada, and the Search for Order in Agricultural Trade*. Montreal: McGill-Queen's University Press.

Dupré, J.S. 1987. "The Workability of Executive Federalism in Canada." In Herman Bakvis and William Chandler, eds., *Federalism and the Role of the State*. Toronto: University of Toronto Press. 236–58.

Globe and Mail. 1997. "$3 billion for your thoughts," 5 December: A1.

Globe and Mail. 1997. "Spending limits irk cabinet," 3 December: A1.

Globe and Mail. 2000. "Penalty killer PM plays rough," 1 December: A4.

Globe and Mail. 2006. "Inside story," 24 November: A1, A4.

Globe and Mail. 2007. "All LAV IIIs to be replaced within a year," 3 April: A1.

Goldenberg, Eddie. 2006. *The Way it Works: Inside Ottawa*. Toronto: McClelland and Stewart.

Greenspon, Edward, and Anthony Wilson-Smith. 1996. *Double Vision: The Inside Story of the Liberals in Power*. Toronto: Doubleday.

Heeney, A.D.P. 1967. "Mackenzie King and the Cabinet Secretariat." *Canadian Public Administration* 10: 366–75.

Johnston, Richard *et al.* 1992. *Letting the People Decide: Dynamics of a Canadian Election*. Montreal: McGill-Queen's University Press.

Kroeger, Arthur. 1998. "A Retrospective on Policy Development in Ottawa." mimeo. Ottawa.

Polsby, Nelson W., and Aaron Wildavsky. 1991. *Presidential Elections: Strategies of American Electoral Politics*. New York: Free Press.

Robertson, Gordon. 1971. "The Changing Role of the Privy Council Office." *Canadian Public Administration* 14, 4: 487–508.

Savoie, Donald J. 1990. *The Politics of Public Spending in Canada*. Toronto: University of Toronto Press.

Savoie, Donald J. 1993. "Introduction." In Donald J. Savoie, ed., *Taking Power: Managing Government Transitions*. Toronto: The Institute of Public Administration of Canada. 1–11.

Savoie, Donald J. 1995. "Globalization, Nation States, and the Civil Service." In B. Guy Peters and Donald J. Savoie, eds. *Governance in a Changing Environment*. Montreal: McGill-Queen's University Press. 82–110.

Savoie, Donald J. 1999. *Governing from the Centre: The Concentration of Power in Canadian Politics*. Toronto: University of Toronto Press.

Savoie, Donald J. 2008. *Court Government and the Collapse of Accountability in Canada and the United Kingdom*. Toronto: University of Toronto Press.

Simpson, Jeffrey. 2005. "From Pariah to Messiah: Send in the Clerk." *Globe and Mail*, 9 March: A15.

Simpson, Jeffery, 2008. "After the Storm." *Globe and Mail*, 5 December: A17.

Sutherland, Sharon L. 1996. "Does Westminster Government Have a Future?" Occasional Paper Series. Ottawa: Institute of Governance.

Sutherland, Sharon. 1991. "Responsible Government and Ministerial Responsibility: Every Reform is Its Own Problem." *Canadian Journal of Political Science* 24, 1: 91–128.

seven

Canada's Minority Parliament

JENNIFER SMITH

Technically speaking, Canada's Parliament is comprised of the elected House of Commons, the appointed Senate, and the Crown (the Queen or her representative here, the governor general), all three of which need to assent to a bill before it becomes law. In the last edition of this book, David Docherty wrote that Parliament Hill — meaning the grand building in the nation's capital in which the House and Senate are located — is the "heart of democracy in Canada" (2004b: 163). Regrettably, he continued, it was not as democratic as it could be, and for this reason, among others, many Canadians had come to consider it irrelevant to their lives. Writing at the conclusion of three back-to-back governing majorities led by Liberal Prime Minister Jean Chrétien, Docherty urged the need for a feisty governing party caucus that would challenge the ministry drawn from its own ranks and strong opposition parties that would hold the government accountable for its actions.

Well, Parliament Hill is still the heart of Canadian democracy because it is at the core of the practice of responsible government. But the era of majority government abruptly ended, to be replaced by minority government, and minority government is a different cat altogether. Certainly there is nothing predictable about it, since a governing party with only a minority of the members of the House of Commons needs the support of some opposition members for its agenda to prevail. Moreover, it is increasingly clear that there has been a sea change in the public policy climate in the country since the Chrétien years. Vastly important public policy choices are being debated and made in the uncertain setting of a minority parliament. Parliament Hill still faces many of the democratic issues that Docherty astutely outlined, but no one can say it does not matter to their lives.

As the title portends, the theme of this chapter is the minority parliament. In the first section there is a brief review of the country's minority parliaments, including the last three governments elected in 2004, 2006, and 2008. The second section features responsible government. Fortunately, this is no longer the dry, forbidding subject it used to be. Lately there have been interesting developments in the evolution of responsible government, and they are definitely worth pondering in the effort to grasp the current state of parliamentary play. In the third section, the leading institutional features of the House of Commons are considered in the context of minority government. These features are party discipline, Cabinet and caucus, legislative committees, and Question Period. The fourth section, improbably, is about the Senate. Normally no one pays attention to the Senate despite the fact that it is an integral part of Parliament. However, the current government is attempting to make radical changes to it, an initiative that warrants the serious attention of students of Canadian government. In the conclusion, there is an appraisal of the strengths and weaknesses of a minority parliament from the standpoint of the democratic standard raised by Docherty.

Minority Parliaments in Canada

People often forget that Canada has a long and close acquaintance with minority parliaments at the federal level. At the time of writing there have been 13 of them, the first and longest from 1921 to 1925 under Liberal Prime Minister Mackenzie King, which lasted three years and 11 months. A further nine were to crop up before the turn of the century, the last of them under Progressive Conservative Prime Minister Joe Clark, whose government endured nine months between 1979 and 1980.

From 1980 onwards there ensued a series of governments that commanded party majorities in the House of Commons. In hindsight it is easy to see the seeds of the minority governments to come in the demolition of the governing Progressive Conservative (PC) party in the general election of 1993. Led by their new leader, Prime Minister Kim Campbell, the PCs won exactly two seats out of a total of 295, and 16 per cent of the popular vote. The party could not withstand the combined assault of the Western-based Reform Party, established in 1987, and the Bloc Québécois (the Bloc), established in 1990. Reform poached conservative voters in Western Canada (Bickerton *et al.,* 1999: 138–39), and the BQ, which ran candidates only in Quebec, poached them in that province (Bickerton *et al.,* 1999: 181). The Liberals under the leadership of Jean Chrétien ran away with the election in 1993 and won the next two as well.

Between 1993 and 2003, the governing Liberal Party faced four opposition parties: the New Democratic Party (NDP), the Bloc, Reform (which became the Alliance Party in 2000), and the PCs. This circumstance contributed mightily in three elections to the party's capacity to transform a minority of the popular vote into a majority of seats in the House — something that Peter Russell calls a "false majority" (2008: 5–6). In 2003, however, Alliance and the PCs finally merged to form the Conservative Party of Canada with the result that the conservative vote in the country could now be consolidated under one banner (Dickerson and Flanagan, 2006: 373). The effect of the consolidation showed in the general election of 2004 that produced the first minority government since the Clark minority in 1979–80. Under their new leader, Prime Minister Paul Martin, the Liberals were unable to hold on to their majority in the House, instead falling back to minority government status with 135 seats out of a total of 308. In the general election of 2006, it was the turn of the Conservatives. Under their leader, Stephen Harper, they formed a minority government with 125 seats. On the hunt for a majority, the Conservatives tried again in October 2008. They increased their share of seats but still fell short of the mark at 143.

The appearance of minority government is cause for some excitement among students of politics, in part because of its unpredictable lifespan — one never knows how long it will last. The Martin minority government was in an especially precarious situation. Liberal member Peter Milliken remained in the position of Speaker of the House, and the Speaker never votes, except to break a tie. That left 134 Liberals who, allied with the 19 NDP members who could be expected to support them, made a voting bloc of 153 in the 308-seat chamber. The Conservatives and the Bloc together counted 153 as well. The lone independent member, former Conservative Chuck Cadman, held the balance of power. The media welcomed the drama of close votes held in the House.

In addition to the element of unpredictability, minority government has the effect of turning the spotlight on the House of Commons and the personalities elected to it. Members of Parliament (MPs) are no longer "no-bodies," as the late Prime Minister Pierre Elliott Trudeau called them, but somebodies whose votes are precious assets in the House and in the committees of the House. Indeed, it is often suggested that minority government shifts power from the prime minister and the Cabinet to the elected members of the House, where it belongs. And there is truth in the suggestion about a shift of power. Precisely because the governing party is dependent upon the votes of some opposition members to get its legislative agenda passed, it needs to be attentive to theirs. To some, this need generates a pleasing picture of members of the House of Commons working together on public policies for Canadians. Nothing could be more misleading.

The fact of the matter is that in Canada, at least, no prime minister has ever wanted to lead a minority government, the current one included. Nor has any prime minister ever shown the slightest interest in coping with the situation by working with an opposition party to develop a legislative agenda — in writing — that guarantees that opposition party's support for the government over a defined period. It is hardly as if no one has ever heard of the idea. On the contrary, in Ontario, Liberal Premier David Peterson ran a minority government from 1985 to 1987 with the support of the NDP. The support was based on a written agreement negotiated by Peterson and NDP leader Bob Rae outlining a legislative agenda that the NDP was prepared to support for two years. At the end of that period, Peterson went back to the electorate and won a majority government.

The other strategy available to a prime minister who leads a minority government, one that is common in many European countries, is a coalition government of two or more parties that together command a majority of the seats in the legislature. The coalition parties negotiate the number of members each is assigned in the Cabinet. The fact that the parties each have seats in the Cabinet is a crucial point, because it means that they must take responsibility for the actions of the government that together they form. Canadian prime ministers, however, are allergic to the very idea of coalition government. The closest the country came to coalition government — and it is not really that close — was the Union government that held office from 1917 to 1921. Briefly, the Conservatives under Prime Minister Robert Borden decided that the country's participation in the First World War required military conscription in particular and a non-partisan governmental effort in general, and they persuaded a significant number of English-speaking Liberals to support the conscription bill that was passed in July 1917 and then to join them in campaigning as "Union" candidates in the general election in December of that year. In many ridings, the incumbent Liberal or Conservative ran as a Union candidate unopposed by the usual rival candidate. (In European-style coalitions, the parties maintain their own names.) In the event, a Union government was returned with 153 seats, while the Liberals under their leader Wilfrid Laurier, who refused to support conscription or Union government, took 82 seats, 62 of them in Quebec (Beck, 1968: 145).

When the war was concluded, the old partisan divide between the Liberals and the Conservatives gradually reasserted itself, despite the efforts of some Unionists to transform the Union party from a coalition into a new party altogether. But the Union government had damaged both parties. The Conservatives, the dominant partner of the coalition, lost the support of Quebec over the conscription issue. The Liberals, meanwhile, were beset by internal discord since the pro-conscription Liberals who had left the fold — and now wanted to return to it — were regarded as betrayers by many of their former colleagues. Even more serious, there were Liberals who had no intention of returning to the fold, in particular, the free-trade Liberals in the West. Caught up in the reinvigorated farmers' movement, they were working to establish the new Progressive Party.

That the Union government had given coalition government a bad name became evident in the general election of December 1921. The new leader of the Liberal Party, William Lyon Mackenzie King, was one of the few English-speaking Liberals who had remained loyal to Laurier throughout the years of the war and the Union government. King was opposed to coalition government. On the other hand, faced with the need to rebuild his party, he prevaricated on the issue. His great problem was the agrarian-based Progressive Party, now prepared to launch its first bid in a federal election. The Progressives turned out to be a disparate group of individuals, some with an agenda of radical democratic reform not shared by all. But they were united in their pursuit of the interests of farmers in such matters as tariffs (low) and transportation (cheap). King thought he could bring many of them back to their Liberal home by showing the similarity between their views and Liberal views. Given the powerful protectionist business wing of the Liberal Party of the day, this was not an easy task.

Seeking to placate the Progressives, King had toyed with the idea of coalition government prior to the election, holding out the prospect that in such a format the Progressives could keep their identity as a party with their own leader. Then he abandoned it for the idea of "coalescence." Here is King: "Deliberately, therefore, I am seeking to bring about, not a coalition, but a coalescence of Liberal and Progressive forces … a new strong, vigorous, united solid Liberal Party, representative of the will and the wish of the great body of the people" (Dawson, 1958: 358). The term, "coalescence," unheard of until King made it up, was a classic fudge.

As the election campaign drew to a close, it was clear that the Progressives would end any chance of a Liberal majority. According to one of King's biographers, even before the votes were counted an irritated King "discouraged any thought of future coalition by stating that Canada wanted no more experiments of that kind" (Dawson, 1958: 356). In the end, the Liberals won 117 out of 235 seats, and the Progressives won 64. King maintained his stand against the idea of a coalition and instead worked hard to gain the support of the Progressives in the House in order to keep his minority government going, which he managed to do for four years. The strategy was to proceed cautiously on an issue-by-issue basis, adjusting the government's legislative proposals somewhat to appeal to the Progressives without alienating the rest of the party. As well, he pursued the longer term objective of bringing them back to the Liberal Party — making them Liberals again — which he eventually managed to do, although not before he had spent nearly the whole decade as the leader of minority governments — 1921–25, 1925, and 1926–30.

King's successors have never veered from his path. This was made abundantly clear once again by the comments of both Martin and Harper when they found themselves leading minority governments. Asked about his plans following the 2004 election, Martin expressed no interest in seeking a coalition with another party on the ground that there was no need for one. He described his minority government as stable because it had a mandate from the voters to proceed on the core items of the party's campaign program; this is the same argument that Joe Clark made in 1979. He said there was sufficient consensus among the voters on these core items (Clark and Fagan, 2004: 1). Interviewed on the same point in the midst of the next election campaign two years later, when it looked like the Conservatives might form the next minority government, Harper refused to consider a coalition government with any of the political parties, terming the idea "unrealistic" and stressing instead his preference for governing on an "issue-by-issue" basis (Taber, 2005: A1). This is nothing, however, compared with the reaction to the opposition coalition that threatened to take down his government in early December 2008.

On December 1, Liberal leader Stéphane Dion announced that his Liberal Party and the NDP were prepared to form a coalition government backed by the support of the Bloc for at least 18 months (Cheadle, 2008b: A1). Since a vote of non-confidence in the government was scheduled a few days hence, the prospect of a European-style coalition government loomed. Harper fought back, arguing that there was no electoral mandate for a coalition government, itself an allegedly "radical" concept, and excoriated the very idea of a government reliant upon the "separatist" Bloc for support (Cheadle, 2008a: A1). In the event, he managed to persuade the governor general to prorogue Parliament, thereby staving off any vote of non-confidence by closing down the institution until late January 2009, when the government promised to bring down its budget (Valpy, 2008: A4). First, however, his party launched a major media effort to convince Canadians of the evils of coalition government. And the effort worked. According to a poll commissioned by one of the country's national newspapers, 58 per cent of Canadians preferred the Conservative government to the coalition, while 38 per cent took the opposite position (LeBlanc, 2008: A6). Meanwhile, the coalition's chief architect, Stéphane Dion, stepped down from the leadership of the Liberal Party earlier than planned, to be succeeded by Michael Ignatieff, who was not a coalition enthusiast.

In office, Harper, like all the other minority prime ministers, has followed King's strategy of seeking opposition support for his legislative program, making adjustments to it where required. The main difference is that King was focused on the Progressives while Harper takes support where he can get it. For example, the government secured the passage of its first budget in May 2006 with the support of the Bloc. It gained that support by promising to concede the validity of Quebec's claim of a fiscal imbalance between Ottawa and the provinces and then finding ways of transferring extra dollars to the provinces to counter it. On the climate change file, by contrast, Harper worked with the NDP, with whom he found common ground on a proposal to legislate the reduction of carbon emissions rather than establish a carbon tax on emitters or a cap-and-trade regime. And finally, in preparation for its 2009 budget, the government sought and received the support of the Liberal Party.

However entertaining is the precariousness of minority governments to observers of political life, it seems obvious why minority prime ministers cannot be expected to enjoy the challenges of their predicament — and it *is* a predicament from their standpoint, a predicament from which they seek to extricate themselves as soon as possible. So they deal with it, all the while looking for the opportunity to pursue a snap election in an effort to gain a majority of the seats, should the polls signal that the time is right. And why would they do otherwise? After all, Canada enjoys a system of responsible government.

Responsible Government

The phrase "responsible government" describes the critical democratic component of the parliamentary system, and yet it is nowhere to be found in the country's written Constitution. This is because it is a convention, that is, an unwritten rule that is followed by the political actors in the system. The convention of responsible government dictates that the government, meaning the prime minister and the Cabinet, must enjoy the support — the confidence — of a majority of the elected members of the legislature. On this basis alone can the government actually govern the country. When it loses that support, the government will advise the governor general to call an election (in the hope of getting a majority), or it will offer to resign to enable the governor general to find an opposition party (or parties) prepared to form a government in its place.

There is always a reason behind a convention, and the reason for the convention of responsible government is democracy. A majority of the elected representatives — the people's representatives — must support the government in order for it to remain in office. The government's need for such support enables the legislature to hold the government accountable to it and through it to the people. Without that support, the government could have no legitimacy in the eyes of the public.

Responsible government is such an elegantly simple concept. And yet from it flow three rules (Smith, 1999: 406–07) that together supply the organizational foundation of the House of Commons. The first is the division of the House (and the Senate, for that matter) into government and opposition, the immediate effect of which is to render it adversarial — we versus them. The government does not share power with the opposition. Instead, the government proposes measures and defends them, while the opposition attacks the measures and occasionally offers alternative options that the government usually ignores. (Incidentally, the opposition is safe from the charge of sedition while on the attack, because the opposition is a constitutional role, a phenomenon captured by the phrase "official" opposition.) The adversarial model of government and opposition applies to almost all of the routines of the House, from formal debates on the government's budget proposals, to the consideration of bills, the organization of legislative committees, and even the daily Question Period.

The second rule of the House of Commons that flows from responsible government is the use of the decision-making rule of a majority of those present and voting (assuming the quorum is met). Finally, there is a third rule — or set of rules — set out in the Constitution Act, 1867 that stipulates first, that taxing and spending bills originate in the House; and second, that such bills be recommended by the governor general. Since the governor general can act only on the advice of the government of the day, the upshot is to restrict the introduction of money bills in the House to Cabinet ministers. No opposition member could get the governor general's agreement to sponsor such bills. As a result, the government holds a constitutional monopoly on this all-important chunk of the country's business.

The net effect of these rules is to establish a zero-sum game that encourages ambitious political leaders to form a *majority* government. A majority government gets to dominate the legislative agenda of Parliament, the proceedings of the House, and the committees of the House. Is it not obvious, then, why a minority prime minister would work hard to gain a majority government rather than remain saddled with a pesky coalition partner or with a document stipulating the policies his government must pursue in a defined period? Or, as is the case of the current prime minister, with the need to troll for opposition support every time there is a vote in the House? Indeed, the urge to escape can even overcome the alleged restriction of the fixed election date. This is worth pausing to consider.

In the 2006 general election, the Conservative campaign platform included a number of planks on the democratic reform of Parliament, among them the promise to establish a fixed election date for the House of Commons (Conservative Party, 2006: 23). The Conservative government kept this promise in legislation that sets the date of the general election at four-year intervals on the third Monday in October, beginning October 19, 2009. It is important to note that nothing in the law compromises — or could compromise — the legal power of the governor general under the Constitution to fix an election on another date altogether. (That would require an amendment of the

Constitution.) Should an election be called for another date, then the four-year interval proceeds from that point. In touting its achievement, the government alleged that the previous Liberal government had "repeatedly abused" the power to set the election date to suit its electoral prospects and said that the new law would eliminate the abuse (Canada, 2007: 1). The prime minister was praised for being prepared to restrict his own invaluable electoral-timing options in favour of the fairness of a fixed date for all of the political leaders and parties — for levelling the playing field, so to speak (Russell, 2008: 141).

As matters transpired, it is clear that whatever democratic credibility the prime minister might have gained on the issue of the fixed election date is nothing in his mind compared to the chance to gain a majority government or even just a strong minority. As indicated above, by the summer of 2008 he had judged his party's electoral prospects to be favourable and wound up having an election called for October 14, a date unrelated to the one established in the new law or even the need to get out from under an opposition looking for every opportunity to bring down his government. The fact of the matter is that none of the opposition parties were interested in an election. That being so, the prime minister needed to manufacture plausible arguments for his move.

All minority prime ministers say they need a mandate from the people — meaning a majority in the House of Commons — for a particular reason or reasons. Harper alleged that his government could not get support from the recalcitrant opposition parties for its legislative agenda — so the House was dysfunctional — and that the country needed a strong Conservative government to steer it through a challenging economic period. Unlike his similarly situated predecessors, however, he also had to deal with the charge from outraged observers (Murphy, 2008: A17) that he was cynically ignoring his own fixed-election law. And he did. He said that the law applies to majority governments, not minority governments that the opposition can combine to defeat at any moment (Kilpatrick, 2008: 1). Whatever the merits of that argument, it should be observed that the rewards of a majority government evidently far outweigh any loss of credibility as a democratic reformer that the prime minister might sustain by making it.

As noted above, the organizational rules of the House of Commons that flow from the system of responsible government have the effect of enabling a majority government to dominate the routines of the House. Such a government can move its agenda forward in a relatively orderly fashion, manage debate in the House in an effort to minimize damaging criticism of its policies and general administrative competence, and reap the benefits of its monopoly over appointments to a wide variety of government and semi-governmental offices. However, these things are impossible without party discipline. No prime minister can reap the rewards of responsible government without maintaining it, not always an easy task. Harper's success in this respect is remarkable. In the review of the House of Commons in the next section, the first topic is party discipline. It sets the stage for the other three: Cabinet and caucus, legislative committees, and Question Period.

House of Commons: Party Discipline

It is ironic that Canada is a leader in party discipline because many Canadians affect to despise it (Dickerson and Flanagan, 2006: 436–37). They prefer to think that the elected representative for whom they vote is an independent-minded individual who is prepared to represent their interests over the political party's interests whenever the two clash with one another (Docherty, 2004b: 176). Certainly one reason behind the appearance of the Reform Party in 1987 was the conviction that the established parties were not sufficiently sensitive to local concerns to give their members some leeway in voicing support for those concerns over party policy (Carty et al., 2000: 8–9). Be that as it may, the public animus against party discipline usually has no effect on the practice of it.

Party leaders are attentive to public criticism of party discipline run amok, at least when they are in opposition. In the 1993 election, the Liberals under Chrétien ran on a "Red Book" that contained their campaign platform, one plank being a promise of more independence for Liberal MPs on votes in the House. In office, however, Chrétien demanded the loyalty of his caucus, and was quick to punish errant members (Thomas, 1997: 7). He considered almost all government bills to be matters of confidence that demand voting on party lines (Docherty, 1997). Harper has followed the same path.

In the 2006 general election, the Conservative campaign platform contained a section on improving democracy, one plank of which was a promise to make all votes except the budget and main estimates "free votes" for ordinary MPs, that is, MPs who are not in the Cabinet (Conservative Party, 2006: 23). This was heady stuff. Once in office, however, Harper jettisoned the free-vote idea altogether and instead demanded and got strict party voting. The example of Bill Casey, member from Cumberland-Colchester in Nova Scotia, shows what happens to a Conservative MP prepared to oppose the party's position on an important money matter (equalization and the Atlantic Accord) *and* how such treatment can backfire.

Casey's problem with his party centred on the Atlantic Accord, an agreement reached between the federal government and Nova Scotia in 1986 on the development and regulation of offshore petroleum resources. As part of the agreement, for a specified period the revenues that the province received from the resources were to be protected, as it were, from any clawback flowing from the receipt of equalization payments. Being a have-not province, Nova Scotia, like other have-not provinces, receives equalization payments from the federal treasury so that it can offer its residents access to public services that are reasonably comparable to those enjoyed by residents of other provinces at levels of taxation that are also reasonably comparable. As a province's revenues increase, equalization payments can be expected to decrease. The Accord established an exception to the rule in order that the province could maximize its revenues from the offshore resources, but only for a time, after which the clawback took effect.

In its budget tabled in March 2007, the Conservative government essentially proposed to terminate the Accord in return for a richer deal on equalization. Nova Scotia eventually signed the deal, but not before the country witnessed weeks of open hostility between the two governments and Casey's decision to vote against the budget legislation. As a result of that decision, Casey was immediately thrown out of the Conservative caucus (Galloway, 2007: A4) and forced to sit as an independent in the House — no-man's land. Moreover, he could not get back in the caucus, even though he sought to do so. This was awkward, since he had already been nominated by the Conservative association in Cumberland-Colchester to run in the next election. The Conservative Party solved that problem by declaring the nomination to be vacant, effectively ordering the local association to nominate someone else. Since candidates need the signature of the party leader in order to run under the party's standard, the Conservative Party was able to assert its position in the matter. Embarassingly for the party, the local association could not find anyone to contest the riding against Casey, who ran as an independent in the 2008 general election and won an overwhelming victory, gaining 69 per cent of the popular vote. The party wound up seizing one of its policy advisers and parachuting him into the riding, where he ran a distant third (McCoag, 2008: A5).

To be fair to Harper, as leader of a minority government he has an extra incentive to insist on the support of his own members. He hardly wants to worry about their allegiance when he needs the support of some opposition members as well in order to pass his legislative agenda. Still, it is interesting to observe that in the fall session of 2007, Harper announced that he would treat a defeat of *any* of his government's bills as a vote of want of confidence in the government (Laghi and Curry, 2007: A1). Therefore, any government member who voted against his party and helped to defeat the government would not only face expulsion from the caucus, like Casey, but then face an election as an independent, normally a tough proposition, the Casey example notwithstanding.

As far as party discipline is concerned, the bottom line is that the institutional incentive for party leaders to maintain it is extremely strong. The objective of any party leader is to run the government, period, not to sit on the opposition benches watching his opponent do it. To run the government requires the support of the majority of the members of the House, and the maintenance of a disciplined caucus makes that a lot easier than an undisciplined caucus. An undisciplined caucus implies that the government would sustain defeats in the House. Thus far in Canadian political history, such defeats spell the end of a government's days in office. By contrast, in the British parliamentary system, the government can and does sustain some defeats in the House without thereby establishing grounds for resignation (Dickerson and Flanagan, 2006: 308–09).

House of Commons: Cabinet and Caucus

The elected members of a political party form the party's caucus. After that, it is necessary to distinguish between the governing party's caucus and the caucuses of the opposition parties. The reason is simple enough. The government caucus includes the prime minister and the members he has chosen to serve in the Cabinet as well as private members (also referred to as backbenchers owing to the fact that they are seated in the rows behind the prime minister and Cabinet). It is a two-tier affair. Government members are expected to support their leader, the prime minister, and the Cabinet.

Government caucus members who are also members of the Cabinet — ministers of the Crown — have more legal power than backbenchers and more influence over the government's policy agenda. Ministers are executives who run departments of government as well as legislators who sit in the House. As already noted, being members of the executive, they alone are empowered under the Constitution to table money bills in the House, that is, bills that involve the expenditure of public money or taxation. Thus, they have a monopoly on a significant element of the legislative agenda. Moreover, these bills are considered matters of confidence that demand the support of the caucus as a whole. All things considered, then, this aspect of responsible government elevates Cabinet members over their caucus colleagues.

In addition to the monopoly over the introduction of money bills in the House, Cabinet members are also members of the various committees of the Cabinet that play a key role in the development of the government's legislative agenda. Being on the inside, as it were, they are better situated to influence public policy than backbenchers. Some are also regional ministers who are assigned political responsibilities in their geographic backyard that range from the recruitment of promising candidates, to advice to the prime minister on patronage appointments, to a say in the expenditure of government money for local purposes.

While they might aspire to a Cabinet position, government backbench MPs perform important functions as well. First, and depending on the proclivities of the prime minister, they can seek to influence the policy direction that the Cabinet proposes to pursue in meetings of the full caucus, subcommittees of the caucus, or meetings with individual ministers. Caucus meetings are *in camera*. Brian Mulroney, Progressive Conservative Prime Minister from 1984 to 1993, was well known for paying close attention to the concerns of the caucus, as well as inspiring their loyalty to his government (Crosbie, 1997: 270–74). By contrast, Prime Minister Harper is thought to run a top-down operation and to expect the loyalty of backbenchers to decisions of the leader and Cabinet that have been made without their participation.

Along with their opposition counterparts, government backbenchers also serve on the committees of the House of Commons in which position they examine bills, possibly conduct hearings on them, and occasionally offer amendments to them. The activities of the committees, discussed in more detail below, are an important part of the workload of MPs. Then there is constituency work, which ranges from the assistance of individuals with government-related problems like immigration issues, to the recognition of the special milestones and accomplishments of particular individuals and organizations, to the pursuit of financial support for various constituency projects. All members, government and opposition, maintain some focus on constituency work.

Since the task of the opposition is to hold the government accountable to the House, the attitude of an opposition member is quite different from that of a government member. It is the attitude of the critic. An opposition member rarely expects to exert an influence on the legislative process by convincing the government to change its mind about a particular bill. Instead, the member seeks to exert such influence by convincing the public that there is a better way of accomplishing the government's objective or that the objective is best dropped altogether in favour of something else. Opposition caucuses are even structured efficiently to attack the government. The party leaders appoint particular individuals from their caucus to cover or "shadow" government ministers. Thus, the finance critic of an opposition party is expected to take the lead in critically questioning the minister of finance in the House.

Finally, mention must be made of the private member's bill. Although the government has a monopoly of the legislative agenda of Parliament, it must be stressed that the House of Commons is the "people's House" (Smith, 2007). The people elect their representatives to participate in the law-making process. Therefore, provision needs to be made to enable MPs to initiate bills in the House despite the recognized press of government business in the contemporary period. The provision is the private member's bill.

Under this system, MPs who are not ministers can prepare two kinds of bills, private and public. Private bills are addressed to matters of particular interest to an individual or corporation rather than the public as a whole. Public bills are addressed to matters under federal jurisdiction that affect the public. Of the two, the private member's public bill is the most interesting since it reveals the broader issues that concern members and their constituents. The House provides legislative counsel to help members craft their bills. Once the bills are introduced into the House and given first reading, they are entered into a draw to determine the numerical order in which they are considered during the time slot of the parliamentary schedule that is devoted to them.

In the course of any one session, very few of these bills get far in the legislative process, although that does not discourage resort to them. For example, when the second session of the 39th Parliament was dissolved for the general election in October 2008, there were 373 private members' bills, the vast majority of which had gotten no further than first reading in the House. However, six received royal assent; they range from C-287 on the establishment of a National Peacekeepers' Day, to C-292 that requires the government to honour its obligations under the Kelowna Accord with Aboriginal communities (Parliament of Canada, 2008). Judging by its use, the private member's bill is regarded by government and opposition members as an important opportunity to participate in a law-making process that is dominated by the concerns of the government of the day. The same can be said for legislative committees.

House of Commons: Legislative Committees

The committee system of the House has undergone many changes over the years, most of them designed to get the right balance between the government's desire for efficient (read quick) disposal of government business and the opposition's desire to hold the government to account for its work and to amend the content of the government's bills for the better, according to their lights. However, two features of committees endure — party discipline and the fact that the membership of the committees reflects the standing of the parties in the House. During minority governments, there are more opposition than government members on the committees, a circumstance that often makes for lively committee meetings.

The workhorses of the committee system are the standing committees, which are appointed for the duration of a Parliament. Each is comprised of a dozen members. The committees correspond to the federal administrative structure — Agriculture and Agri-Food is the name of the government department as well as the standing committee. The standing committees carry heavy responsibilities in relation to the subject areas assigned to them. The House routinely sends them bills to review and report back on, the estimates of the money needed by the government to pay for its activities and programs, reports that the government has tabled in the House, and government nominees for non-judicial appointments. The committees can conduct reviews of government departments and initiate studies within their subject area. They are assisted by an expert staff.

Given the importance of the standing committees in the work of the House, it is easy to see why a government would want to maintain control of them so that they support the government's legislative agenda. Clearly, this is a challenge for a minority government, not just because government members are outweighed by opposition members, but because the committees elect their own chair and vice-chairs from among the government members (although there are exceptions, like the Public Accounts committee, which elects an opposition chair). But which government members? Prime Minister Harper selected the Conservative chairs in advance in the full expectation that no other Conservative member would oppose his choice by standing for the position. And he has relied on these chairs to keep the committees from taking courses of action that challenge the government. An example is the tactic of the filibuster.

The filibuster is a tactic in which a member talks as long as possible in order to delay proceedings. It is the tactic of the opponent of a government bill. In a majority government, it is not a terribly effective one in committee because the government chair, backed by the government majority on the committee, can easily forestall or at least keep the talking to a minimum. However, in the 39th Parliament, the *government* has employed the tactic in an effort to forestall opposition initiatives in committee. And of course it is much more successful in this circumstance, because the government chair who is in charge of keeping order in the proceedings can be rather relaxed about the job. An example is the standing committee on Procedure and House Affairs. With the connivance of the chair, Conservative members launched a successful filibuster to prevent the committee from approving a motion to review allegations that the Conservative Party overstepped its spending limits in the 2006 general election (Curry, 2008: F8).

The Conservatives pioneered another tactic in the 39th Parliament — even simpler but evidently just as effective. It is a tactic of the chair who downs tools. Thus, the Conservative chair of the standing committee on Justice and Human Rights simply walked out of the meeting whenever he faced an opposition motion that the committee investigate allegations that in 2005 the Conservatives — then in opposition — offered Independent MP Chuck Cadman inducements to vote against the budget of the minority Liberal government (Gérin-Lajoie, 2008: 55).

Obviously a minority government does not have the numbers that make for easy control in a parliamentary setting. Well aware of this circumstance, the Conservative government appears to have developed some interesting new tactics to try to keep a grip on opposition moves against it in committees.

House of Commons: Question Period

The daily Question Period presided over by the Speaker of the House of Commons continues to be the set piece of the proceedings of the House that is best known to Canadians because it features dramatic conflict between partisan foes and because it is often used as backdrop by the broadcast media in their coverage of federal politics. Question Period is not a courteous exchange of views. It is rude and noisy and as a result often the subject of irate commentary by Canadians who deplore what they see as childishness. Nevertheless, it puts the accountability function of responsible parliamentary government on the public stage for all to see. It is a visible presentation of the opposition demanding that the government account to the House for its actions.

The oral Question Period lasts about 45 minutes. In the Canadian version, members who pose questions to ministers are not obliged to give advance notice of the questions to anyone. Right off the bat this lends the proceedings an air of unpredictability. Further, supplementary questions are allowed. Thus, members can pursue a promising line of questions that prove awkward for the government to field. By contrast, in the British case ministers receive advance notice of the questions that they will face later in the day, thus gaining time in which to find and rehearse suitable answers.

The House has developed guidelines for Question Period, among them an order of precedence among questioners. The Speaker generally recognizes the leader of the official opposition party first, then the leaders of each of the other opposition parties. Depending on the time, other members of the opposition parties might be recognized as well. Occasionally the Speaker also permits government MPs to pose questions to ministers, although there is no urgency to do so since theirs are mostly "bouquets" in any event.

The government is not compelled to answer questions that it would prefer to ignore. However, not answering looks terrible, and so ministers almost always do supply answers, trying to dodge bullets in the course of doing so. They mostly do, but there are exceptions, one of the more painful being the experience of the environment minister — Rona Ambrose — in the Cabinet

Harper put together following the 2006 general election. The Harper government repudiated the Kyoto Protocol to reduce greenhouse gas emissions to combat global warning that was signed in 1997 by the predecessor government of Jean Chrétien and in its place initially proposed a system of emission reduction targets for industry to meet. The minister was subjected to a withering attack by the opposition day after day as she sought to explain and defend the government's policy. It was difficult to do. Evidently dissatisfied with her performance on the file, the prime minister eventually pulled her from the job and assigned her to a less important position in his Cabinet instead.

Question Period is often followed by a "scrum" in the hall outside the chamber, in which the media surround a chosen minister or member whom they regard as newsworthy, often on the basis of an exchange that has taken place in the House just moments before. Once again, the visual watched by millions of Canadians is a rough-and-tumble political encounter, this time between the media and a politician. However unpleasant the experience might appear, most members are prepared to engage it for the sake of being on television. Indeed, according to long-time journalist (now Conservative Senator) Mike Duffy, practically all of them are agreeable to answering in scrums — all except Harper. Says Duffy, "He's one of the very few people here who is not interested in the kind of fame and validation most politicians get from being on TV" (Doyle, 2008: R2).

Senate Reform

The Canadian Senate is one of the few remaining non-elected second chambers in the world's liberal democracies. In some respects it was modelled after the British House of Lords (Smith, 2004: 47–50), and even that body has been the subject of incremental reform over the past few years, although at the time of writing the reform is still a work in progress. The main function of the Senate is the exercise of sober second thought in relation to proposed bills. It performs other functions as well, including the study and preparation of acclaimed reports on a variety of public policy issues.

On the nomination of the prime minister, senators are appointed by the governor general to serve until age 75. The composition of the Senate is regional. Each of four regions of the country — the four Western provinces, Ontario, Quebec, and the three Maritime provinces — is assigned 24 seats. Newfoundland and Labrador has six seats and the northern Territories one seat each. Under the Constitution the legal powers of the Senate are nearly the same as the House, except that money bills must originate in the House. In addition, the Senate has only a six-month suspensive veto on constitutional amendments.

For the most part, the Senate has worn its outdated mode of selection modestly, attending to its work of legislative review and rarely confronting the public policy objectives of the government of the day. There are always exceptions to the rule, of course, and the current one is fascinating indeed. The Senate — or at least the majority of the members, who are Liberal — objects to the Conservative government's bills to reform it and thus far has managed to hold up their passage, although to be fair to the Senate these bills were unlikely to find easy passage in either house anyway. What does the government propose?

The government has two proposals, the first being to change the term of senators from retirement at age 75 to a non-renewable eight-year term. The second is to elect senators in so-called consultative elections. As noted above, under the Constitution the prime minister nominates someone to fill a Senate vacancy and the governor general makes the appointment. Thus, the Crown has the legal power of appointment, and that power cannot be compromised by ordinary statute. It can only be changed by an amendment to the Constitution. So, in order to proceed by ordinary statute law, the government proposes that elections be held to produce candidates for the Senate whom the prime minister will advise the governor general to appoint. Nominally, nothing changes. Practically, everything does — the country moves from the appointment to the election of senators.

The Conservative government's proposals are not unusual in and of themselves. Certainly the ideas of fixed terms and the election of senators have been around for a long time. What is unusual is the strategy of moving on a statutory basis alone instead of seeking an amendment to the Constitution, a process that would immediately require that the government gain the agreement of the provinces to the changes. Even more unusual are the hard-ball tactics that the prime minister has adopted to push along his unilateralist strategy. Initially he refused to appoint anyone to fill a vacant Senate seat who was not elected for the purpose. Since Alberta is the only province that has deigned to hold "Senate elections" — the prime minister appointed "senator-in-waiting" Bert Brown from the province — the predictable result was a rise in the number of vacancies. Given the palpable lack of support for the government's reform measures in the country and the fact that they have stalled in Parliament, the prime minister backtracked on his vow not to appoint senators and instead announced in December 2008 that he would fill the 18 vacancies with appointees who are wedded to his reform project. Apparently Conservatives fear that, should their government fall, another government would take the opportunity to appoint their own partisans to the Senate — individuals not interested in the idea of an elected Senate (Curry, 2008: A5). That would finish off the project for at least a generation.

It is widely appreciated that the formulas that govern the amendment of the Constitution set the requirement of a high standard of consensus for change among the formal participants of the system, namely Parliament and the provincial legislatures. Therefore, it is not terribly surprising to find an enterprising prime minister attempting to get around the amendment procedure by insisting that Parliament alone can make the change he has in mind. Still, it is somewhat disconcerting to watch the fate of a foundational institution of the country being played out in this fashion.

Conclusion

As noted at the outset, five years ago Docherty argued that Canada's parliamentary system had become less democratic than it should be, his point of reference being the three back-to-back majority governments of Jean Chrétien. During this period, party discipline in the House and in committees remained tight, giving members little opportunity to stray from the party line and express their own views or those of their constituents on matters of public policy. The government faced a weak and divided opposition and was able to impose its legislative agenda on the country without much difficulty.

It might be expected that, almost by definition, a minority parliament would be more democratic than a majority parliament. After all, in this circumstance the majority sits on the opposition side of the line. The government needs to convince some opposition members to support its agenda. It needs to reach out to opponents, to show some appreciation of their point of view. Has this happened during the Martin and Harper minorities? Arguably not.

The Conservative Party's 2006 campaign platform included more items of democratic reform than the fixed election date, itself implemented and then ignored when the government called the next election a year earlier than required under the new law. The government has introduced legislation to increase the seats in the House assigned to Ontario, British Columbia, and Alberta, provinces underrepresented there now, as well as legislation to establish an elected Senate. Both items are mired in controversy. There were two other important promises not acted upon at all. One was to stipulate that all votes except the budget and main estimates be "free votes" on which members can make up their own minds with impunity, that is, without fear of punishment by the party leadership. The other was to increase the power of House committees to review the spending estimates of departments and to hold ministers to account before them.

Interestingly, on the issue of free votes, the Conservative minority government has gone in the opposite direction of its campaign platform by insisting that bills other than the budget and the estimates are confidence measures too on which there can be no freedom for Conservative members to vote differently than the leadership. Not only that, the government has pursued the tactic of including non-budgetary items in a budget omnibus bill in order to strengthen its hand in demanding disciplined voting. Of course, had the party not promised a free vote on everything except financial measures, it would not have needed to resort to such a ruse.

As far as committees are concerned, there is no evidence that the government has adopted measures to increase their power in relation to the spending estimates, the accountability of ministers, or anything else. On the contrary, being in a minority position on the committees, the government has gone in the opposite direction, reportedly schooling the government chairs in tactics designed to frustrate any committee actions that are not supportive of itself or its agenda.

One could do worse than conclude that in Canada the logic of responsible government trumps all other concerns. The aim of the old-line parties — the Conservatives and the Liberals — is to form a majority party government. When they fall short of the mark and form a minority government instead, they try to maintain themselves in office with the minimum opposition support necessary, all the while waiting for the opportunity to appeal to the electorate for a majority. Once they have successfully made such an appeal, they revert to their standard behaviour of ignoring the opposition whose support they no longer need. This is the norm.

The old-line political parties have not shown an interest in coalition government and have not developed the attitudes and skills that coalition politics would appear to require. As a result, the public has little understanding of coalition government and is easily led into considering it a problem rather than a solution to the challenge of a minority parliament. As noted earlier, the Harper government had no difficulty convincing the public that the Liberal-NDP coalition formed in early December 2008 to replace it was a bad idea. Indeed, in addition to making the predictable point that the deteriorating economy ruled out political experimentation, the prime minister went so far as to state that the proposed coalition was undemocratic because no one had voted for it and unpatriotic because it had negotiated the support of the Bloc Québécois (Cheadle, 2008: A1, A3). Since the fact of the matter is that Canadians elect a House of Commons, which in turn is expected to generate and sustain a government — minority, majority, or coalition — the prime minister's rhetoric was breathtaking. Yet obviously effective. The doomed coalition can only serve to redouble the efforts of each of the old-line parties to form a single-party, majority government — the brass ring of Canadian politics.

References and Suggested Readings

Beck, J.M. 1968. *Pendulum of Power: Canada's General Elections*. Scarborough: Prentice-Hall.

Bickerton, James, Alain-G. Gagnon, and Patrick J. Smith. 1999. *Ties That Bind: Parties and Voters in Canada*. Toronto: Oxford University Press.

Canada. 2007. "Canada's New Government Delivers on Fixed Date Elections." http://www.democraticreform.gc.ca/eng/media.asp?media_category_id=1&id=1381. 3 May: 1–2.

Carty, R. Kenneth, William Cross, and Lisa Young. 2000. *Rebuilding Canadian Party Politics*. Vancouver: University of British Columbia Press.

Cheadle, Bruce. 2008a. "Gov. Gen. winging her way back to Canada to deal with turmoil." *The Chronicle Herald*, 3 December: A1, A3.

Cheadle, Bruce. 2008b. "Opposition tells Governor General they're prepared to run Canada in a liberal-led coalition." *The Chronicle Herald*, 2 December: A1, A2.

Clark, Campbell, and Drew Fagan. 2004. "Day after election victory, Martin rules out coalition." http://www.theglobeandmail.com/servlet/story/RTGAM.20040629.wndp0629/BNPrint/.

Conservative Party of Canada. 2006. *Stand up for Canada*. http://www.conservative.ca/media/20060113-Platform.pdf. 23.

Crosbie, John. 1997. *No Holds Barred: My Life in Politics*. Toronto: McClelland and Stewart.

Curry, Bill. 2008. "Take a bathroom break? Order pizza? The new filibuster is for sissies." *Globe and Mail*, 3 May: F8.

Dawson, R. McGregor. 1958. *William Lyon Mackenzie King: A Political Biography, 1874–1923*. Toronto: University of Toronto Press.

Dickerson, Mark O., and Thomas Flanagan. 2006. *An Introduction to Government and Politics*, 7th ed. Toronto: Thomson Nelson.

Docherty, David C. 1997. *Mr. Smith Goes to Ottawa: Life in the House of Commons*. Vancouver: University of British Columbia Press.

Docherty, David C. 2004a. *Legislatures: The Canadian Democratic Audit*. Vancouver: University of British Columbia Press.

Docherty, David C. 2004b. "Parliament: Making the Case for Relevance." In James Bickerton and Alain-G. Gagnon, eds. *Canadian Politics*, 4th ed. Peterborough: Broadview Press. 163–83.

Doyle, John. 2008. "Behind the scenes, some great TV." *Globe and Mail*, 7 February: R1.

Galloway, Gloria. 2007. "Tory MP kicked out of caucus over budget vote." *Globe and Mail*, 6 June: A4.

Gérin-Lajoie, Catherine. 2008. "House of Commons." *Canadian Parliamentary Review* 31, 2 (Summer): 54–56.

Kilpatrick, Sean. 2008. *The Canadian Press*. "Harper strongly suggests fall election coming, dismisses fixed election date," 27 August: 1–2. http://canadianpress.google.com/article/ALeqM5jFxzeM7zpCGhxKsRMBHu5KplVNGw.

Laghi, Brian, and Bill Curry. 2007. "Harper's election ultimatum." *Globe and Mail*, 4 October: A1.

LeBlanc, Daniel. 2008. "Majority prefers keeping Conservative government." *Globe and Mail*, 5 December: A6.

McCoag, Tom. 2008. "Chants of 'Bill, Bill, Bill' greet victorious Casey." *Globe and Mail*, 15 October: A5.

Murphy, Rex. 2008. "Was it all a 'pious hope' dream?" *Globe and Mail*, 23 August: A17.

Parliament of Canada. 2008.."39th Parliament, 2nd Session, Private Members' Bills."
http://www2parl.gc.ca/HouseBills/BillsPrivate.aspx?Parl=39&ses=2&Language=E
&Mode=1.

Russell, Peter H. 2008. *Two Cheers for Minority Government: The Evolution of Canadian
Parliamentary Democracy*. Toronto: Emond Montgomery.

Savoie, Donald J. 2008. *Court Government and the Collapse of Accountability in Canada and the
United Kingdom*. Toronto: University of Toronto Press.

Smith, David. 2007. *The People's House of Commons: Theories of Democracy in Contention*.
Toronto: University of Toronto Press.

Smith, Jennifer. 1999. "Democracy and the Canadian House of Commons at the Millennium." *Canadian Public Administration* 42, 4 (Winter): 398–421.

Smith, Jennifer. 2004. *Federalism: The Canadian Democratic Audit*. Vancouver: University of
British Columbia Press.

Taber, Jane. 2005. "Harper rules out coalition: Tory minority government would operate
on issue-by-issue basis, leader says." *Globe and Mail*, 23 December: A1, A8.

Thomas, Paul G. 1998. "Caucus and Representation in Canada. *Parliamentary Perspectives*
1 (May): 2–10.

Valpy, Michael. 2008. "G-G made Harper work for prorogue." *Globe and Mail*, 6 December:
A4.

eight

The Dynamics of Canadian Federalism

RICHARD SIMEON & IAN ROBINSON

Introduction

Federalism is perhaps the most visible and distinctive element in Canadian political life. More than in most other advanced industrial countries, our politics have been conducted in terms of the conflicts between regional and language groups and the struggles between federal and provincial governments. Many of our most important political issues — from the building of the postwar welfare state, to the energy wars in the 1970s, to the constitutional wars of the 1980s and 1990s, to more recent economic and fiscal crises — have been fought in the arena of federal-provincial relations and shaped by the institutions of the federal system. The very structure of Canadian federalism, with its ebb and flow of power between federal and provincial governments, has been at the heart of our political debates. Indeed, for many observers, what makes Canada distinct is the highly decentralized character of its federal system.

We can think of federalism in several ways. Federalism refers, first, to a particular set of governing *institutions* (the classic definition comes from K.C. Wheare, 1964). It is a system in which political authority is divided between two or more constitutionally distinct orders or levels of government. Each has a set of constitutional powers; each has an independent base of political legitimacy in the electorate. In Canada, we talk of federal and provincial governments. Municipal governments are also important in the lives of Canadians, but they do not have independent constitutional status. On the other hand, Aboriginal governments may one day constitute a "third order of government," parallel to federal and provincial governments (Royal Commission on Aboriginal Peoples, 1993).

Several other elements are central to the design of federal institutions (Watts, 1996). There is the *constitution*, which sets out *the division of powers* and the relationships among the governments. In the Canadian context, there has been increasing debate about whether it is necessary for all provinces to have identical powers ("symmetrical federalism") or whether powers can either formally or informally vary according to the needs and characteristics of individual provinces, as in the case of Quebec ("asymmetrical federalism.") (Smiley and Watts, 1985). Most federal constitutions also create a Supreme Court, one of whose central purposes is to act as umpire between levels of government, and an *amending formula* establishing procedures for altering the division of powers and other elements in the constitution. Since one of the central characteristics of all federal systems is the wide range of shared and overlapping responsibilities (*interdependence*), federal institutions also include a set of *mechanisms of intergovernmental relations* (first ministers' conferences and the like) through which the governments deal with each other. Associated with these mechanisms is a complicated set of *fiscal arrangements* dividing up the revenue pie, financing shared responsibilities, and assisting the poorer provinces through equalization payments. Almost unique among federal countries, Canada is largely lacking in one other institution — that is, a *second chamber* in the national Parliament explicitly designed to represent the states or provinces within central decision-making. Unlike the American Senate or the German Bundesrat, the Canadian Senate has conspicuously failed to play this role, thus forcing struggles within our federal system to be worked out between governments whose relations sometimes take on the character of international negotiations, or "federal-provincial diplomacy" (Simeon, 1972, 2006).

Federalism, then, is at heart an *institutional structure* — joining parliamentary or Cabinet government and, since 1982, the Charter of Rights and Freedoms, as one of the three institutional pillars of Canadian government. Each of these pillars embodies a somewhat different conception of democracy; they coexist in a dynamic tension.

Second, federalism can be seen as *a characteristic of the society*. We talk of Canada as a "federal society" (Livingston, 1956). By that we mean the salience of differences that are organized and expressed largely on the basis of region or territory. Such differences may be rooted in language, history, and culture or in differences of economic interest. They interact strongly with the institutional dimension of federalism: Canada has federal institutions largely because of the initial differences in interest and identity among the founding provinces. But federal institutions, in turn, perpetuate these regional differences and reinforce Canadians' tendency to see politics in regional terms. Beyond simple regional differences, Canada is also a binational state (Quebec and the Rest of Canada) or even a multinational state when the First Nations or Aboriginal peoples are included.

Third, federalism is underpinned by *multiple identities*. Citizens are members of both the national community, embodied in the national government, and of provincial communities reflected in their provincial governments. If the balance falls too far to one side, there remains little to hold the system together in the face of demands for provincial independence; if it falls too far the other way, there is little to prevent the aggrandizement of federal power and movement towards a unitary state. Federalism is thus about the coexistence of multiple loyalties and identities; about divided and shared authority; "national standards" and provincial variation; "self-rule" and "shared rule"; "coming together" and "coming apart." Finding the right balance among these is the trick. Much survey evidence confirms that Canadians are, indeed, federalists in this sense, valuing both their national and their provincial identities (Graves *et al.*, 1999; Cutler and Mendelsohn, 2001). Federalism is often justified as a means by which different regional/linguistic communities can live together in a single state. On the one hand, it helps preserve local communities by assuring them the opportunity to manage their own affairs through their provincial government without fear of domination by the majority; on the other hand, it allows them to pursue their common interests through the federal government. Federalism thus combines "*shared rule* through common institutions and *regional self rule* for the governments of constituent units" (Watts, 2008: 1).

Indeed, it is hard to imagine any country as regionally and nationally diverse as Canada being governed as a unitary state. Yet in some such countries, federalism is sometimes seen as the "F-word," its critics believing that it institutionalizes, perpetuates, and exacerbates the very conflicts it is designed to manage and that powerful provincial governments may use their political, bureaucratic, and financial resources to press for greater and greater autonomy, leading eventually to secession. The answer is that successful federalism is double-sided. Not only does it "build out" by devolving power to constituent units, but also it "builds in" by ensuring representation and inclusion within the institutions and practices of the central government.

Other ideas have also been used to justify federalism. In the American political tradition, federalism is seen, along with the Bill of Rights and the separation of powers between president and executive, as a way to check and limit excesses of governmental power through the separation of powers and "checks and balances." And in democratic theory, federalism serves the interests of popular sovereignty by placing governments closer to the people and by allowing citizens to pursue their interests through several governments (Simeon, 1982–83).

In this chapter, we will talk about all three dimensions of Canadian federalism. Our focus is primarily on what drives the federal system and what accounts for the changes over time. In this sense, for the most part we treat federalism as a *dependent variable*. What explains, for example, the relative balance of power and influence between federal and provincial governments?

What explains the nature and level of conflict or disagreement among them? What accounts for the ways they manage their interdependence?

Relative to other federations, Canada is one of the most decentralized, in terms of political authority, powers, and financial resources. The relationship between governments is more often seen as an equal partnership than as a hierarchy. It is also more competitive and adversarial than in most other federations.

We can also look at federalism as an *independent variable*. Here we focus on the consequences of federalism. Does federalism make a difference? What are its effects on public policy or the structure of identities? Do some groups or interests benefit by federalism; are others weakened? How does federalism structure our party system or the role and strategies of interest groups? Many answers to such questions have been given, and most assume that federalism does shape our political life in profound ways. The links between the politics and institutions of federalism and specific outcomes, however, are often very difficult to trace (Fletcher and Wallace, 1986; Bakvis and Skogstad, 2008).

To see federalism as an independent variable quickly shades into a third kind of question: evaluation or judgement. Does federalism contribute to the quality of Canadian democracy? To making public policy that is timely and effective? To the successful management of the diverse social groups that make up the Canadian population?

On all these dimensions, federalism seems to point in two directions. It offers the democratic virtues of governments closer to the people and to lo- cal needs, but the closed nature of much intergovernmental decision-making has led many to complain of a "democratic deficit" (Simeon and Cameron, 2003). Federalism suggests effective ways to balance national and regional concerns in public policy, but again it can be criticized for slowing policy responses in areas where the responsibilities of governments overlap. This is the so-called "joint decision trap" (Scharpf, 1988). Finally, federalism does provide valuable tools for accommodating differences, providing regional and linguistic minorities with provincial governments they can use to pursue their own interests and resist control by the national majority. But at the same time, federal institutions help institutionalize and perpetuate these same divisions (Simeon and Conway, 2001).

Evaluation, of course, also depends on the perspective and criteria one brings to the task. An important distinction in assessments of federalism in Canada is that scholars in Quebec tend to see it as centralized and Ottawa-driven, subordinating Quebec's autonomy. English-speaking scholars tend to stress how decentralized it is and how much autonomy provinces enjoy. Thus, similar facts can produce quite different views.

Evaluative questions quickly spill over into questions about reform. Many elements of the federal system have been and remain hotly contested in Canadian politics. And the stakes have been high: at some times even the very survival of the country. Traditionally, reform efforts stressed the operation of federal structures such as fiscal arrangements, the division of powers, and the amending formula. Since the 1960s, however, the issues have become more fundamental: the place of Quebec in the federal system and whether it should have distinct status or powers; Senate reform to accommodate better in Ottawa the interests of the smaller provinces; self-government for Aboriginal peoples within the federal system; and the implications of federal arrangements for disadvantaged groups such as women, many of whom have felt neglected by one or another aspect of federalism (Russell, 1992).

No single theoretical approach can possibly account for the evolution of the federal system over more than a century. We bring together elements of both societal and state-centred approaches, and we focus on the *interaction* between them. The causal arrow flows both ways. In particular we emphasize the impact of economic and social forces in setting the basic context within which federalism operates. But how these forces are channelled and expressed, and how successful they will be, is in turn greatly influenced by the federal structure and by the choices made by individual leaders.

We begin with the Confederation settlement, then trace the period from 1867 to the 1920s, showing how the centralized federalism, based in part on the extension to Canada of the British colonial model, was replaced by a more province-centred and classical form of federalism. Then we look at the crises that faced Canadian federalism in the Depression and Second World War, followed by the development of the Keynesian welfare state through *co-operative federalism*. The period from 1960 to 1982 saw the intensification of federal-provincial conflict, driven first by Quebec nationalism and later by the resurgence of provincialism, especially in the West. We call this *competitive federalism*. Following 1982, we trace the conflicting pressures on federalism engendered on the one hand by the continuing need to resolve regional and linguistic tensions and on the other by the need to respond to newly mobilized social forces, armed with the Charter of Rights and Freedoms, which challenged many aspects of federal politics. This was the period of *constitutional federalism*. Woven through these social divisions were profound economic changes, which also challenged many elements of contemporary federalism. By the late 1990s, after the failures of constitutional federalism, attention turned to alternative ways to adapt and modernize the federation and to develop new ways for provincial and federal governments to work collaboratively on economic and social issues (Lazar, 1998). We call this emerging pattern *collaborative federalism*. But this was also the era of globalization (which some saw as hollowing out central governments and shifting power upwards to international corporations and institutions and downwards to smaller governments); of debts, deficits, and fiscal restraint that generated new tensions in the federal system; and of neoliberal strategies for economic development and public management, which also had implications for federalism (Lazar, Telford, and Watts, 2003). By 2008–09, the global economic crisis was again shifting the environment to which federal institutions would have to respond. As we shall see, change is seldom moving in one direction, and the economic and social pressures are not always synchronized.

The Confederation Settlement

Three sets of concerns drove the fiercely independent clutch of British colonies in British North America to create the Canadian federation in 1867. The first was political. The attempt to join what is now Quebec and Ontario into the single united province of Canada in 1840 had resulted in political deadlock that frustrated both language groups. The second was economic. Britain was dismantling colonial preferences that had given Canadian exports a competitive edge in Britain; the small separate colonies, deep in debt, were increasingly unable to borrow the funds needed for their economic development. The solution appeared to be the creation of a new national market reaching from sea to sea. That would require the creation of a new national state. The third reason was security, as the weak Canadian colonies feared the dominance of their powerful and expansionist neighbour to the south and sought strength in greater numbers. But what form would this new country take?

Sir John A. Macdonald, his eye on nation-building, would have preferred a powerful unitary state on the British parliamentary model. But this was unacceptable to Quebec, which feared the dominance of the English-speaking majority, and to the other colonies, fearful of losing their independence. If there was to be a new country, it would have to be a federal one, like the United States. Even then, the Atlantic colonies were reluctant brides, and Prince Edward Island and Newfoundland initially remained outside the union.

And what kind of federalism would it be? Would it be weighted to a dominant central government or to strong provinces? Would it share responsibilities across the governments or divide powers into exclusive areas of jurisdiction or "watertight compartments?" Which level of government would control the financial levers? Would there be a strong Senate to represent provincial interests in Ottawa? How would federalism be reconciled with the parliamentary model inherited from Britain? Again, the colonial negotiators had different ideas and different models to choose from.

In the end, the British North America Act (the BNA Act, later renamed the Constitution Act, 1867) was a compromise, adopting elements from among the competing views. On its face, though, the new Constitution leaned towards the centralized model. The federal government was given the powers thought to be essential to creating the new economic union — jurisdiction over trade and commerce, interprovincial transportation, banking, currency, and the like. It was also given responsibility for Aboriginal peoples and for protecting some minority religious and language rights. It had the power to raise money by any mode of taxation. More generally, the BNA Act seemed to place the federal government in much the same relationship to the provinces as Britain had been to its former colonies. Section 91 gave Ottawa the broad general power to make laws for the "Peace, order and good government of Canada," and it was not initially clear that the list of specific responsibilities following was any more than a set of examples. The federal government was to appoint the lieutenant-governors of the provinces, and they were to have the power to "reserve" provincial legislation for the pleasure of the governor general. Moreover, Ottawa had a broad "declaratory power," which would allow it to bring "works and undertakings" in the provinces under federal control. On top of that was an unlimited power to "disallow" or invalidate any or all provincial laws (Simeon and Papillon, 2006).

On the other hand, provinces were given wide responsibilities as well, especially in matters of local and provincial concern, such as education, health, and what later came to be described as social policy. Many of these provincial powers were later to gain vastly increased importance as the modern welfare state was created. The provinces also had a broad, imprecise, residual power in "property and civil rights," which again was to expand as the regulatory role of the state increased in social, economic, and environmental affairs. Thus, the Constitution reflected differing and potentially competing models of federation. It also left some notable gaps: the Senate was to provide equal representation to regions, but unlike the American Senate, members were to be appointed by the federal government, thus vitiating its role as a strong regional voice. Nor was there a method for future amendment of the Constitution: that was to remain in British hands, on the request of the federal government. Also missing was a judicial umpire to resolve intergovernmental disputes. The federal government was empowered to create a Supreme Court, but ultimate judicial authority was to remain with Britain's highest court, the Judicial Committee of the Privy Council, until 1949. All these omissions and ambiguities meant that different groups could interpret the federal bargain very differently, each drawing on those aspects of the Constitution that appeared to support their preferred vision and interests. They also meant that the federal system would be adaptable enough to respond to shifting visions and policy agendas.

Colonial Federalism

After 1867 the federal government vigorously pursued the nation-building project. Western settlement led to the creation of the province of Manitoba, and later Saskatchewan and Alberta. British Columbia joined with the promise of a railway to link it to the East. The transcontinental railway became a cornerstone of the Conservative government's National Policy of 1878. Western producers were expected to consume tariff-protected Canadian farm implements and supplies, while selling their products largely in international markets.

Initially, Sir John A. Macdonald's government vigorously asserted the extraordinary powers of disallowance and reservation. Provincial governments resisted. They favoured a more provincialist model. Ontario and Quebec organized the first interprovincial conference in 1887 to coordinate their demands and strategy against the federal government. In contrast to the colonial model, with its implied subordination of the provinces, Ontario Premier Oliver Mowat argued that Confederation was a "compact" among the provinces, which implied that the federal government was a creature of the provinces. This debate has reverberated through much of the subsequent history of the federation.

Macdonald's aggressive assertions of federal authority rested on precarious foundations. They were not accompanied by the anticipated prosperity that could have cemented federal dominance. Growing Protestant-Catholic and French-English conflict fuelled pressures for a more decentralized federalism.

Most profound was the growing alienation of French Canada. The federal government's decision to let Louis Riel hang following the Rebellion of 1885, along with its failure to use its constitutional power to protect the rights of Catholics and French-speakers under attack by provincial legislatures, led many Quebecers to believe that they were destined to become a diminishing minority in Canada outside Quebec.

The moral of the story seemed obvious to many French Canadians: only where they were a majority — which was to say, only in Quebec — would their religious and linguistic rights be secure. Even then, they would be safe only if the government of Quebec had the final say on these matters within that province. These conclusions led inexorably towards the identification of language and religion with the provincial rather than the national community and to a constitutional orientation bent on strengthening the powers of the provincial government rather than improving minority rights at the federal level. In other words, the "French Canadians" became *les Québécois*.

Classical Federalism

Thus — with the notable exception of emergency centralization during the First World War — the pendulum swung to the provinces. Much of the new resource and industrial development took place largely under provincial jurisdiction. Provincial revenues swelled, reducing their dependence on federal subsidies. The federal government's powers of reservation and disallowance were rarely used (though they remained in the Constitution), and in the era of the minimal state, federal and provincial responsibilities seldom overlapped. With important exceptions, such as battles between Ontario and Ottawa over resources and timber exports, intergovernmental conflict was relatively muted.

All this ended with the Great Depression of the 1930s. The resulting crisis of the state was also a crisis for federalism. With unemployment above 20 per cent, there was enormous pressure for welfare and relief, which fell largely on the provinces; at the same time their revenues shrivelled. Several provincial governments were driven to the brink of bankruptcy. A variety of ad hoc federal relief programs were put together, and in 1937 the federal government established the Rowell-Sirois Commission to recommend reforms to the federal system. In the United States the primary legislative response to the crisis was Franklin Roosevelt's New Deal, which was eventually declared constitutional by the American Supreme Court. These landmark decisions, based on a broad interpretation of the American trade and commerce power, effectively established the predominance of the central government in the American federal system. In Canada the Conservative Prime Minister R.B. Bennett sought to emulate Roosevelt with his "Bennett New Deal." His successor, Mackenzie King, referred the package to the Judicial Committee of the Privy Council, which ruled its key provisions *ultra vires* — beyond the powers of the federal government. The courts also reinforced the classical and decentralized model of federalism in other cases, as in the *Labour Conventions* case (1937).

This experience led many observers, especially on the left, to mount a fundamental critique of the federal system. For the British scholar Harold Laski, federalism was "obsolete," unable to deal with the problems of a complex industrial society or to manage fiscal crisis. To Canadian critics, such as F.R. Scott (1977), the "dead hand" of the federal Constitution was a fundamental barrier to progressive reform. The Second World War temporarily halted such debates, as Ottawa assumed virtually all the powers of a unitary government under the emergency powers of the War Measures Act. But what sort of federalism would peacetime bring?

Many commentators built on the critics of the 1930s. Modernization, in this view, would inexorably push towards centralization. The emergence of national — and international — economic actors meant that the regulatory reach of the state had to be similarly expanded. Industrialization and urbanization inevitably meant that "traditional" identities rooted in language, ethnicity, and region would decline in significance to be replaced by interests and identities defined in class terms. Moreover, the economic and social roles of the state were changing as governments began to play a greater role in the management of the economy and in building a redistributive welfare state. Only central governments, with a national perspective and control of the major fiscal, jurisdictional, and bureaucratic resources, it was felt, could effectively play these new roles. Thus, writers like Alec Corry predicted a steady flow of influence to Ottawa, echoing John A. Macdonald's much earlier hope that the provinces would one day be reduced to the role of municipalities. Provincial governments, however, had no wish to concede powers to Ottawa, and they possessed important constitutional and institutional powers to resist massive centralization.

The result of the interplay of these forces was that the new roles for the state were adopted with remarkably few changes to the federal Constitution. The major elements of social security — unemployment insurance and pensions — were shifted to Ottawa through constitutional amendments. But the primary instrument of adaptation was the federal spending power — the largely unchallenged ability of the federal government to spend money even on matters that lay within provincial jurisdiction. Since the new roles of government cut across jurisdictional lines, interdependence, overlapping, and sharing of responsibilities became the hallmarks of modern federalism in Canada as in all other federations. Along with this increased interdependence came an increased need for fiscal and administrative arrangements to manage intergovernmental relations. Hence, there was a steady increase in the number and scope of intergovernmental meetings. By 1970 Donald Smiley was to identify "executive federalism" — negotiations among officials and ministers of the federal and provincial governments — as a central characteristic of the Canadian policy-making process.

Postwar Canadian federalism can be divided into four periods, though no neat markers separate them: cooperative federalism, lasting until the early 1960s; competitive federalism, from the 1960s to the early 1980s; constitutional federalism in the following decade; and a more policy-focused collaborative federalism as the next century arrived.

Cooperative Federalism

In 1945 the federal government placed before the provinces a comprehensive set of proposals known as the Green Book proposals. Ottawa would assume responsibility for some areas, such as pensions and unemployment insurance (already achieved in a 1940 amendment), and achieve national programs in other aspects of health and welfare through the sharing of costs with the provinces. In return, Ottawa would retain control over major tax fields and would make compensating grants to the provinces. These centralizing proposals were flatly rejected by wealthy Ontario, supported by British Columbia and Quebec. But over the next few years, most of their elements were put into place.

Unemployment insurance, pensions, and family allowances gave Ottawa responsibility for the basic income security system. The rest of the welfare state programs came about through the use of the federal spending power in the form of shared cost, or conditional grant, programs. These included hospital insurance in 1955, expanded to full medical care in 1968; assistance to post-secondary education; provisions for aid to disadvantaged groups, consolidated in the Canada Assistance Plan of 1968; and a host of smaller programs. Thus, the "complexities of federalism" may have slowed, but did not prevent, the implementation of the postwar project common to most advanced industrial countries (Banting, 1987).

This process was achieved without major federal-provincial conflict. The postwar agenda did not divide Canadians sharply on regional lines. Provinces in most cases accepted federal leadership and welcomed the financial assistance that enabled them to spend "50-cent dollars." Provincial pressure also was able to ensure that, unlike American "grant-in-aid" programs, the conditions in most programs were relatively loose and accommodating to provincial priorities. Intergovernmental relations tended to be conducted among officials within the various program areas. Provinces often complained of onerous federal conditions or the distortion of provincial priorities by the lure of federal spending, but fundamental constitutional issues were pushed aside: federalism was largely an administrative matter.

There was one major exception to this generally harmonious pattern. From the very outset of the modern period, Quebec governments were strongly opposed to the expansion of federal policy influence. Quebec governments of all political stripes favoured a decentralized form of classical federalism, a vision clearly articulated by the Tremblay Commission in 1956. In the Duplessis years, the Quebec government was closely allied with the conservative wing of the Catholic Church and business interests that strongly objected to the expansion of the postwar welfare state into areas previously left to the Church and voluntary organizations. Thus, Quebec rejected both the content of the postwar model and the means by which it was achieved. Throughout the 1940s and 1950s, therefore, its strategy was largely to resist federal encroachments rather than to expand provincial powers.

Competitive Federalism

Competitive federalism refers to a number of changes from the postwar cooperative model: the escalation of inter-regional and intergovernmental conflict, stronger pressures for decentralization, expansion by both levels of government into new policy fields in a form of "competitive expansionism" or "province-building versus nation-building," and increasing efforts by both levels of government to mobilize their populations around competing images of federalism and how it should work. The process was triggered by the Quiet Revolution in Quebec.

The election of Jean Lesage's Liberal government in 1960 swept away the conservative coalition that had dominated Quebec politics. The Quiet Revolution embraced the secular modern bureaucratic state and its policy agenda. But Quebecers were to become *maîtres chez nous* (masters in our own house) — Quebec, not Ottawa, was to be the instrument. Hence, Quebec governments went beyond the resistance exemplified by Duplessis to seek the powers and financial resources with which they could undertake the same kinds of policies on behalf of the Québécois nation that the federal government was undertaking on behalf of the English-Canadian nation, without constitutional interference or financial penalty.

At first, Quebec's demands focused on fiscal arrangements and specific programs. Quebec led successful renegotiations of federal-provincial fiscal arrangements to give provinces a greater share of tax revenues and to enrich the equalization program. It also was able to achieve a measure of *de facto* special status in a number of areas: the establishment of a separate Quebec Pension Plan and the "opting out" of a number of shared-cost programs in return for a greater share of taxes.

It was not long, however, before the debate escalated to the constitutional level. Lesage's successor, Daniel Johnson, sought more fundamental changes, expressed in the slogan "*égalité ou indépendance*." The Constitution should recognize Canada as a partnership of two nations, one centred in Ottawa, the other in Quebec City. More important, in 1968 René Lévesque founded the Parti Québécois from disaffected Liberals and other nationalist groups and led the party to power in 1976. The PQ model was "sovereignty-association," an independent Quebec that would maintain ties with the rest of Canada in a binational framework. Federalism, Lévesque argued, frustrated both sides:

English Canada could not have the strong central government it desired; Quebec could not have the freedom it sought. Thus, among Quebec leaders the debate was now between those who sought greater autonomy for Quebec within a federal structure and those who argued for independence.

The alternative model was expressed by Pierre Trudeau, who came to Ottawa in 1965 expressly to battle what he considered a retrograde Quebec nationalism. Quebec's future, he argued, lay in a bicultural, bilingual, united Canada, in which Quebecers were strong participants in the national government and enjoyed rights from sea to sea. Recognition of Quebec as the primary political expression of Quebec society was to him an anathema; even the modest steps towards *de facto* asymmetry, he believed, were leading down a slippery slope, whose outcome could only be separation. Thus, Trudeau insisted both on a strong central government and on the equality of all the provinces. The politics of federalism became dominated by a much larger debate over the future of Quebec and the country. The process culminated in the 1980 Quebec referendum, in which the PQ lost by a significant margin its request for a "mandate" to negotiate sovereignty-association. The subsequent constitutional negotiations, resulting in the Constitution Act, 1982, gave Canada a Charter of Rights and an amending formula but rejected not only the sovereigntist position but also that of Quebec federalists.

By the 1970s other provinces, especially the larger wealthier ones, were also mounting a challenge to the Ottawa-dominated federalism of the postwar period. In part this reflected the growing resources, competence, and confidence of provincial governments and their bureaucracies, which, fuelled by federal transfers, had been growing much faster than the federal government. As issues such as the environment entered the public agenda, both levels of government competed to enter the field. Provincial governments were less willing to accept federal definitions of national priorities. More generally, the rapid economic growth of the postwar period had ended, and Canada, like other countries, entered a period of economic volatility and instability that exacerbated regional tensions and forced a rethinking of Keynesian economic policy. Increasingly, provinces sought to control the policy levers to assure their ability to manage the economy — a phenomenon that came to be known as "province-building."

Nowhere were these economic difficulties more evident than in the field of energy. The energy shocks of the 1970s provoked profound regional conflict, pitting energy-producing — or potentially producing provinces, like Newfoundland — against central Canada. The producers sought to move towards world energy prices, to retain the proceeds of their provincially owned resources, and to enhance their capacity to manage energy development. Consuming provinces looked to the federal government to keep prices down and to ensure that oil and gas revenues would be shared across the country. The escalating conflict culminated in the federal National Energy Program (NEP) of 1980, in which the federal government asserted sweeping control over the industry — provoking Alberta briefly to limit the flow of oil to the rest of the country. The battle also tapped deeply held grievances in the West and in the smaller provinces about their economic and political subordination to central Canada and the federal government.

Thus, a provincial reform agenda emerged alongside Quebec's: on one hand, the provinces sought to limit the federal spending power and its ability to intervene in areas of provincial jurisdiction; on the other, they wanted to strengthen their own financial resources and powers in areas important to them. Also expressed was the idea of "we want in": a greater role for regions at the centre, reflected in the demand for Senate reform and in the growth of the Reform Party in the West. Increasingly, debates within federalism took the form of rival conceptions of the very nature of the system — the province-centred view, which saw Canada as a "community of communities" and governing Canada as a partnership between Ottawa and the provinces; and the "Canada-centred" view, which saw Ottawa as the primary order of government.

Intergovernmental relations also became much more conflictual. Fundamental policy debates about what should be done and who should do it replaced the earlier pattern of bargaining over administrative details. Governments took a more strategic approach to federalism, many of them creating dedicated ministries or central agencies to oversee the federal-provincial battles. It all culminated in the drawn-out battle over the Constitution following the 1980 Quebec referendum. The 1982 constitutional settlement, while excluding Quebec, was otherwise a compromise: the nation-centred view was reflected in the Charter of Rights and Freedoms, to be enforced by the Supreme Court; the province-centred view was reflected in the amending formula, which ensured a strong provincial role in future amendment.

Constitutional Federalism

Thus, by the early 1980s, Canadian federalism had come to be dominated by the "high politics" of the Constitution. After 1982 there was a brief hiatus in the conflict; a more harmonious federal-provincial relationship seemed likely when the Progressive Conservatives under Brian Mulroney were elected in 1984. The Mulroney government had all the authority of a sweeping mandate, with a majority of seats in every province. Moreover, by winning over many Quebec nationalists while maintaining its Western base, the Mulroney coalition seemed to bridge the fundamental divide in Canada. In his election campaign, Mulroney promised to find a way to "bring Quebec back into the Constitution with honour," to kill the NEP, and to govern Canada as a collaborative partnership between the two levels of government.

The Quebec goal was achieved in the Meech Lake Accord of 1987. However, public opinion turned against the Accord, and three newly elected provincial governments, which had not been party to the original agreement, sought fundamental changes. Three years later the Accord died in a welter of recriminations. In Quebec the demise of Meech Lake was seen as a rejection of even a minimal set of objectives, adding insult to the exclusion of 1982. But in English Canada the mood was very different. Meech Lake had revealed a profoundly different political climate in the rest of the country. The advent of the Charter had shifted the constitutional discourse: now it was less about governing the relations among governments than a vehicle for popular sovereignty, defining the relations between citizens and governments. It was a Constitution more for citizens than for governments. The constitutional agenda broadened vastly, and the legitimacy of making constitutional change in the closed-door setting of first ministers' conferences was fundamentally challenged. So was the idea that compromise carefully crafted by élites could not be allowed to unravel in the legislative ratification process.

The changed climate in English Canada threatened key elements of the Quebec agenda. Many groups rejected any form of asymmetry or special status for Quebec: the Constitution should reflect the equality of citizens and the equality of the provinces; there should be no hierarchy of rights in which the rights of language groups would be privileged over the rights of women, multicultural groups, or Aboriginal peoples; Ottawa's ability to establish and enforce national standards in areas of provincial jurisdiction should not be limited. Moreover, there were new items on the constitutional agenda, notably the call for a "Triple E Senate" — equal, elected, and effective — and the Aboriginal peoples' call for the right to self-government.

The federal-provincial process was renewed in 1991. Now the leaders of the Aboriginal peoples and of the two territories were at the table. The resulting Charlottetown Accord sought to respond to the diverse forces at play, but the divisions were too wide to bridge and the process had lost its legitimacy. The consequence was the defeat of the Accord in the referendum of October 1992.

Constitutional federalism had failed. It did not disappear — the 1995 Quebec referendum on "sovereignty-partnership" and the subsequent federal Clarity Act saw to that. But now the emphasis would be on "making the federation work better" through "non-constitutional renewal," including, for example, passage of a federal resolution recognizing Quebec as a nation within Canada and a federal commitment not to support any constitutional amendment without the consent of Quebec (Lazar, 1998).

Collaborative Federalism

Constitutional federalism focused primarily on the character of Canada as a political community — on Quebec and Canada, the role of national and provincial governments, and the ability of federalism to accommodate the emergence of new identities and interests. But throughout this period Canada was also undergoing a wrenching set of economic changes in the face of an integrating global and North American economy, competition from newly industrialized nations, increased integration of financial markets, and the like. In some sense the Canada–US Free Trade Agreement and its successor, the North American Free Trade Agreement, constitute an "economic constitution" that parallels Canada's political constitution, with profound implications for the future of the Canadian political economy. The changed economic climate also raised questions about the relative responsibilities of the two orders of government.

Trade also raised the question of the economic links among Canadian provinces. Ontario's manufacturing economy was turned 90 degrees from a tariff-protected east–west orientation to an open-border north–south one. Canada's economic regions were becoming less linked to each other than they were to other parts of the world, with important implications for regional disparities, for the ability to generate national policies, and for the long-run commitment to equalization or inter-regional sharing. Some argued that this suggested the need for a stronger federal government; for others, it was provinces that were more capable of forging the links among business, government, and labour necessary for economic success (Courchene, 1992).

Whatever the final answer, it is clear that globalization meant that federalism no longer stopped at the border: international forces reached deep into Canadian life to affect provinces and municipalities, and the tensions within Canadian federalism were projected into the international arena. This was dramatically illustrated by a drawn-out dispute with the United States over exports of softwood lumber. Managing competing domestic interests was almost as difficult as managing the Canadian–American relationship, allowing American negotiators many opportunities to pursue divide and rule strategies.

A second fundamental challenge to federalism arose from the escalation of government debt and deficits at both levels of government. In the 1990s we saw a "federalism of restraint" as governments competed to reduce their deficits and avoid political blame. Thus, the 1995 federal budget rolled transfers for health care, welfare, and post-secondary education into a single "block grant," the Canada Health and Social Transfer (CHST). While there were fewer federal controls over how the money would be spent, this was accompanied by a dramatic reduction of $6 billion, or 37 per cent, over two years. This in turn helped drive up provincial deficits and threatened to erode the federal government's ability to shape national priorities through its use of the spending power: with its share in the cost of major social programs plummeting, what right would it have to call the tune? Thus, the elaborate structure of intergovernmental transfers that had been a hallmark of Canadian federalism came under profound challenge.

For some commentators the combination of continued pressures for decentralization and the fiscal crisis suggested that Canada should move towards a more confederal model. This is one in which — as in the European Union — the federal government is essentially a creature of the provinces. Thomas Courchene (1997) argued that provinces must take much greater collective responsibility for "preserving and promoting social Canada." André Burelle (1995) argued for "partnership federalism" in which a permanent Council of First Ministers would establish national goals and standards, replacing federal standards enforced through the federal spending power. Ottawa would be responsible only for those matters that cannot be managed with full justice and efficiency by the provinces. (For a critique of these approaches, see Gibbins, 1997.)

These pressures — combined with constitutional fatigue — helped fuel calls for a focus on the need for Canadian governments to work together. The first manifestation of this collaborative, non-constitutional approach to improving the management of the Canadian federal system was the Agreement on Internal Trade (AIT) in 1994. Concern about reducing barriers to trade among provinces and strengthening the Canadian economic union was of long standing. With Ottawa and the provinces unable to agree on a constitutional solution, the alternative was for both to negotiate a set of rules and standards, along with mechanisms to resolve future disagreements (Trebilcock and Schwanen, 1995). The essential point was that if Ottawa lacked the authority to impose national standards itself — and if there were to be such standards — they would emerge from intergovernmental collaboration.

Attention then turned to the "social union," the complex set of intergovernmental agreements through which the major elements of social policy — health, post-secondary education, and welfare — are developed and delivered. Here the issue was whether and how Canadians across the country could enjoy national standards while also permitting the variations in policy necessary to meet the needs of different provinces. A Provincial-Territorial Ministerial Council on Social Policy Reform and Renewal was formed. Its work eventually led to a meeting of first ministers in February 1999, at which "A Framework to Improve the Social Union for Canadians" (SUFA) was adopted. This agreement set out a number of principles respecting the social union that all governments were committed to, including equality of treatment across the country, access by all Canadians to adequate social programs wherever they live, the reduction of barriers to mobility among provinces, and greater transparency and accountability. In addition, the governments committed themselves to "mutual respect" and to working "more closely together to meet the needs of Canadians" (SUFA, 1999), including an obligation to plan social policy together and to consult before introducing new programs.

For its part, Ottawa agreed that when using conditional transfers, it would "proceed in a cooperative manner that is respectful of the provincial and territorial governments and their priorities" (SUFA, 1999). A year's notice would be given before any change in funding. Moreover, it would not introduce any new program without the prior agreement of a majority of the provinces. Provinces would be responsible for "detailed program design," and where they already had a program in place, they would still receive the new funds, which could be used in related areas. This went some way to meeting provincial concerns that federal funding could distort provincial priorities. However, Ottawa did not concede any limitations — except for a commitment to prior notice and consultation — on its power to make direct grants to individual Canadians in areas within provincial jurisdiction (for example, direct grants to post-secondary students). The agreement also included a commitment by the governments to develop mechanisms for avoiding and resolving intergovernmental disputes that would be "timely, efficient, effective, transparent, and non-adversarial." In short, it would operate as a collaboration or partnership between the two orders of government.

The SUFA did not explicitly provide for provinces to opt out of new shared programs and still receive federal funding, as an earlier interprovincial draft had suggested. This has been a long-standing goal of successive Quebec governments. Its omission led Quebec Premier Lucien Bouchard to refuse to sign the agreement. The actual impact on Quebec's finances would probably be minimal, but symbolically the isolation of Quebec meant that the distinct society status that had proved so difficult to achieve in the constitutional forum was becoming a reality in the daily practice of Canadian federalism.

Collaborative federalism also includes some change in the institutions of intergovernmental relations. This complex machinery includes First Ministers' Conferences or Meetings on specific issues such as health care funding, the Annual Premiers' Conference, an array of Ministerial Councils or Committees on specific policy areas, and an array of daily contacts among senior officials.

In 2004 the provinces established a "Council of the Federation" to deepen and extend these efforts (see IIGR, 2003). Overall, however, despite calls to recognize the centrality of intergovernmental relations (for example, by requiring annual First Ministers' Conferences), intergovernmental relations remain very informal. They still have no constitutional or statutory base; they take no votes; and the agreements they sign have no enforceable legal status. Each government remains accountable only to its own legislature.

In many ways this informality may facilitate the success of intergovernmental relations. It is adaptable and flexible, and it allows governments at both levels to use their policy levers to meet their own goals without always needing to find intergovernmental consensus. But the informality has its costs as well. Without clear rules and principles, intergovernmental wrangling ends up a competition for turf and status, with basic policy issues taking a back seat. "One-off" deals have often replaced carefully planned agreements and common action. With respect to fiscal arrangements, there have been long debates about whether or not there is a "fiscal imbalance" in the federation, about the equalization program for poorer provinces, and about whether provinces such as Ontario are receiving their "fair share" of federal spending. The fact that intergovernmental agreements have no legal status means that a shift in government may unravel carefully crafted arrangements, as happened with the Kelowna Accord (2005). It involved massive intergovernmental cooperation with Aboriginal groups, but was repudiated when a new Conservative government came to power in Ottawa. As well, without clear rules and principles, public accountability and legislative oversight of executive federalism become more difficult.

Assessments of collaborative federalism vary. Some question whether governments are fully committed to the mutual trust and cooperation that collaboration requires. Agreements are often vague, reflecting the lowest common denominator of what governments can agree to rather than hard choices and commitments. Activists in areas such as social and environmental policy worry that the focus on power and position, combined with a preoccupation with the flow of money between federal and provincial governments, diverts attention from the substance of issues. Despite powerful criticisms about meetings behind closed doors, little progress has been made in opening the process to the public. Indeed, it is striking that despite the massive economic and social changes in Canada, the institutions and processes for the conduct of federalism and the dynamic of intergovernmental relations seem to have changed very little in recent decades (Simeon, 2006).

As we have seen, many labels have been applied to Canadian federalism over time: cooperative, collaborative, dualist, competitive, and so on. The most recent, coined by Prime Minister Stephen Harper is "Open Federalism"

(IIGR, 2006). It includes a mix of policies — respecting provincial jurisdiction, limiting the federal spending power, redressing the "fiscal imbalance," and responding to Quebec's concerns. The words are distinctive, but the direction is consistent with the evolution of Canadian federalism in recent decades.

Conclusion

Federalism, it has been said, is a "process" rather than a steady state. This has been abundantly true of Canadian federalism throughout its history, as the governments and institutions that make it up have responded to changing circumstances and shifting policy agendas. We conclude with a few of the current and future challenges that the system faces.

1. *Alleviating the "democratic deficit."* How can intergovernmental relations be rendered more open and transparent to citizens? This could involve opening the process to more citizen participation or strengthening the role that parliaments and legislatures play in debating and scrutinizing the conduct of intergovernmental relations.
2. *Alleviating the "policy deficit."* Here the concerns are how to shift federal-provincial debates from often sterile debates over turf, money, and status to a greater concern for the substance of issues. Behind that is the question of how to find the right balance between "national standards" that will apply across the whole country and the variations in policy that federalism is designed to encourage. And there is the further question of whether effective policy is more likely to emerge from close collaboration between governments or through more vigorous and open competition and debate between them. Another continuing challenge is getting the roles and responsibilities — and the financial resources to pay for them — right. Provinces have recently complained of a "fiscal imbalance," arguing that the chief areas of growing government spending lie largely in their jurisdiction while Ottawa has more access to revenues. The solution, they say, is not in greater use of the federal spending power to act in areas of provincial jurisdiction but to move more taxing powers to the provinces. Social policy advocates have often worried that a declining federal role may lead to the erosion of national standards and a "rush to the bottom" in provincial programs. There is little evidence of this, however (Harrison, 2005).
3. *Accommodating difference.* Many of the difficulties in reconciling East and West, French- and English-speakers in Canada lie not in federalism itself, but in larger elements of our institutional structure discussed

elsewhere in this book — an ineffective Senate, an electoral system that exaggerates regional differences, a regionally fragmented party system, and a parliamentary system that is dominated by the executive, leaving little room for individual MPs to speak for their local interests. This analysis suggests that simply improving the institutions of intergovernmental relations is insufficient. With respect to Quebec, the continuing question is how much "asymmetry" — whether formal or informal — is possible or desirable in the Canadian federation.

4. *From federalism to multilevel governance.* Local governments provide a vast array of services, yet are constitutionally subordinate to the provinces. Local governments — especially the large urban areas that are the centres of economic growth and multiculturalism — are now calling for greater recognition and authority, for greater financial resources, and for seats at the intergovernmental table. Whether, and how, they will be integrated into the Canadian pattern of multilevel governance is an important question for the future. The same is true for Aboriginal governments. The idea that they would constitute a "third order of government" in Canada was included in the 1993 Charlottetown Accord and was a central recommendation of the Royal Commission on Aboriginal Peoples, but it has not been enacted. Nevertheless, court decisions and political negotiations are moving towards self-government and critical questions remain about how they will relate to both federal and provincial governments in the future.

5. *Reform at the centre.* The practice of Canadian federalism focuses on the interstate dimension — the relation between the orders of government. But another aspect of federalism has been labelled intrastate federalism, which focuses on the representation of the federal characteristics within central institutions. One reason for the strength of Canadian provinces is the weakness of Canada's federal government in this regard: an electoral system that emphasizes and exaggerates regional differences, a Parliament where party discipline makes it difficult for members to speak for their regional and local interests, and a Senate that fails to represent either provincial governments or regional populations (Smith, 2004; Simeon and Nugent, 2008).

6. *Responding to crisis.* In earlier times of national crisis such as the Great Depression, Canadians have tended to look to the federal government for leadership. In 2009, as Canadians faced an economic crisis at once local, national, and global, it is worth asking whether this pattern will be repeated, whether governments will be able to collaborate on coordinated solutions, or whether competing interests will frustrate coordinated action.

References and Suggested Readings

Essential resources for all students of federalism and intergovernmental relations in Canada and elsewhere are: The Institute of Intergovernmental Relations, School of Policy Studies, Queen's University, Kingston (http://www.iigr.ca), the Forum of Federations (http://www.forumfed.org), and the Institute for Research on Public Policy (http://www.irpp.org).

"A Framework to Improve the Social Union of Canadians" [SUFA]. 1999. An agreement between the Government of Canada and the Governments of the Provinces and Territories. 4 February. Ottawa: Treasury Board of Canada Secretariat. http://www.tbs-sct.cg.ca.

Bakvis, Herman, Gerald Baier, and Douglas Brown. 2009. *Contested Federalism: Certainty and Ambiguity in the Canadian Federation.* Toronto: Oxford University Press.

Bakvis, Herman, and Grace Skogstad, Eds. 2008. *Canadian Federalism: Performance, Effectiveness and Legitimacy,* 2nd ed. Don Mills: Oxford University Press.

Banting, Keith. 1998. "The Past Speaks to the Future: Lessons from the Postwar Social Union." In Harvey Lazar, ed., *Canada: The State of the Federation, 1997.* Kingston: Institute of Intergovernmental Relations. 36–69.

Banting, Keith. 1987. *The Welfare State and Canadian Federalism,* 2nd ed. Montreal: McGill-Queen's University Press.

Brown, Douglas M. 2002. *Market Rules: Economic Union Reform and Intergovernmental Policy-Making in Australia and Canada.* Montreal: McGill-Queen's University Press.

Burelle, André. 1995. *Le mal canadien.* Montréal: Fides.

Cairns, Alan C. 1977. "The Governments and Societies of Canadian Federalism." *Canadian Journal of Political Science* 10: 695–725.

Cairns, Alan C. 1979. "The Other Crisis in Canadian Federalism." *Canadian Public Administration* 22: 175–95.

Cairns, Alan C. 1991. *Disruptions: Constitutional Struggles from the Charter to Meech Lake,* ed. Douglas Williams. Toronto: McClelland and Stewart.

Cameron, David, and Richard Simeon. 2002. "Intergovernmental Relations in Canada: The Emergence of Collaborative Federalism." *Publius: The Journal of Federalism.* 32, 2: 49–72.

Courchene, Thomas. 1992. *Rearrangements: The Courchene Papers.* Toronto: Mosaic Press.

Courchene, Thomas. 1996. "ACCESS: A Convention on the Canadian Economic and Social System." *Canadian Business Economics* 4, 4: 3–26.

Cutler, Fred, and Matthew Mendelsohn. 2001. "What Kind of Federalism do Canadians (outside Quebec) Want?" *Policy Options* (October): 23–29.

Fletcher, Frederick J., and Donald C. Wallace. 1986. "Federal-Provincial Relations and the Making of Public Policy in Canada." In Richard Simeon, ed., *Division of Powers and Public Policy.* Toronto: University of Toronto Press. 125–206.

Fortin, Sarah, Alain Noel, and France St. Hilaire. 2003. *Forging the Canadian Social Union: SUFA and Beyond.* Montreal: Institute for Research on Public Policy.

Gagnon, Alain-G., and Hugh Segal. 2000. *The Canadian Social Union Without Quebec.* Montreal: Institute for Research on Public Policy.

Gibbins, Roger. 1982. *Regionalism: Territorial Politics in Canada and the United States.* Toronto: Butterworths.

Gibbins, Roger. 1997. *Time Out: Assessing Incremental Strategies for Enhancing the Canadian Political Union.* Toronto: C.D. Howe Institute.

Frank L. Graves *et al.* 1999. "Identity and National Attachments in Canada." In Harvey Lazar and Tom McIntosh, eds., *How Canadians Connect. Canada: The State of the Federation, 1998/1999.* Kingston: Institute of Intergovernmental Relations.

Harrison, Kathryn, Ed. *Racing to the Bottom? Provincial Interdependence in the Canadian Federation.* Vancouver: University of British Columbia Press.

Hueglin, Thomas, and Alan Fenna. 2006. *Comparative Federalism: A Systematic Enquiry.* Peterborough: Broadview Press.

Institute of Intergovernmental Relations, School of Policy Studies, Queen's University. 2003. *Special Series on the Council of the Federation.* http://www.queensu.ca/iigr/working/archive/Fed/EN.html.

Institute of Intergovernmental Relations, School of Policy Studies. 2006. *Open Federalism: Interpretations, Significance.* Kingston: The Institute.

LaSelva, Samuel V. 1996. *The Moral Foundations of Canadian Federalism: Paradoxes, Achievements, and Tragedies of Nationhood.* Montreal: McGill-Queen's University Press.

Lazar, Harvey, Ed. 1998. *Canada: The State of the Federation, 1997.* Kingston: Institute of Intergovernmental Relations.

Livingston, William. 1956. *Federalism and Constitutional Change.* New York: Oxford University Press.

McRoberts, Kenneth, and Patrick Monahan, Eds. 1993. *The Charlottetown Accord, the Referendum, and the Future of Canada.* Toronto: University of Toronto Press.

McRoberts, Kenneth, and Dale Posgate. 1980. *Quebec: Social Change and Political Crisis.* Toronto: McClelland and Stewart.

Meekison, J. Peter, Hamish Telford, and Harvey Lazar, Eds. 2004. *Reconsidering the Institutions of Canadian Federalism.* Kingston: Institute of Intergovernmental Relations, School of Policy Studies.

Porter, John. 1965. *The Vertical Mosaic: An Analysis of Social Class and Power in Canada.* Toronto: University of Toronto Press.

Romanow, Roy, John Whyte, and Howard Leeson. 1984. *Canada ... Notwithstanding: The Making of the Constitution 1976–1982.* Toronto: Carswell/Methuen.

Royal Commission on Aboriginal Peoples. 1993. *Partners in Confederation: Aboriginal Peoples, Self-Government, and the Constitution.* Ottawa: Minister of Supply and Services.

Russell, Peter. 1992. *Constitutional Odyssey: Can Canadians Be a Sovereign People?* Toronto: University of Toronto Press.

Scharpf, Fritz. 1988. "The Joint Decision Trap: Lessons from German Federalism and European Integration." *Public Administration Review* 66: 239–78.

Scott, F.R. 1977. *Essays on the Constitution: Aspects of Canadian Law and Politics.* Toronto: University of Toronto Press.

Simeon, Richard. 1972. *Federal-Provincial Diplomacy: The Making of Recent Policy in Canada.* Toronto: University of Toronto Press.

Simeon, Richard. 1975. "Regionalism and Canadian Political Institutions." *Queen's Quarterly* 82: 499–511.

Simeon, Richard. 1982-83. "Criteria for Choice in Federal Systems." *Queen's Law Journal* 18: 131–57.

Simeon, Richard, and David Cameron. 2002. "Intergovernmental Relations and Democracy: An Oxymoron If Ever There Was One?" In Herman Bakvis, and Grace Skogstad, eds., *Canadian Federalism: Performance, Effectiveness and Legitimacy,* 1st ed. Don Mills: Oxford University Press. 278–95.

Simeon, Richard, and Amy Nugent. 2008. "Parliamentary Canada and Intergovernmental Canada: Exploring the Tensions." In Herman Bakvis, and Grace Skogstad, eds.,

Canadian Federalism: Performance, Effectiveness and Legitimacy, 2nd ed. Don Mills: Oxford University Press. 89–111.

Simeon, Richard, and Martin Papillon. 2006. "Canada." In Akhtar Majeed, Ronald L. Watts, and Douglas M. Brown, eds., *Distribution of Powers and Responsibilities in Federal Countries.* Global Dialogue on Federalism, Vol. 2. Montreal: McGill-Queen's University Press. 91–122.

Simeon, Richard, and Ian Robinson. 1990. *State, Society, and the Development of Canadian Federalism.* Research Studies for the Royal Commission on the Economic Union and Development Prospects for Canada, Vol. 71. Toronto: University of Toronto Press.

Simmons, Julie. 2004. "Securing the Threads of Cooperation in the Tapestry of Intergovernmental Relations: Does the Institutionalization of Intergovernmental Ministerial Conferences Matter?" In J. Peter Meekison, Hamish Telford, and Harvey Lazar, eds., *Reconsidering the Institutions of Canadian Federalism.* Kingston: Institute of Intergovernmental Relations, School of Policy Studies. 285-314.

Skogstad, Grace. 2002. "International Trade Policy and Canadian Federalism: A Constructive Tension?" In Herman Bakvis, and Grace Skogstad, eds., *Canadian Federalism: Performance, Effectiveness and Legitimacy,* 1st ed. Don Mills: Oxford University Press. 159–77.

Smiley, D.V. 1974. *Constitutional Adaptation and Canadian Federalism Since 1945.* Document of the Royal Commission on Bilingualism and Biculturalism. Ottawa: Information Canada.

Smiley, D.V., and R.L. Watts. 1985. *Intrastate Federalism in Canada.* Toronto: University of Toronto Press.

Smith, Jennifer. 2004. *Federalism.* The Canadian Democratic Audit. Vancouver: University of British Columbia Press.

Stevenson, Garth. 1977. "Federalism and the Political Economy of the Federal State." In Leo Panitch, ed., *The Canadian State.* Toronto: University of Toronto Press. 71–100.

Swinton, K.E., and C.L. Rogerson, Eds. 1988. *Competing Constitutional Visions: The Meech Lake Accord.* Toronto: Carswell.

Trebilcock, Michael, and D. Schwanen, Eds. 1995. *Getting There: An Assessment of the Agreement on Internal Trade.* Toronto: C.D. Howe Institute.

Watts, Ronald. 1996. *Comparing Federal Systems in the 1990s.* Kingston: Institute of Intergovernmental Relations.

Wheare, K.C. 1964. *Federal Government,* 4th ed. New York: Oxford University Press.

Whitaker, Reginald. 1983. *Federalism and Democratic Theory.* Kingston: Institute of Intergovernmental Relations.

nine

The (Re)Emergence of
Aboriginal Governments

MARTIN PAPILLON

Aboriginal peoples are engaged in a struggle to redefine their relationship with the Canadian state.[1] As other Indigenous populations facing the legacy of colonialism, they have defined their claims in terms of self-determination — that is, in its broadest sense, the possibility to freely define the rules, norms, and institutions governing their lands, their communities, and their relationship with the dominant society. Not surprisingly, these self-determination claims have encountered much resistance. Aboriginal peoples not only challenge powerful economic interests, they also question deeply embedded assumptions about the organization of state authority in the Canadian federation.

In response, the federal government, the provinces, and the territories have embraced the idea of Aboriginal self-government. If expectations vary widely as to what exactly self-government means, it has nonetheless become a central aspect of Aboriginal-state relations in Canada. In fact, the recognition of various forms of Aboriginal government — in Nunavut, British Columbia, or the Yukon for example — is arguably one of the most significant developments in the institutional landscape of the Canadian federation in recent times. To put these developments into perspective, one needs to look back 40 years to the ill-fated White Paper of 1969, in which the federal government of the time proposed to do away with treaties and any form of special status in order to fully integrate First Nations communities into the broader Canadian polity as municipalities under provincial jurisdiction.

The shift in perspective in the past few decades is certainly remarkable. However, not everyone agrees it represents a significant break with Canada's colonial past. Relatively few self-government agreements have been successfully negotiated, and Aboriginal nations who have done so face frustrating delays and ongoing administrative battles as they seek to transform the letter of their agreements into governance practices. More significantly, many nations and

---

1. Following the practice in the Canadian literature, the term "Aboriginal peoples" is used in this text interchangeably with the more internationally recognized term "Indigenous peoples" to refer to the descendants of the original inhabitants of the continent. The Canadian Constitution recognizes three groups of Aboriginal people: American Indians (now often referred to as First Nations), the Métis, and Inuit. Distinctions between these groups are made in this text when necessary.

communities refuse to engage in the negotiation of self-government agreements under the existing federal policy framework, arguing that the conditions offered amount to a denial of their inherent right to govern themselves. For Indigenous scholar Taiaiake Alfred, self-government, as it exists today, is simply a new form of colonial domination (Alfred, 2005: 37).

So, what should we make of self-government today? What does it mean for Aboriginal peoples? And for Canadian federalism? Is self-government a new form of shared sovereignty or, as Alfred argues, a new form of political containment? The objectives of this chapter are first to explain what self-government is and how it came about in the Canadian context and, second, to assess its impact on the relationship between Aboriginal peoples and the Canadian state. I argue that the emergence — or more accurately the re-emergence since the first inhabitants of the continent have long been governing themselves — of Aboriginal self-government has the potential to transform the Canadian federation, but this potential has yet to be realized.

A careful examination of recent self-government agreements suggests there remains a fundamental gap between the ideal of self-government, as understood by Aboriginal peoples, and the reality on the ground. By and large, Aboriginal governments are still limited in their capacity to act as agents of self-determination by the overarching framework of Canadian federalism. In analytical terms, the ongoing institutionalization of self-government can be understood more as a process of incremental adaptation of Canadian federalism than as a radical shift in the configuration of constitutional authority in Canada.

To explain this process of incremental adaptation and assess its potential impact, it is important to locate recent changes in their broader historical context. Politics matter here. Self-government is largely the result of Aboriginal political and legal pressures on federal and provincial authorities. But ongoing changes must also be located in the ideological, political, and economic context of the past 30 years. For example, the constitutional battles of the 1980s proved a fertile ground for Aboriginal peoples to have their governing rights recognized by Canadian governments. Beyond constitutional battles, Canada's changing political economy has also shaped the nature of self-government. It is largely through the negotiation of land claims settlements in regions of the country undergoing rapid expansion of their resource-based economy that the most significant developments with regards to self-government have taken place. Self-government finally gained currency in the policy discourse at a time when neoliberal perspectives advocating for a leaner and less heavy-handed state were also gaining ground, creating openings for Aboriginal communities who embrace a market-based conception of their development. They also contributed to the conflation of self-government with more limited forms of administrative decentralization.

It is in this context, as constitutional principles encountered neoliberal governance, that the battle for self-government was initially fought, leading to the development of what can be defined as competing narratives about what self-government is and how it should be positioned in relation to Canadian federalism. I discuss these competing narratives in the second section of this chapter, before taking a more detailed look at existing models of self-government, their limits and transformative potential. First, however, it is important to locate self-government in its historical context.

Challenging the Colonial Legacy

There are a little over a million Aboriginal people in what is now Canada, representing 4 per cent of the total population.[2] It is a highly diverse group, with more than 800 First Nations, Inuit, and Métis communities scattered across the country, some of them linked together through ancient or more recent political ties, forming, according to the Royal Commission on Aboriginal Peoples (RCAP), 60 to 80 self-defined nations. Aboriginal peoples also vary considerably in their institutional relationship with the Canadian federation. While all were recognized as having the same rights under the Constitution Act, 1982, there are significant differences in the governance regime of each nation. Not all have a treaty-based relationship with the Canadian state, and if most First Nations are, at least formally, governed under the regime of the federal Indian Act, Inuit and Métis are not. To further complicate the portrait, more than half of Aboriginal people in Canada now live in urban centres, where issues of status, membership, and political authority become far more complex. This diversity in conditions and history explains in part why any generalization about an "Aboriginal perspective" on self-government is a hazardous enterprise. Aboriginal peoples do, however, share a common experience with colonialism. Moving beyond this colonial legacy is certainly a common objective. -

Indigenous peoples were governing themselves long before the arrival of European settlers. In its final report, RCAP (1996, vol. 1) explains some of the governing practices of the original inhabitants of the land. In the Haudenosaunee (Iroquois) and Mi'kmaq confederacies, for example, relations between communities and nations were governed through a complex set of rules, equivalent to constitutional conventions, transmitted through oral tradition from one generation to another. French and British authorities recognized these governing structures and engaged in diplomatic relationships

---

2. These numbers are based on Statistics Canada estimates from the 2006 Census. It is important to note that a number of First Nations communities refuse to participate in the Census.

with these peoples in order to secure military alliances or gain access to the fur trade routes at the centre of the early colonial economy (Dickason and McNab, 2008).

The expansion of the settlers' society led to growing pressure on Aboriginal lands and traditional forms of governance. From early land cession treaties in Ontario and the Prairie provinces to the absence of Aboriginal representatives during the negotiations leading to the creation of the Canadian federation in 1867, Aboriginal peoples were increasingly marginalized politically and geographically. The adoption of the Indian Act in 1876 and the expansion of the reserve system, followed by the imposition of the band council governance regime in First Nations communities, are all part of a long process of displacement of traditional Aboriginal governing structures and economic relationships to the land (Tobias, 1991).[3] Despite significant resistance in a number of communities, previously self-governing and culturally distinct societies were progressively subjugated politically and legally to the authority of the federal government and forced to adopt the cultural codes, norms, and social practices of the dominant society.

Aboriginal Resistance

The rise to prominence of self-government as a political ideal can be traced to the resurgence of Aboriginal political activism in the postwar period, in particular in the aftermath of the federal government's *Statement on Indian Policy* of 1969, otherwise known as the White Paper. At the same time as the Canadian government was proposing undifferentiated citizenship as a solution to socio-economic disparities between First Nations communities and other Canadians, the decolonization and civil rights movements were influencing the political thinking of marginalized Indigenous populations around the globe. Newly formed pan-Canadian Aboriginal organizations, such as the National Indian Brotherhood (which later became the Assembly of First Nations), rejected the notion that their differentiated status was the source of their disastrous socio-economic conditions. To the contrary, Cree leader Harold Cardinal argued in his famous reply to the White Paper, this status must be recognized to its full extent in order for Aboriginal peoples to regain their sense of dignity and political agency (Cardinal, 1969).

Aboriginal leaders used the language of human rights and self-determination to assert their claims for proper recognition of existing treaties, for control over their lands, and for greater recognition of their status as politically

---

3. Most dispositions of the Indian Act never applied to Métis and Inuit communities, who were largely ignored by governments until the middle of the twentieth century.

autonomous nations. The Dene declaration of 1975 is a classic example of this emerging discourse:

> We the Dene insist on the right to be regarded as a nation.... Our plea to the world is to help us in our struggle to find a place in the world community where we can exercise our right to self-determination as a distinct people and as a nation. What we seek then is independence and self-determination within Canada.[4]

By the mid-1970s, then, Aboriginal peoples were increasingly challenging not only existing colonial institutions, such as the Indian Act, but also the very legitimacy of federal and provincial authority on their lands and communities. Regaining some degree of political autonomy was seen as key to the protection of Aboriginal cultures and traditions, but it was also a way to regain control over Aboriginal lands in order to establish the foundation of a better and healthier economy and, most significantly, to establish the basis of a new, more equal relationship with the Canadian state. It is in this context that self-government rose to prominence, both as an ideal and a concrete policy alternative to existing models of governance.

What Is Self-Government? Competing Narratives

What exactly is self-government, and how can it be implemented? There is no single answer to these questions. Given their diverse history, geographic situation, and status in relation to the Canadian state, not all Aboriginal nations conceive of self-government in the same way. As Belanger and Newhouse (2008) suggest, the idea of self-government has also evolved significantly in the past 30 years. At the risk of oversimplifying, we can identify at least three narratives that have informed political debate and policy development related to self-government during this time. These narratives are grounded in fundamentally different understandings of the status of Aboriginal peoples in relation to the institutions of Canadian federalism.

Self-Government as Delegated Authority

Self-government can firstly be defined as a delegation of federal, provincial, or territorial authority to local Aboriginal governments. The transfer to band councils of some degree of responsibility for local affairs is not a new idea. As early as the 1930s, Ottawa was encouraging band councils to take charge of

---

4. The *Dene Declaration* of 1975 is available at http://www.denenation.com/denedec.html.

local services. The federal government also initiated a series of experiments with local management of education, community development, and social services in the 1960s in order to foster "local empowerment" in First Nations communities (Weaver, 1981: 27). With the rise of self-government on the political agenda in the late 1970s, however, the federal government proposed a more comprehensive approach to the transfer of administrative and legislative authority to band councils. It offered First Nations the possibility to "opt out" of the closely regulated governance regime of the Indian Act and exercise instead a form of delegated authority through federal legislation in a number of policy areas.

At a time when neoliberal ideas promoting a scaled-down, more efficient state were gaining ground in Canada, decentralization became simultaneously an answer to Aboriginal claims for more autonomy and a way "to enhance program effectiveness" and "reduce the administrative costs of delivering programs to geographically dispersed communities."[5] In this perspective, self-government is first and foremost defined as self-administration. Aboriginal autonomy is achieved through a diffusion of state authority at the local level, much like municipalities, rather than through the recognition of Aboriginal nations as autonomous political entities (Abele and Prince, 2006: 572). Not surprisingly, Aboriginal peoples have largely rejected this conception of self-government.

An Inherent Right

If self-government was initially understood as a form of delegation of authority, an alternative narrative, more closely tied to the principle of self-determination, rapidly gained currency in Aboriginal political and academic circles. For the vast majority of Aboriginal peoples today, political autonomy is a fundamental right that derives not from Parliament or the Canadian Constitution, but from their status as distinct nations who were governing themselves long before the creation of the Canadian federation.

The principle of self-government as an inherent right of nations first received pubic attention in a report of a special committee of the House of Commons on Indian Government (Canada, 1983). The Penner Committee

---

5. The link between fiscal control and the progressive disengagement of the federal government from Aboriginal program administration was made explicit in a report of the Task Force on Program Review commissioned by the newly elected Progressive Conservative government in 1985. In order to contain escalating costs, the Neilsen Task Force suggested the federal Indian and Inuit programming should be scaled back "to its strict constitutional and legal obligations" and Aboriginal peoples should be "encouraged to assume more responsibilities for their own development" (Canada, Deputy Prime Minister's Office, 1986: 21).

not only recognized the inherent nature of self-government rights, it also endorsed the principle of a "third order" of Aboriginal governments in the Canadian federation. The inherent right to self-government became a focal point of the constitutional battles of the 1980s and early 1990s, as Aboriginal organizations were engaged in negotiations with federal and provincial authorities for the definition of Aboriginal rights under section 35(1) of the Constitution Act, 1982.

Despite the ultimate failure of the constitutional process, it clearly shaped future debates over Aboriginal self-government. In 1995 the federal government released a policy statement in which it recognized the principle of self-government as an inherent right as a basis for future negotiations (Canada, 1995). RCAP also endorsed the principle as a cornerstone of a renewed nation-to-nation relationship between Aboriginal peoples and the Canadian federation in its 1996 report. While the Supreme Court of Canada has not explicitly recognized self-government as an Aboriginal right under section 35(1) of the Constitution Act, 1982, a number of legal analysts suggest its recent jurisprudence points in that direction (Macklem, 2000; McNeil, 2004).

Behind this apparent unanimity over the notion of self-government as an inherent right, fundamental divergences remain when it comes to translating what is a relatively abstract principle into practical governance norms and rules. From the federal government's perspective, the inherent right to self-government exists within the existing framework of the Canadian federation. This is the position developed in the 1995 federal policy statement: Aboriginal peoples have a right to self-government, but the modalities of exercise of this right still depend on federal and provincial legislative consent. RCAP insists instead on the principle of continuing Aboriginal sovereignty as the basis of a renewed nation-to-nation relationship between Aboriginal peoples and the Canadian state. As previously self-governing political communities, each Aboriginal nation should be entitled to negotiate a new division of responsibilities with the federal and provincial governments, thus forming a third order of governments within the Canadian federation (RCAP, 1996, vol. 2: 215).

Coexisting Sovereignties

The articulation of self-government as a fundamental right remains central to Aboriginal discourse today, but the RCAP model and the federal policy statement of 1995 have their limits. Aboriginal self-government is assumed to operate *within* the predetermined boundaries of the Canadian Constitution. As such, even if Aboriginal governments are recognized to predate the

Canadian federation, they are ultimately still operating within a constitutional structure defined without their consent or involvement.

As an alternative to incorporating Aboriginal governments *within* the existing federation as a third order, a number of Indigenous and non-Indigenous scholars have argued for the reaffirmation of Aboriginal sovereignty *outside* the institutions of Canadian federalism. In this perspective, partly inspired by theories of legal pluralism, pre-existing Aboriginal governing practices and institutions should be fully recognized for what they are: the expression of distinctive constitutional orders that continue today to co-exist in parallel with Canada's own Constitution (Ladner, 2005). Aboriginal governance regimes were recognized as such by European powers, who engaged in the negotiation of treaties and alliances as if it were diplomatic relations between sovereign entities. According to Sakej Henderson (1994), these early alliances and treaties effectively created a form of federal alliance between mutually consenting polities. It is, according to Henderson, this "treaty federalism" that should be revived as the basis of contemporary relationships between Aboriginal nations and the Canadian federation. Building on a similar perspective, James Tully (1995) argues that Canada should be conceived as a double confederation: the treaty-based partnership between Aboriginal peoples and the Crown and between Aboriginal peoples and the newer federal-provincial federation.

The revitalization of Indigenous constitutional traditions is, of course, fraught with legal and political difficulties. Not only is this a direct challenge to orthodox conceptions of state sovereignty, but it also raises a number of very concrete institutional challenges. For example, it is not clear how, or even if, Aboriginal peoples would be represented in the shared institutions of a two-level federal system. Should all nations, no matter their size, have equal representation in what would become an extremely complex structure of executive federalism? Moreover, as Alan Cairns (2000: 191) argues in his critique of nation-to-nation conceptions of Aboriginal governance, it is not evident how one can reconcile a treaty-based association with a substantive conception of shared citizenship, a necessary condition, in his view, to foster a sense of solidarity and cooperation across communities that are bound to live together on a common territory. More pragmatically, a treaty-based regime assumes a degree of fiscal autonomy that may not be realistic for many Aboriginal nations or communities. Even with access to land-base revenues, most Aboriginal communities would remain dependent on fiscal transfers from the federal government.

These obstacles are not insurmountable, but they illustrate the challenges in moving from theoretical constructs to more concrete institutional reforms. They also show the distance between conceptions of self-government as a form of devolution of powers, under which the foundations of Canadian federalism remain largely intact, and alternative models for coexistence between nations, which call for a fundamental rethinking of Canada's constitutional framework.

From Principles to Practice: Negotiating Self-Government

So far, I have discussed self-government in relatively abstract terms, as a principle to be recognized, more than in concrete institutional terms. Throughout the 1980s and 1990s, a number of Aboriginal nations engaged in the negotiation of self-government agreements with the federal government, the provinces, and the territories.[6] The competing narratives discussed above influenced these negotiations, but other pragmatic considerations also shaped the processes and their outcomes. For one, most self-government agreements negotiated so far in Canada are the result of larger land claims settlement processes. In 1973, in the *Calder* case, the Supreme Court of Canada acknowledged the possibility that Aboriginal title could have survived the assertion of Canadian sovereignty in areas where no treaties were previously signed. As the natural resource extraction economy expanded further north, the clarification of Aboriginal rights in these areas became a driving force compelling federal and provincial authorities to negotiate alternative governance arrangements with Aboriginal peoples. Land claims settlements offered legal certainty for governments and resource extraction industries. In exchange, Aboriginal peoples faced with growing pressures on their traditional lands sought to regain a voice in the management of their communities and territories.

A First Model: The James Bay and Northern Quebec Agreement

The first self-government experiences were limited in scope and consisted essentially of administrative decentralization. One such example is the governance model established pursuant to the James Bay and Northern Agreement (JBNQA) of 1975 for the Cree Nation of Eeyou Istchee (the James Bay Cree) and the Inuit of Nunavik. The JBNQA was negotiated in a few months while the construction of the James Bay hydroelectric complex was already underway. Under time pressure, both groups negotiated the cession of any potential rights to most of their traditional territory in exchange for monetary compensations; specific hunting, trapping, and fishing rights; and a series of new administrative arrangements under which

---

6. For a more complete overview of the nature of the various agreements negotiated in the past 30 years, see Morse, 2008.

they were to manage most government programs in their communities. Regional boards under the legislative authority of the province were created to administer services such as education and health care in Cree and Inuit communities. At the local level, the Inuit chose a public form of government under Quebec's municipal regime, while Cree communities opted to remain under federal jurisdiction.

With the adoption of the Cree-Naskapi (of Quebec) Act by the federal government in 1984, a new framework outside the Indian Act was established for the local governance of Cree communities and their neighbour, the Naskapi. While this was a significant development, the new governance regime did not constitute a major break from the underlying logic of the Indian Act. Cree bands were granted marginally greater bylaw powers and their administrative decisions were no longer subject to the ministerial veto. But otherwise, Cree bands were still considered creatures of the federal government, largely dependent on the latter for their funding and limited in their capacity to adopt policies outside of the legislative and policy frameworks established in Ottawa.

The James Bay Cree and the Inuit rapidly discovered the limits of administrative decentralization. The newly created regional governance structures were compelled to follow the policies established in Quebec City or in Ottawa. Budgets were also set unilaterally by governments, based on guidelines that had little to do with the costs of running services in the North. Financially constrained and limited in their policy margins, Cree and Inuit regional bodies could hardly be considered more than regional and local arms of federal and provincial authorities.

Both the Cree and the Inuit have sought to modernize their limited self-government structures in recent years. The Paix des Braves agreement between the Cree and Quebec paved the way to greater Cree involvement in the management of forestry and other resource extraction activities in the region, in addition to securing funding for economic development in the communities. The Cree are also in the final stages of ratification of a more comprehensive regional self-government agreement with the federal government. The Inuit have embarked on a similar project of regional government, a public model under the legislative authority of the province (Wilson, 2008).

A Second Generation of Self-Government Agreements

The limits of the JBNQA model rapidly became apparent to other Aboriginal peoples contemplating self-government. Not only did it reproduce the top-down logic of the Indian Act, it also was inconsistent with conceptions of self-government based on the recognition of pre-existing Aboriginal sovereignty. As discussed earlier, by the late 1980s the focus had shifted away from devolution perspectives to a debate on the constitutional foundations of self-government. With the failure of the Charlottetown Accord in 1992, the constitutional window closed and the focus shifted again to the negotiation of specific agreements. Future arrangements, however, would have to recognize that Aboriginal governments are more than administrative arms of the state. Self-government was now considered an inherent right of distinct nations.

It is once again via the land claims negotiation process that the second generation of self-government agreements took shape. The Yukon Umbrella Final Agreement of 1993, the Nisga'a Final Agreement of 1998, and the Tlicho Agreement signed in 2003 are broadly similar in this respect. While self-government arrangements were negotiated separately from the land claims in the case of the Yukon First Nations, both Nisga'a and Tlicho self-government provisions are directly included in their treaty. They are thus protected under section 35 of the Constitution Act, 1982. The Nisga'a Final Agreement was signed after 25 years of negotiation. It is the first comprehensive self-government agreement that establishes a distinctive Aboriginal legislative authority within a province. It provides for self-governing control of approximately 2,000 square kilometres of land in the Nass Valley in British Columbia, including surface and subsurface resources. The agreement establishes law-making authority for the Nisga'a Lisims government and four village governments. These governments operate according to the Nisga'a Constitution and have primary jurisdiction over a number of areas, including the management of community lands, education, environmental regulation, citizenship, and local matters.

The Nisga'a, Tlicho, and Yukon First Nations agreements are quite significant. Federal, provincial, and territorial signatories did recognize the legislative authority of Aboriginal governments in key areas of jurisdiction. In this respect, they go much further than the Cree-Naskapi Act of 1984. There are nonetheless significant limits to these second-generation self-government agreements. First, their land base is limited and so are the possibilities of raising independent sources of revenues. Despite provisions for a tax base, they will therefore remain, at least for the foreseeable future, dependent on federal, territorial, and provincial financial support. Second, even in areas where their legislative power is recognized, Aboriginal governments remain subject to significant constraints. The law-making authority of the Nisga'a Lisims government, for example, only prevails in certain areas in case of conflict with federal and provincial laws, and only as long as the Nisga'a law is consistent with equivalent federal and provincial legislations. It is thus hard to define these governments as a "third order" of governments on par with their federal and provincial counterparts.

Self-Government as Public Government

The Nisga'a, Tlicho, and Yukon land claims and self-government agreements were negotiated with First Nations previously under the Indian Act. Their structures and operations do bear, to a certain degree, the legacy of Canada's colonial legislation. For example, they chose to reproduce the Aboriginal-only model of political membership so central to the Indian Act logic. Only members of the Nisga'a Nation can vote in Nisga'a regional elections. The Inuit were not subjected to the Indian Act and do not share the same legacy of status-based politics. The demographic pressures on their communities are also clearly not the same, as they still form a substantive majority on their traditional lands. Self-government in the North thus takes a very different form.

The Inuit in Nunavut opted for public government when they negotiated their own land claim settlement, the Nunavut Land Claims Agreement, signed in 1992. The agreement led to the creation of the Nunavut territory in 1999 and to the establishment of a territorial government elected by all residents of the territory but effectively controlled by the Inuit majority. The government of Nunavut is similar in structure to other territorial governments, with the important exception that there are no political parties. As a result, members of the legislative assembly choose the executive, including the premier.

Like the other two territories, Nunavut does not have the constitutional status of a province. Its authority is delegated through federal legislation. In practice, however, its authority is equivalent to that of a province in most areas of provincial jurisdiction, with the important exception of natural resources on Crown lands, which remain under federal jurisdiction. Although it is a public government, the Nunavut government promotes, as a matter of policy, the interests, culture, and traditions of the Inuit majority. It is thus arguably a form of *de facto* self-government (Henderson, 2008).

As with other self-government experiences developed as offshoots of land claims settlements, the Nunavut model has significant limits. Its funding structure, while far more stable and predictable than that of First Nations self-government agreements, remains ultimately in the hands of the federal Parliament. The territorial government struggles with limited budgets and significant social and economic challenges in Inuit communities. Its impact on the quality of life of Inuit has been limited so far (Sénécal and O'Sullivan, 2006). More significantly, while explicit attempts have been made to adopt a working philosophy that corresponds to Inuit values (under the principle of *Inuit Qaujimajatuqangit*, or Inuit knowledge), the relatively rigid operational logic and institutional culture associated with Canadian-style public government, most notably the focus on hierarchical authority and concerns over efficiency and accountability, have proven difficult to adapt (Tester and Irniq, 2008). The public government established in Nunavut thus largely reproduces in its structure and operating logic the rational bureaucratic model of any Canadian-style government, leaving some to question its success as a self-government experiment designed to promote the interests, perspectives, and values of the Inuit (Henderson, 2008: 236).

Alternatives to Self-Government Agreements

Land claims settlements have clearly been the driving force behind self-government. Very few agreements have been successfully negotiated outside the context of a land claims process. One example is the agreement with the Sechelt Band of British Columbia negotiated in 1986. The Sechelt were recognized as exercising delegated, municipal-type authority in a number of policy areas of local interest. More recently, the Westbank First Nation in British Columbia negotiated an agreement with the federal government for the exercise of legislative authority outside the Indian Act. These, however, are exceptions. An agreement signed by the federal government and the Anishnaabe of Ontario was rejected in a referendum in the communities in 2005, as was an Agreement-in-Principle with the Mohawks of Kahnawake in 2001.

Clearly, the negotiation of a formal self-government agreement is a complex affair. It is time-consuming (the Nisga'a negotiated for more than 25 years, the Anishnaabe for almost 20 years before the process ultimately fell apart) and draining for the leadership of small communities who also have to deal with very concrete social and economic challenges. Formal self-government, however, is not the sole avenue for reconfiguring Aboriginal governance. In fact, some of the most significant transformations have come not from grandiose agreements but from the slow, ongoing, and steady process of administrative decentralization that has continued to characterize Aboriginal governance in the past 35 years.

While it was no longer associated with formal self-government agreements, administrative transfers to local Aboriginal authority continued to figure prominently on the federal policy agenda through the 1990s. Under the impetus of neoliberal and "Third Way" ideas, Indian and Northern Affairs Canada undertook a massive transfer of responsibilities for the management of programs and services to Aboriginal organizations and local authorities. By the mid-1990s, close to 80 per cent of the department's budget was directly managed by band councils, Inuit local authorities, or Aboriginal regional organizations. Numbers have remained stable since (Canada, INAC, 2005).

Decentralization through "partnership agreements" in specific policy fields, such as education, human resources, and economic development or the administration of justice, is now the norm in Aboriginal governance. Most agreements remain administrative in nature, but some sector-specific agreements do create a form of legislative authority. In 1998 the federal government transferred jurisdiction over education to the Mi'kmaq of Nova Scotia. A similar province-wide agreement was reached with First Nations in British Columbia in 2005.[7] Under these agreements, the Indian Act provisions regarding on-reserve education no longer apply and are replaced by provisions established directly by First Nations. Provinces and territories are also increasingly engaged in similar sector-specific agreements with Aboriginal communities.

As a result of these multiple sector-specific transfers, Aboriginal governance has evolved over the past two decades from a highly centralized and homogenous system to what is now a largely decentralized, place-specific, and multilevel structure of governance in which Aboriginal governments and organizations play a growing role in the implementation of policies and programs. To be sure, this is not self-government. These transfers obey a very different logic. Federal and provincial governments are motivated at least as much by efficiency and cost savings as they are by the ideal of Aboriginal autonomy. Accounting and reporting mechanisms are even more constraining than under more comprehensive self-government agreements, and budgets are highly vulnerable to ministerial discretion. The impact of these transfers of program administration to band councils and other Aboriginal governing bodies should not be entirely dismissed. It does create a significant margin for Aboriginal authorities to develop their own policy expertise and capacity. More importantly, it creates *political*, if not legal, space for the development of alternative approaches to governance in the communities, especially those willing to embrace a vision of their development consistent with neoliberal ideas.

With the federal and provincial governments withdrawing from the daily management of policies in the communities, a growing number of First Nations have sought to fill the void with their own proactive policies in various areas such as economic development, the delivery of services, or the administration of justice. In other words, First Nations are simply asserting their jurisdiction over certain policy areas. A number of First Nations are

---

7. For information on the British Columbia First Nation education agreement, see http://www.fnesc.ca/jurisdiction/index.php.

going further, developing their own constitutions as parallel legal regimes coexisting with federal and provincial authorities outside of any formal self-government agreement.

One example of this is the Mohawk community of Kahnawake, near Montreal. For a number of years now, the Mohawk Council of Kahnawake (MCK), formally a band council under the Indian Act, has been adopting laws and creating institutions — such as a police service, a membership code, and an alcohol and gaming commission regulating a flourishing online gambling industry in the community — that operate in parallel to federal and provincial regulatory frameworks. The MCK is not opposed to negotiations with federal and provincial authorities. In fact, it has negotiated a number of administrative agreements with Quebec and Ottawa on policing and other matters. But these agreements have taken a very specific form: the MCK has agreed to harmonize its own laws and institutions with federal and provincial regulations in exchange for recognition by the latter of the legitimacy of pre-existing Mohawk institutions. In other words, governments are expected to recognize these Mohawk institutions as products of Mohawk authority rather than as administrative or legislative creatures of the Canadian state.

This type of unilateral action, followed by semi-formal recognition by the state, has found fertile ground under the ideological premises of neoliberal restructuring. As governments seek to reduce their expenditures and foster local autonomy, they also are more tolerant of asymmetries in the definition of policies at the regional or local level when these initiatives foster autonomous market-driven development. Autonomy is encouraged outside of any formal institutional framework as long as it corresponds to the broader (neoliberal) framework under which Aboriginal governance should operate.

Conclusion

The re-emergence of Aboriginal governments is undoubtedly a significant change in the institutional landscape of the Canadian federation. There is little doubt that Aboriginal governments are here to stay and are likely to play a growing role in Canadian politics. Change, however, is desperately slow. Very few agreements have been ratified, largely because of the ideological distance between Aboriginal conceptions of their relationship with the Canadian state and the models of self-government available to them. Despite the obvious advances made since the first experiences with self-government negotiated under the JBNQA, there remains a significant gap between conceptions of Aboriginal self-determination advanced by RCAP or under theories of treaty federalism and existing self-government agreements and governance practices.

As our brief review of the Nisga'a, Yukon, or Nunavut models suggests, Aboriginal governments are still today considered a second tier of legislative authority in relation to federal and provincial parliaments. Beyond issues of jurisdiction, the implementation of agreements has also proven difficult. Fiscal constraints and accountability requirements play an important role in limiting the autonomy of Aboriginal governments no matter their legal and constitutional status. In fact, it is not clear that formally self-governing First Nations have all that much more autonomy than those who have taken advantage of the policy void created by neoliberal approaches to governance to unilaterally establish their own institutions and policies. With or without self-government agreements, First Nations, Inuit, and Métis communities have become much more involved in the governance of their communities, and those embracing neoliberal models of development are certainly at an advantage in the current context.

This pressure on Aboriginal communities to embrace a certain form of autonomy, coupled with the experiences of the James Bay Cree, the Nisga'a, or the Inuit in Nunavut with various forms of institutional autonomy, also raises difficult questions about the objectives of self-government. Clearly, self-government is not just about jurisdiction. It is ultimately about a community's capacity to decide on its future orientations and collective well-being. Doing so according to governance practices that correspond to one's culture and values is perhaps as important as the outcome of the process itself. So far, it has been a constant challenge for Aboriginal governments to make room for culturally relevant practices in the development of policies or negotiations with their federal or provincial counterparts. No matter their degree of institutional autonomy, existing Aboriginal governments tend to reproduce, both in their operating logic and policy outcomes, what non-Aboriginal governments do.

In this respect, Taiaiake Alfred may well be right when he argues self-government is a new form of political containment that ultimately contributes to the assimilation of Indigenous peoples through the penetration of Western values and ideas in governance structures that are, unlike previous ones, willingly embraced by the communities. Whether this can be avoided at all is debatable. After all, Aboriginal governments are modern governments operating in a complex policy environment, traversed by ideologies and economic dynamics that have little to do with the context under which traditional governance practices were developed. But the broader issue of whether or not self-government can actually contribute to the development of alternative, culturally relevant governance practices is certainly a pertinent question.

Ultimately, the transformation of Aboriginal-state relations is a slow and frustrating process. The resistance encountered along the way should not be surprising given the stakes. Federal, territorial, and provincial governments have little interest in jeopardizing their control over resource-rich areas of the country, or in creating precedents that could lead to an unworkable patchwork of institutional arrangements. Given the profound power imbalance between the parties involved and the inherent resistance to change in what are, after all, deeply embedded conceptions of governance, radical breakthroughs are ultimately unlikely. Instead, incremental transformations, similar to the ones we have seen over the past 30 years, are likely to continue to reshape Aboriginal-state relations. In the long run, these cumulative changes could lead to a more significant redefinition of Canadian federalism.

References and Suggested Readings

Abele, Frances, and Michael Prince. 2006. "Four Pathways to Aboriginal Self-Government in Canada." *American Review of Canadian Studies* 36: 568–95.

Alfred, Taiaiake. 2005. *Wasáse: Indigenous Pathways of Action and Freedom*. Peterborough: Broadview Press.

Belanger, Yale D., and David Newhouse. 2008. "Reconciling Solitudes: A Critical Analysis of the Self-Government Ideal." In Yale Belanger, ed., *Aboriginal Self-government in Canada. Current Trends and Issues*, 3rd ed. Saskatoon: Purich. 1–19.

Cairns, Alan. 2000. *Citizens Plus*. Vancouver: University of British Columbia Press.

Canada. 1969. *Statement of the Government of Canada on Indian Policy (The White Paper)*. Ottawa: Department of Indian Affairs and Northern Development.

Canada. 1995. *Aboriginal Self-government, Federal Policy Guide: The Government of Canada's Approach to the Implementation of the Inherent Right and Negotiation of Aboriginal Self-government*. Ottawa: Public Works and Government Services.

Canada. Deputy Prime Minister's Office, 1986. *Task Force on Program Review 1985*.

Canada. House of Commons. 1983. *Report of the Special Committee on Indian Self-Government*. Ottawa: Supply and Services Canada.

Canada. Indian and Northern Affairs Canada. 2005. *Performance Report for the Period Ending March 31, 2005*. Ottawa: Public Works and Government Services Canada.

Cardinal, Harold. 1969. *The Unjust Society*. Edmonton: M.G. Hurtig.

Dickason, Olive, and David McNab. 2008. *Canada's First Nations: A History of Founding Peoples from Earliest Times*, 4th ed. Don Mills: Oxford University Press.

Henderson, Ailsa. 2008. "Self-Government in Nunavut." In Yale Belanger, ed., *Aboriginal Self-government in Canada. Current Trends and Issues*, 3rd ed. Saskatoon: Purich. 222–39.

Henderson, James Youngblood (Sakej). 1994. "Empowering Treaty Federalism." *Saskatchewan Law Review* 58, 2: 241–329.

Ladner, Kiera L. 2005. "Up the Creek: Fishing for a New Constitutional Order." *Canadian Journal of Political Science* 38, 4: 923–53.

Macklem, Patrick. 2000. *Indigenous Difference and the Constitution of Canada*. Toronto: University of Toronto Press.

McNeil, Kent. 2004. *The Inherent Right of Self-government: Emerging Directions for Legal Research*. Report prepared for the First Nations Governance Centre.

Morse, Bradford. 2008. "Regaining Recognition of the Inherent Right of Aboriginal Governance." In Yale Belanger, ed., *Aboriginal Self-government in Canada. Current Trends and Issues*, 3rd ed. Saskatoon: Purich. 55–84.

Royal Commission on Aboriginal Peoples (RCAP). 1996. *Final Report*, 5 vols. Ottawa: Canada Communication Group Publishing.

Sénécal, Sacha, and Erin O'Sullivan. 2006. *The Well-Being of Inuit Communities in Canada*. Ottawa: Indian and Northern Affairs Canada.

Tester, Frank James, and Peter Irniq. 2008. "*Inuit Qaujimajatuqangit:* Social History, Politics and the Practice of Resistance." *Arctic* 61, suppl. 1: 48–61.

Tobias, John L. 1991. "Protection, Civilization, Assimilation: An Outline History of Canada's Indian Policy." In J.R. Miller, ed., *Sweet Promises: A Reader on Indian-White Relations*. Toronto: University of Toronto Press. 128–44.

Tully, James. 1995. *Strange Multiplicity. Constitutionalism in an Age of Diversity*. Cambridge: Cambridge University Press.

Weaver, Sally. 1981. *Making Canadian Indian Policy: The Hidden Agenda, 1968–1979*. Toronto: University of Toronto Press.

Wilson, Gary. 2008. "Nested Federalism in Arctic Quebec: A Comparative Perspective." *Canadian Journal of Political Science* 41, 1: 71–92.

ten

The Judiciary and the Charter

RAYMOND BAZOWSKI

There was a time not too long ago when students of Canadian politics paid scarcely any attention to courts and the judicial process. While texts of the day would contain sections describing the make-up of courts and those constitutional rulings thought to be important to the evolution of federalism, the prevailing sentiment was that the judiciary was altogether a minor branch of government. This view of the courts ostensibly finds support in the principle of parliamentary supremacy according to which Parliament (in the Canadian context, given the reality of executive dominance, this means primarily the prime minister and Cabinet) is said to enjoy ultimate decision-making authority. The fact that courts always have had the power to invalidate legislative measures on constitutional grounds was never regarded as a genuine departure from the principle of parliamentary supremacy because constitutional jurisprudence in Canada prior to 1982 was confined largely to questions of which level of government, federal or provincial, was entitled under the 1867 British North America Act (BNA Act) to legislate on some contested subject matter. A metaphor frequently used to describe the court's unassuming constitutional role was that of an umpire impartially administering the rules defining the Canadian game of federalism. While umpires might be essential to the successful conduct of any game, they are hardly expected to displace the players themselves, but rather are intended to remain in the background, rulebook always at the ready.

This portrait of a court passively and more-or-less invisibly adjudicating constitutional questions in the manner of an umpire hardly seems an accurate depiction of current judicial practices. On the contrary, it is commonplace today to speak of a conspicuous *judicialization* of politics that materialized after the Charter of Rights and Freedoms was added to the Constitution in 1982. The term "judicialization of politics," it is worth noting, has at least two interrelated meanings. Most directly it implies that courts have intruded into the policy-making arena to an extent not contemplated by the classic doctrine of the separation of powers, which holds that well-ordered government consists of distinct functional branches best kept within their own spheres of competence. But it also means that conflicts that are at root political are increasingly being transformed into legal issues to be resolved through a categorical judicial language in an impenetrable institutional setting by an appointed and largely unaccountable body. As a well-known authority on the courts had warned early on, this process could only accelerate the flight from politics by contributing to a "deepening disillusionment with the procedures of representative government and government by discussion as a means of resolving fundamental questions of political justice" (Russell, 1982: 32).

Are the critics right in deploring a trend towards the judicialization of politics in Canada? In this chapter it will be argued that misgivings about the political role of the modern judiciary are in part overstated and otherwise are offered up in a way that usually is too decontextualized to afford us a truly useful perspective on the relationship between law and politics. To this end it will be necessary briefly to recount the history of courts and constitutional jurisprudence, if only to show that a conception of courts as a non-political institution supplying narrow technical interpretations of the law has always been problematic.

The Courts and the Constitution Before the Charter

It must be conceded that the image of the Court as an umpire in constitutional affairs does have a certain compelling force. After all, when the Canadian Constitution consisted primarily of the BNA Act, virtually the only constitutional disputes that ever arose concerned the division of powers. In the circumstances, it makes eminent sense to assume that some institution — and who better than the courts — be able to settle authoritatively any arguments over which level of government is empowered to regulate particular activities. Created in 1875 through a simple act of Parliament and staffed by judges appointed solely on the discretion of the prime minister, the Supreme Court was devised with this role of constitutional adjudication especially in mind. But from the very beginning there were suspicions, particularly among provincial governments like that of Quebec, that the court's responsibility for deciding constitutional matters might be more than a little adulterated by politics. Provincial wariness concerning a federally contrived Supreme Court was not ill-founded. After all, when he first introduced legislation to create a general appellate court, Prime Minister John A. Macdonald did not conceal its intended political objective, proposing that its jurisdiction in constitutional law be restricted to examining only provincial legislation. Established eventually not by Macdonald's Conservatives but by the Liberal government of Alexander Mackenzie, the court's constitutional purview was expanded to include federal legislation, though many parliamentarians still anticipated it would act to invalidate primarily provincial legislation, thereby accomplishing more circumspectly the same nationalizing results that hitherto had been produced through the heavy-handed federal power of disallowance (Smith, 1983: 125-26; Snell and Vaughn, 1985: 5–10).

If the Supreme Court was initially thought to be a tool of Ottawa to fashion the still young federal state according to its own centralist design, it proved not to be particularly adept at the task. There were several reasons for this. To begin with, the judges of the early Court disappointed many of their provincial counterparts with the legal quality of their rulings, thus failing to inspire the kind of confidence that is indispensable for a national appellate court in a unified legal system. Its authority undermined by its own un-impressive legal performance, the Supreme Court also faced the embarrassing fact that it was only nominally supreme because, somewhat controversially, the legislation which created it allowed for a continuation of appeals to the imperial tribunal for the British colonies, the Judicial Committee of the Privy Council (JCPC).[1] Even more confounding was the fact that decisions from provincial courts of appeal could be appealed directly to the JCPC, a measure that could only intensify skepticism about the capability of the Supreme Court. Not surprisingly, such *per saltum* appeals became a common feature of Canadian jurisprudence in the first few decades following the establishment of the Supreme Court, in no small measure because provincial governments expected the imperial tribunal to be more dispassionate in resolving disputes over the division of powers.[2] An obliging JCPC repaid the trust that provin-cial governments reposed in it with a series of inventive rulings in cases such as *Attorney General of Ontario v. Attorney General of Canada [1896]*, re *Board of Commerce Act and Combines and Fair Prices Act [1919, 1922]*, and *Toronto Electric Commissioners v. Snider [1925]*. With these judgements the JCPC, it is generally conceded,[3] altered the Canadian Constitution by diluting the fed-eral government's authority over trade and commerce and its general power to legislate in the interests of peace, order, and good government, while at

---

1. The Supreme Court Act of 1875 contained a backbencher's amendment, clause 47, which was supposed to make judgements of the Canadian Court "final and conclu-sive," except for those appeals granted by Royal Prerogative. Persuaded by imperial authorities that this clause left intact the established appeal process, the Canadian government ignored the letter of its own law and did not foreclose constitutional appeals to the JCPC for the next 75 years (Russell, 1987: 336).
2. Figures cited by Peter Russell indicate that almost half (77 out of 159) of all appeals to the JCPC prior to its withdrawal from Canadian judicial affairs were *per saltum*, the majority of which came in the early post-Confederation years (Russell, 1987: 336).
3. Not all scholars, it should be noted, concur that the JCPC's constitutional legacy was in the main the furtherance of provincial powers. See, for example, Andrée Lajoie (2009), who forcefully argues that while the JCPC indeed displayed a classical federal approach to its division of powers cases, thereby preserving for the provinces those powers afforded them by the text of the Constitution, the British tribunal nonethe-less fashioned a series of dubious interpretative doctrines that a subsequent Supreme Court of Canada used systematically to enhance the federal powers.

the same time enhancing provincial powers over property and civil rights and matters of a local and private nature.

This reordering of the relative powers of the federal and provincial governments by a distant imperial body — whose experience of federalism was entirely academic — did attract its share of criticism, principally from English-Canadian nationalists and other partisans of a strong central government (Cairns, 1971). But the JCPC also had its defenders, including the political essayist Pierre Elliott Trudeau, who once remarked that the British tribunal had helped keep Quebec in Confederation by fashioning a more accommodating division of powers than that envisaged by the original designers of the BNA Act (Trudeau, 1968: 198). Yet even defenders of the JCPC have been hard-pressed to say its disputed judgements were legally correct because it is only too evident that they were intrinsically political judgements, not simply in their consequences, but in their source. Indeed, it is almost impossible to imagine any court giving substance to the letter of constitutional law without drawing upon conceptions of justice, political ideals, theories of government, administrative assumptions, and a host of other considerations that can only be characterized as political. Whatever the exact reasons behind its provincialist inclinations, the JCPC, particularly in the interwar years, was anything but an impartial umpire, and the political landscape of Canada became different as a result.

Political too were the circumstances that led the Canadian government finally to abandon appeals to the JCPC in 1949. A series of detested rulings on the so-called Bennett New Deal legislation that hampered the federal government's efforts to respond boldly to the economic hardships brought on by the Great Depression,[4] together with sentiments of an increasingly self-confident nationalism, drew together federal politicians of all parties to support a motion to abolish appeals to the JCPC. Unsaid but certainly wished for in many quarters was that the Supreme Court, unshackled from its judicial superior, would reverse the decentralizing momentum the JCPC had facilitated. Initially these hopes were indulged by the Supreme Court, as in *Johannesson v. West St. Paul [1952]* where it offered an interpretation of the "peace, order and good government" clause of the Constitution more commodious to the federal government. But, for the most part, the Supreme Court did not disturb to any great extent the precedents established by the JCPC, and at least for the first two decades of its newly minted judicial supremacy, it moved cautiously and often inconsistently in constitutional cases.

---

4. The rulings in question were: *Attorney General of Canada v. Attorney General of Ontario (Employment and Social Insurance Act Reference) [1937]*; *Attorney General of British Columbia v. Attorney General of Canada (Natural Products Marketing Act Reference) [1937]*; and *Attorney General of Canada v. Attorney General of Ontario (Labour Conventions Case) [1937]*.

This was true not only of its federalism cases but also of its incipient civil rights cases, for which a potential constitutional justification had emerged in the form of the "Duff doctrine." Enunciated by Chief Justice Duff in what amounted to a judicial conjecture in *Reference Re Alberta Statutes [1938]*, this doctrine suggested that the preamble to the BNA Act implicitly contains a guarantee of those freedoms, such as freedom of speech, which are essential to the functioning of democratic government. Although occasionally cited by subsequent judges, notably in a series of civil rights cases in Quebec in the 1950s, the Duff doctrine failed to reach the level of a binding precedent and the prospect of an activist court spiritedly safeguarding civil liberties was never realized during this period. Not even when the federal government passed a Bill of Rights in 1960 did the courts eagerly take up the assignment it seemed to offer. An ordinary piece of legislation, and only applicable to actions of the federal government, the Bill of Rights had so uncertain a constitutional status that in the main, the courts ignored its provisions.[5]

Commentators have frequently remarked on the conservatism of the Supreme Court in constitutional and civil rights matters during the 1950s and 1960s, and its almost slavish adherence to common law precedents established by British judicial authorities, even after it had become the final appellate court in Canada (Bushnell, 1992). No doubt this is true as a description of the court's jurisprudence, but there is a political context to this judicial diffidence. By the time the Supreme Court had become the court of last resort in division of powers cases, federal and provincial governments were embarking on concerted efforts in taxation and social policy in what came to be called the era of cooperative federalism. The relative political harmony that ensued made the court's constitutional role less momentous if only because fewer federalism disputes were litigated. Significantly, once this cooperative era began to languish in the 1970s, and as private corporations fought to escape unwanted regulations, the number of division of powers cases multiplied, and the Court assumed a much larger role in the political affairs of Canada.

As for the court's reluctance to use its legal resources to vigorously defend civil rights prior to the introduction of the Charter, there again is a political background that needs to be taken into account. In his comparative study of judicial activism, Charles Epp has suggested that courts are much more likely to be emphatic champions of civil liberties if there already exists within society institutional and cultural support structures that can reinforce

---

5. The Supreme Court upheld rights claims under the Bill of Rights only five times, four of which involved reading into federal criminal law due process requirements. The lone federal law that the Court invalidated under the Bill of Rights was a provision of the Indian Act in *The Queen v. Drybones [1970]* (Morton, 1986: 5).

an emboldened judiciary (Epp, 1998). The relative absence in Canada in the early postwar years of such a foundation for judicial activism goes some way in explaining the Supreme Court's disappointingly intermittent concern for protecting civil liberties. By the same token, the subsequent decades-long campaign for a constitutionally entrenched Charter of Rights, the multiplication of public interest groups prepared to include legal action in their repertoire of political tactics (helped in some instances by government programs designed for just such a purpose), the demonstration effect of successful civil rights undertakings in the United States under the Warren Court, changes in professional legal education, as well as assorted efforts to make legal knowledge more widely available to the general public, all acted to produce an environment more conducive to judicial activism.

Alongside the influence of these various political and social forces, there were some important transformations occurring in the Supreme Court itself that prepared it for a more activist role. Introduced during the tenure of Pierre Trudeau as Justice Minister and later Prime Minister, these changes included reforming the appeal process to give the Court virtually complete control over which cases it would hear and therefore the capacity to determine which areas of the law it would influence through its judgements.[6] One very visible result of this revised appeal process was the heightened prominence the Court began to give to *public* as opposed to *private* law cases. Another less formal but equally consequential change involved judicial appointments. In an effort to enhance its legitimacy, the Trudeau government inaugurated a pattern of appointments to the Supreme Court, imitated by subsequent prime ministers, in which partisan connections and political experience were downplayed in favour of academic reputation and judicial experience. As one judicial scholar has observed, this "revolution by appointment," which began in earnest with the pre-Charter Laskin court, "delivered on the hopes of those who wanted a powerful court playing a strong public role" (McCormick, 2000: 103).

One rather clear sign of the metamorphosis taking place in the Supreme Court occurred in a 1976 reference case, re *Anti-Inflation Act [1976]*. Reference cases, it must be pointed out, are a peculiarity of the Canadian judicial system and illustrate just how tenuous the distinction between judicial and political

---

6. Prior to amendments to the Supreme Court Act made in 1975, anyone had a right to appeal a civil law case to the highest court if it involved a monetary matter in excess of $10,000 and any criminal law case involving a capital crime. Such appeals by right occupied a disproportionate amount of the Supreme Court's time. After 1975 appeals by right (aside from reference questions, which constitute a different order of pleading) are available only in criminal law cases where there is at least one dissenting judge at the level of the provincial court of appeal (McCormick, 2000: 86).

functions can be.[7] The reference procedure allows the federal government to refer to the Supreme Court legal issues for an advisory opinion. Usually, though not exclusively, constitutional questions related to a federal law or proposed policy (occasionally the federal government refers provincial laws), reference questions, strictly speaking, have no legal consequences because they do not involve an actual legal dispute. Since the court's opinion in these circumstances is only advisory, it is conceptually more in the nature of political counsel than legal ruling, though governments have always treated the court's response to a reference question as authoritative (Hogg, 2002: 8.6.d). The reference procedure calls into question the separation of powers doctrine, not simply because the Court is called upon to provide what amounts to political advice, but because the process lends itself to political exploitation. It is only too easy for a government that wishes to delay the introduction of a law for political reasons,[8] or stake out a claim in a federalism dispute,[9] or avoid squarely confronting a controversial issue[10] to hand over to the Court responsibility for the problem with hopes that a judicial pronouncement will facilitate a desired political outcome. While the *Anti-Inflation Act* reference was not devised for any such blatant political purpose, it did nonetheless exhibit features that would become commonplace in the subsequent Charter era, including granting standing to groups with a valid public interest in the outcome of the case and, perhaps more notably, deciding to admit social scientific evidence relevant to the issue at dispute. What bears comment about these practices is that by engaging in them, the Court places itself in a position of judging not simply the legal qualifications but also the substantive merits of a disputed government measure. By so inquiring into the policy justifications of a law, it can be argued that courts are straying illicitly into the legislative domain, a charge that becomes familiar in the era of the Charter, although the exercise is already prefigured in *re Anti-Inflation Act*.

Judicial Activism in the Era of the Charter

Changes in types of judicial appointments, changes in the way the Court chooses and administers its caseload, changes in its evidentiary rules — all

---

7. Just how unique the Canadian reference procedure is can be seen by comparing the experiences of other common law countries with constitutional courts. For example, both the United States Supreme Court and the Australian High Court have refused to supply advisory opinions on grounds that it would offend the principle of the separation of powers (Hogg, 2002: 7.3.a).
8. As arguably happened in the Bennett New Deal reference cases. See note 3.
9. As was the case in *re Secession of Quebec [1998]*.
10. As in the reference on same-sex marriage consequent on the ruling in *Halpern et al. v. Attorney-General of Canada et al. [2003]*.

signalled a Supreme Court ready to become more actively engaged in the policy domain. But without doubt it was the introduction of the Charter of Rights and Freedoms that did most to augment the court's power of judicial review. This power to evaluate the constitutionality of government actions, and to strike down those found to be unconstitutional, could not but be magnified after 1982 for the simple reason that the Charter explicitly proscribes certain kinds of state conduct. Considering its reluctance to seize upon a civil rights agenda when provided the opportunity with the earlier Bill of Rights, it remained to be seen whether the Court would be more favourably disposed to wield its enhanced power under the Charter. As it turned out, the Supreme Court initially proved a Charter enthusiast, awarding victories in decisions that were almost always unanimous to more than half of the claimants who had invoked its constitutional guarantees in the period 1982–84. Thereafter, however, the success rate for Charter challenges has declined, ranging from a third to as little as a quarter as was the case in 2007. At the same time, disagreements in the Court have become more commonplace. While the latter might be taken as a sign that ideological camps are solidifying in a manner comparable to what has occurred in the United States, students of the attitudinal characteristics of Canadian Supreme Court Justices have concluded that for the most part simple liberal/conservative ideological distinctions are inadequate in accounting for the incidence of concurrences and dissents in the Court (Ostberg and Wetstein, 2007; McCormick, 2004). If anything, as Patrick Monahan suggests, the emergence of different voting blocs in recent years might best be explained by the degree of deference different groups of judges are prepared to show to elected governments, particularly in disputes that have fiscal consequences (cited in Makin, 2008).

Success rates for Charter challenges and the frequency of dissents do not, however, tell us all that much about the impact of Charter jurisprudence on public policy. More revealing are the patterns discernable among the over 400 Charter cases heard by the Supreme Court in its first quarter century and the interpretative strategies the Court has developed over this period. The Charter, it should be recalled, has some unique features that were meant to guide courts in their interpretation of its enumerated rights. For example, the general legal right contained in Section 7 guaranteeing the right to life, liberty, and security of person is qualified by the phrase "in accordance with the principles of fundamental justice" to indicate broadly the circumstances where governments may be justified in depriving citizens of this right. Or again, Section 15 guaranteeing equal treatment before and under the law, and equal protection and benefit of the laws, has an additional phrase implying that its purpose is to protect against specific types of discrimination, such as that based on race or religion or sex. Moreover, Section 15 is followed by a clause exempting from Charter challenge affirmative action programs, thereby reinforcing the notion that it should be seen primarily as a remedial right aimed at those historically disadvantaged by prejudices and intolerance.

The internal limitations and interpretative clues contained in these and other rights in the Charter are further qualified by three pivotal application clauses: Sections 1, 24, and 33. Section 1 instructs courts to treat the rights and freedoms of the Charter as only conditionally guaranteed, as they are subject to "such reasonable limits prescribed by law as can be demonstrably justified in a free and democratic society." This latter phrase permits governments to defend a *prima facie* Charter breach by arguing that it is a reasonable limitation on the infringed right. Should a Charter violation be found to exist and not be justified under Section 1, courts are charged under Section 24 with devising a remedy they consider "appropriate and just under the circumstances." This enforcement section confers on the courts discretionary power in deciding just how to respond to a Charter violation, which means that when totalling up Charter victories one should always pay heed to the remedy ordered up because a Charter "win" does not automatically mean that the victor obtains the sought-after result. Finally, Section 33 acts to bracket almost all the fundamental rights of the Charter by allowing the federal Parliament or provincial legislatures to override Sections 2 and 7 through 15 through simple statutory declarations for repeatable periods of five years. This controversial "notwithstanding" clause was a concession the federal government made during constitutional negotiations leading up to the Charter to those provincial premiers who were hesitant to relinquish the principle of parliamentary supremacy, though it should be noted that this same provision had also been a part of the 1960 Bill of Rights.[11] While Section 33 seems to impose a considerable restriction on the Charter, and hence on the Court's power of judicial review, in practice this has not been the case. Except for a period in the 1980s when the government of Saskatchewan used the notwithstanding clause to try to pre-empt a constitutional challenge to back-to-work legislation, and governments in Quebec for symbolic political reasons used it to insulate as much of that province's legislation as possible from Charter challenge and, later, to override an adverse court ruling on its language laws, Section 33 has become increasingly a less credible option for governments as its public legitimacy declined in the intervening years.

Alongside these assorted cues and directives, the Supreme Court has developed a number of its own interpretative strategies to give substance to Charter rights. One such strategy has been to interpret the purpose of the rights contained in the Charter, that is, the values they are designed to

---

11. For opposing views on the wisdom of including Section 33 in the Charter, see Whyte, 1990 and Russell, 1991.

protect or advance, by canvassing their historical, political, or philosophical sources. This "purposive approach" to Charter interpretation, first articulated by Chief Justice Dickson in his ruling in *Hunter v. Southam [1984]*, ensured that the Court would not confine itself to legally narrow representations of the newly entrenched constitutional rights. Another interpretative approach favoured by the Court has been called "contextualism." The contextual approach, first elaborated by Justice Wilson in *Edmonton Journal v. A.G. Alta [1989]*, invites courts to be more sensitive to the complexities of individual rights claims by acknowledging that "a particular right or freedom might have a different value depending on the context" (1355–56). By endorsing a contextual approach, the Court has signified that it is indisposed to rely on a simple formula to decide upon the validity of a rights claim, preferring instead to examine the underlying circumstances and competing values that might clarify what actually is at stake in the claim.

Understandably, there are those uncomfortable with the interpretative latitude the Court seemingly enjoys when it uses a purposive approach to define the meaning of Charter rights and a contextual approach to decide upon their relative weight in concrete legal disputes. Likewise, there are those who are disconcerted by how the courts have come to interpret the limitations clause of Section 1. In an early Charter case, *The Queen v. Oakes [1986]*, Chief Justice Dickson outlined a four-part analysis to determine when a government might be justified in infringing a Charter right. The so-called *Oakes* test, originally devised to be quite rigorous but subsequently relaxed in practice, requires governments found in violation of a Charter right to satisfy the Court that a pressing and substantial public purpose is being served by the controverted measure, that it is rationally connected to that purpose, that the affected right has been impaired in a minimal fashion, and that the public benefits of the measure outweigh the costs of this impairment. Significantly, the way the *Oakes* test has been construed invariably involves the Court in policy assessments, for there is no other practical way for it to conclude whether a disputed law or government action is rationally connected to the public purpose it is meant to serve, or, even more acutely, whether a right has been minimally impaired, except to compare policy alternatives. Predictably it is at the Section 1 stage of a Charter hearing that courts are most vulnerable to the charge of subverting the democratic process by substituting their own policy preferences for those of elected legislatures.

Whether an unelected judiciary has indeed used its heightened power of judicial review to illicitly inject its values into the field of democratic policymaking is something that can best be determined by first trying to get a sense of the kinds of Charter-based nullifications the courts have dispensed. In the period between 1982 and 2007, the Supreme Court ruled that 86 federal or provincial statutes or regulations contravened the Charter or Section 35 of the Constitution Act, 1982, the latter containing guarantees of Aboriginal and treaty rights that are not a part of the Charter but that have been approached by the Court in a manner analogous to its Charter jurisprudence.[12] Of these 86 constitutional invalidations, 47 involved federal and 39 provincial statutes or regulations. The majority of federal laws or regulations found to be unconstitutional (27 of 47) were faulted for procedural rather than substantive matters, which has meant in principle that Parliament could with relative ease remedy the problem with amended legislation or new regulations. In the case of impugned provincial statutes and regulations, the majority (30 out of 39) have been judged unconstitutional on substantive grounds, which means that it has been comparatively harder, though again not impossible, for these governments to repair the legislation or regulation.

The contrast between federal and provincial experiences with the Charter on the face of it seems to support the view that implicit in the Charter's design was a nationalizing mission to harmonize provincial legislation and regulatory practices (Russell, 1983; Cairns, 1992; Laforest, 1992). Yet closer analysis of the actual disposition of Charter cases suggests that such a national alignment among provincial laws has not taken place to any significant degree. For instance, in the area of language rights, which many thought had the greatest potential to produce federal homogenization, it turned out that after interpreting these provisions relatively strictly during the first few years of the Charter, the Supreme Court has lately been much more willing to approve provincial variations in language and cultural policies.[13] These and other trends in Charter jurisprudence have led the constitutional commentator, Yves De Montigny, to report that the "Charter has not had the devastating impact on the legislative authority of Quebec (and the other provinces) that some may have feared" (Montigny, 1997: 21). Likewise, his statistical analysis of Charter cases has caused James Kelly to conclude that the Charter has had "a minimal impact on federal diversity" (Kelly, 1999: 685).[14]

---

12. This data is taken from Kelly, 1999; Monahan, 2002; and from a statistical analysis of Supreme Court cases between 2002–07 undertaken by the author.

13. It should be noted that language cases have not disappeared entirely from the purview of the Court. Thus, in both *Société des Acadiens et Acadiennes du Nouveau-Brunswick Inc. v. Canada [2008]*, and *Doucet-Boudreau v. Nova Scotia (Minister of Education) [2003]* the Supreme Court was compelled to return to some of the constitutional language issues with which it had been preoccupied in the 1990s.

14. Again it is worthwhile pointing out that there are alternative views on this matter, particularly among scholars in Quebec. For example, Lajoie argues that the era of the Charter coincided with a broad centralizing thrust in which the Supreme Court tended to support federal efforts to secure free trade both within and without the borders of Canada and that, in terms of Charter cases, the Court was more receptive

If the Supreme Court has not used the Charter to further the national-izing project often attributed to it, there are nonetheless some general motifs evident among its Charter rulings, which suggests it is appreciative of both the perils and possibilities of its enhanced political role. The most conspicuous of these patterns has been the extent to which legal rights dominate Charter jurisprudence. Most frequently invoked in Charter litigation (Section 7 argu-ments in particular outnumber all others), legal rights claims also have tended to be the most successful. Not surprisingly, the Supreme Court, just as it had done in a much more modest fashion with the Bill of Rights, has proved most receptive to Charter arguments in a realm of the law — the criminal justice system — for which it feels it possesses a special competence. This relative concern for the rights of the accused, which the Court has hitherto exhibited, does not mean that it will always be firmly wedded to a due process model of law enforcement, and indeed recent trends point to a court more willing to side with the police in legal rights cases (Makin, 2008).

As for fundamental freedoms — freedom of expression, religion, associa-tion, and assembly — the Court has in the past tried to establish a balanced approach, though in the process it has also laid itself open to the charge of constitutional capriciousness. For instance, in *The Queen v. Big M Drug Mart Ltd [1985]*, the Court struck down the Federal Lord's Day Act on grounds that it infringed the guarantee of freedom of religion, but it subsequently upheld the validity of Ontario's Retail Holiday Act in *Edwards Book and Art Ltd v. the Queen [1986]*, ruling that the latter was a justifiable limitation on the same right. Freedom of expression cases have also come in for some rather variable treatment. In *R. v Keegstra [1990]*, for example, the Court upheld a federal law on hate speech under Section 1, but in *R. v. Zundel [1992]* it declared another federal hate speech law unconstitutional because it was deemed to be overly broad and for this reason an objectionable en-croachment on freedom of speech. In pornography cases, the Supreme Court has upheld the federal obscenity law in *R. v. Butler [1992]*, although it also effectively read that law down to narrow its application. Likewise in *R. v. Sharpe [2001]* the Supreme Court upheld the federal law on the possession of child pornography but at the same time read in exceptions to that law to cover situations it believed posed no risk of harm to children. The Court has thus far been willing to countenance abridgements to free speech in the realm of erotica so long as they can be justified under a notoriously vague "community standards test."

The Court's equality jurisprudence has been especially notable for its doctrinal difficulties and, as in other Charter cases, has entailed contrasting

---

to so-called national as opposed to Quebec (or other minority cultural or social) values in instances where the latter threatened federal sovereignty (Lajoie, 2009).

rulings.[15] For example, the Court refused arguments that various provisions in the Income Tax Act discriminated against women in *Symes v. Canada [1993]* and *re Thibaudeau and the Queen [1995]* but allowed the argument that failure to provide translation services for deaf patients in British Columbia hospitals constituted a violation of Section 15 in *Eldridge v. B.C. [1997]*. If the *Eldridge* ruling signalled the advent of a substantive interpretation of the equality section of the Charter, it was a short-lived episode as evidenced by the ruling in *Auton v. British Columbia [2004]* where the Court decided not to order the provincial government to fund costly specialized treatment for autistic children.

One of the most demonstrable instances of the Court's shifting constitutional position on equality rights has been its response to claims of discrimination brought forward by gays and lesbians. A bare majority of the Court, for example, found that the federal government's refusal to extend spousal allowance benefits under the Old Age Security Act to gay and lesbian partners in long-term relationships was an acceptable departure from the Charter's equality guarantee in *Egan et al. v. the Queen [1995]*. But within a few years the Court altered its approach and in *Vriend v. Alberta [1998]* found the Alberta government contravened Section 15 by failing to provide gays and lesbians protection from discrimination in its provincial human rights act. In the same vein, the Court ruled in *M. v. H. [1999]* that by excluding same-sex couples from provisions in its Family Services Act, which allow domestic partners to sue for support in the event of a marital breakdown, the Ontario government had violated their equality rights. And in *Attorney General v. Hislop [2007]* the Court repudiated entirely the approach it had taken in *Egan* by ruling that the federal government's attempt to limit the time period in which a surviving partner of a same-sex union could claim survivor benefits under the Canada Pension Plan breached the equality guarantee of Section 15.

The vacillations exhibited in these and other rulings seem to illustrate not so much a court seized with Charter hubris but one that has been rather gingerly muddling through with its enhanced power of judicial review, usually choosing to nullify laws for procedural defects or for being overly broad rather than reproving of them in their entirety. This is not to say that courts have not produced controversial Charter judgements. Whether extending

---

15. Chief Justice Beverley McLachlin, for instance, has protested that the Charter right to equality is the "most difficult right" (McLachlin, 2001). The Supreme Court's jurisprudence certainly bears out this observation as evidenced by the often sharp disagreements among the justices over how to understand this constitutional guarantee. And even after its collegial effort to produce an authoritative interpretation of Section 15 in *Law v. Canada [1999]*, the Court continues to split over the proper application of this right.

to corporations the same legal rights available to individuals in *Hunter v. Southam* [1984], or invalidating the federal abortion law in *R. v. Morgentaler [1988]*, or nullifying Quebec's sign law in *Ford v. Quebec [1988]*, or declaring the common law definition of marriage unconstitutional thereby opening the door to gay marriage in *Halpern et al. v. Attorney-General of Canada et al. [2003]*, courts have periodically handed down highly contentious decisions that arguably have encroached upon the policy prerogative of legislatures. Significantly, when the Court has produced politically divisive rulings, it has done so in the manner of an equal opportunity antagonist by alternately disturbing left- and right-wing constituencies.

Two recent cases illustrate this propensity of the Court to attract censure from opposing ideological camps. In *Sauvé v. Canada (Chief Electoral Officer) [2002]* (otherwise known as *Sauvé 2*), a bare majority of the Supreme Court ruled that the federal government's amendment to the Canada Elections Act found in Section 51(e), which denied to prisoners serving sentences of two years or more the right to vote — an amendment prompted by an earlier successful court challenge by the same litigant — was a violation of the Charter's basic democratic guarantee in Section 3. This ruling was decried by many a conservative commentator as an altogether inappropriate judicial repudiation of Parliament's role in defining the scope of Charter rights, especially considering that the disputed amendment to the Canada Elections Act represented Parliament's calculated response to the Court's previous ruling on what was entailed by the Charter's guarantee of the right to vote (see, for example, Manfredi, 2007). A few years later another deeply divided court ruled in *Chaoulli v. Quebec (Attorney General) [2005]* that the provision in Quebec's Health Insurance Act and Hospital Insurance Act prohibiting citizens of that province from obtaining private insurance to cover health care services already available under the provincial public health care plan was a violation of the guarantee to life found both in the Quebec Charter of Human Rights and Freedoms and the Canadian Charter of Rights and Freedoms. This was a ruling that invited an equally harsh share of criticism from liberal or left-wing commentators because of the way the majority of the Court found a constitutional violation by drawing its own conclusion about the efficacy of a publicly funded medicare plan in supplying reasonably prompt medical services, in the process laying open all other provincial medicare plans to constitutional challenge on similar grounds (see, for example, Flood, 2006).

How can one possibly justify permitting unrepresentative and unaccountable judges to replace the policy preferences of elected officials with their own, as they arguably did in these two cases? It is instructive to observe that both left- and right-wing analysts of the Court refer to this counter-majoritarian dilemma when sounding the alarm about the judicialization of

politics.[16] But there are significant differences between left and right apprais-
als of judicial politics that are worth recounting. Left critics have generally
been concerned that judges, by virtue of their class background and training,
will invariably tend to be conservative in outlook. A principal fear is that
this conservative judiciary will use the Charter, in particular its ostensibly
libertarian components such as Section 7, to reinforce the already powerful
position business interests possess at common law.[17] A related concern is that
the Charter conveys a beguiling message to progressives by suggesting that
genuine social reform is possible through courtroom forensics, something
that not only is unlikely but also debilitating for truly effective political action
(Petter, 1987; Mandel, 1994; Hutchinson, 1995; Bakan, 1997).

While some of the force of this left critique had dissipated over the years
as the Supreme Court repeatedly refused to employ Section 7 to fortify economic rights (but by the same token also declining to use this section to
help those who sought a constitutional guarantee for welfare and other social
rights), the *Chaoulli* decision has certainly revived left-wing apprehensions
about rights-based jurisprudence. But in the event, it has been the right-wing
critics of the Court who have become more influential in the debate about
the judicialization of politics, a fact that perhaps should not be surprising
given the late twentieth-century growth of political conservatism (Morton
and Knopff, 2000; Manfredi, 2001; Leishman, 2006). For the right, the over-
riding trepidation is that the Court will exploit the egalitarian sections of the
Charter, principally Section 15, to advance a radical redistributive agenda.[18]
Given the prominence the writings of F.L. Morton and Rainer Knopff have
gained in both academic and political circles, their arguments on this score re-
pay close attention. Morton and Knopff's main contention is that self-serving
special interest groups such as feminists, gays and lesbians, and ethnic and other
identity-based groups, which they call the Court Party, have allied themselves
with the *jurocracy* (a shorthand for legal professionals and advocates within law
schools, the bureaucracy, and the judiciary who are Charter enthusiasts) to

16. The term, "counter-majoritarian" was coined by the American legal scholar,
    Alexander Bickel (1986) when writing about the civil rights jurisprudence of the
    Warren Court.
17. The cautionary tale left critics of the Court most frequently invoke when warning of
    the reactionary potential of a bill of rights is the regrettable *Lochner* era in American
    constitutional history. For most of the first three decades of the twentieth century, a
    very conservative American Supreme Court elevated the reference to property rights
    in the Fourteenth Amendment into nothing short of a constitutional warrant for
    laissez-faire capitalism, in the process continually striking down progressive legislation
    passed by state and federal governments.
18. For right critics it is also an American judicial episode — the vigorous civil rights
    program of the Warren Court — that stands as the embodiment of all that can go
    wrong with an unbridled judiciary.

get through the courts what they have not been able to secure through the ordinary legislative process. This Court Party, they protest, typically inflates its claims when employing the vocabulary of rights in a way that is inhospitable to the spirit of compromise and conciliation supposedly characteristic of the legislative arena. Morton and Knopff have frequently been criticized for assimilating a deliberately selective cast of characters into what amount to ideological categories of Court Party and jurocracy, and for using a disingenuous conception of democracy as a normative foundation for their critique of the courts (Smith, 2002). But the impression of a furtive style of politics conducted in courtrooms remains powerful enough to have summoned a variety of justificatory arguments for the power of judicial review.

The most straightforward defence of the Court's constitutionally enhanced role under the Charter is that the capacity to strike down legislation in order to protect vulnerable minorities from the depredations of legislative majorities is precisely what is intended by a bill of rights in the first place (Bayefsky, 1987). A more refined version of this proposition relies on a process-based conception of democracy. According to this argument, judicial review based on a bill of rights actually promotes democracy by giving the courts the power to ensure that the mechanisms of political representation operate fairly, with special consideration given to the plight of minorities who might otherwise be effectively excluded from the political process (Monahan, 1987). On either view, an activist court is ordinarily regarded a success rather than a problem. To reinforce this optimistic characterization of the power of judicial review, Charter supporters often point out that public opinion is always much more favourable to courts than to legislatures and that polls have consistently shown Canadians are more likely to agree than disagree with controversial Supreme Court rulings (Fletcher and Howe, 2000; CRIC, 2002). Judicial adversaries are generally not persuaded by such observations, however, maintaining on the one hand that public opinion can be notoriously inconstant[19] and, on the other, that the very fact that courts are unaccountable hardly qualifies them for presuming to act as guardians of democracy.

Because courts are forever susceptible to this latter charge, their supporters have lately fastened on another justificatory strategy in which it is asserted

---

19. Public opinion surveys continue to provide conflicting evidence about how well the Charter is received by Canadian citizens. For example, in a poll commissioned by the journal *Policy Options* on the occasion of the twenty-fifth anniversary of the Charter, a significant majority of respondents did not identify Charter values as a central component of "Canadian values" and were for the most part uninformed about the mechanics of judicial review. At the same time, a majority of respondents reported that they supported the Charter, and, tellingly, a large majority thought sexual orientation should be protected under the Charter and that the courts should have the last word in interpreting Charter guarantees. See Nanos, 2007.

that judges do not have the final word on the disposition of individual rights and freedoms but rather are engaged in a dialogue with elected legislatures over their interpretation. Proponents of the judicial dialogue thesis contend that so long as a judicial decision is capable of being reversed, modified, or avoided by ordinary legislative means, then the relationship between courts and legislatures should be regarded as a colloquy (conversation) rather than one of subordination and superordination (Hogg and Bushell, 1997; Roach, 2001). The Charter supposedly facilitates this dialogue because it features such clauses as Sections 1 and 33, which offer legislatures room to contribute their own interpretations of contested constitutional values and, in some instances, ignore entirely their judicial explication. In one of the more compelling versions of this argument, Peter Hogg and Allison Bushell have ventured proof of a dialogue by surveying the laws invalidated by the Supreme Court on Charter grounds, finding that in two-thirds of the cases the relevant legislative body responded with amended laws, most of which incorporated minor refinements that did not compromise the objectives of the original legislation (Hogg and Bushell, 1997).[20]

Hogg and Bushell's evidence of dialogue, it should be pointed out, has been disputed,[21] and even proponents of the thesis disagree over whether courts, legislatures, or executives guide the process (Hiebert, 2002; Kelly, 2005). These reservations notwithstanding, courts are for obvious reasons attracted to the dialogue thesis because it makes judicial review appear a benign exercise in value discovery. It is not surprising, therefore, that shortly after the Hogg and Bushell article was published, Justice Iacobucci, writing for the majority of the Supreme Court, cited it approvingly in the *Vriend* case, remarking that "dynamic interaction among branches of government … has aptly been described as a 'dialogue'…" (para. 139). Even more telling, Chief Justice McLachlin and Justice Iacobucci, again writing for the majority in *R. v. Mills [1999]*, referred to the dialogue thesis in support of their decision not to overrule the federal government's amended "rape-shield" law, even though that law departed from what the Court had previously announced would be constitutionally acceptable (para 57). Governments also have gravitated to this portrayal of judicial power. For instance, after courts in British Columbia, Ontario, and Quebec ruled separately that marriage

---

20. Just how influential the Hogg and Bushell argument has been can be gathered from the fact that the *Osgoode Hall Law Journal* produced a special issue debating the merits of the dialogue thesis on the tenth anniversary of their original article. See *Osgoode Hall Law Journal Special Issue: Charter Dialogue Ten Years Later* 45:1 (Spring 2007).

21. See Manfredi and Kelly, 1999, and the reply furnished by Hogg and Thornton, 1999. See also Sujit Choudhry and Claire Hunter, 2003, whose study of judicial activism casts doubt on the claim that the Supreme Court frequently strikes down majoritarian legislation.

must be open to same-sex couples, the federal government decided not to appeal, electing instead to recruit the Supreme Court as a political advisor by submitting to it a set of reference questions related to the constitutionality of same-sex marriage. Significantly, the Department of Justice declared that in "taking this course of action, the Government of Canada is ensuring, through a dynamic dialogue between the Courts and Parliament, that our laws reflect the fundamental values of the Charter" (Canada, Department of Justice, 2003).

This manifest concern for public acceptance on the part of both the Supreme Court and the federal government, in the first instance for the power of judicial review, in the second for a potentially unpopular law, suggests that there is a much more fundamental process underlying the judicialization of politics than its critics are prepared to grant. This more fundamental process is nothing less than the recurrent legitimation crises experienced by executive-centred governments in the postwar period. Legitimation crisis is routinely described in social scientific literature as a situation where government fails to elicit sufficient allegiance to its authority. The roots of these crises are typically complex and multi-faceted. In Canada, for example, legitimacy crises of varying intensity emerged as the postwar pattern of elite accommodation, predicated on the creation of a regulatory and welfare state, began to decompose in face of accelerated social change. Among these changes was a breakdown in the political compromise between French and English Canada at a time when other identities demanded acknowledgement in something other than a narrowly construed binational state. This period also witnessed a growing economic enfranchisement of women with accompanying demands for equal treatment. At the same time the ideal of the nuclear family increasingly became contested and the presumptive norms of heterosexuality more openly defied. Added to these various bids for recognition and equitable treatment, struggles between capital and labour, never entirely displaced during the formation of the welfare state, gained a new salience as neoliberalism emerged as a dominant economic and political paradigm. And that paradigm itself, no less than its welfarist predecessor, encountered escalated attacks by opponents of immoderate economic growth and a consumerist culture.

While these diverse political currents presented challenges to settled democratic norms and practices, they were also more-or-less vigorously opposed by the very interests and institutions most closely associated with the postwar regulatory and welfare state. In these circumstances, where many of the new movements found their claims marginalized and their political ventures effectively organized out of established democratic pathways, it is not surprising that some would seek to influence public policy through the courts. Nor should it be surprising that the judiciary might sometimes be solicitous of these otherwise powerless groups. After all, one of the by-products of the postwar political settlement was the relative decline of the Supreme Court's constitutional purpose as witnessed in its dwindling number of federalism cases. The Charter made it possible for the Court to redefine its constitutional role as defender of so-called "discrete and insular" minorities[22] just at the time that the legitimacy of existing democratic practices, and the distribution of goods and services they have underwritten, increasingly came to be assailed, and politics-as-usual became more difficult to pursue.[23]

It is in the confluence of these events that the judicialization of politics gains its significance, both as an emerging political reality and as an object of normative critique. While this phenomenon has provoked a great deal of concern and demands for reform ranging from a more transparent appointments procedure to an outright curbing of the courts, rather less attention has been paid to the underlying circumstances that have sustained the judiciary's growing political prominence and the counter-tendencies that have worked to moderate it. Of the latter, suffice it to say that as courts become more of a focal point in the public policy debates that polarize Canadians, they too risk having their legitimacy undermined, particularly when they are involved in fundamental questions about entitlements, both public and private. Perhaps it has been a recognition of just such a risk that has led to the marked decrease in Charter cases reaching the Supreme Court. While the Court averaged over 25 Charter cases a year in its first two decades, that number has declined notably this decade, reaching a low of around ten cases annually between 2005 and 2007. This waning of Charter jurisprudence is matched by another noteworthy development — the growing inclination of the Court to construe Charter violations more narrowly either as instances of misconduct on the part of state officials (for example, police officers) or procedural defects in impugned legislation, thereby averting direct quarrels with legislatures over substantive issues in law. It may well be, as Kelly suggests, that this latter tendency has coincided with the cultivation by the federal executive of a bureaucratic apparatus more competent in the ways of drafting legislation

---

22. The phrase "discrete and insular minorities" was introduced by Justice Stone of the American Supreme Court in his oft-cited footnote in *United States v. Carolene Products Co. [1938]* where he proposes that the Court defer to the legislatures in economic policy but subject to "more exacting judicial scrutiny" legislation that relies on prejudices against minorities. The same phrase appeared in Canadian jurisprudence as the Canadian Supreme Court attempted to devise a credible test for applying the Section 15 equality right (Hogg, 2002: 52.7.g).

23. Doubtless it was this sense of political paralysis that led a chagrined Chief Justice Lamar to complain that the reason the Supreme Court has become involved in policy issues in the era of the Charter is because "too often timid politicians have been afraid to confront them directly" (Lamar, cited in Greene *et al.*, 1998: 194).

that would survive Charter challenges, thereby signalling that the Cabinet and its officials are becoming as important in defining Charter values as the Court (Kelly, 2005). Either way, whether it is a Supreme Court becoming more deferential in response to legitimacy concerns, or a federal executive becoming more aggressive in asserting the Charter credentials of its own laws, a full-scale judicialization of Canadian politics against which so many critics have sounded dire warnings seems not to have taken place.

All this is not to say that the Court has disappeared from politics, as its disputed rulings in *Sauvé* and *Chaoulli* so amply demonstrate. Nor is it likely, given the way the Charter has come to inspire litigation strategies involving public law, that the Court will withdraw from politically charged cases in the future, cases in which its own members are frequently as divided as the rest of the population. Detractors of judicial politics too often imagine a judiciary somehow limited to a world of legal principles safely distanced from the contests over power that obtain in the democratic arena. If, however, political power and legal principles are not so easily separable, as has been argued throughout this chapter, then the vision of a sequestered Court may not only be illusory, but it may distract us from more fruitful lines of empirical inquiry concerning the process of democratic demand-setting and the periodic eruption of judicial policy-making.

References and Suggested Readings

Bakan, Joel. 1997. *Just Words: Constitutional Rights and Social Wrongs*. Toronto: University of Toronto Press.

Bayefsky, Ann. 1987. "The Judicial Function under the Canadian *Charter of Rights and Freedoms*." *McGill Law Journal* 32: 791–833.

Bickel, Alexander. 1986. *The Least Dangerous Branch: The Supreme Court at the Bar of Politics*, 2nd ed. New Haven: Yale University Press.

Bushnell, Ian. 1992. *The Captive Court: A Study of the Supreme Court of Canada*. Montreal: McGill-Queen's University Press.

Cairns, Alan C. 1971. "The Judicial Committee and Its Critics." *Canadian Journal of Political Science* 4: 301–45.

Cairns, Alan C. 1992. *Charter versus Federalism*. Montreal: McGill-Queen's University Press.

Canada, Department of Justice. 2003. *Backgrounder: Reference to the Supreme Court*.

Centre for Research and Information on Canada (CRIC). 2002. "The Charter: Dividing or Uniting Canadians." *The CRIC Papers 5*. Montreal: Centre for Research and Information on Canada.

Choudhry, Sujit, and Claire E. Hunter. 2003. "Measuring Judicial Activism on the Supreme Court of Canada: A Comment on Newfoundland (*Treasury Board v. NAPE*)." *McGill Law Journal* 48: 525–62.

Epp, Charles R. 1998. *The Rights Revolution: Lawyers, Activists, and Supreme Courts in Comparative Perspective*. Chicago: University of Chicago Press.

Fletcher, Joseph, and Paul Howe. 2000. "Public Opinion and the Courts." *Choices* 6: 4–56.

Flood, Colleen M. 2006. "*Chaoulli's* Legacy for the Future of Canadian Health Care Policy." *Osgoode Hall Law Journal* 44: 273–310.

Greene, Ian, Carl Baar, Peter McCormick, George Szablowski, and Martin Thomas. 1998. *Final Appeal: Decision-Making in Canadian Courts of Appeal*. Toronto: James Lorimer.

Hein, Gregory. 2000. "Interest Group Litigation and Canadian Democracy." *Choices* 6: 3–30.

Hiebert, Janet L. 2002 *Charter Conflicts: What is Parliament's Role*. Montreal: McGill-Queen's University Press.

Hogg, Peter W. 2002. *Constitutional Law in Canada*, Student ed. Toronto: Carswell.

Hogg, Peter W., and Allison Bushell. 1997. "The Charter Dialogue between Courts and Legislatures (Or Perhaps the Charter of Rights Isn't Such a Bad Thing After All)." *Osgoode Hall Law Journal* 35: 75–124.

Hogg, Peter W., and Allison Thornton. 1999. "Reply to 'Six Degrees of Dialogue.'" *Osgoode Hall Law Journal* 37: 529–36.

Hutchinson, Alan C. 1995. *Waiting For CORAF: A Critique of Law and Rights*. Toronto: University of Toronto Press.

Kelly, James B. 1999. "The Charter of Rights and Freedoms and the Rebalancing of Liberal Constitutionalism in Canada, 1982-1997." *Osgoode Hall Law Journal* 37: 625–95.

Kelly, James B. 2005. *Governing with the Charter: Legislative and Judicial Activism and Framers' Intent*. Vancouver: University of British Columbia Press.

Laforest, Guy. 1992. "La *Charte* canadienne des droits et liberté au Québec: nationaliste, injuste et illégitimate." In François Rocher, ed., *Bilan québécois du fédéralisme canadien*. Montreal: VLB.

Lajoie, Andrée. 2009. "Federalism in Canada: Provinces and Minorities — Same Fight." In Alain-G. Gagnon, ed., *Contemporary Canadian Federalism: Foundations, Traditions, Institutions*. Toronto: University of Toronto Press.

Leishman, Rory. 2006. *Against Judicial Activism: The Decline of Freedom and Democracy in Canada*. Montreal: McGill-Queen's University Press.

Makin, Kirk. 2008. "Top court takes more time on fewer decisions." *Globe and Mail*, 18 April: A4.

Mandel, Michael. 1994. *The Charter of Rights and the Legalization of Politics in Canada*, rev. ed. Toronto: Thompson Educational Publishing.

Manfredi, Christopher P. 2001. *Judicial Power and the Charter: Canada and the Paradox of Liberal Constitutionalism*, 2nd ed. Don Mills: Oxford University Press.

Manfredi, Christopher P. 2007. "The Day the Dialogue Died: A Comment on *Sauvé v. Canada.*" *Osgoode Hall Law Journal* 45: 122.

Manfredi, Christopher P., and James Kelly. 1999. "Six Degrees of Dialogue: A Response to Hogg and Bushell." *Osgoode Hall Law Journal* 37: 513–27.

Martin, Robert I. 2003. *The Most Dangerous Branch: How the Supreme Court Has Undermined Our Law and Our Democracy*. Montreal: McGill-Queen's University Press.

McCormick, Peter. 2000. *Supreme At Last: The Evolution of the Supreme Court of Canada*. Toronto: James Lorimer.

McCormick, Peter. 2004. "Blocs, Swarms, and Outliers: Conceptualizing Disagreement on the Modern Supreme Court." *Osgoode Hall Law Journal* 42, 1: 99–139.

McLachlin, Beverley C.J. 2001. "Equality: The Most Difficult Right." *Supreme Court Law Review* 14: 17-27.

Monahan, Patrick. 1987. *Politics and the Constitution: The Charter, Federalism, and the Supreme Court of Canada*. Toronto: Carswell/Methuen.

Monahan, Patrick. 2002. "The Charter at Twenty." Paper presented at *The Charter at Twenty* Conference. Professional Development Program Centre (Osgoode Hall), Toronto, 13 April.

Montigny, Yves De. 1997. "The Impact (Real or Apprehended) of the Canadian Charter of Rights and Freedoms on the Legislative Authority of Quebec." In David Schneiderman and Kate Sutherland, eds., *Charting the Consequences: The Impact of the Charter of Rights and Freedoms on Canadian Law and Politics.* Toronto: University of Toronto Press.

Morton, F.L. 1986. "The Political Impact of the Charter of Rights." Occasional Papers Series, Research Study 2.2. Calgary: Research Unit for Socio-Legal Studies, University of Calgary.

Morton, F.L., and Rainer Knopff. 2000. *The Charter Revolution and the Court Party.* Peterborough: Broadview Press.

Morton, F.L., Peter H. Russell, and Troy Riddell. 1994. "The Canadian Charter of Rights and Freedoms; A Descriptive Analysis of the First Decade, 1982–1992." *National Journal of Constitutional Law* 5: 1–69.

Nanos, Nik. 2007. "Charter Values Don't Equal Canadian Values: Strong Support for Same-Sex and Property Rights." *Policy Options* 28, 2: 50–55.

Ostberg, C.L., and Matthew E. Wetstein. 2007. *Attitudinal Decision-Making in the Supreme Court of Canada.* Vancouver: University of British Columbia Press.

Petter, Andrew. 1987. "The Immaculate Deception: The Charter's Hidden Agenda." *The Advocate* 45: 857–66.

Roach, Kent. 2001. *The Supreme Court on Trial: Judicial Activism or Democratic Dialogue.* Toronto: Irwin Law.

Russell, Peter H. 1982. "The Effect of a Charter of Rights on the Policy-making Role of Canadian Courts." *Canadian Public Administration* 25: 1–33.

Russell, Peter H. 1983. "The Political Purposes of the Canadian *Charter of Rights and Freedoms.*" *Canadian Bar Review* 61: 30–54.

Russell, Peter H. 1987. *The Judiciary in Canada: The Third Branch of Government.* Toronto: McGraw-Hill Ryerson.

Russell, Peter H. 1991. "Standing Up for Notwithstanding." *Alberta Law Review* 29: 293–309.

Smith, Jennifer. 1983. "The Origins of Judicial Review in Canada." *Canadian Journal of Political Science* 16: 115–34.

Smith, Miriam C. 2002. "Ghosts of the JCPC: Group Politics and Charter Litigation in Canadian Political Science." *Canadian Journal of Political Science* 35: 13–29.

Snell, James G., and Frederick Vaughn. 1985. *The Supreme Court of Canada: History of the Institution.* Toronto: University of Toronto Press.

Trudeau, Pierre Elliott. 1968. *Federalism and the French-Canadians.* Toronto: Macmillan of Canada.

Whyte, John D. 1990. "On Not Standing for Notwithstanding." *Alberta Law Review* 28: 347–57.

PART III
Democracy and Representation

eleven

Reforming Representative Democracy: Taming the "Democratic Deficit"

A. BRIAN TANGUAY

On October 14, 2008, just under 59 per cent of Canada's registered voters went to the polls to elect a second successive minority Conservative government led by Stephen Harper. This marked an all-time low for voter turnout in Canadian federal elections, breaking the former record low of 61 per cent set in the 2004 general election (see Figure 11.1).[1] Not even 50 per cent of registered voters in Newfoundland and Labrador, the Northwest Territories, and Nunavut bothered to cast a ballot in 2008.[2] In the aftermath of this election result, many observers in the media, academe, and the political world worried that low turnout was but one symptom of a broader disengagement of voters from the political system and wondered whether far-reaching reforms of representative institutions — parties, elections, legislatures — were necessary to restore the health of democracy in Canada.

One politician who spoke frequently of the urgent need to reinvigorate and revitalize democratic institutions in the country was Paul Martin, when he was Minister of Finance in Jean Chrétien's government. In a speech on parliamentary reform and public ethics that he delivered at Osgoode Hall in the fall of 2002, for example, Martin pointed to the precipitous drop in voter turnout in recent federal elections as a symptom of more fundamental problems in our democratic system: in the general elections of 1997 and 2000, he noted, non-voters outnumbered those who supported the winning party by a considerable margin. Martin acknowledged that particular circumstances in each election might account for some of the drop in political interest among voters, but he nonetheless argued that "at some stage we have to face

---

1. Figure 11.1 indicates that official turnout in the 2000 federal election was also 61 per cent, but this number was depressed artificially by the duplication of almost a million names on the permanent voters' list. "Using the wrong number, [Elections Canada] estimated that 61.2 per cent of voters had cast ballots [in 2000], a sharp drop from the 67 per cent who showed up in 1997. In fact ... the number was closer to 64.1 per cent" (CBC News, 2004). Elections Canada did not bother to revise the official figure because that was what was reported in the House of Commons.

2. Nunavut recorded the lowest turnout among the provinces and territories at 47.4 per cent, followed by Newfoundland and Labrador and the Northwest Territories, both at 47.7 per cent. The highest turnout rate was in Prince Edward Island, where 69 per cent of registered voters cast a ballot (Elections Canada, 2008: Table 4).

up to the fact: *something is going wrong here, and in a fundamental way.* Casting a ballot is the most basic function of our democratic system. That so many Canadians choose not to do so is the political equivalent of the canary in the coalmine ... far too many Canadians cannot be bothered to vote because they don't think their vote matters" (Martin, 2002–03: 11; emphasis added). Martin singled out the "mindless adversarialism" in the House of Commons, the centralization of power in the Prime Minister's Office,[3] and rigid party discipline as primary factors contributing to the growth of what many political commentators now label the "democratic deficit."

This chapter examines the perception that Canada is indeed suffering from a democratic deficit. What is this thing; what are its symptoms; and what did Jean Chrétien, Paul Martin, and Stephen Harper attempt to do about it? The analysis proceeds in six stages: the first section consists of a discussion of the notion of a democratic deficit, along with a survey of the evidence that Canada suffers from one. The following four sections provide an examination of the initiatives undertaken by the various provincial governments in recent years to reduce the perceived democratic deficit, as well as those implemented by three successive prime ministers — Jean Chrétien, Paul Martin, and Stephen Harper — during their terms in office. A brief conclusion considers the argument made by a number of scholars that low voter turnout is not necessarily such a bad thing, that it may in fact have beneficial consequences for democratic politics (Rodriguez, 2008; Rosema, 2007; Rubenson *et al.*, 2007).

What Is a "Democratic Deficit" ... and Does Canada Have One?

The term "democratic deficit" first entered popular discourse in Western Europe in the late 1970s, as the drive for a unified Europe gathered momentum.[4] Those who were skeptical of the creation of a European "superstate" worried that decision-making authority would inevitably leach away from national governments to the European bureaucracy in Brussels. At the same time, they claimed, the democratic institutions that were being created to represent the interests of Europe's citizens were insufficiently accountable, transparent, and effective. Real power, these "Euroskeptics" argued, resided with the unelected technocrats in the European Commission and, in particular, in the Council of Ministers, which often met in secret. While members of the European

---

3. Martin notes that the "one question that everyone in Ottawa believes has become the key to getting things done [is]: 'Who do you know in the PMO?'" (2002–03: 11).

4. The website of the Jeunes européens fédéralistes (JEF) claims that its manifesto of 1977 marked the first recorded use of the term "democratic deficit." The URL is http://www.federalunion.org.uk/archives/democraticdeficit.shtml.

Figure 11.1 Voter Turnout in Federal Elections, 1945–2008

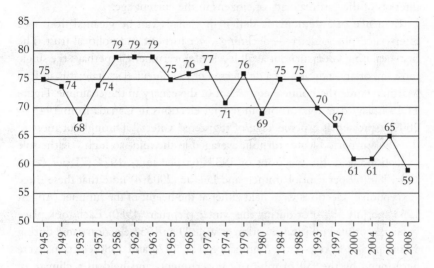

Source: http://www.elections.ca/content.asp?section=pas&document=turnout&lang
=e&textonly=false

Parliament were directly elected (beginning in 1979), European elections tended to be "decentralized, apathetic affairs, in which a relatively small number of voters select among national parties on the basis of national issues," with little discussion of questions directly relevant to Europe as a whole (Morovcsik, n.d.: 2–3). These misgivings about the undemocratic nature of the European Union were, and still are, especially pronounced among the poor, women, the economically marginalized, and those dependent on the welfare state. These groups tend to believe that the European Union (EU) is much more interested in freeing up the market for investors than it is in protecting those harmed by its untrammelled operation, revealing an inherent class bias in the EU's policy outputs (Morovcsik, n.d.: 3).

In recent years, "democratic deficit" has become a favourite buzzword among journalists and scholars alike, and its constant repetition may have debased its meaning somewhat. Nonetheless, the term can be used meta-phorically to describe the perceived loss of control over their own political destinies experienced by many citizens in an age of rapid globalization: "All around the world, citizens are watching power and control shift to points further and further away from their communities; we are all losing the power to plan our economies" (Klein, 2002: 7). There is a widespread sense among voters in the industrialized nations that the traditional mechanisms of rep-resentative democracy — political parties, elections, and territorially based legislatures — are simply not up to the task of articulating or defending the interests of the vast majority of citizens in the current age.

Evidence of a democratic deficit in Canada can be gleaned from two interrelated phenomena — declining voter turnout and political trust. The first, declining voter turnout at all levels of government, is perhaps the single most important indicator of a disaffected or indifferent electorate; it is, in Paul Martin's words, the political equivalent of the canary in the coalmine. Figure 11.1 displays data for turnout in federal elections in Canada from 1945 to 2008, expressed as a percentage of registered voters.[5] Throughout most of the postwar period, voter turnout averaged in the mid- to high 70s; the sole exceptions were the elections of 1953 (68 per cent), 1974 (71 per cent), and 1980 (69 per cent). Pammett and LeDuc (2003: 4) note that these three "exceptional" elections were held either at the height of the summer (August 1953 and July 1974) or during the winter (February 1980). Each took place in an exceptional political situation as well: "The 1953 election came during a long period of one-party dominance. The 1974 and 1980 elections were occasioned by the fall of minority governments and held in a climate of relative public dissatisfaction with politics in general."

Since 1988, however, turnout has declined in almost every successive election: from 70 per cent in 1993, to 67 per cent in 1997, and to a then all-time low of 61 per cent in 2000 and 2004.[6] The 2006 election, in which the Conservative Party succeeded in ousting the Liberals after 13 years in power, witnessed a significant upsurge in voter turnout, to 65 per cent. The competitiveness of this particular election, with the two major parties so evenly matched and the stakes of the outcome so high, was undoubtedly a contributing factor to this increase in turnout. In the 2008 election, however, a number of factors — confusing rules regarding voter identification and the existence of a contingent of demoralized Liberal voters, who could not bring themselves to support Stéphane Dion and his Green Shift program (Heard,

---

5. Voter turnout can be calculated as a percentage of registered voters or of the voting age population (all citizens above the legal voting age). The United States employs voting age population to determine voter turnout, while Canada uses registered voters. The two methods yield quite different results. According to the International Institute for Democracy and Electoral Assistance (International IDEA, 2003), the voting age population figures tend to be more accurate in countries where large numbers of voters are, for whatever reason, left off the register. Blais, Massicotte, and Dobrzynska (2003: 3), however, note that both methods have their biases, since voting age population figures often include people who are not eligible to vote (such as recent immigrants), thus depressing the actual voter turnout figure.

6. As noted above in note 1, however, the figure for 2000 was artificially low, the by-product of problems with the permanent voters' list. Actual turnout in 2000 was closer to 64 per cent.

Table 11.1 Voter Turnout (percentage of registered voters) in Provincial Elections Since 1990

Province	First	Second	Third	Fourth	Most Recent
British Columbia	64 (1991)	59 (1996)	55 (2001)	58 (2005)	53 (2009)
Alberta	60 (1993)	54 (1997)	53 (2001)	45 (2004)	41 (2008)
Saskatchewan	83 (1991)	65 (1995)	66 (1999)	71 (2003)	76 (2007)
Manitoba	69 (1990)	69 (1995)	68 (1999)	54 (2003)	57 (2007)
Ontario	64 (1990)	63 (1995)	58 (1999)	57 (2003)	52 (2007)
Quebec	82 (1994)	78 (1998)	70 (2003)	71 (2007)	57 (2008)
New Brunswick	80 (1991)	75 (1995)	76 (1999)	69 (2003)	68 (2006)
Nova Scotia	75 (1993)	69 (1998)	68 (1999)	66 (2003)	60 (2006)
Prince Edward Island	81 (1993)	86 (1996)	85 (2000)	83 (2003)	84 (2007)
Newfoundland and Labrador	84 (1993)	74 (1996)	70 (1999)	70 (2003)	61 (2007)

Sources:
British Columbia: http://www.elections.bc.ca/index.php/resource-centre/statistics-and-surveys
Alberta: http://www.elections.ab.ca/Public%20Website/files/Reports/Part8.pdf
Saskatchewan: http://www.elections.sk.ca/faq-general.php
Manitoba: http://www.electionsmanitoba.ca ,
Ontario: http://www.elections.on.ca/NR/rdonlyres/686AD8BE-2042-4316-8A64-89B6DB8F47FF/0/StatisticalSummary.pdf
Quebec: http://www.electionsquebec.qc.ca/en/stat_gen.asp
New Brunswick: http://www.gnb.ca/elections/06prov/06provresults-e.asp
Nova Scotia: http://electionsnovascotia.ns.ca/results/Comparative%20Stats%202006.pdf
Prince Edward Island: http://www.electionspei.ca/provincial/historical/ceoreports/turnout/turnout.pdf
Newfoundland and Labrador: http://www.elections.gov.nl.ca/elections/PDF/2007/GeneralElection-October09-Report.pdf

2008) — contributed to the precipitous drop in turnout, to an historic low of 58.8 per cent.

Nine of the ten provinces have also experienced drops in voter turnout since 1990, as Table 11.1 demonstrates. Only Prince Edward Island bucks the trend, experiencing a rise in turnout from 81 per cent in 1993 to 84 per cent in 2007 (after peaking at 86 per cent in 1996). In the most recent election held in each province, turnout has been lower than 60 per cent of registered voters in five of the ten provinces: Alberta (41 per cent in 2008), Ontario (52 per cent in 2007), Manitoba (57 per cent in 2007), Quebec (57 per cent in 2008), and British Columbia (59 per cent in 2009). Nova Scotia (60 per cent in 2006), Newfoundland and Labrador (61 per cent in 2007), and New Brunswick (68 per cent in 2006) had turnouts between 60 and 70 per cent. Only two provinces had comparatively high turnouts: Saskatchewan (76 per cent in 2007) and Prince Edward Island (84 per cent in 2007).

It should be pointed out that Canada is not unique in experiencing a marked drop in voter turnout since the end of the Second World War. In 17 of 19 Organization for Economic Cooperation and Development (OECD) countries recently surveyed by a team of researchers, turnout figures during the last ten years are in most cases substantially lower than those of the early 1950s. In Switzerland, turnout in the two most recent elections before 2000 was 24 percentage points lower than the figure for the first two elections of the 1950s. Comparable declines occurred in New Zealand (18 points), France (13 points), and Austria (12 points). Only Denmark and Sweden resisted this trend: in each, there has been an increase in turnout of 4 percentage points over this period. As Wattenberg observes (2000: 71), "[i]t is rare within comparative politics to find a trend that is so widely generalizable."

Without a doubt the most important factor underlying the decline in electoral participation in Canada (and elsewhere) is the effect of age on a voter's political attitudes and behaviour. As Thomas Axworthy puts it, "turnout has not declined in the electorate as a whole but it has fallen like a stone among Canadians born after 1970" (2003–04: 16). Pammett and LeDuc's study of non-voters in the 2000 federal election demonstrated that Canadians 25 years and under were far less likely to vote than their elders. Only 22 per cent of voters between the ages of 18 and 20, and 28 per cent of those aged 21 to 24, bothered to vote. Voter turnout increased with each successive age cohort: 83 per cent of voters 68 years or older cast a ballot in 2000, as did 80 per cent of those aged 58 to 67.

These findings have been confirmed in a more recent study undertaken by Paul Howe (2007: 10). His data show that habitual non-voters (those who never vote) and intermittent non-voters (those "who vote sometimes but not always") are much more prevalent among the young than any other age cohort in Canada. Howe points out that in the 1974 federal election, "there were very few habitual non-voters in the population as a whole" and "there were no more habitual non-voters among the younger respondents than in older age groups." In the 2004 federal election, by contrast, habitual non-voters constituted almost 16 per cent of the voting population under the age of 30; the percentage of habitual non-voters among the entire population was only 5.4 per cent. Intermittent non-voters were also much more numerous in the under-30 age cohort than in any other age group. Howe concludes that "a considerable change has occurred in the composition of the non-voting population, especially in the younger age groups. Habitual non-voting is more significant nowadays among young people" (2007: 12).

Young voters are not necessarily more cynical about politics than their older counterparts — in fact they are slightly less so (Blais *et al.*, 2002: 54) — but they are markedly less interested in or informed about politics than any previous generation. They are, in the words of Gidengil *et al.*, a "tuned out" generation rather than a "turned off" one (2003: 11; cf. Blais *et al.*, 2002: 57, 61). In addition to their lack of interest in politics generally and in the nuances of particular election campaigns, young voters (aged 18 to 25) are more likely to experience problems with the registration process (getting their names on the permanent voters' list) than any other group of voters, apart from those over 65 years of age. Young voters are also most likely to report that they were simply too busy with work or family or school to get out to the polling station (Pammett and LeDuc, 2003: Table 12). This suggests that a combination of administrative reasons and lack of interest and knowledge about politics prevent young Canadians from voting in higher numbers. The former, at least, might be rectified through the use of new technologies — like the Internet — for registration and voting itself. The latter, however, constitutes a much more intractable problem: strategies for increasing young voters' awareness of and interest in politics include more intensive instruction of civics and government at the high school level, but there is no guarantee that this will make even a dent in the turnout rates among youth (see the discussion in Pammett and LeDuc, 2003: 52–59).

It could plausibly be argued that the sharp drops in political participation among young voters are simply the product of the "life cycle," since young voters of every previous generation have been less politically active than their elders. But as Gidengil *et al.* point out, the decline in voting among voters under 30 years of age is in fact a generational phenomenon: "There is something about this generation of young Canadians that makes them less likely to vote than their parents or their grandparents were when they were in their twenties" (2003: 9–10).[7] There is absolutely no reason to suggest that these trends towards increasing political disengagement among the young will be reversed or halted at any time in the near future, and thus turnout rates are likely to decline even further in upcoming elections.

---

7. The authors go on to note that turnout "was 10 points higher among those born in the 1960s when they were young and 20 points higher among baby boomers when they were the same age…. Turnout has held more or less steady for the three older generations; it is only among the young that voting has decreased" (Gidengil *et al.*, 2003: 10).

Figure 11.2 Voter Disaffection in Canada, 1968-2006

1. "Quite a few of the people running the government are a little crooked."

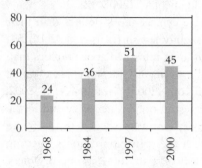

2. "People in the government waste a lot of the money we pay in taxes."

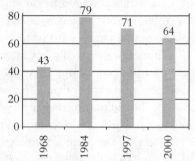

3. "I do not think that the government cares much what people like me think."

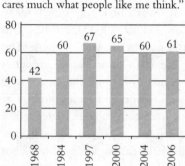

4. "People like me don't have any say in what the government does."

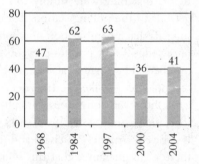

The second trend considered by many observers to be additional evidence of a growing democratic deficit in the industrialized democracies is to be found in the declining levels of political trust among most voters. In their important study of non-voters in Canada, Pammett and LeDuc (2003: 7) note that an overwhelming majority of Canadians — almost 70 per cent — cite "negative public attitudes toward the performance of … politicians and political institutions" as the principal factor underlying declining voter turnout in the country.[8] Politicians have become a lightning rod for voter discontent in Canada, as they have elsewhere in the industrialized democracies. Pammett and LeDuc remark that there "is a widespread perception that politicians are untrustworthy, selfish, unaccountable, lack credibility, are not true to their word, etc" (2003: 7).

---

8. Pammett and LeDuc (2003: 1) base their study on a survey conducted by Decima Research in 2002. Short screening interviews were held with 5,637 Canadians, followed by longer interviews with 960 reported voters and 960 reported non-voters in the 2000 general election.

Figure 11.2 (continued)

5. "Generally, those elected to Parliament soon lose touch with the people."

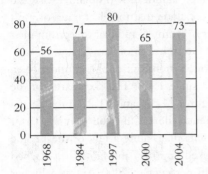

6. "Politics and government seem so complicated that a person like me can't understand what's going on."

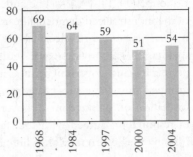

Source: These data are drawn from the Canadian National Election Studies and were made available by the Institute for Social Research at York University in Toronto. The author wishes to thank the Laurier Institute for the Study of Public Opinion and Policy (LISPOP) and Greg Whitfield of Wilfrid Laurier University for their assistance in retrieving the data.

Note: Not all six questions were included in every election study conducted since 1965. Question wordings varied slightly over time, as did the response categories for questions: in 1968, respondents were given only two options (agree/disagree), while after 1984 there were four categories (strongly agree, agree, disagree, strongly disagree). For 1984, 1997, and 2000, 2004, and 2006 the strongly agree and agree categories have been collapsed into one. Those with no opinion or who refused to answer the question have been included in the calculation of percentages. It should be noted that the 1968 survey did not contact voters under the age of 21. All of these qualifications suggest that the data must be interpreted cautiously.

This public mistrust of politicians and government has been growing stronger over the past three decades or so, not only in Canada but in most of the established democracies. A recent analysis of survey data from about 20 of the so-called Trilateral democracies[9] concluded that between the mid-1970s and the present there has been a steady decline in public confidence in politicians in 12 out of 13 countries for which data are available; a similar decline

---

9. The Trilateral countries include those of North America, Western Europe, and Japan. The Trilateral Commission, an influential private think-tank founded in 1973 to foster cooperation among the three major democratic industrialized areas of the world on common problems facing them, issued a report on "governability" entitled *The Crisis of Democracy* (Crozier, Huntington, and Watanuki, 1975). The volume of essays edited by Pharr and Putnam was published to commemorate the twenty-fifth anniversary of the publication of this earlier Trilateral Commission study.

in confidence in legislatures has occurred in 11 out of the 14 countries. Over the same period, membership in political parties in most of these countries has plummeted, and the percentage of citizens expressing a partisan attachment (party identification) has also declined significantly (Putnam, Pharr, and Dalton, 2000: 14, 17, 19). The authors conclude that the electorates of most of the industrialized democracies are very "grumpy," and that this grumpiness is clearly a cause for concern about the future health of democracy.

Figure 11.2 provides some indication of trends in public confidence in politicians and government in Canada since 1968. The six charts can be grouped into three sub-categories. Figures 11.2.1 and 11.2.2 provide information on public trust of government: whereas in 1968 only a quarter of respondents agreed with the statement that "quite a few of the people running the government are a little crooked," by 1997 this figure had reached 51 per cent, dipping only slightly to 45 per cent in 2000. An even higher percentage of voters believe that the government wastes "a lot" of tax money: 43 per cent of respondents were in agreement with this statement in 1968, increasing to 79 per cent in 1984, and dropping a bit in 1997 (71 per cent agreement) and 2000 (64 per cent).

Figures 11.2.3, 11.2.4, and 11.2.5 are all indicators of government responsiveness; all three are generally included together as key components of *political efficacy* — the "feeling that individual political action does have, or can have, an impact on the political process" (Campbell, Gurin, and Miller, 1954: 187, cited in Craig, Niemi, and Silver, 1990: 290). The data indicate that in 2000 almost two-thirds of voters agreed that government does not care much what people like them think, up from 42 per cent in 1968. This figure dropped slightly, to 60 and 61 per cent, in the 2004 and 2006 elections, respectively. Just over 60 per cent of voters in 1984 and 1997 agreed that they did not have any say in what the government does," up from 47 per cent in 1968. This figure plunged to 36 per cent in 2000, and rose slightly to 41 per cent in 2004. Almost three-quarters (73 per cent) of voters in 2004 agreed with the statement that "those elected to Parliament soon lose touch with the people"; this figure was down from a high of 80 per cent in 1997, but up from 56 per cent in 1968 and 65 per cent in 2000. Finally, Figure 11.2.6 shows that only about half of respondents (54 per cent in 2004) agree with the statement that "politics and government seem so complicated that a person like me can't understand what's going on," down substantially from 69 per cent in 1968. This item, which is also usually included as one of the components of political efficacy, indicates that a growing number of citizens feel sufficiently knowledgeable to understand the worlds of politics and government; this clearly reflects the higher levels of education of today's voters as compared to those of the 1960s and 1970s. Combining these results with the data in Figure 11.2.4, we might conclude that Canadian citizens feel fairly positive about their own role in the political system but are highly skeptical about the responsiveness of the political actors who represent them.

This overview of recent research on voter attitudes and behaviour, both in Canada and in the other industrialized democracies, suggests that while there is evidence of a serious democratic *malaise* in most of these countries, this does not mean that a crisis of democracy currently afflicts the West. When the Trilateral Commission published *The Crisis of Democracy* in 1975, in the immediate aftermath of the first OPEC crisis and its attendant economic dislocation, it could plausibly be argued that the future of liberal democracy itself was in peril. Conservatives, like the members of the Trilateral Commission, agreed with Marxists such as James O'Connor (1973) and Erik Olin Wright (1978) on this pessimistic prognosis. Yet today the commitment to the *ideal* of democracy appears to be more widespread and more intense than ever before (Putnam, Pharr, and Dalton, 2000: 7). Approximately 70 per cent of Canadians in 2000 expressed satisfaction with "the way democracy works in Canada" (Howe and Northrup, 2000: 6). In the 2006 Canadian National Election Survey, 59 per cent of respondents indicated that they were very or fairly satisfied with the way democracy works in Canada.[10] This indicates that the vast majority of Canadians are devoted to the democratic ethos, but at the same time they are quite critical of the operation of most of the traditional institutions of representative government — political parties, elections, and legislatures. A distressingly high proportion of voters in the industrialized democracies simply feel that their representatives are not listening to them. It is in this sense that Canada can be said to suffer from a *democratic deficit*.

Moreover, the fact that so many countries — with vastly different constitutional orders and electoral systems — are exhibiting symptoms of a democratic malaise should convince us that there is no simple institutional "fix" that will revitalize democratic politics, in this country or elsewhere. Nevitte has theorized that shifting public attitudes towards representative democracy are part of a larger, "possibly generationally driven, public reaction against *all* hierarchical institutional arrangements that limit the opportunities for meaningful citizen participation" (1996: 62; emphasis in the original). The following sections of the chapter will provide an overview of the efforts made by provincial and federal governments to reform Canada's representative institutions.

---

10. See Figure 11.2 for the sources of this data.

Addressing the Democratic Deficit at the Provincial Level

In a number of provinces in Canada, the political class's concern with the democratic deficit led to a spate of reform initiatives in the early part of the twenty-first century. In March 2003 the Quebec government's Estates-General on the Reform of Democratic Institutions (better known as the Béland Commission) issued a report in which the democratic deficit was highlighted as a prominent theme. Over the course of its public consultations, the Béland Commission encountered numerous citizens who registered a number of complaints about existing democratic institutions:

- that they seem to lack real power;
- that decision-making authority is centralized in the hands of the political executive (and in Canada that means party leaders and their entourages);
- that excessive party discipline emasculates elected representatives;
- that women, ethnic minorities, and Aboriginal peoples continue to be under-represented in the legislature and other government bodies (Quebec, Comité directeur des États-généraux sur la réforme des institutions démocratiques, 2003: 22–23).

The Commission made a number of far-reaching recommendations to improve democratic performance in the province, among them the adoption of a new electoral system based on regional proportional representation, fixed dates for elections, a law permitting citizen initiatives, and direct election of the head of government. To date, none of these recommendations has made its way into legislation.

In British Columbia, the Liberal government of Gordon Campbell adopted a law setting a fixed date for provincial elections, which are now held every four years on the second Tuesday in May. It also created an independent Citizens' Assembly consisting of individuals drawn randomly from the provincial voters' list (two from each of the 79 constituencies) and charged it with reviewing the strengths and weaknesses of the existing first-past-the-post (FPTP) electoral system (Gibson, 2002; Ruff, 2003). In November 2004 the Assembly recommended that the province adopt a version of the single transferable vote, which it named BC-STV, a type of proportional electoral system similar to the one employed in Ireland and Malta. This option was put to voters in a referendum held concurrently with the provincial election in May 2005. In order for the referendum to be binding, a "supermajority" was required: at least 60 per cent of those casting ballots and at least 50 per cent of voters in 60 per cent of the province's ridings (48 out of 79) had to vote "Yes." While the referendum easily cleared the second hurdle, garnering more than 50 per cent of the vote in 77 of the province's 79 ridings, it failed to pass the first threshold; 57.7 per cent of voters cast a ballot for the BC-STV electoral system (Elections BC, 2005: 9). The Campbell government, which won a second consecutive majority, pledged to hold another referendum on electoral reform — with the same requirements for a supermajority — at the next provincial election on May 12, 2009 (Stephenson and Tanguay, forthcoming; Tanguay, 2007: 478, 483). In the event, the Campbell government was returned to power, but support for electoral system reform fell sharply to 39 per cent with a majority in favour of reform in only seven ridings (Elections BC).

In Ontario, the Liberal government of Dalton McGuinty established a Democratic Renewal Secretariat during its first mandate that sought "to reach out to Ontarians and engage them in the most ambitious democratic renewal process in Ontario history, including fixed election dates, new ways to engage young people and innovative tools that could include Internet and telephone voting" (Ontario, Ministry of the Attorney General/Democratic Renewal Secretariat, 2003). The McGuinty government passed legislation to establish fixed dates for elections in the province, which are now held every four years, starting in 2007, on the first Thursday in October (Ontario, Office of the Premier, 2004; Stephenson and Tanguay, forthcoming). It also implemented measures to make voting more convenient, increasing the number of advance polling days from six to 13 and modernizing the ballot paper by including party labels for the first time. Finally, in early 2006, the government created a Citizens' Assembly consisting of 103 randomly selected individuals, one from each of the provincial constituencies. Fifty-two of the members were female, and 51 were male. The appointed Chair — George Thomson, a former provincial court judge and deputy minister in both the Ontario and federal governments — brought the total membership of the Ontario Citizens' Assembly to 104. After studying the merits and drawbacks of the various electoral systems in use around the world, the Citizens' Assembly recommended that the province's existing single-member simple plurality, or FPTP, be replaced by a Mixed Member Proportional (MMP) system similar to those found in Germany and New Zealand.

A referendum was held concurrently with the provincial election in Ontario in October 2007. Voters were asked whether they wished to adopt the MMP system or to retain the existing FPTP system. In order to be binding, the referendum required a supermajority of voters: 60 per cent of those casting ballots and at least 50 per cent of those voting in 60 per cent of the province's ridings (64 out of 107) had to endorse MMP. In the end, the outcome was not even close: 63 per cent of the voters in the province were in favour of retaining FPTP and only 37 per cent endorsed MMP. A majority of voters supported MMP in only five of the province's ridings, all of them in the City of Toronto.[11]

In New Brunswick, Premier Bernard Lord fulfilled one of his election promises by establishing a Commission on Legislative Democracy, whose mandate was to "examine and make recommendations on strengthening and modernizing New Brunswick's electoral system and democratic institutions and practices to make them more fair, open, accountable and accessible to New Brunswickers" (New Brunswick, 2003). The Commission submitted its final report on December 31, 2004. It proposed the creation of a regional MMP electoral system, in which 36 members would be elected in single-member constituencies by a simple plurality of votes and the remaining 20 would be selected from party lists in four regional districts of approximately equal size, based on each party's share of the provincial vote. Voters would cast two ballots — one for their preferred candidate in their riding, the other for one of the parties — and there was to have been a 5 per cent threshold that a party needed to reach before it would be eligible to win any list seats (New Brunswick, Commission on Legislative Democracy, 2004: 17–18).

The Progressive Conservative government responded to the Commission report by promising to hold a binding referendum on electoral reform on May 12, 2008. Bernard Lord lost his razor-thin (one-seat) majority in 2006, however, and a provincial election was called for September 18 of that year. Shawn Graham's Liberal Party won a narrow, three-seat majority in that election, but ironically came in second in the popular vote, thereby illustrating one of the principal defects of the FPTP system (the election of so-called wrong winners). The newly installed Liberal government issued its own response to the Commission on Legislative Democracy report, in which it promised to implement fixed election dates and allow for online registration in order to increase voter turnout. On the subject of electoral reform, the government pledged to conduct a "thorough review" of existing initiatives in other provinces, with a view to improving the operation of New Brunswick's system of voting. It explicitly rejected the recommendation to hold a binding referendum on MMP (New Brunswick, Executive Council Office, 2007; Stephenson and Tanguay, forthcoming).

Finally, the government of Pat Binns in Prince Edward Island set up a one-man Commission on Electoral Reform under the Honourable Norman Carruthers, which issued its final report in December 2003. Carruthers also recommended the adoption of a MMP electoral system, in which two-thirds (21) of the members of the provincial assembly would be elected in

---

11. See Stephenson and Tanguay (forthcoming) for a discussion and analysis of the referendum outcome.

constituencies by means of the existing simple plurality electoral system, and the remaining one-third (ten) would be drawn from party lists, based on party shares of the provincial vote (Prince Edward Island, Commissioner of Electoral Reform, 2003: ch. 9). A five-person Commission on Prince Edward Island's Electoral Future was created in February 2005 and charged with designing a plebiscite question and conducting a public education campaign on the issue. On November 28, 2005, an overwhelming majority of the province's voters — 63 per cent of those who cast ballots[12] — opted to retain FPTP. Some observers have argued that this apparently decisive result might not represent the final word on electoral reform in Prince Edward Island, since advocates of MMP can plausibly argue that "a lack of public education and a lack of funding for Elections PEI resulted in … relatively low voter turnout" in a province renowned for high turnout (Canada, Library of Parliament, 2007: 9).

At the provincial level, then, concern with the democratic deficit has produced a flurry of investigations and studies, especially of such measures as on-line voting, which *might* encourage more young people to vote. It also has led to some not insignificant legislative changes, especially the adoption of fixed election dates in a number of provinces. The latter are seen as a possible means of lessening voter cynicism, because many voters and pundits are convinced that governments in a Westminster-style system play with the timing of the dissolution of Parliament or the legislature in order to extract maximum partisan advantage from incumbency. However, far-reaching reforms, such as a switch to MMP or STV electoral systems, have not yet been adopted by any province. Voters in Ontario, Prince Edward Island, and most recently British Columbia massively rejected electoral reform proposals put to them in referendums. This appears to lend support to the findings of Johnston, Krahn, and Harrison (2006: 178), who in their study of Alberta voters concluded that "concerns over the health of democracy are much more immediately rooted in a widespread general distrust in government as being too powerful and secretive than in concerns about the inadequacy of political institutions."

The next sections of the chapter discuss the initiatives undertaken (or not, as the case may be) by Prime Ministers Chrétien, Martin, and Harper in order to address the democratic deficit at the federal level.

---

12. Elections PEI (2005) noted that no official count of electors was available for the plebiscite, since no enumeration was conducted: "An *approximate* idea of voter turnout can be calculated using the 2003 Provincial General Election figure of 97,180 eligible electors." A total of 32,265 voters cast ballots in the plebiscite, putting the unofficial turnout at a meagre 33.2 per cent.

Jean Chrétien and the Democratic Deficit: "What, Me Worry?"

During his ten years as prime minister, Jean Chrétien gave few indications that he thought the modernization and revitalization of the structures of representative democracy were urgent priorities for his government. Chrétien was a reactive rather than an innovative leader, content to work within the institutions and mores of political life as he had found them when he assumed office. It was only when Paul Martin's accession to the leadership of the Liberal Party became inevitable that Chrétien began to think about his legacy as prime minister and focus on restoring public confidence in representative government. His hand was also forced by Auditor General Sheila Fraser's report in the spring of 2002, which first raised concern about questionable spending under the sponsorship program, and by a number of other comparatively minor scandals at this time.[13]

On June 11, 2002, Chrétien outlined an eight-point action plan on ethics in government in a speech in the House of Commons (Canada, House of Commons, 2003: 2849). Along with proposed guidelines for fundraising by Cabinet ministers and new rules governing relations between ministers and Crown corporations, a key item in this Action Plan was a proposed overhaul of the Canada Elections Act in order to ban contributions by corporations and trade unions to political parties. Chrétien's intention was to restore the public's faith in the democratic system, which was being eroded by the perception — rooted in ignorance, in the view of many Liberal MPs — that large contributions to political parties by their friends in the corporate sector were buying access to government decision-makers and favourable policies.

Chrétien's proposals sparked a storm of controversy within his own party.[14] The most vocal opponents of the proposal tended to be supporters of Paul Martin, who himself stated publicly that he was not in favour of the idea — not surprisingly, since he was in the process of amassing a war chest of almost $11 million to bankroll his bid for the leadership of the Liberal Party, much of it from his allies in the corporate sector (Francoli, 2003a; Persichilli, 2003).

---

13. Art Eggleton was forced to resign as Minister of Defence in May 2002, and Don Boudria was demoted as the result of improprieties — Eggleton for awarding a research contract to a former girlfriend in violation of the government's guidelines on conflict of interest, and Boudria for having taken a free family vacation at the summer home of the president of a Montreal public relations firm that had received millions of dollars in contracts under the sponsorship program. These and other scandals are itemized in Martin, 2003: 358–63.

14. Stephen LeDrew, the party president, remarked that whoever had come up with the idea of banning corporate political contributions was "dumb as a bag of hammers" (quoted in Francoli, 2003b).

Chrétien mused publicly about calling a snap election if his caucus refused to fall in line. Reluctantly, most of the rebels eventually did just that.

Bill C-24, "An Act to Amend the Canada Elections Act and the Income Tax Act (Political Financing)," was tabled in the House of Commons on January 29, 2003, and received royal assent on June 19 of that year. The legislation was modelled after similar laws adopted by the Parti Québécois government in Quebec (1977) and by the NDP government in Manitoba (2000). At the time of its introduction, Don Boudria, House Leader, claimed that the proposed law would enhance "the fairness and transparency of our political system by ensuring that full disclosure of contributions and financial controls would apply to all political participants.... Together these reforms [will] increase the confidence of Canadians in our electoral system" (Canada, House of Commons, 2003: 2849). The bill represented the most significant reform of Canada's election finance laws since the 1974 Election Expenses Act established the existing regime of party finance, one based on spending limits for candidates and parties, disclosure of campaign expenses and contributions, and partial public reimbursement of election expenditures (Canada, Library of Parliament, Parliamentary Research Branch, 2003: 1–2).

The principal provisions of Bill C-24 were as follows:

- with some minor exceptions, only individual voters may contribute to political parties, candidates, riding associations, or candidates for a party's leadership;
- individual contributions may total $5,000 a year to *each* party and its candidates;
- unions, professional associations, and corporations may contribute up to $1,000 per year to a party or its candidates;
- riding associations, now called *electoral district associations*, must now register with Elections Canada, and candidates for nomination in any riding will be subject to spending limits (up to 20 per cent of the amount to which the candidate in that riding was entitled during the previous election);
- candidates for nomination must disclose their contributions;
- candidates for the leadership of a party will have to report the source of their contributions and their expenses; they will be able to "take advantage of a separate annual contribution limit of $5,000 per individual ... No limits are imposed on the costs of leadership campaigns" (Canada, Library of Parliament, Parliamentary Research Branch, 2003: 13);
- rates of reimbursement of election expenses for registered political parties are to be raised from 22.5 per cent of expenses to 60 per cent;

- individual candidates will qualify for reimbursement of 50 per cent of their election expenses if they win at least 10 per cent of the vote in a riding, down from 15 per cent previously;
- registered political parties will receive an annual allowance equal to $1.75 per vote received by the party in the previous election, provided they obtained at least 2 per cent of the national vote in the previous election or 5 per cent of the vote in those ridings where they presented candidates;
- tax credits for individual political donations will be increased — the amount eligible for a 75 per cent reimbursement will increase from $200 to $400 — up to a maximum credit of $650 for donations of $1,275 or more.

This legislation introduced significant — and controversial — reforms to Canada's election finance regime. Unlike the 1974 Election Finances Act, which focused on regulating party and candidate expenditures, Bill C-24 "is largely concerned with restrictions on contributions" (Canada, Library of Parliament, Parliamentary Research Branch, 2003: 10). For the first time, constituency associations and leadership campaigns were brought under the regulatory ambit of Elections Canada. The law should succeed in enhancing the transparency and fairness of election contests, which are its principal objectives, and this *might* help to restore public confidence in our political institutions, although there is no guarantee of this.

While the new law was a marked improvement over previous legislation, Bill C-24 was not without its flaws. Probably the most controversial provision in the legislation was the one concerning annual public subsidies of registered political parties. The law set the subsidy at $1.75 per vote received by the party in the previous election. In the original draft of the legislation, the subsidy was set at $1.50 per vote, but the figure was raised after a number of Liberal backbenchers complained bitterly in committee hearings about being starved for funds in future election campaigns. Many observers believe, however, that the original $1.50 per vote subsidy was already more than generous; $1.75 per vote will provide the parties with far more money than they used to obtain from corporate or trade union donations. The rich get richer under this regulatory scheme, although small parties can make significant gains as well. Aaron Freeman, one of the founders of the advocacy group Democracy Watch, notes that the Green Party in particular should benefit under the new regime: "[W]ith the new law, a vote for a party that has no chance of electing an MP will suddenly become meaningful, as that vote will help direct publicly-financed dollars to the party" (2003). With just under 7 per cent of the popular vote in the 2008 federal election, the Green Party received a public subsidy of $1.29 million, which compares rather favourably to "the paltry $82,000 they received in small donations in the 2000 election year" (Freeman, 2003).[15]

Combined with other more generous reimbursements of campaign expenditures included in the law, Bill C-24's overall effect on the public purse will likely be in the neighbourhood of $35 to $40 million annually. While it can be argued that $40 million a year is a relatively small price to pay for a more transparent and equitable system of financing parties, these large state subsidies come at a time when public attitudes towards political parties are corrosively hostile. There is potentially a more fundamental problem with state funding of political parties, however, beyond the fact that a cynical electorate might view it as another instance of the political class helping itself to a bigger share of the taxpayer-generated revenue pie. In debates on the second reading of Bill C-24, Clifford Lincoln, a Liberal MP from Quebec and former member of the provincial Liberal Cabinet of Robert Bourassa, remarked that one of the positive features of Quebec's party finance law was that it

> made it possible to get additional funding directly to the political parties [and] allowed the parties to worry less about funding and focus more on policy, research, and groundwork with the voters. In fact, the party I belonged to had hundreds of thousands of members. It was always a lively and dynamic membership. There was no link between the legislation and decreased support in the party. On the contrary, it stimulated support within the party (Canada, House of Commons, 2003: 3485).

This may well have been true during the first 15 years or so in which the legislation was in effect. The need to solicit numerous small donations from individual voters to replace corporate and trade union funding forced both major parties to attend to their grassroots, and the Liberals eventually became something of a mass party, just like their competitor, the Parti Québécois. State funding served as a kind of emergency reserve for the parties, providing them with the necessary resources to fulfill their policy development and education functions between elections more successfully than many or even most other provincial political parties. Over time, however, there has been growing concern that state funding is crowding out individual contributions as the main source of party revenue: the three main provincial parties

---

15. Data on the amount of the subsidies received by each eligible party are available from the Elections Canada website.

in Quebec may have become addicted to state funds, robbing them of the ability to reach into and communicate with civil society.[16]

The risk with legislation like Bill C-24, then, is that over time party memberships will decline even more dramatically, the parties themselves will become professional machines and wards of the state, and the gap between the electorate and their representatives will widen. It is worth noting that Young, Sayers, and Jansen (2007: 352), in their assessment of the federal party financing legislation, conclude that "there is little evidence to suggest that state funding has liberated the parties to engage in more meaningful ways with the electorate. Parties have not taken on a more prominent role in policy development, mobilization of citizens, or public education with their new funds." Canada's parties continue in the main to be vote-harvesting machines.

Other elements of Jean Chrétien's record as prime minister are less positive from the standpoint of enhancing democracy. In particular, his iron-fisted control of caucus and his attitudes towards patronage came in for considerable criticism within his own party (Martin, 2003: 237–40, 348–63). One of the things that made Paul Martin so attractive to dissident Liberal MPs was his promise to do politics differently as prime minister and to change the political culture in Ottawa. In the next section we briefly examine Martin's proposals to make democracy work better.

Paul Martin: Democratic Deficit Slayer?

As noted earlier, Paul Martin sought to portray himself as a politician committed to taming the democratic deficit, much as he was the principal architect, as Finance Minister from 1993 to 2002, of the policies that eliminated Canada's fiscal deficit (Axworthy, 2003-04: 15,19). After becoming prime minister, Martin appointed a Minister Responsible for Democratic Reform, Jacques Saada. His government enacted an "Action Plan for Democratic Reform" in early February 2004 that was intended to reconnect Parliament to Canadian citizens and to restore the ability of individual MPs to shape government decision-making (Canada, Privy Council Office, 2004: ii). Contending that "[d]emocracy is an active process — one that requires ongoing engagement between citizens and their elected representatives," the action plan proposed "a fundamental change in parliamentary culture, a rebalancing of the relationship between the Cabinet and the House" (Canada, Privy Council Office, 2004: 1, vi). Its principal recommendations were as follows:

---

16. See the discussion of Quebec's party finance legislation and its effects in Tanguay, 2004: 237-38.

- "The creation of an independent Ethics Commissioner and a Senate Ethics Officer reporting to their respective Chambers" (3).
- Much greater freedom for MPs to voice their opinions, mainly by distinguishing between *one-line free votes* on issues where members are free to vote their conscience and *two-line free votes* on which "the government will take a position and recommend a preferred outcome to its caucus." Parliamentary secretaries and Cabinet ministers will be bound to support the government's position in two-line votes, but caucus members will be "free to vote as they wish." Only *three-line votes* will be considered votes of confidence, and the action plan states that these will be few in number: "Most votes will be either two-line or one-line free votes, and Ministers will be unable to take approval for granted. Achieving parliamentary consent will be an exercise in coalition building, and Ministers must earn the support of Members through hard work and active engagement" (4).
- "Bills subject to two-line and one-line free votes will be routinely referred to Committee before second reading so that MPs have a greater capacity to shape and influence legislation" (5).
- In order to promote the independence of parliamentary committees, their chairs will be elected by secret ballot (7).
- Appointments to "certain key agencies, including heads of Crown Corporations and agencies, should be subject to prior parliamentary review" (12). This process should extend to nominations to the Supreme Court of Canada, although the government will consult with the appropriate parliamentary committees in order to determine the best way of implementing this procedure in this sensitive case.

The Action Plan concluded by stating that, if adopted, these measures would "greatly empower Members of Parliament to more effectively do the jobs they were elected to do. This will ensure that Parliament will once again be the place where the great debates of the nation occur" (15).

Predictably, the opposition parties castigated these proposals as inadequate or mere window-dressing (proving once again that "the perfect is the enemy of the good"). This kind of Pavlovian response on the part of the opposition parties is precisely one of the aspects of the existing parliamentary culture that Martin said he was attempting to eradicate. This proved to be no easy task, however, and there were signs within the Liberal caucus of a brewing power struggle over what should constitute a vote of confidence. For instance, the minister in charge of the controversial gun registry disagreed with his parliamentary secretary on whether a vote to extend the program would be a three-line vote or a free vote.

Thomas Axworthy, former principal secretary to Prime Minister Pierre Trudeau, argued that the democratic deficit ought to be "Paul Martin's next big idea." He asserted that "[d]emocratic accountability could do for Paul Martin what the Just Society did for Pierre Trudeau: give his government an easily understood conceptual framework" (Axworthy, 2003–04: 19). One could argue, of course, that the Democratic Deficit ended up being for Martin precisely what the Just Society was for Pierre Trudeau: a catchy slogan, but one that was thin on substance. Martin created enormous expectations, both within his party and in the broader electorate, about his ability to enact *real* change and to constitute a *real* alternative to his predecessor. That he failed to live up to these expectations, and was in part punished by the voters for this failure in the 2006 general election, should come as no real surprise.

Stephen Harper: Democratic Reform in the Service of Partisan Advantage

In its first Speech from the Throne in April 2006, the Conservative government of Stephen Harper pledged to make government accountable to its citizens in a way that previous administrations had failed to accomplish in order to remove the stain of the so-called Sponsorship Scandal, or Adscam. To fulfill this promise, the government passed Bill C-2, The Federal Accountability Act, in the fall of 2006. Among the provisions of this omnibus legislation were revisions to the Canada Elections Act that went further than Bill C-24 by banning all corporate and trade union contributions to parties and candidates and limiting individual contributions to parties, candidates, leadership candidates, or electoral district associations to $1,000 annually in each case.[17] The law also banned "secret donations" to political candidates (gifts that might be perceived as influencing them), strengthened the role of the federal Ethics Commissioner, and toughened the Lobbyist Registration Act by, among other things, creating "an independent Commissioner of Lobbying with a strong mandate to investigate violations under the new *Lobbying Act* and *Lobbyists' Code of Conduct*" (Canada, Treasury Board Secretariat, 2006).

The Harper government also pledged in its initial Speech from the Throne to "involve parliamentarians and citizens in examining the challenges facing Canada's electoral system and democratic institutions. At the same time, [the government] will explore means to ensure that the Senate better reflects both the democratic values of Canadians and the needs of Canada's regions" (Canada, Office of the Prime Minister, 2006). The government hired the

---

17. This figure was indexed to inflation and rose to $1,100 in 2007. See Canada, Library of Parliament, 2008: 3.

polling firm Compas Inc. and the Frontier Centre for Public Policy to hold 12 citizens' forums — one in each of the provinces, one in the territories, and one for youth — between March and May 2007. Participants were asked to provide their views on five interrelated themes: the role of the citizen in a democracy, the role of the House of Commons, the role of the Senate, the role of political parties, and the desirability of electoral reform (Canada, Minister of State for Democratic Reform, 2007). The authors of the report noted that the project was commissioned in part to respond to what the government perceived to be "moderate discontent with the operation of Canada's democratic institutions and moderate concern about the public's gradual disengagement from the democratic process" — precisely the themes that have served as the backdrop to this analysis (Compas, 2007: 9). Among its principal findings were:

- that governments do not consult citizens regularly or, if they do, the consultation is often "not genuine" (Compas, 2007: 4);
- that stronger civics education for youth might remedy some of the democratic malaise;
- that Canadians lack knowledge of the ways in which the House of Commons and Senate operate;
- that an overwhelming majority of Canadians (79 per cent) favour an elected Senate (Compas, 2007: 6);
- that parties are "not interested in recruiting members or hearing from ordinary citizens, not good at communicating, not accountable, somewhat secretive, and not sufficiently honest in their communications, promises and platforms" (Compas, 2007: 6–7); and
- that the "ideal electoral system should above all produce clear winners" (Compas, 2007: 7-8).

To date, the Harper government has made very little effort to address any of the themes explored in the citizens' forums. In fact, many observers have been struck by Harper's willingness to sacrifice his nominal commitment to strengthening representative democracy to the dictates of political expediency. An elected and effective Senate had been a cherished plank in the platform of the Reform Party (under whose banner Harper was originally elected), yet one of Harper's first acts as prime minister was to appoint Michael Fortier to the Senate so that he could serve as Minister of Public Works and political lieutenant for Quebec. In December 2008 Harper announced that he would appoint 18 new senators with Conservative Party credentials to the upper chamber, a move that was denounced by one NDP MP as "a hog-troughing orgy" and was characterized by some observers as being at the very least contradictory to the Conservative Party platform on Senate reform (CTV. ca, 2008). On this and other matters of democratic reform — such as a commitment to fixed election dates[18] — Harper has proven to be a political pragmatist (some uncharitable critics might say opportunist) rather than a principled visionary. In other words, he has proven to be much more of a Tory than a Reformer, at least when the survival of his government is at stake.[19]

Conclusion

This chapter has reviewed the evidence that Canada is suffering from a "democratic deficit." Even if this term has been cheapened through overuse, it does seem to apply to the current state of affairs in Canada, where voters stay home in droves, seem less interested or engaged in politics than previously, and are reflexively hostile towards the political class and traditional political institutions like Parliament and parties. Young voters in particular appear to be "tuned out," and political elites are scrambling to find ways to get them interested in politics. Canada is by no means unique in this regard, since almost all of the industrialized democracies are experiencing similar trends. This indicates that the symptoms of democratic malaise in the West are likely the product of long-term generational shifts in attitudes towards politics and all structures of authority.

Some observers have argued that the present levels of political disengagement in Canada and the other established democracies might not be such a bad thing after all. Harking back to one of the classics of voting research — *Voting*, written by Bernard Berelson, Paul Lazarsfeld, and William McPhee, and first published in 1954 — journalist Gregory Rodriguez of the *Los Angeles Times* contends that widespread apathy might be *functional* for the system as a whole: "[A] healthy democracy needs the uncommitted middle, the fence straddlers and the apathetic as much as the firebrand activists. Indeed, in a nation so torn by the passions of partisans, it is those of us who aren't all that enamoured of either side who give politicians the room to compromise, which ... is the art that politics is supposed to be all about" (2008). The alternative viewpoint is that politicians in the established democracies have been given *too much leeway* by a disengaged and apathetic electorate. Low levels of political participation threaten to destroy the feedback loop whereby informed citizens hold their representatives accountable. Widespread lack of

---

18. A commitment that Harper managed to circumvent when manoeuvring for a dissolution of Parliament in 2008.

19. An observation made by Rob Leone, Department of Political Science, Wilfrid Laurier University. Personal communication with the author.

citizen involvement in elections means that what is rightly regarded as the centrepiece of the democratic experience has little chance of educating or informing voters, as lofty and utopian an ideal as that may seem.

References and Suggested Readings

Axworthy, Thomas S. 2003-04. "The Democratic Deficit: Should This Be Paul Martin's Next Big Idea?" *Policy Options* 25, 1 (December-January): 15–19.

Bakvis, Herman. 2000–01. "Prime Minister and Cabinet in Canada: An Autocracy in Need of Reform?" *Journal of Canadian Studies* 35, 4 (Winter): 60–79.

Blais, André, Elisabeth Gidengil, Richard Nadeau, and Neil Nevitte. 2002. *Anatomy of a Liberal Victory: Making Sense of the Vote in the 2000 Canadian Federal Election.* Peterborough: Broadview Press.

Blais, André, Louis Massicotte, and Agnieszka Dobrzynska. 2003. "Why is Turnout Higher in Some Countries than in Others?" Elections Canada. March. http://www.elections.ca.

Campbell, Angus, Gerald Gurin, and Warren E. Miller. 1954. *The Voter Decides.* Evanston: Row, Peterson.

Canada. House of Commons. 2003. *Debates.* 37th Parliament, 2nd Session. January–June.

Canada. Library of Parliament. Law and Government Branch. 2008. *Political Financing,* Sebastian Spano. Cat. PRB 07-50E.

Canada. Library of Parliament. Parliamentary Information and Research Service. 2007. *Electoral Reform Initiatives in Canadian Provinces,* Andre Barnes and James R. Robertson. Cat. PRB 04-17E.

Canada. Library of Parliament. Parliamentary Research Branch. 2003. *Bill C-24: An Act to Amend the Canada Elections Act and the Income Tax Act Political Financing — Legislative Summary.* Cat. LS-448E 5 February, revised 11 February.

Canada. Minister of State for Democratic Reform. 2007. *Public Consultations on Canada's Democratic Institutions and Practices.* http://www.democraticreform.gc.ca/index.asp?lang=eng&Page=news-comm&Sub=news-comm&Doc=20070910-eng.htm.

Canada. Office of the Prime Minister. 2006. *Speech from the Throne.* 4 April. http://pm.gc.ca/eng/media.asp?id=1087.

Canada. Privy Council Office. 2004. *Ethics, Responsibility, Accountability: An Action Plan for Democratic Reform.* Ottawa. http://www.pco-bcp.gc.ca.

Canada. Treasury Board Secretariat. 2006. *Federal Accountability Act Becomes Law.* http://www.tbs-sct.gc.ca/media/nr-cp/2006/1212-eng.asp.

CBC News. 2004. "Elections Canada defends error-plagued voters' list," 25 June. http://web.archive.org/web/20041205031003/http://www.cbc.ca/story/election/national/2004/06/25/elxn2_kingsley040625.html.

Compas. 2007. *Public Consultations on Canada's Democratic Institutions and Practices: A Report for the Privy Council Office.* http://www.democraticreform.gc.ca/docs/news-comm/news-comm/docs/20070910/rpt-eng.pdf.

Craig, Stephen C., Richard Niemi, and Glenn E. Silver. 1990. "Political Efficacy and Trust: A Report on the NES Pilot Study Items." *Political Behavior* 12, 3: 289–314.

Crozier, Michel, Samuel P. Huntington, and Joji Watanuki. 1975. *The Crisis of Democracy.* Report on the Governability of Democracies to the Trilateral Commission. New York: New York University Press.

CTV.ca. 2008. "Harper Senate appointments slammed by opposition," 11 December. http://www.ctv.ca/servlet/ArticleNews/story/CTVNews/20081211/senate_folo_081211?hub=Canada.

Elections BC. 2005. *Statement of Votes: Referendum on Electoral Reform*. Victoria, BC. 17 May. http://www.elections.bc.ca/docs/rpt/SOV-2005-ReferendumOnElectoralReform.pdf.

Elections Canada. 2008. *Official Voting Results, 40th General Election*. http://www.elections.ca/scripts/OVR2008/default.html.

Elections Canada. 2008. *Quarterly Allowances to the Registered Political Parties*. http://www.elections.ca/content.asp?section=pol&document=qua2008&dir=pol/qua&lang=e&textonly=false.

Elections Prince Edward Island. 2005. *Plebiscite on Mixed Member Proportional Representation System — Official Results*. http://www.electionspei.ca/plebiscites/pr/results/detailed/index.php.

Francoli, Paco. 2003a. "Paul Martin thanks his fundraisers." *The Hill Times*, 10 November. http://www.thehilltimes.ca/html/index.php?display=story&full_path=/2003/november/10/francoli.

Francoli, Paco. 2003b. "PM should leave political financing bill to successor: Grit MP Harvard." *The Hill Times*, 20 January. http://www.thehilltimes.ca/html/index.php?display=story&full_path=/2003/january/20/legislative_process/.

Freeman, Aaron. 2003. "New fundraising rules: Profound changes." *The Hill Times*, 14 July. http://www.thehilltimes.ca/html/index.php? display=story&full_path=/2003/july/14/freeman/.

Gibson, Gordon. 2002. *Report on the Constitution of the Citizens' Assembly on Electoral Reform*. Vancouver, December 23.

Gidengil, Elisabeth, André Blais, Neil Nevitte, and Richard Nadeau. 2003. "Turned Off or Tuned Out? Youth Participation in Politics." *Electoral Insight* 5, 2 (July): 9–14.

Heard, Andrew. 2008. "Historical Voter Turnout in Canadian Federal Elections and Referenda, 1867-2008." http://www.sfu.ca/~aheard/elections/historical-turnout.html.

Howe, Paul. 2007. *The Electoral Participation of Young Canadians*. Working Paper Series on Electoral Participation and Outreach Practices. Ottawa: Elections Canada.

Howe, Paul, and David Northrup. 2000. "Strengthening Canadian Democracy: The Views of Canadians." *Policy Matters* 1, 5 (July). Montreal: Institute for Research on Public Policy.

International IDEA [Institute for Democracy and Electoral Assistance]. 2003. "Voter Turnout — A Global Survey." http://www.idea.int/vt/survey/voter_turnout.cfm.

Johnston, W.A., Harvey Krahn, and Trevor Harrison. 2006. "Democracy, Political Institutions, and Trust: The Limits of Current Electoral Reform Proposals." *Canadian Journal of Sociology* 31, 2 (Spring): 165–82.

Klein, Naomi. 2002. "What Is This Movement?" In Mike Prokasch and Laura Raymond, eds., *The Global Activist's Manual*. New York: Thunder's Mouth Press/Nation Books. 1–9.

Law Commission of Canada. 2004. *Voting Counts: Electoral Reform in Canada*. Report submitted to the Minister of Justice (March). Ottawa: Ministry of Justice.

Martin, Lawrence. 2003. *Iron Man: The Defiant Reign of Jean Chrétien*. Toronto: Viking.

Martin, Paul 2002–03. "The Democratic Deficit." *Policy Options* 24, 1 (December–January): 10–12.

Morovcsik, Andrew. n.d. "In Defense of the 'Democratic Deficit': Reassessing Legitimacy in the European Union." *Center for European Studies Working Paper No. 92*, Harvard University, Cambridge. MA. http://www.ces.fas.harvard.edu/working_papers/Moravcsik92.pdf.

Nevitte, Neil. 1996. *The Decline of Deference.* Peterborough: Broadview Press.

New Brunswick. 2003. "Premier Bernard Lord creates Commission on Legislative Democracy." *News Release,* 19 December. http://www.gnb.ca/cnb/news/ld/2003e 1208ld.htm.

New Brunswick. Commission on Legislative Democracy. 2004. *Final Report and Recommendations.* Fredericton.

New Brunswick. Executive Council Office. 2007. "Government response to Committee on Legislative Democracy Report." *News Release,* 28 June. http://www.gnb.ca/cnb/ news/ex/2007e0859ex.htm.

O'Connor, James. 1973. *The Fiscal Crisis of the State.* New York: St. Martin's Press.

Ontario. Ministry of the Attorney General/Democratic Renewal Secretariat. 2003. "McGuinty government to strengthen our democracy and improve the way government serves people." *News Release,* 8 December. http://www.attorneygeneral.jus.gov. on.ca/english/news/2003/20031208-dr1.asp.

Ontario. Office of the Premier. 2004. "Remarks announcing fixed election dates." http:// www.premier.gov.on.ca/news/Product.asp?ProductID=339.

Pammett, Jon H., and Lawrence LeDuc. 2003. "Explaining the Turnout Decline in Canadian Federal Elections: A New Survey of Non-Voters." Elections Canada (March). http:// www.elections.ca.

Persichilli, Angelo. 2003. "EXTRA! EXTRA! Civil war brewing in Liberal caucus." *The Hill Times,* 27 January. http://www.thehilltimes.ca/html/index.php?display= story&full_path=/2003/january/27/angelo/.

Prince Edward Island, Commissioner of Electoral Reform. 2003. *Report,* 18 December. http://www.gov.pe.ca/photos/original/er_premier2003.pdf.

Putnam, Robert D., Susan J. Pharr, and Russell J. Dalton. 2000. "Introduction: What's Troubling the Trilateral Democracies?" In Susan J. Pharr and Robert D. Putnam, eds., *Disaffected Democracies.* Princeton: Princeton University Press. 3–27.

Quebec. Comité directeur des États-généraux sur la réforme des institutions démocratiques [Béland Commission]. 2003. *Prenez votre place! La participation citoyenne au coeur des institutions démocratiques québécoises.*

Rodriguez, Gregory. 2008. "Lack of voter interest may be good for democracy." *The Kitchener-Waterloo Record,* 30 May: A13.

Rosema, Martin. 2007. "Low Turnout: Threat to Democracy or Blessing in Disguise? Consequences of Citizens' Varying Tendencies to Vote." *Electoral Studies* 26: 612–23.

Rubenson, Daniel, André Blais, Patrick Fournier, Elisabeth Gidengil, and Neil Nevitte. 2007. "Does Low Turnout Matter? Evidence from the 2000 Canadian Federal Election." *Electoral Studies* 26: 589–97.

Ruff, Norman. 2003. "BC Deliberative Democracy: The Citizens' Assembly and Electoral Reform 2003-2005." Paper presented to the annual conference of the Canadian Political Science Association, Halifax, NS, 1 June.

Stephenson, Laura, and A. Brian Tanguay. forthcoming. "The 2007 Ontario Electoral System Referendum: Information, Interest, and Democratic Renewal." Institute for Research on Public Policy.

Tanguay, A. Brian. 2004. "Sclerosis or a Clean Bill of Health? Diagnosing Québec's Party System in the Twenty-First Century." In Alain-G. Gagnon, ed., *Québec: State and Society,* 3rd ed. Peterborough: Broadview Press. 221–43.

Tanguay, A. Brian. 2007. "The Paradoxes of Direct Democracy." In Alain-G. Gagnon and A. Brian Tanguay, eds., *Canadian Parties in Transition,* 3rd ed. Peterborough: Broadview Press. 467–89.

Wattenberg, Martin P. 2000. "The Decline of Party Mobilization." In Russell J. Dalton and Martin P. Wattenberg, eds., *Parties without Partisans: Political Change in Advanced Industrial Democracies.* Oxford: Oxford University Press. 64–76.

Wright, Erik Olin. 1978. *Class, Crisis, and the State.* London: New Left Books.

Young, Lisa, Anthony Sayers, and Harold Jansen. 2007. "Altering the Political Landscape: State Funding and Party Finance." In Alain-G. Gagnon and A. Brian Tanguay, eds., *Canadian Parties in Transition*, 3rd ed. Peterborough: Broadview Press. 335–54.

twelve

Representation and Political Parties

WILLIAM CROSS

Political parties are the central players in Canadian politics. Public opinion data reveal that a large majority of citizens view political parties as essential to their democratic life. Voters' inability to imagine a national politics without parties is undoubtedly influenced by their experience with parties dominating key democratic institutions. Canadians participate in national politics, and view their democratic institutions, largely through the prism of political parties. As Carty, Cross, and Young (2000: 3) have written: "Making sense of Canada has always meant making sense of its party politics."

Election campaigns are contests fought among political parties. Most voters decide which party they wish to govern and cast a ballot for the local candidate endorsed by that party. Media coverage of election campaigns is dominated by the parties, and the single most covered event is a televised debate among the parties' leaders. Candidates independent of political parties stand in each election but they are almost always bit players. Candidates representing political parties received more than 99 per cent of the votes cast in the 2008 election, and in the past seven federal elections only one MP has been elected to Parliament in the first instance as an independent. Parties' electoral campaigns are heavily subsidized from the public purse while all other organizations wishing to participate are subject to strict spending limitations, ensuring they are unable to compete on a level footing with the parties in attempting to win the attention of voters.

Similar to elections, our legislatures are organized along party lines. Whether members sit on the government or opposition benches depends upon the relative electoral strength of their party. Members are organized into party caucuses that determine nearly every aspect of their parliamentary careers, from the committees they serve on to whether they actively participate in the daily Question Period. Voting in the House of Commons is largely a party-driven affair with rates of party cohesion significantly higher than those in other comparable democracies such as the United States and the United Kingdom. Canadian governments are formed by a single party, with Cabinet and ministry representation reserved for the largest parliamentary party.

Given this centrality of parties to our democratic life, it is essential to consider who the parties represent. Many political observers have been critical of parties as being out-of-touch and non-responsive to the views of regular Canadians. Some have criticized them as being elite-driven, hierarchical organizations while others have criticized them for a lack of inclusivity and diversity. This is especially troubling considering that one of the central roles traditionally ascribed to parties is a linkage function between civil society and government (King, 1969).

A principal reason for the existence of parties is size — both geographically and in terms of population. There are simply too many Canadians living too far from one another to allow for a citizen-based democracy of the type practiced in ancient Greece. Instead, Canadians organize themselves into political parties, and representatives of these parties make up our legislatures and governments. The parties take on the task of connecting citizens in their far-flung communities with political power exercised in Ottawa. Contemporary democratic norms demand that the parties are inclusive of the many different components of Canadian society both so that voters see themselves represented within the parties and thus within their legislatures and governments, and so that all perspectives are reflected in public policy decision-making.

Pitkin (1967) identifies both these symbolic and substantive dimensions of representation. From a symbolic perspective it is important that various groups see themselves represented so that they feel included in the communities' democratic institutions and are thus more likely to view outcomes as legitimate. From a substantive perspective, there is considerable literature suggesting that representatives of different groups bring different styles, perspectives, and priorities to politics. Their presence brings a unique viewpoint to policy debates and raises the salience of different issues; in short, their inclusion in the decision-making body affects policy priorities and outcomes (see, for example, Brodie, 1988; Norris and Lovenduski, 1989; and Mansbridge, 2003).

This chapter contributes to a consideration of "democracy and representation" by examining how inclusive the parties are in terms of how well they reflect the diversity of Canadian society. We will consider three different faces of political parties — legislative, electoral, and organizational. All three are captured through an examination of the parties' parliamentary caucuses, election candidates, grassroots activists, and organizational structures. The characteristics considered are age (focusing on the representation of young voters), gender, and ethnicity. Consideration of these characteristics provides a good overview of how inclusive and representative our political parties are in their various dimensions.

Young Voters

There has been a great deal written regarding low participation rates of young Canadians in traditional methods of democratic engagement. Young Canadians are voting at record low numbers and at rates significantly lower than other age cohorts. Estimates of voter participation among Canadians ages 18 to 25 range from just 25 per cent in the 2000 federal election (Leduc and Pammett, 2003) to 38 per cent in 2004 (Kingsley, 2005) and 44 per cent in 2006 (Elliott, 2008). In all three cases, these are dramatically lower participation rates than those for older age cohorts, resulting in overall participation rates in the 60 per cent range.

Political parties have not fared any better at attracting youth to their activities. The most comprehensive study of Canadian party members found the average age of members to be 59 and that fewer than one in 20 was younger than age 25 (Cross and Young, 2004). This is consistent with findings from surveys of the general population showing young Canadians the least likely to report party membership (Howe and Northrup, 2000).

While we cannot be certain why so few young Canadians are joining political parties, there is considerable literature suggesting that it is related to a preference for alternative methods of civic and political participation. O'Neill reports that young Canadians are four-and-one-half times more likely to belong to an interest group than a political party while older Canadians are more likely to choose participation in a political party. O'Neill's findings (2007: 21) suggest that the youngest "generation is not 'dropping out' of politics but shifting to new and different forms of participation."

Partial explanation of young activists' preference for interest groups over parties is found in Cross and Young's (2008a) study of young political activists. They find that many young activists reject political parties on grounds related to both internal and external efficacy. They view decision-making within political parties as elite-dominated and do not believe that ordinary members can play a significant role in influencing party decision-making. They also do not perceive political parties as effective vehicles for accomplishing social and political change. By large numbers, young Canadians are choosing interest groups over political parties largely because they feel they can play a more consequential role in shaping these advocacy organizations and because they believe these groups are significantly more effective at achieving policy change than are political parties.

It is important to note that this phenomenon is not unique to Canada's parties. There has been a general decline in party membership numbers across Western democracies. In a study of party membership in 22 European countries, Whiteley finds that the overall decline in party activism is almost completely attributable to a dramatic decline in the number of young voters joining parties. Agreeing with O'Neill, Whiteley (2007: 2) contends that: "Young cohorts of political activists prefer to get involved in single interest pressure groups and in other types of voluntary organizations, rather than in parties." Similar findings have been reported in recent studies of parties in

Table 12.1 Canadian Party Members (2000 postal survey)

In the past year, how much time did you devote to federal party activities *in an average month?* (by age) (percentages reported)

	older than 25	25 and younger
none	40.1	15.9
less than 1 hour	21.2	16.7
1–3 hours	16.5	22.3
3–5 hours	8.5	13.5
more than 5 hours	13.7	31.6
N	3,645	146

Ireland, the United Kingdom, and Denmark, among others (Pedersen *et al.*, 2004; Gallagher and Marsh, 2002; and Seyd and Whiteley, 1992, 1994). For example, Seyd and Whiteley find the average age of British Conservative Party members is 62, and Gallagher and Marsh find the average age of Irish Fianna Fail members is 52.

The low levels of youth membership have a negative effect on overall activism rates within parties. This is because, as illustrated in Table 12.1, young party members tend to be significantly more active within parties than are their older counterparts. While approximately two in five older members of parties are completely inactive in party affairs, more than eight in ten members age 25 and younger participate in party activity on a monthly basis. Thus, the under-representation of young Canadians within parties means their overall vitality at the grassroots level is diminished. O'Neill's finding that young Canadians report higher rates of volunteerism than older cohorts suggests that these voters are diverting their efforts away from political parties to other organizations. Cross and Young (2008b) suggest that this has a long-term effect on the strength of the parties' local volunteer corps as they find that members who join a party while young are considerably more likely to be active in party activity in their later years than are those who join later in life. They examine party members ages 35 to 55 and find significantly higher activism rates for members who join before turning 25 than for those who join when older. This means that the paucity of young members in parties today will likely have an effect on the vitality of local party associations for decades to come.

There is a significant difference in the manner in which the parties organize their young members. All of the parties allow Canadians under the voting age of 18 to join. The minimum age in the Bloc Québécois (the Bloc) is 16, the Liberals and Conservatives allow 14-year-olds, while the minimum age in the New Democratic Party (NDP) varies by province and is as low as 12 years in some such as British Columbia. Most of the parties have organs dedicated to recruiting and involving young Canadians in their affairs. In the Liberal Party, for example, members age 25 and younger belong to the Young Liberals of Canada. The Young Liberals have their own organizational structure in each province and territory reaching from local constituencies and post-secondary institution clubs to provincial and national executives. The Young Liberals operate at arms-length from the party and adopt their own policy resolutions, which are often at odds with positions taken by the party as a whole. This quasi-independence offers youth activists a venue for party participation that is not made to feel ineffective by virtue of control by party elites. The party also ensures representation of its young members on key decision-making bodies through mechanisms such as including the president of the Young Liberals as a voting member of the party's national executive. Youth clubs are also guaranteed representation at party conventions and in decisions such as selection of the party leader; and, in addition, a minimum proportion of leadership convention delegates chosen by local constituency associations (separate from youth and university clubs) must be filled by members under the age of 26 (4 of 14 for the 2006 contest). The result of these rules is that young party members form a significant block of participants at all party conventions, often in excess of one-third of total delegates.

While the Bloc and NDP organize their youth members in a fashion similar to the Liberals (through New Democratic Youth Canada for members under 26 and the Forum Jeunesse for Bloc members under 30), the Conservative Party takes a different approach. At its inaugural convention in 2005, the party explicitly decided not to have separate party organs dedicated to different types of members including youth. Rather, all members are formally organized through local electoral district associations. This was a somewhat controversial decision and should not be read to mean that the party does not actively recruit young members. In fact, its constitution charges the National Executive with responsibility for "Encouraging the participation and recruitment of youth" (article 8.6.4). There also is an informal organization called CPC Energy that supports Conservative Party clubs at post-secondary institutions, but, unlike those in other parties, these are not formally recognized by the party, do not have a separate national organization, and are not entitled to representation on party decision-making bodies including conventions. The result is that young Conservatives join the party like all other members and are on equal footing with them in terms of representation in party decision-making (with the exception that at least one in ten local association convention delegates must be younger than age 26).

One result of this lack of formal representation for youth within the party is that there are fewer youth and campus clubs in the Conservative Party than in the Liberals. Cross and Young (2008b) find that the presence of youth-based party associations makes a significant difference in terms of increasing youth activism. They find that members who belong through a youth or campus-based party association are significantly more active in party affairs than are similarly aged members who belong solely through a local constituency association. This is likely related to the young members' perceptions of the efficacy of their participation. Organizations dedicated to young members, coupled with significant representational guarantees, allow these activists to perceive their participation in party affairs as more meaningful as the youth groups engage in activities such as adopting their own policy resolutions and form significant voting blocks in important party decisions such as leadership selection.

The parties' parliamentary caucuses reflect the age bias of the wider membership, with young Canadians dramatically under-represented and seniors over-represented. As of January 2009, the average age of an MP was 52 years. There is little deviation among parties: the average age of Conservative MPs is 50 years and for the other three parties approximately 52.5. Only four MPs are younger than 30, and almost one in four are 60 or older. In a study of youth representation in the House of Commons, Lewis (2006) finds that younger cohorts of Canadians have always been under-represented. While approximately half of Canadians are younger than 40, in the seven most recent Parliaments fewer than one in five MPs belonged to this age cohort. And the election of young MPs is generally in decline. In the 11 parliaments between 1957 and 1984, an average of 21.8 per cent of MPs was younger than 40, reaching a high of 29.1 per cent in 1974. For the seven subsequent Parliaments, the average is 13.8 per cent, reaching a low of 11 per cent for the 1997 and 2000 elections.

It is interesting that the Conservative Party has in recent elections elected the largest number of young MPs. In the 39th Parliament, the five youngest members all belonged to the Conservative caucus, and 24 of their members were under age 40 compared with six Liberals, one NDP, and seven Bloc members. This trend continues in the 40th Parliament with five of the seven youngest members belonging to the Conservative caucus. Twenty-five Conservative members are under age 40 compared with eight Bloc members, seven Liberals, and four NDP. In recent elections, the Conservatives (and one of its predecessors, the Canadian Alliance) highlighted its ability to attract young candidates and elect young MPs as evidence of its inclusivity and outreach to young Canadians, notwithstanding the party's unique approach to the organization of its youth members.

Table 12.2 Gender of Party Members (2000 mail survey, percentages reported)*

	Overall	Progressive Conservatives	Canadian Alliance	Liberal	NDP	Bloc
Female members	38	33	32	47	46	36

* The Progressive Conservatives and Canadian Alliance have subsequently merged to form the Conservative Party of Canada.

Women

There is a considerable body of literature that both describes and explains the under-representation of women in Canadian political life (Bashevkin, 1993; MacIvor, 1996; Tremblay and Trimble, 2003; Young, 2000). Much of this work focuses on the role of political parties as the key gatekeepers to political power. Underscoring this key role parties play in our democratic life, Young (2000) argues that the rate of women's involvement in political parties is positively related both to the number of women elected to public office and to parties' responsiveness to women's policy interests. The under-representation of women, then, at nearly every level of party organization helps to explain the relatively low numbers of women in elected office and what many consider to be the relative lack of responsiveness by the parties to issues of primary concern to female voters.

Similar to O'Neill's findings concerning youth voters, Young and Cross (2003) suggest that women are more likely to express greater confidence in interest groups than in political parties and are thus less likely than men to channel their political and community activism through parties. Young and Cross suggest that women generally find political parties to be overly hierarchical and partisan and that many instead prefer the more egalitarian environment found in interest groups.

The large-scale study of party members in 2000 confirmed the under-representation of women in Canada's political parties. Cross and Young (2004) report that more than six in ten party members are male. These results are consistent with surveys of the general population, which find that many more men than women have belonged to a political party (Howe and Northrup, 2000). As shown in Table 12.2, there is considerable variance among parties with the Liberals and NDP approaching gender parity while two-thirds of Conservative Party members are male. This under-representation of women is not unique to the Canadian case. Studies of party membership in other countries routinely find a disproportionate number of male members (Pedersen *et al.*, 2004; Gallagher and Marsh, 2002; Seyd and Whiteley, 1992).

Not only do fewer women than men belong to parties but they tend to be less active and are less likely to hold positions of influence. In terms of time contributed to party affairs generally, male members are 24 per cent less likely to be inactive than are female members, and men are 11 per cent more likely to spend in excess of three hours per month on party activity. The difference also extends to holding party office. Male members are 26 per cent more likely than female members to have served on a constituency association executive and are 29 per cent more likely to have sought their party's nomination for a federal election. The earlier findings of Bashevkin (1993) suggest that these are long-term patterns. In her study of party activism, Bashevkin found that female party activists were over-represented in positions of low prestige and influence, such as local association secretaries, and significantly under-represented in influential positions such as party executive committees and campaign managers.

The different approaches taken by the parties to the representation of women within their organizational structures largely resemble the approaches taken for youth members described above. For example, the Liberal Party's constitution establishes the National Women's Liberal Commission, which has branches in local constituencies that elect delegates to national policy and leadership conventions. In addition, the party requires that half of all convention delegates chosen by local associations are female. Female members are also guaranteed representation on most parties' national decision-making bodies. For example, in the NDP the chair of the party's Participation of Women Committee is a member of the national executive, and at least half of the representatives of labour affiliates and of the geographic regions to the national executive must be female.

The difference between the Conservative Party and the others concerning the organization of women in the party is even starker than it is for youth. The party's constitution includes no general provision encouraging the participation of women, there is no informal organization dedicated to the participation of female members, there is no guaranteed representation for women on the party's decision-making bodies, and there is no provision for a guaranteed number of female delegates to party conventions. One result of this is that three of the 18 members of the party's National Council (as of January 2009) are female. This contrasts with the 12 of 20 female members on the NDP executive.

Similar to youth members, females who participate in a party organ dedicated to women are more active in party affairs than are those who participate only through their constituency association. In both the NDP and the Liberal

Table 12.3 Female Candidates by Party

(1997–2008 federal elections, as percentage of all candidates)

	1997	2000	2004	2006	2008
Bloc	21	23	24	31	27
Liberal	28	22	24	26	37
NDP	36	31	31	35	34
Conservatives	–	–	12	12	20
PCs	19	13	–	–	–
Reform/Alliance	10	10	–	–	–

Party, members active in a women's group are significantly more likely to have served on a constituency association executive than are those who participate only through their local riding association. Similarly those active in a women's association devote more time to party affairs. For example, in the NDP, 37 per cent of those belonging to a women's group contribute three hours or more to party affairs per month compared with 9 per cent of female partisans who participate only through a constituency association.

Parties nominate women for public office in far lower numbers than their male counterparts. In the 2008 federal election, none of the major parties came close to nominating a representative number of female candidates. The Liberals nominated the largest proportion with 37 per cent of their candidates being female, compared with 34 per cent of NDP candidates, 27 per cent of Bloc candidates, and 21 per cent of Conservatives. As illustrated in Table 12.3, these numbers generally represent a modest increase over recent elections.

Many reasons have been advanced to explain the lack of female candidates nominated by the parties, and it seems that the problem is both one of supply and demand. On the demand side, the two major parties have at times guaranteed the re-nomination of their existing MPs. Because these groups are overwhelmingly male, this practice ensures that most candidates nominated by the parties in the ridings they are most likely to win (i.e., those they won in the most recent election) are male. This leaves women to seek nominations in less hospitable electoral terrain. On the supply side we find relatively few women seeking party nominations. There is no systematic evidence of voter bias on the part of local party members against female candidates for nominations, but the challenge seems to be to attract more women to seek public office. All party leaders have expressed their concern over the low numbers of female candidates, but little concrete action has been taken to remedy the situation. (For a broader discussion of the status of women in Canadian politics, see Chapter 14 in this volume).

The exception to this is the NDP, which through its "Nomination and Affirmative Action Policy" has put in place substantial measures to combat the under-representation of women among its parliamentary candidates. The NDP's rules stipulate that before a local association may nominate a candidate it must certify that it is in compliance with the following requirements: "A) a Candidate Search Committee has been established reflecting the diversity of the riding; and B) there are one or more candidates for nomination from affirmative action groups." The party places special emphasis on recruiting female candidates where it has achieved electoral success in the past, setting a target of nominating female candidates in 60 per cent of these ridings. The focus on "winnable" ridings ensures that female candidates are not ghettoized to ridings the party has no hope of winning. The result is that in recent elections women generally comprise a similar share of the NDP parliamentary caucus as they do general election candidates. By contrast, in the Liberal Party 37 per cent of 2008 candidates were female as is 25 per cent of the party's current elected caucus. This means women were disproportionately nominated in ridings lost by the party. For example, more than half of the party's candidates in Alberta were women — this in a province where Liberals had no realistic hope of electing any MPs.

Given the relatively low rates of women nominated by the parties, and the parties' collective electoral dominance, it is not surprising to find a continued under-representation of women in Parliament. Ever since Agnes Macphail was elected to the House of Commons in 1921, women have been elected in each election with the lone exception of 1949. The percentage of female MPs today is approximately 22 — a number that has essentially remained constant over the past decade. While the proportion of women elected to the House of Commons doubled between 1980 and 1984 (from 5 to 10 per cent) and reached 20 per cent by 1997, it did not move in the four subsequent elections. There is no evidence that general election voters are biased against female candidates; rather, the relatively low number of women elected to the Canadian Parliament seems directly related to the low number of women nominated by the parties in electoral districts they are likely to win in a general election.

Canada does not compare particularly favourably with other countries in terms of the proportion of female legislators. Of similarly placed liberal democracies, as illustrated in Table 12.4, northern European countries with a much deeper commitment to gender equality far outpace Canada in this regard.

The parties remain crucial to the representation of women in Canada partially because of the effects of our single-member plurality electoral system.

Almost all of the countries ranking above Canada in terms of the proportion of elected female representatives have a proportional electoral system, while relatively low-ranking countries such as Australia, the United Kingdom, and the United States join Canada in having single-member districts. The key difference is that in proportional systems, voters choose more than one candidate to represent them and the parties nominate slates of multiple candidates in each electoral district. Proportional systems facilitate a greater representation of minority candidates as the contests are not zero sum with only one candidate presented by each party in each district (MacIvor, 2003). While it is impossible to apportion one MP among different genders or other representational groups, in multi-member proportional systems parties are able to present a number of candidates in each district and often balance these lists between women and men.

Table 12.4 Percentage of Women in Selected Lower Houses (as of 31 October 2008)

Sweden	47
Finland	42
Argentina	40
Netherlands	39
Denmark	38
Spain	36
Norway	36
Belgium	35
Iceland	33
New Zealand	33
Germany	32
Australia	27
Canada	22
United Kingdom	20
United States	17

Source: Inter Parliamentary Union, http://www.ipu.org/wnn-e/classif.htm

The principal Canadian parties have done little to increase the number of women elected to Parliament in recent elections. Without leadership on their part, it is likely that the current stagnation in female representation will continue for some time. While voters are not opposed to electing women to the legislature, their ability to do so is restricted by the parties' unwillingness to take the necessary measures to present voters with a representative number of female candidates in competitive ridings.

Visible Minorities

Canada is a diverse community of immigrants. In addition to the three founding nations of Aboriginal peoples, French, and English, Canada has a long history of welcoming large numbers of immigrants primarily from European nations. This pattern changed dramatically towards the end of the last century with significantly greater diversity in the origins of newcomers to Canada. In the 2006 census there were more than 200 different ethnic origins reported, with 34 of them claimed by more than 100,000 respondents and 11 by more than one million. The census found that 16 per cent of respondents were visible minorities, an increase from 13.4 per cent in 2001 (Statistics Canada, 2008). In 2007 Canada admitted approximately 237,000 immigrants largely from non-European countries (Citizenship and Immigration Canada, 2008). The degree of change from earlier immigration patterns is evident in the list of the most common countries of origin for recent immigrants: China, India, Philippines, Pakistan, United States, United Kingdom, Iran, South Korea, Columbia, and Sri Lanka. The result is a Canada made up of very different ethnic communities than that of even one generation ago and with an ever-increasing number of visible minorities.

Formally, the parties welcome the participation of new arrivals. None of them restricts membership to Canadian citizens, but most have a residency requirement. The strictest requirement is in the Conservative Party, which offers membership to citizens or "permanent residents" of Canada. The Liberals require that members "ordinarily live in Canada," and NDP membership is open to "every resident of Canada." The Bloc membership form explicitly states that members may live anywhere in the world. Despite this liberal approach to membership, none of the parties' activist base resembles the diversity of Canadian society. The 2000 study of party members found that virtually all of them (99 per cent) are Canadian citizens (Cross, 2004). Because citizenship takes a number of years to acquire after arrival in Canada, this finding suggests that there are virtually no new arrivals participating in the parties. The lack of diversity is also apparent in the paucity of members who are born outside Canada — only one in ten. There is some diversity among parties in this regard, with one in five NDP members born abroad compared to one in 33 Bloc members (Cross, 2004).

For the parties that compete in English Canada, the most common ancestry reported by their members is British followed by Irish/Celtic. Nine in ten Progressive Conservative members reported this ancestry as did approximately two-thirds of Liberal, NDP, and Alliance members. Their remaining members were primarily of German/Austrian, French, Russian, and Scandinavian descent with virtually no members from Africa, Asia, or India — the areas providing the largest numbers of new immigrants. More than nine in ten Bloc members report being of French ancestry (Cross, 2004).

There is some evidence that this under-representation of new immigrant groups may be beginning to change, at least modestly. In a mail survey of young Liberal Party members (younger than age 26) conducted by Cross in 2004, somewhat more representation of these communities is found. While the vast majority of members continue to be of European descent, there is some representation from the Indian (3 per cent), Chinese (2 per cent), and

Sikh (1.5 per cent) communities. While these are very small numbers, they do suggest that at least among the newest and youngest members of the Liberal Party there is the beginning of greater cultural diversity.

The NDP is the only party to have a constitutionally mandated organ dedicated to the participation and representation of visible minorities. The Participation of Visible Minorities Committee is charged with outreach to these ethnic communities and to encourage their participation in party affairs. The Committee is also guaranteed representation on party decision-making bodies such as the National Executive. Both the Liberals and NDP have organized Aboriginal committees that are similarly charged with outreach and provided with representation within the party.

The under-representation of new immigrant communities is apparent in the pools of candidates nominated by the parties. Table 12.5 displays the number and percentage of visible minority candidates presented by each of the parties in the 2004 election. While visible minorities comprised about 15 per cent of the Canadian population that year, none of the parties came close to nominating this proportion of visible minority candidates. Nonetheless, the overall percentage of 9.3 per cent (for the four major parties) represents a significant increase from previous elections in which the estimates were in the 4 per cent range. Black and Hicks (2006) consider the percentage of visible minority candidates as a ratio of the visible minority share of the population and find that it was remarkably consistent in the .37 range before increasing significantly to .62 in 2004. Black and Hicks (2006) and Tossutti and Najem (2002) find that the parties are more likely to run minority candidates in ridings with significant visible minority communities. Furthermore, they find that, generally speaking, visible minority candidates are not ghettoized to unwinnable ridings but are as likely as non-visible minority candidates to be nominated in a riding where their party has a chance for electoral success. Taken together, these two points suggest that the parties see the nomination of visible minority candidates as a tool to be used to maximize their electoral chances in ethnically diverse electoral districts. If this is the case, and given the significant increase in the number of visible minority voters, we can expect the parties to continue to increase the number of visible minority candidates in districts where such a candidacy might energize a minority community — if only for their electoral self-interest.

Considering the under-representation of visible minority candidates offered by the major parties, it is not surprising that this community is also under-represented in Parliament. The 2006 campaign resulted in the election of 23 visible minorities representing 7.5 per cent of all MPs and an increase of one MP from the 2004 election. These numbers suggest that visible minority candidates are elected at a lower rate than are candidates generally.

To some extent, this results from the incumbency effect. The vast majority of incumbents are non-visible minorities, and almost by definition they contest each party's safest seats. As suggested above, it does not appear to be the case that parties are nominating their visible minority candidates disproportionately in unwinnable ridings. Of the Conservative effort Black and Hicks note: "It would seem then that the party not only nominated the largest contingent of visible minority candidates but did so with a degree of commitment to have more of them elected" (2006: 31).

Table 12.5 Visible Minority Candidates Nominated by Party in 2004

	total candidates	
	N	%
Bloc	5	6.7
Conservatives	33	10.7
Liberals	26	8.4
NDP	29	9.4
Total	93	9.3

Source: Black and Hicks, 2006: 18.

The increased diversity in the House of Commons is made evident by examining the countries of origin of the 36 members who were born outside Canada (as of January 2009). They come from a very diverse set of countries including, for example, India, Ivory Coast, Vietnam, China, Paraguay, Brazil, Tanzania, Japan, Argentina, Hong Kong, and Trinidad. The generational change is highlighted by the fact that five MPs in the 40th Parliament were born in France or England and eight were born in China, India, or Tanzania. Change may be slow in coming, but there is no denying that in terms of ethnic diversity, the House of Commons is undergoing considerable reform.

Conclusion

In a wide-ranging evaluation of the status of Canadian democracy at the outset of the twenty-first century, the Canadian Democratic Audit project chose inclusiveness as one of three principal benchmarks by which the health of our democratic institutions could be measured (Cross, 2001). This reflects the primary importance the "auditors" gave to the democratic norm of ensuring that all groups are equitably represented in public decision-making bodies. Had the audit been conducted a generation earlier, it is unlikely that inclusiveness would have been so central to the assessment. Democratic norms evolve over time, and in recent years the demands that the different groups comprising Canadian society be represented equitably in public decision-making institutions have intensified. While region and language have always been important representational imperatives in Canada, representation by gender, age, and ethnicity are now also salient concerns.

Much of the literature concerning representation of these groups in Canadian politics appropriately focuses on political parties. This is because of the primary place of parties in our politics. Parties make important decisions such as setting the public policy agenda and selecting party leaders who serve as premiers, prime minister, and opposition leaders. They also serve as gatekeepers to elective office. As the literature reviewed here suggests, the practices of parties in organizing their candidate selection processes have significant influence in determining the representation of these groups in our legislatures.

The data suggest that parties are not doing an adequate job of including these groups of Canadians. Youth, women, and visible minorities are under-represented in party membership, among grassroots party activists, among candidates nominated by the parties, and in the House of Commons. There is evidence that when parties reach out to these groups and encourage them to participate in public life the response is positive. The challenge seems to be that party politics do not appear welcoming and the parties have not consistently reached out to under-represented groups and ensured their inclusion in party affairs.

References and Suggested Readings

Bashevkin, Sylvia. 1993. *Toeing the Lines: Women and Party Politics in English Canada.* Toronto: Oxford University Press.

Black, Jerome H., and Bruce Hicks. 2006. "Visible Minority Candidates in the 2004 Federal Election." *Canadian Parliamentary Review* (Summer): 15–20.

Brodie, Janine. 1988. "The Gender Factor and National Leadership Conventions in Canada." In George Perlin, ed., *Party Democracy in Canada: The Politics of National Party Convention.* Scarborough: Prentice Hall. 172–87.

Carty, R.K, William Cross, and Lisa Young. 2000. *Rebuilding Canadian Party Politics.* Vancouver: University of British Columbia Press.

Citizenship and Immigration Canada. 2008. "Facts and Figures 2007." http://www.cic.gc.ca.

Cross, William. 2001. "Canada Today: A Democratic Audit," *Canadian Parliamentary Review* 24,4: 37–55.

Cross, William. 2004. *Political Parties.* Vancouver: University of British Columbia Press.

Cross, William, and Lisa Young. 2004. "The Contours of Political Party Membership in Canada." *Party Politics* 10, 4: 427–44.

Cross, William, and Lisa Young 2008a. "Factors Influencing the Decision of the Young Politically Engaged to Join a Political Party: An Investigation of the Canadian Case." *Party Politics* 14, 3: 345–69.

Cross, William, and Lisa Young. 2008b. "Activism Among Young Party Members: The Case of the Canadian Liberal Party." *Journal of Elections, Public Opinion and Parties* 18, 3: 257–81.

Elliott, Nathan 2008. "The youth vote: has the tide turned?" *Calgary Herald*, 4 October 2008.

Gallagher, Michael, and Michael Marsh. 2002. *Days of Blue Loyalty: The Politics of Membership in the Fine Gael Party*. Dublin: Political Science Association of Ireland Press.

Howe, Paul, and David Northrup. 2000. "Strengthening Canadian Democracy: the Views of Canadians." *Policy Matters* 1, 5. Ottawa: Institute for Research on Public Policy.

King, Anthony. 1969. "Political Parties in Western Democracies: Some Sceptical Reflections." *Polity* 2, 2: 111–41.

Kingsley, Jean-Pierre. 2005. "The 2004 General Election." *Electoral Insight* (January): 1–5.

Leduc, Larry, and Jon Pammett. 2003. *Explaining the Turnout Decline in Canadian Federal Elections: A New Survey of Non-Voters*. Ottawa: Elections Canada.

Lewis, J.P. 2006. "Identities and Ideas: Participation of Young Legislators in the Canadian House of Commons." *Canadian Parliamentary Review* 29, 2: 12–20.

MacIvor, Heather. 1996. *Women and Politics in Canada*. Peterborough: Broadview Press.

MacIvor, Heather. 2003. "Women and the Canadian Electoral System." In Manon Tremblay and Linda Trimble, eds., *Women and Electoral Politics in Canada*. Toronto: Oxford University Press. 22–36.

Mansbridge, Jane. 2003. "Rethinking Representation." *American Political Science Review* 97, 4: 515–28.

Norris, Pippa, and Joni Lovenduski. 1989. "Women Candidates for Parliament: Transforming the Agenda?" *British Journal of Political Science* 19: 106–15.

O'Neill, Brenda. 2007. *Indifferent or Just Different? The Political and Civic Engagement of Young People in Canada*. Ottawa: Canadian Policy Research Network.

Pedersen, Karina, Lars Bille, Roger Buch, Jorgen Elklit, Bernhard Hansen, and Hans Jorgen Nielsen. 2004. "Sleeping or Active Partners? Danish Party Members at the Turn of the Millennium." *Party Politics* 10, 4: 367–84.

Pitkin, Hanna F. 1967. *The Concept of Representation*. Berkeley: University of California Press.

Seyd, Patrick, and Paul Whiteley. 1992. *Labour's Grassroots: The Politics of Party Membership*. Oxford: Clarendon Press.

Statistics Canada. 2008. *Canada's Ethnocultural Mosaic*. Ottawa: Ministry of Industry.

Tossutti, Liviana, and Tom P. Najem. 2002. "Minorities and Elections in Canada's Fourth Party System." *Canadian Ethnic Studies* 34, 1: 85–112.

Tremblay, Manon, and Linda Trimble, Eds. 2003. *Women and Electoral Politics in Canada*. Toronto: Oxford University Press.

Vickers, Jill, and Janine Brodie. 1981. "Canada." In Joni Lovenduski and Jill Hills, eds., *The Politics of the Second Electorate: Women and Public Participation*. London: Routledge. 52–82.

Whiteley, Paul. 2007. "Are Groups Replacing Parties? A Multi-level Analysis of Party and Group Membership in the European Democracies." Paper presented at the workshop on Partisanship in Europe: Members, Activists, and Identifiers. European Consortium for Political Research Joint Sessions, Helsinki.

Young, Lisa. 2000. *Feminists and Party Politics*. Vancouver: University of British Columbia Press.

Young, Lisa, and William Cross. 2003. "Women's Involvement in Canadian Political Parties." In Manon Tremblay and Linda Trimble, eds., *Women and Electoral Politics in Canada*. Toronto: Oxford University Press. 91–108.

thirteen

Are Interest Groups Useful or Harmful?

ÉRIC MONTPETIT

Political discourses and commentaries typically present interest groups as harmful to policy-making processes, as "hijacking" policy-makers to better serve their "special interest." Policies are thereby prevented from serving the common good. In this chapter, I argue that alternative views of interest groups are possible. In fact, I show that under some conditions, interest groups can contribute to policy-making in ways that are not inconsistent with serving the common good.

What is an Interest Group?

Language rarely describes reality in a neutral fashion. The biases of language cannot be anymore evident than with interest groups. For example, some analysts use the expression "pressure group" to speak about interest groups (e.g., Pross, 1995). In the expression, the word "pressure" refers to the action of groups in exerting pressure to obtain decisions government would not otherwise be inclined to make. The image behind the expression of pressure group is one of adversarialism between government and groups. Groups do not help government by providing advice or expertise but press them to adopt policies against its will. Below, I will argue that this image of adversarialism is incorrect, as the relationship between government and groups is often one of cooperation.

Other analysts prefer the expression "advocacy groups" (e.g., Young and Everitt, 2004; Seidle, 1993). Instead of exerting pressure, the key action of groups consist in advocating in favour of their ideas or beliefs. Here, the image of adversarialism disappears. The word "advocacy" projects an image of groups as primarily motivated by ideas, without *a priori* assumption about the hostility or acceptance of those ideas by government. In fact, those who use this expression often notice that groups are not exclusively turned towards government but seek to convince just about everyone about the validity of their ideas. This expression does not always match reality either. If groups are involved in advocacy, they also participate in political processes, where exerting power is the goal and strategy is more important than ideas. In these latter processes, alliances and money feature prominently.

Other analysts refrain from using a universal expression to describe groups, preferring distinctive expressions for different groups. For example, some analysts use "public interest groups" to distinguish groups that have a wide membership with weak material interests from "private interest groups" with a narrower membership primarily motivated by their material interest (Young and Forsyth, 1991; Phillips, Pal, and Savas, 1992). A group advocating for women's rights would thus be considered a public interest group, while a group representing an industry would form a private interest group. In empirical research, the distinction between the two types of groups is not always easy to establish (Stanbury, 1993). In addition, the dichotomy between public and private interest groups lends itself too easily to value judgements, suggesting the former are good groups and the latter bad ones (Montpetit, 2004). Yet even groups representing narrow material interests can make a valuable contribution to governance.

In my own work, I prefer using the expression "interest groups" in a universal fashion, despite all the limitations associated with this choice. As I will show, interest groups display important differences, which are not conveyed by any universalistic expression. Moreover, the word "interest" projects an image of groups as motivated by their material interests rather than by their arguments and ideas. In fact, I would be hard-pressed if I were asked to decide whether groups have interests or ideas, as both phenomena are difficult to delineate. In several political situations, the interest of groups depends as much on perceptions, which evolve, than on a stable material reality (Stone, 1997). Several political scientists overcome this analytical difficulty by assuming that interests and ideas are subsumed into the policy preferences expressed by groups (Scharpf, 1997). In short, my choice of expression — interest group — is somewhat arbitrary, possibly stemming from its common use in comparison to alternative expressions.

Inspired by Pross (1995; 1986), I define interest groups as follows: *organizations created to facilitate the collective action of members who share interests or ideas, with the objective of making a contribution to governance, without seeking public office.* It follows that interest groups are different from social movements, which are more spontaneous and not as organized. Interest groups, however, can be located at the centre of social movements and can act as social movement organizations (see Scala, Montpetit, and Fortier, 2005). Interest groups are also distinct from political parties, which, in contrast to groups, seek election to public office.

Groups differ among themselves with regard to their organization. For the sake of simplicity, I distinguish between two ideal typical organizational forms: peak associations and unitary groups. The members of peak associations are other groups, while the members of unitary groups are individuals.

Peak associations have elaborated rules, codified into constitutions, whereby leaders are selected and exercise their authority. Unitary groups frequently function with a less formalized set of rules and may be led by charismatic leaders. The rules of peak associations enable an internalization of debates among members, while debates are frequently external to unitary groups. Lastly, peak associations deal with a wider range of issues than unitary groups. Most groups fall somewhere between these two ideal types, sometimes closer to peak associations, sometimes closer to unitary groups.

For example, the Canadian Federation of Agriculture falls close to being a peak association. Its membership is made up of other farm groups, organized at the provincial level, frequently representing commodity sectors. It is led by two vice-presidents who are elected according to a formal set of rules. Lastly, the Federation devotes important efforts to unite the Canadian farming community behind a single voice. It has elaborate procedures to bridge differences among members in developing its policy positions on a wide range of issues. Like most peak associations, the Federation is not always successful in this latter endeavour, with some competing groups making their dissonant voice heard effectively on a number of issues. However, the presence of a peak association in the Canadian agricultural sector contributes to internalizing the debates over agricultural policy.

In several policy sectors, peak associations are much less successful than in agriculture. The environment provides a good example of such a sector. The environmental sector is indeed characterized by the presence of a large number of small unitary groups. These tend to be specialized, focusing on climate change, water quality, or the protection of specific geographical areas, but rarely do they concern themselves with a wide range of environmental issues at once. Greenpeace works on a carefully selected set of issues, even though the group presents itself as a general environmental group. The members of most environmental groups are individuals, that is, environmental groups have members and not simply financial contributors, such as Greenpeace does. Lastly, the debates in the environmental sector tend to take place *among* groups as opposed to *within* groups. Environmental groups will often challenge industry groups, but they also debate among themselves as they promote frequently competing policy preferences. Because peak associations are not as successful in the environmental sector as they are in the agricultural sector, the former sector appears more fragmented to policy-makers than the latter.

Finally, interest groups carry out a range of activities, including the direct provision of services to their members. However, they are of interest to political scientists primarily because they seek to make a contribution to governance. As discussed in the next section, this can take several forms. Sometimes, groups contribute in a simple manner, transmitting their preferences to

Table 13.1 Four Contributions to Governance by Interest Groups

		Group/Government interactions	
		1. Puzzling	2. Voice
Scope of issues	1. Wide	Participating in Policy-making	Advocating
	2. Narrow	Self-Regulating	Lobbying

policy-makers in hopes of obtaining their incorporation into public policy. However, they can also be motivated genuinely by the search for the best possible solution to collective problems. When this is the case, they are not as wedded to their own perceived interests and ideas. And they are not as harmful to policy-making as they are frequently depicted to be in political discourses and commentaries.

What Does an Interest Group Do?

The forms of the various contributions of interest groups to governance can be distinguished using a simple two by two table (Table 13.1). Columns 1 and 2 correspond to the nature of the relationship between the group and government. Before explaining this, I will focus on the lines that refer to the scope of the issues over which groups and government interact.

Groups naturally differ with regard to the ideas and interests they represent and, therefore, the policy issues over which they interact with government. Some groups address only a limited set of issues. As mentioned above, carefully selecting issues is common among unitary groups, whereas peak associations tend to have wider preoccupations. However, peak associations can also choose to focus on given issues, while unitary groups can choose to adopt a comprehensive approach. The choice of focusing on a narrow or a wide range of issues will often depend on organizational capacity.

Organizational capacity also encourages the development of contrasting forms of interactions with government. Naturally, the attitude government adopts towards groups is an additional influence on those interactions. To better understand differences in group/government interactions, it is useful to summarize political science knowledge on political behaviour.

At least two types of political behaviour are to be found. The first is *strategic action*, that is, political actors interact with each other in view of securing the incorporation of their preferences into public policy. The concepts of "exit" and "voice," developed by Albert Hirschman (1970), belong to such a strategic view, and a number of studies on interest groups are based on these concepts (Cohen, 1998). Strategic groups voice their preferences and expect government to act accordingly. Where groups have competing preferences, however, government simply cannot satisfy everyone. Under these circumstances, government has to choose among groups' preferences. And groups most likely to have their preferences transposed into government policy are those that have the possibility to end their cooperation — to exit — at a cost to government. For example, mobile businesses that voice their preferences for subsidies or tax advantages are likely to receive a favourable hearing from government because they have the possibility of investing abroad, slowing down growth and job creation (see Lindblom, 1977). Therefore, large inequalities among groups persist where voice is the only form of interaction between interest groups and government.

Paraphrasing Hirschman, Walzer (2004: 76) writes that "loyalty has to be a central value of any decent associational life." Indeed, loyalty refers to actors' unwillingness to exit even when their immediate preferences are not satisfied. Loyalty requires a sense of belonging to a community. It is closely associated with a second kind of political behaviour, known as *problem-solving* in the German literature (Scharpf, 1997; Risse, 2000) and *deliberation* in the Anglo-Saxon world (Mansbridge, 1992). In this alternative to strategic action, behaviours take the form of puzzling, truth-seeking, and argumentation. Here, actors are motivated by the search for the best argument, and therefore they are curious about alternative perspectives, even those coming from the "other side" (Mutz, 2006). When they adopt this behaviour, interest groups cooperate with government in the development of policy for the betterment of the community. Where this behaviour prevails, interest groups accept preferences that are not as stable as when they conduct themselves strategically.

Following this distinction between problem-solving and strategic action, the two columns in Table 13.1 differentiate between puzzling and voice. Although tempting, one should avoid treating puzzling as helpful to governance and voice as harmful, simply on the ground that the latter behaviour is strategic action. As underlined below, both voice and puzzling can make positive contributions to governance. Moreover, puzzling is not preferred by generous groups and voice by selfish ones. As underlined above, groups' behaviour depends on organizational capacities, which are not distributed equally among sectors (Olson, 1965). To puzzle efficiently, groups need expensive expertise. In contrast, voicing preferences is cheap. Table 13.1 thus suggests that interest groups can make four contributions to governance: lobbying, advocating, participating in policy-making, and self-regulating.

Lobbying typically involves voicing preferences or transmitting demands to government, exclusively on behalf and for the benefit of members. This contribution to governance is typically made by unitary groups, with a narrow membership. Although the exact origin of the term "lobbying" is uncertain,[1] at the end of the nineteenth century it was used to refer to the private meetings between representatives of interest groups and government legislators in the lobby of the American Congress (Milbrath, 1968: 441–42; Boivin, 1987: 23–24). Given the lack of transparency of these meetings, all the activities included under the term "lobbying" are treated with suspicion. To make lobbying more transparent, many governments, including Canada and the United States, have adopted constraining regulations (Chari, Murphy, and Hogan, 2007; Holtmann, 1993). Again, it bears insisting that not all lobbying is detrimental. When citizens think about lobbying, they often have in mind large resourceful businesses seeking rents from government. In fact, a small association of street residents engages in lobbying when transmitting demands to city government through a simple letter — asking for an improvement of cleanliness on their street, for example. In turn, the information the demand carries about the lack of cleanliness can make a useful contribution to policy-making, helping the city administration to allocate resources where they are most needed, even though improving resource allocation is not the prime motivation of the group.

In fact, a better resource allocation is a side benefit of the demand for a cleaner street. Rational choice policy analysts describe improvement in resource allocation as a positive externality. Unlike a cleaner street, a better allocation of resources is a benefit beyond that desired by the members of the group and for which they do not have the exclusive enjoyment. Goods for which exclusive enjoyment is impossible are known as public goods. Interestingly, some interest groups choose to demand the provision of more public goods by government. In other words, they seek policies that will im-prove the conditions of a large number of people, well beyond group mem-bership. Groups advocating for a reduction in social inequalities, a cleaner environment, or a deepening of democracy are examples. Unlike groups that lobby, the prime motivation behind advocating (top right cell in Table 13.1) is the improvement of conditions for all rather than the material interest of specific group members. Although the possibility that policies satisfying the demands of these groups will benefit members is real, group representatives who prefer advocating over lobbying insist on the positive externality of their preferences.

---

1. Sekwat (1998: 1293) in the *International Encyclopedia of Public Policy and Administration* attributes British origins to lobbying, whereas Milbrath (1968: 441) in the *International Encyclopedia of the Social Sciences* places its origins in the United States.

Interest groups that advocate often do so because they lack the organizational capacity needed to participate in policy-making.[2] In fact, participating in policy-making involves puzzling, and puzzling is costly. In a perfect world, in which organizational capacities would be distributed equally, all groups would participate in policy-making. As I will argue below, an interest group makes its greatest contribution to governance by such participation. Before providing additional details about what policy-making participation entails, I will say a few words on self-regulation (the bottom left cell in Table 13.1).

Some issues are so narrow and specialized that government just cannot resort to its own expertise to make good policies. In such cases, highly specialized interest groups play a prominent role in puzzling over policy solutions. Expert knowledge being a prime exigency in the medical field, the regulation of medical practice, for example, is done essentially by the colleges of doctors and surgeons in collaboration with the various associations of specialists. Wolfgang Streeck and Philippe Schmitter (1985) have explained well how certain interest groups set up "private interest governments" outside of governmental hierarchies. If only because they provide a needed expertise, groups engaged in self-regulation make a useful contribution to governance. However, just like group representatives who advocate rather than lobby, those involved in self-regulation frequently are suspected of being too motivated by the benefits self-regulation entails for their members and not enough by self-regulation's positive externalities.

In sum, interest groups can contribute to governance by performing four types of activities: lobbying, advocating, self-regulating, and participating in policy-making. If some of these activities can harm democratic processes occasionally, all have the potential to make a helpful contribution to governance. I have argued, however, that of all four contributions, policy-making participation is unsurpassed. I now focus on this latter contribution to governance, represented by the top left cell of Table 13.1.

What Is It That Interest Groups Do That Is Useful to Policy-making?

Here I focus on two key aspects of policy-making: policy formulation and policy implementation. Policy formulation refers to discussions among actors and eventually their decisions about policy objectives, the nature of related collective problems — their causes in particular — and the various instruments likely to correct those problems. Policy implementation refers to the administrative efforts required by the instruments to meet policy objectives.

---

2. In fact, some groups try to pursue both simultaneously, but they face serious difficulties (Montpetit, Scala, and Fortier, 2004).

Figure 13.1 Interest Groups' Usefulness to Policy-making

	UNCERTAINTY		
SANCTION	2. Groups useful to policy formulation	4. Groups very useful to policy formulation and implementation	NO SANCTION
	1. Groups less useful	3. Groups useful to policy implementation	
	CERTAINTY		

Figure 13.1 is a useful simplification of the challenges facing policy-makers in both policy formulation and policy implementation.

Policy formulation can be characterized by low or high uncertainty. When certainty is high over a policy issue, actors agree on clear policy objectives, on the nature of the main problems, and on the best solutions to correct those problems. In contrast, when uncertainty prevails, policy actors do not have a clear understanding of objectives, problems, and solutions. To implement policies, policy-makers frequently resort to coercive policy instruments, including prohibitions and sanctions for violators. Indeed, coercion is a key governmental instrument, as the state possesses a monopoly over the legitimate use of force in modern societies (Weber, 1971). However, the use of coercion to deal with several collective problems is inefficient because sanctions can be difficult to apply. In some cases, violators simply cannot be caught; in other cases, sanctions demobilize target populations and worsen problems (Schneider and Ingram, 1997). In short, from issue to issue, the degrees of uncertainty during policy formulation and the possibility to resort to sanction vary. Depending on these variations, policy-makers will be faced with different challenges, and interest groups are not of equal help in surmounting these challenges. The extent to which interest groups can be helpful in surmounting policy-making challenges is summarized in Figure 13.1.

I begin with the easiest policy-making challenges, represented in Quadrant 1 of Figure 13.1. Here, a great deal of certainty surrounds policy formulation. If all objectives cannot be entirely shared by all actors, they agree on some of them. More importantly, they know the causes behind the problems preventing goal attainment and they know what instrument to apply to attain the goal. Here, sanction is an option that can improve policy implementation. Under such circumstances, government can make policy alone. Groups are of little use.

Water quality in a river along which a number of industrial plants operate provides a good example of a situation where actors can be confident during policy formulation and resort to sanctions to correct problems. Industrial plants produce end-of-pipe or point source pollution; that is, they release into the air or into water the residues of their industrial processes. In other words, when water quality in a river is degraded by the residues of industrial processes, the source of the problem can be found with certainty. In fact, a simple comparison of the content of industrial run-offs with the various pollutants found in the river should make for an easy identification of the polluters. Once polluters are identified, improvement in water quality can be achieved without too much difficulty. In fact, government can adopt regulations imposing environmental release standards on polluters and sanction violators. In other words, government does not need the assistance of interest groups to improve water quality in a river polluted by industrial plants. Because the source of the problem and the instrument needed to correct it are known, puzzling with groups can improve policy formulation at the margin only. Moreover, given the small number of potential polluters, the application of sanctions can be handled efficiently by civil servants.

In Quadrant 2, puzzling with groups can improve policy formulation because more uncertainty prevails than in the first quadrant. Improvement in road safety illustrates this situation. In most countries, the number of car accidents causing death or serious injuries is considered a serious problem. In the early 1970s, policy-makers believed that impaired driving was the main cause of the problem, and therefore the road safety policies developed during this decade were to discourage people from driving while under the influence of alcohol. At the outset, it was not entirely clear how the influence of alcohol could be measured. To develop regulations prohibiting drunk driving, policy-makers needed a precise standard to decide what drunk driving was and was not. In other words, policy-makers had to puzzle over this issue with various experts, some belonging to interest groups. It was through such puzzling that a decision was made to use the presence of alcohol in blood as the measuring device necessary to set a standard. The setting of the standard was also the object of puzzling. Policy-makers had to decide whether the standard should be set at zero, thereby prohibiting drivers from having a glass of wine with their dinners, or whether a reasonable limit should be set. What constituted a reasonable limit was itself subject to much uncertainty. Several groups, including health professionals, police associations, automobile clubs, and restaurant owners, felt they had something to contribute to policy formulation. Moreover, their participation in policy debates, problem-solving, and deliberation (called puzzling in Table 13.1) was appreciated by policy-makers who were uncertain about the course of action on which they should settle. Puzzling helped reduce their uncertainty. After having heard all sides and tested some arguments, policy-makers could decide which was most convincing. And decisions are made easier when interest groups do not cling rigidly to their preferences but persuade each other about the validity of their respective arguments.

Interestingly, 20 years of policy efforts have contributed to the sharp decline of impaired driving in the developed world. This success can be attributed in part to severe sanctions for drunk drivers. However, the number of casualties on roads continues to be considered problematic in most countries. Consequently, the puzzling over this policy issue goes on. In fact, it has expanded far beyond the issue of impaired driving, with government puzzling conjointly with interest groups on matters as diverse as youths' attitudes towards driving, the use of cell phones while driving, and appropriate speed limits. In other words, the expansion of the issue of road safety beyond impaired driving has increased uncertainty and therefore calls for the expansion of the range of interest groups involved in policy formulation.

In some policy issues policy-makers value the participation of groups to policy-making for their role during policy implementation rather than their role in policy formulation. This is true when certainty prevails during policy formulation, thereby reducing the importance of puzzling, while sanction is not an option during implementation (Quadrant 3 in Figure 13.1). Think for example of river wildlife endangered by the propagation of a non-native seaweed transported from its native ecosystem by pleasure boaters. In this case, the cause of the problem is well known: non-native seaweed transported by pleasure boats. The solutions are also known: the removal of the non-native seaweed and the prevention of future contamination by pleasure boats. The problem here is not so much related to the formulation of a policy than its implementation. Indeed, removing seaweed cannot be accomplished through sanction, nor does sanction provide the best instrument to prevent future contamination. It is unlikely that government alone is capable of overcoming the challenges of policy implementation over such an issue. Interest groups, however, can help.

Interest groups representing the users of the river can help locate areas where the seaweed is present and needs to be removed. Government employees can certainly inspect the river, but their inspection would be all the more efficient if they can be alerted about problematic areas by those who spend time on the river, including fishers, hunters, birdwatchers, and pleasure boaters, as well as the members of various environmental groups. Concerned about the efficiency of their work, government employees responsible for the inspection of the river will be in contact with group representatives who can sensitize their members to the problem and encourage the transmission of information. In any event, government employees are not sufficiently numerous to handle the removal of the seaweed by themselves. They need concerned citizens to help in this task, and interest groups are naturally well placed to mobilize such citizens.

Sanctioning pleasure boaters might not be the best instrument to prevent future contamination. First, the inspection of boats to find violators would not be a simple task. It would require underwater inspection for seaweed trapped in keels and propellers. In the peak of the boating season, such inspections would be expensive, requiring a large number of qualified government employees. Under these circumstances, sanction is unlikely the best instrument. It would probably be preferable to sensitize pleasure boaters about the importance of carrying out their own inspection regularly. Again, the representatives of the various associations of pleasure boaters are those who have the easiest access to pleasure boaters and are therefore well placed to help government carry on information campaigns.

Quadrant 4 represents issues for which groups are helpful for both policy formulation and implementation. It includes issues such as the promotion of public health, the improvement of education, the reduction of non-point source environmental contamination, etc. Uncertainty prevails about the causes and solutions to these problems. For example, policy-makers used to believe that health problems only required curative health care systems. This certainty no longer prevails, with health problems related as frequently to social conditions as they are to biological pathologies. Much puzzling is currently going on over the causes and solutions to health problems in developed countries. Meanwhile, sanctions appear inefficient as solutions to resolve these problems. For example, sanctioning high school dropouts to raise the level of education of a society can be grossly counterproductive. Sanctions might increase the number of students in class and even graduation rates. Forcing kids to attend school might also cause alienation and deprive them of a taste to contribute to society. Clearly, persuading them that education is stimulating and necessary to their future welfare is a better option than sanction. It is in this context that the contribution of community and public education groups to the promotion of education among disadvantaged youth has been valued by government.

In short, governments need the help of interest groups to formulate and implement policies. In fact, most policy issues facing modern governments are located within the fourth quadrant of Figure 13.1. Policy-makers around the world realize the complexity of collective problems and therefore the uncertainty surrounding policy development. Consequently, they value groups that puzzle over ways to address these problems. Long experience with the use of coercion and accompanying sanctions also has taught policy-makers that they have to consider a wider range of policy instruments, several of which the state cannot implement alone efficiently. In other words, government increasingly needs the involvement of interest groups in the policy-making process.

Are There Constraints on Interest Group Participation in Policy-making?

Government increasingly needs interest groups, but interest groups frequently fail to make the expected contribution. I have already mentioned that groups have different organizational capacities, sometimes preventing effective participation in puzzling. Clearly, peak associations in agriculture are likely to have more resources to gather expertise and contribute valuable ideas to policy formulation than the small unitary groups characterizing the environmental sector. Peak associations also have more staff available to assist civil servants in the implementation of policy than small unitary groups. The interest group literature explains variation in group capacity based on differences in the nature of the good they seek (Olson, 1965). Groups advocating the provision of a public good should remain weak, as members are not incited to make large contributions whose benefit escapes them in good part, spreading to the wider population. In contrast, groups that lobby for a good that is exclusive to their members should obtain more support from members, since the size of member contributions could affect the provision of the good, while failure to contribute might endanger this outcome. Thus, farmers should make larger contributions to groups lobbying for farm subsidies than environmentalists to groups advocating for cleaner air. Clean air can be enjoyed by everyone, even individuals who refuse to make a contribution to environmental groups, while subsidies are exclusive to farmers, granted that farm groups have sufficient resources to lobby effectively for these subsidies.

However, the nature of goods does not explain all differences in groups' capacity and willingness to contribute to policy-making. It does not explain why peak associations of farm groups, for example, frequently choose to participate in policy-making rather than confining themselves to lobbying strategies. History frequently provides a useful complement to the nature of goods in explaining variations in the contribution of groups to governance. In every sector of every country over time, national institutions, political parties, policies, and circumstances have combined in different ways to shape patterns of relationships between interest groups and government (Martin and Swank, 2008). Sometimes, these relationships have developed into cooperation and sometimes into adversarialism between interest groups and government. These relationships and their patterns are known as policy

Table 13.2 Forms of Policy Networks

Form of network	Openness	State autonomy	Expertise distribution	Interest group contribution to governance
Pluralist	High	High	Equal	Constrained by the number of groups
Corporatist	Weak	Weak	Equal	Constrained to a limited number of groups
Dirigist	High	High	Unequal	Almost or entirely absent
Clientelist	Weak	Weak	Unequal	Limited to a single group

networks (Coleman and Skogstad, 1990). In other words, interest groups do not choose (or not) to participate in policy-making; they simply find themselves (or not) in networks particularly conducive to such participation. An interest group might want to change the network within which it operates with a view to improving its contribution to governance. Unfortunately, the shape of such a structure, built over a long period of time, evolves though the combination and recombination of circumstances rather than the will of any single actor. In other words, the contribution of interest groups to governance is severely constrained by the form of the policy networks within which they happen to find themselves. The four policy network forms most frequently encountered in the literature are presented in Table 13.2, along with key characteristics.

Pluralist networks are common in Canada and the United States. Access to these networks is open, that is, any group can enter and exit easily. Because of their openness, pluralist networks typically comprise a large number of unitary groups at any time. Because of this large number of groups, they voice a wide range of policy preferences, contributing to the autonomy of government officials in decision-making. In other words, government officials in pluralist networks are free to make policies that best match their own preferences or those of the groups of their choosing. However, pluralist networks distribute expertise equally between the state and interest groups. Therefore, interest groups in these networks can provide reasonable arguments to explain their dissatisfaction with policy choices, encouraging adversarial debates.

Interest groups that find themselves in pluralist policy networks will often make a limited contribution to governance. They are likely to reason that their sheer number makes for difficult conditions to puzzle, let alone become partners of government in policy implementation. Under these conditions, they should limit their investment in the development of their expertise, which anyway runs high risks of being received with hostility or of being ignored. Under these conditions, interest groups will invest just enough to make their policy preferences credible, but probably not enough to puzzle effectively. In short, interest groups in pluralist networks often advocate and lobby rather than participate in policy-making.

Corporatist networks are common in Europe, but they can also be found in some sectors in North America. In contrast to pluralist networks, they are closed around a limited number of interest groups, which are frequently peak associations. New actors do not have easy access to corporatist networks and therefore do not exit once inside. The range of ideas represented in corporatist networks thus is narrower than in pluralist networks. These ideas are also less polarized. However, corporatist networks are not made up of actors holding entirely cohesive ideas. Frequently, they include groups representing segments of society with distinctive interests. For example, a corporatist network can include unions representing workers and groups representing business. Under such circumstances, the corporatist network serves to mediate actors' preferences, which would otherwise be competing. To achieve mediation, actors who belong to the network develop cooperative rather than adversarial relationships. Actors consider each other as partners. Therefore, state actors cannot make decisions autonomously when they find themselves in corporatist networks. Rather, they make decisions in concert with their network partners. Likewise, sustaining trust among the partners in the network is easier in the absence of a gross imbalance in the distribution of expertise.

Interest groups that find themselves in corporatist networks can make a significant contribution to policy-making. Along with their partners, they can puzzle around collective problems, their causes, and potential solutions (Öberg, 2002). The more varied the interests included in a corporatist network, the wider the range of solutions over which puzzling occurs. At the same time, corporatist networks cannot reflect the range of interests and ideas found in society to the same extent as pluralist networks do. If actors in these networks consider themselves as trustworthy partners, it is precisely because their number is limited. In other words, puzzling, the upside of corporatist networks, is closely related to their downside, which is the exclusion of many interest groups.

Dirigist and *clientelist* networks are least common in North America and in Europe. Nevertheless, they do exist in some places and can provide a powerful explanation of policy failure (Montpetit, 2003). In fact, these networks are least conducive to interest groups' contribution to policy-making. While clientelist networks are closed to all groups but one, dirigist networks are open. However, their openness is deceiving as state actors do not value the contribution of these interest groups, whatever form it takes. Consequently, group density in dirigist networks is low, as citizens and interests have too few reasons to organize into groups. In dirigist networks, it is more rewarding for citizens to join the state, the civil service for instance, than to join interest groups. In fact, government actors in dirigist networks, frequently large bureaucracies, enjoy considerable autonomy in the making of policy decisions. In addition, they are resourceful, creating an imbalance in the distribution of expertise that disadvantages interest groups. Clientelist networks are similar, but the advantage in terms of expertise distribution and autonomy is with the only interest group included in the network. In clientelist networks, government is subservient to the group. To the extent puzzling requires at least two actors, very little of it can occur in either clientelist or dirigist networks.

All this is to say that while interest groups may be genuinely motivated to participate in policy-making, they will face constraints, severe in some networks and less so in others. Fortunately, pluralist and corporatist networks, which allow some contribution to governance by groups, are more common than clientelist and dirigist networks. Even in pluralist and corporatist networks, however, constraints exist. In pluralist networks, interest groups frequently cannot contribute to governance to their full potential, frustrating policy-makers who expect more. In corporatist networks, some groups enjoy full and effective participation in policy-making, but many others are excluded and disappointed. All the political noise created by this frustration and disappointment sometimes leaves citizens with a sense that they are being badly governed. In fact, interest groups and government frequently search together for policy solutions that provide widespread benefits, collaborating effectively, if imperfectly, over their implementation.

Conclusion

Are interest groups useful or harmful? Do groups prevent policy-makers from serving the common good? Answers to these questions are more complex than the questions themselves. A simple yes or no would be unconvincing. In fact, no consensus exists among analysts on the substance of policies that would serve the common good. Under these circumstances, analysts of interest groups simply observe group behaviours and decide whether they are likely to influence the adoption of policy that could not be understood as serving the common good under any circumstances. In this chapter, I have pointed out the adoption of behaviour by interest groups that is not inconsistent with serving the common good. Puzzling over policy solutions and contributing to their implementation are examples of behaviour unlikely to be averse to the common good. In other words, interest groups can be useful to policy-makers and citizens.

This being said, interest groups are not entirely free to make the contribution they would like to make to governance. They find themselves in policy networks that constrain their behaviour. Unfortunately, analysts of interest groups too often focus on these constraints, forgetting that networks commonly encountered in the Western world also present opportunities for groups to make valuable contributions to governance. For example, I have illustrated how corporatist networks enable some interest groups to participate in policy-making as partners of state actors and how pluralist networks enable the expression of a plurality of policy arguments. In addition, one should not exaggerate the deterministic character of policy networks; interest groups are sometimes successful at overcoming the constraints posed by networks, contributing to policy-making above and beyond what is expected of them.

References and Suggested Readings

Boivin, Dominique. 1987. *Le lobbying: ou le pouvoir des groupes de pression*. Montréal: Éditions du Méridien.

Chari, Raj, Gary Murphy, and John Hogan. 2007. "Regulating Lobbyists: A Comparative Analysis of the United States, Canada, Germany, and the European Union," *The Political Quarterly* 78, 3: 422–38.

Coen, David. 1998. "The European Business Interest and the Nation State: Large-firm Lobbying in the European Union and Member States." *Journal of Public Policy* 18: 75–100.

Coleman, William D., and Grace Skogstad, Eds. 1990. *Policy Communities and Public Policy in Canada: A Structural Approach*. Mississauga: Copp Clark Pitman.

Hirschman, Albert O. 1970. *Exit, Voice, and Loyalty: Responses to Decline in Firms, Organizations and States*. Cambridge: Harvard University Press.

Holtmann, Felix. 1993. *Sur la voie de la transparence: révision de la loi sur l'enregistrement des lobbyistes*. Ottawa: Rapport du Comité permanent de la consommation et des affaires commerciales et de l'administration gouvernementale.

Lindblom, Charles. 1977. *Politics and Markets*. New York: Basic Books.

Mansbridge, Jane J. 1992. "A Deliberative Theory of Interest Representation." In M. Petracca, ed., *The Politics of Interest: Interest Groups Transformed*. Boulder: Westview Press. 32–57.

Martin, Jo Cathie, and Duane Swank. 2008. "The Political Origins of Coordinated Capitalism: Business Organizations, Party Systems, and State Structure in the Age of Innocence." *American Political Science Review* 102: 181–98.

Milbrath, Lester W. 1968. "Lobbying." In D.L. Sills, ed., *International Encyclopedia of the Social Sciences*. New York: The Macmillan Company and the Free Press.

Montpetit, Éric. 2003. *Misplaced Distrust: Policy Networks and the Environment in France, the United States, and Canada*. Vancouver: University of British Columbia Press.

Montpetit, Éric. 2004. "Governance and Interest Group Activities." In James Bickerton and Alain-G. Gagnon, eds., *Canadian Politics*, 4th ed. Peterborough: Broadview Press. 305–22.

Montpetit, Éric, Francesca Scala, and Isabelle Fortier. 2004. "The Paradox of Deliberative Democracy: the National Action Committee on the Status of Women and Canada's Policy on Reproductive Technology." *Policy Sciences* 37: 137–57.

Mutz, Diana C. 2006. *Hearing the Other Side: Deliberative versus Participatory Democracy.* Cambridge: Cambridge University Press.

Öberg, Perola. 2002. "Does Administrative Corporatism Promote Trust and Deliberation?" *Governance* 15, 4: 455–75.

Olson, Mancur. 1965. *The Logic of Collective Action: Public Goods and the Theory of Groups.* Cambridge: Harvard University Press.

Phillips, Susan D. 1993. "Of Public Interest Groups and Sceptics: A Realist's Reply to Professor Stanbury." *Canadian Public Administration* 36, 4: 606–16.

Phillips, Susan D., Leslie A. Pal, and Daniel J. Savas. 1992. *Interest Groups in the Policy Process.* Working Paper Series. Ottawa: Carleton University, School of Public Administration.

Pross, Paul A. 1986. *Group Politics and Public Policy*, 2nd ed. Toronto: Oxford University Press.

Pross, Paul A. 1995. "Pressure Groups: Talking Chameleons." In Michael S. Whittington and Glen Williams, eds., *Canadian Politics in the 1990s.* Toronto: Nelson Canada. 252–75.

Risse, Thomas. 2000. "'Let's Argue!': Communicative Action in World Politics." *International Organization* 45, 1: 1–39.

Scala Francesca, Éric Montpetit, and Isabelle Fortier. 2005. "NAC's Organizational Practices and the Politics of Assisted Reproductive Technologies in Canada." *Canadian Journal of Political Science* 38: 581-604.

Scharpf, Fritz W. 1997. *Games Real Actors Play: Actor-Centered Institutionalism in Policy Research.* Boulder: Westview Press.

Schneider, Anne Larason, and Helen Ingram. 1997. *Policy Design for Democracy.* Lawrence: University Press of Kansas.

Seidle, Leslie F. 1993. "Interest Advocacy through Parliamentary Channels: Representation and Accommodation." In F. Leslie Seidle, ed., *Equity & Community: The Charter, Interest Advocacy, and Representation.* Montreal: Institute for Research on Public Policy. 189–225.

Sekwat, Alex. 1998. "Lobbying." In Jay M. Shafritz, ed., *International Encyclopedia of Public Policy and Administration*, Vol. 3. Boulder: Westview Press.

Stanbury, William T. 1993. "A Sceptic's Guide to the Claims of So-Called Public Interest Groups." *Canadian Public Administration* 36, 4: 580–605.

Stone, Deborah. 1997. *Policy Paradox: The Art of Political Decision Making.* New York: W.W. Norton and Company.

Streeck, Wolfgang, and Philippe C. Schmitter. 1985. "Community, Market, State and Associations? The Prospective Contribution of Interest Governance to Social Order." In Wolfgang Streeck and Philippe C. Schmitter, eds., *Private Interest Government.* London: Sage Publications. 1–29.

Walzer, Michael. 2004. *Politics and Passion: Toward a More Egalitarian Liberalism.* New Haven: Yale University Press.

Weber, Max. 1995. *Économie et société / 1.* Paris: Plon.

Young, Lisa, and Joanna Everitt. 2004. *Advocacy Groups.* Vancouver: University of British Columbia Press.

Young, R.A., and Shirley M. Forsyth. 1991. "Leaders' Communications in Public-Interest and Material-Interest Groups." *Canadian Journal of Political Science* 24, 3: 525–40.

fourteen

Women (Not) in Politics: Women's Electoral Participation

LISA YOUNG

Comparing Canada to much of the rest of the world, it is evident that Canadian women enjoy considerable political freedom, legal equality, and educational and economic opportunity. These advantages are a product of decades of women's activism, both inside and outside the halls of power. Fundamental political freedoms like the right to vote, to run for office, and to be considered "persons" under the law were won by activists insisting that women were both qualified and entitled to participate in the democratic life of their country.

In many respects, these activists were successful: Canadian women now enjoy full equality under the law; the Canadian Charter of Rights and Freedoms and various human rights acts explicitly ban discrimination based on gender. Women vote in Canadian elections in numbers similar to men and face no formal barriers to holding elected office. Both the chief justice of the Supreme Court of Canada and the governor general are women, and a woman has served briefly as prime minister. Women comprise the majority of undergraduate students on Canadian campuses and have made remarkable inroads into many previously male-dominated occupations. Although women still earn less, on average, than men, the gap is decreasing and is smaller than that found in many countries. Canadian women have access to universal health care services and are largely able to control their reproductive functions.

In light of this, it would be reasonable to expect that Canada would be a world leader in terms of women's political representation. In fact, this is not the case. As of 2007, Canada ranked forty-seventh internationally in a comparison of women's representation in national legislatures, lagging behind countries in Scandinavia and elsewhere in Western Europe, as well as behind emerging democracies like Afghanistan, Argentina, and Rwanda (IPU, 2007). This chapter provides an overview of Canadian political scientists' efforts to understand the barriers to the representation of women in the formal political arena. It does not address the studies that examine women's extensive participation in informal but equally political arenas such as activism through interest groups, social movements, and community organizations. By focusing exclusively on the world of voting, parties, and elections, this chapter overlooks an important part of the story of Canadian women's political participation but illuminates the extent to which the electoral arena remains foreign territory to many Canadian women.

A discussion of the patterns of women's involvement and non-involvement in the formal political arena must begin with some consideration of women's ambivalence towards electoral politics. Despite all the gains women have made in terms of education, participation in the workforce, and participation in public life, survey findings still report that they are less likely than men to be interested in politics and are less knowledgeable about the formal political arena. In a recent study, Gidengil *et al.* (2003a) found that women are consistently less knowledgeable about political parties' policy stances and leaders than are men. Even women's growing access to education does not diminish the gap: university-educated women score lower on measures of political knowledge than university-educated men. It is not clear why women are less interested in and knowledgeable about politics than are men. Perhaps the fact that men remain the majority of politicians and political leaders sends a subtle message to women that this world is closed to them. Perhaps the relative absence of women from political life means that the issues that matter to them are not constructed in a way that many women consider to be relevant to their lives. And, quite possibly, the social legacy of politics being "men's business" lives on, despite women's entry into all sorts of arenas that were just as exclusionary in the past. No matter what their source, these gender differences in political knowledge and interest are crucially important: knowledge is an essential resource for political activism of any kind, and if women lack it, they will remain marginal to political life.

Other scholars have examined women's different political priorities and attitudes and concluded that they constitute a discernible sub-culture within the Canadian political culture (O'Neill, 2002). If we accept that this is the case, then an ambivalent relationship to formal politics is certainly a salient aspect of this sub-culture. This ambivalence provides the underpinnings for examining studies of women's participation in, and exclusion from, the formal political life of Canada; it provides at least a partial explanation for the title of this chapter, which notes that the examination of women's involvement in Canadian political life focuses as much on their absence as it does on their presence.

To organize this discussion of women's electoral participation, I divide the research into two broad categories: studies that ask "where are the women in the political process?" and studies that ask "what do women do when they get there?" The former category encompasses studies of women as voters, women's participation in political parties, and women as candidates for election. The focus of these studies, for the most part, is on women's relative absence from the formal political process and probes the reasons for this. The latter category concentrates on what women do once they have entered the formal political arena, be it as political party members or legislators. A portion of these studies focus on women's experiences of discrimination within political institutions — as legislators who are subjected to abuse by their colleagues or as party leaders who face extra scrutiny from the mass media. The larger body of literature addresses the question of whether women's participation in the formal political arena makes a difference in terms of their behaviour or policy outcomes.

Where Are the Women?

Although women's representation in political elites has increased steadily over the past three decades, it remains low when compared to many other countries and to the democratic ideal of representation proportionate to women's presence in the population. It is noteworthy that more than 30 years after Jill Vickers (1978) published an article in *Atlantis* asking "Where Are The Women In Canadian Politics?" we are still asking the same question. The consistent theme that emerges through these studies is: *where power is, women are not*. This applies equally to studies of women in municipal politics and analyses of the composition of the current federal Cabinet. The focus of much of this literature, then, has been to document this pattern and to explain it, usually with a view to suggesting some remedy.

Women as Voters

The most basic and fundamental form of participation in the formal political arena is voting. This fundamental democratic right was denied to most Canadian women until 1920, women in Quebec until 1940, and many Aboriginal women until the 1960s. In the period after women won the vote, turnout tended to be lower among women than among men, but since the 1970s women have been as likely, if not more likely, than men to cast a ballot.

Has the vote turned into a powerful political resource for women? Given that women constitute over half the electorate and are slightly more inclined to vote than their male counterparts, women have the theoretical potential as a numeric majority to exercise considerable control over the political process. For the most part, however, this theoretical possibility has not been realized. Like men, women do not vote as a bloc. They differ in their fundamental political perspectives and their political interests and their voting behaviour varies accordingly. To the extent that there have been systematic patterns of difference between the voting behaviour of men and women — referred to as an electoral "gender gap" — political parties have shown some responsiveness to concerns specifically associated with women.

There are persistent gender gaps in party preference in Canada at the federal level. Men are somewhat more likely to support parties on the right (Reform/Canadian Alliance, and now the Conservative Party), and women more likely to support parties on the centre and left of the political spectrum (the Liberals and NDP). These gender gaps in party preference are reflective of consistent patterns of gender difference in policy attitudes, with women "more sceptical of the virtues of free enterprise, more supportive of the welfare system, and more reluctant to endorse market solutions than men" (Gidengil *et al.*, 2003b: 154; see also Gidengil *et al.*, 2005; Everitt, 1998; Gidengil, 1995). Analysis of gender differences in attitudes and party preference indicate that electoral gender gaps are best understood as "cultural" in character, as they are rooted in men's greater support for free enterprise, closer ties to the United States, and social conservatism (Gidengil *et al.*, 2006).

These gender gaps in voting have, however, seldom been parlayed into a source of influence for women. Canadian feminist leaders have not followed the lead of their American counterparts in trying to construct a political meaning for gender differences in voting, thereby turning the gender gap into a political resource. This is due in part to the pattern of gender differences among Canadian voters, with the Liberal Party rather than the more feminist NDP historically tending to benefit the most from gender gaps (Young, 2000: 202).

Women in Political Parties

Women were involved in Canadian political parties throughout most of the twentieth century, but until the 1970s their participation tended to be channelled into supportive roles. Women's involvement in the two major parties at the time (the Liberals and the Progressive Conservatives) took the form of activism in ladies' auxiliary organizations that supported the party but played no role in directing it. By the late 1960s, attitudes about women's roles in society were coming into question, and this led women inside the parties to challenge the character of their involvement in party affairs. In 1970 the Report of the Royal Commission on the Status of Women encouraged this, advocating that the parties should disband their ladies' auxiliaries and encourage women to participate in the mainstream of party life. Through the 1970s, women's organizations in the party were converted into feminist organizations that promoted women's participation in the parties on an equal footing.

Despite the activism of women in the three major federal political parties at the time, women remained under-represented in most facets of party life through the 1980s. The most comprehensive study of women's under-representation in party politics in English Canada is Sylvia Bashevkin's *Toeing the Lines* (1993). Bashevkin found that the more electorally competitive the party, the greater the under-representation of women within it. She also found that women's participation in parties tended to be channelled into traditional roles such as secretary of the riding association, thereby creating "pink collar ghettoes" within the parties. Some parties, most notably the NDP at the federal level and in some provinces, have adopted internal affirmative action programs, and these have gone some distance towards improving women's representation within the party (Praud, 1998). In her analysis of the women's committee of the Parti Québécois, Jocelyne Praud (2003) found that the activism of that committee resulted in moderate numerical gains for women, generally exceeding that of the Liberal Party of Quebec.

A survey of members of the five major national political parties in 2000 (prior to the merger of the Canadian Alliance and Progressive Conservatives) found that women remain a minority among party members. Young and Cross (2003) report that only 38 per cent of party members in their survey were women. This proportion varies somewhat by party, with parties that have maintained organizations focused on women's participation (the Liberals and NDP) exceeding those that have eschewed them (the Progressive Conservatives and Canadian Alliance). In addition, this corresponds generally with the patterns of gender difference in electoral support for the parties. Examining patterns of recruitment into the parties, the study finds that women are more likely than men to have been asked to join the party, rather than taking the initiative themselves. Women were also more likely to have been recruited into the party to support a candidate for the party's nomination or leadership. According to these findings, once women have been recruited into the party, their activities differ little from those of their male counterparts. Despite this, the study finds that female party members see themselves as insufficiently influential within their parties and are (with the exception of members of the Canadian Alliance) generally supportive of measures to increase their influence and the number of women holding elected office.

The under-representation of women in political parties reflects gender differences in evaluations of political parties versus interest groups. In a study of politically active young people on Canadian university campuses, Young and Cross (2007) found that women were more likely to join interest groups than the youth wing of political parties and that they were more negative in their evaluations of political parties than were young men.

Women as Candidates

The focus of much of the women in politics research in Canada is on the issue of why women remain under-represented in numeric terms in the House of Commons, provincial legislatures, and city councils. These institutions are at the heart of representative democracy in Canada; city councils act as decision-making bodies in their own right, and legislatures are the institutions from which Cabinets are drawn and to which Cabinets must answer. Exclusion of women from these representative institutions signifies exclusion from political decision-making. It is not surprising, then, that women's under-representation in these elected bodies has been the focus of much research.

Feminist political scientists began to study the barriers to women's election in the 1970s, roughly the time when the numbers of women elected gradually began to increase from few or no women to the roughly 20 per cent of provincial and federal elected representatives we now have. At first, studies examined the role political parties played as gatekeepers, consistently choosing men over women in electoral districts the party expected to win but willing to nominate women in ridings where the party's prospects were poor. Other studies have emphasized the rules governing nomination campaigns, political culture, the party system, and women's unwillingness to run for office.

One would expect that the level of government for which the election is held makes some difference to the representation of women. There has been a perception that local governments have been more open to women than provincial or federal governments. The Federation of Canadian Municipalities (2007) reports, however, that women comprise approximately 20 per cent of the members of elected municipal governments. Women's representation in federal and provincial legislatures is at a similar level, holding steady at just over 20 per cent federally and ranging from a low of 11 per cent to a high of 27 per cent in the provinces and territories (Equal Voice, 2007).

There is no evidence that the electorate is responsible for the under-representation of women. Studies at both the federal level (Denton, 1984) and the municipal level (Kushner et al., 1997) show that voters do not discriminate against female candidates. How, then, has women's relative absence from the formal legislative sphere been explained?

- *The electoral system*: Like Britain and the United States, Canada uses a single-member plurality electoral system. Not coincidentally, Britain and the United States have comparably low levels of women's representation to Canada. In a single-member system, it is more difficult to design a quota system that ensures that a certain number of seats are set aside for women. In list-based proportional representation systems, it is possible to "zip" the lists so that it alternates between the names of women and men. Women's representation tends to be much higher under such systems. In recent years, several Canadian provinces have considered moving to some form of proportional representation system, but these proposals have all been defeated in referendums.

• *Party gatekeepers*: Initial studies identified political parties as the "gatekeepers" preventing women from winning party nominations (Brodie, 1985). Candidate nomination in Canadian political parties is a decentralized affair, with party members in each electoral district voting to elect the party's candidate. Analysing patterns of nomination between 1975 and 1994 at the provincial level, Studlar and Matland (1996) conclude that there was evidence supporting the contention that parties tended to nominate women disproportionately in ridings they were unlikely to win in the 1970s, but there is no evidence that this took place systematically after the mid-1980s. The exception to this is Jerome Black's (2003) finding that minority women candidates report being encouraged by party officials to run, but they tended to be placed in ridings where their party was normally expected to lose. Some parties, notably the federal NDP, have undertaken explicit affirmative action campaigns for women and members of minority groups, which have yielded promising results (Erickson, 1998). The Liberal Party of Canada has, on occasion, appointed female candidates, circumventing the usual nomination process. In advance of the 2008 federal election, the Liberal Party formally committed itself to ensuring that one-third of its candidates would be women; one-quarter of the current Liberal caucus is female. Since it was formed in 2004, the Conservative Party has not made any formal efforts to nominate or elect women, who comprise 16 per cent of its current caucus.

• *Characteristics of the district*: At the municipal level, where parties do not act as gatekeepers, the size of the community appears to have some effect on the number of women elected. Both Kushner *et al.* (1997) and Gidengil and Vengroff (1997) found that women were more likely to be elected either in the smallest or the largest municipalities. This is in keeping with Studlar and Matland's (1996) finding at the provincial level that women were more likely to be elected from urban constituencies.

• *Political culture*: Political culture has been employed as an explanation for why the Atlantic provinces consistently lagged behind other provinces in the rate of increase in the number of women nominated and elected (see Arscott and Trimble, 1997). More recently, in a comparative analysis of rates of election to provincial and American state legislatures, Louise Carbert (2002) found evidence that higher rates of election of women are partially a consequence of a populist legacy, predominantly in Western states and provinces. More recently, however, there have been sharp increases in the representation of women in the legislatures of Ontario, Quebec, Prince Edward Island, and Newfoundland and Labrador. Arguably, Quebec stands out as the province where women's representation is highlighted, with women making up half the members of the province's Cabinet.

- *Party systems*: Some analyses suggest that the constellation of parties present in the system affect the likelihood that women will be nominated in winnable ridings. Studlar and Matland (1996) found evidence that the NDP played a crucial role in accelerating the rate at which women's representation increased. Similarly, analyzing patterns of election of women at the provincial level, Arscott and Trimble (1997) found that election of NDP governments in three provinces in the 1990s was accompanied by sharp increases in the number of women elected. The province with the highest proportion of women in its legislature is Manitoba, which the NDP has governed for over a decade. In the case of Ontario, the defeat of the NDP Rae government by the Progressive Conservative Harris government also saw a decline in the proportion of women in the provincial legislature (Tolley, 2000).

- *Women's unwillingness to run for office*: In her analyses of patterns of women's candidacy, Erickson (1991, 1993) concludes that the major explanation for the relatively low number of women running for office is a question of supply: women are unwilling to come forward and run for office. There are two aspects to this. The first relates to women who might well be interested in running for office, but are not inclined to step forward, instead waiting to be asked. In cases such as these, Erickson's recommendation that party constituency associations employ search committees to encourage well-qualified candidates to run is relevant. The second and more intractable aspect of this is some degree of disinterest among women in pursuing political careers. It is difficult, if not impossible, to gauge the extent of this. Women's reasons for not wanting to enter the formal political arena are undoubtedly complex. Tolley's (2000) interviews with municipal politicians in Ontario suggest that role strain (the difficulty of combining family with a political career) is a significant factor at all three levels of government, but it is even more acutely felt at the provincial and federal levels where extensive travel to a geographically distant capital is often a requirement of the job. Studying individuals in professions from which politicians are usually recruited in the United States, Fox and Lawless (2004) find that women are less likely to harbour political ambitions or to see themselves as qualified to run for political office. Similar factors are likely at play in the Canadian context.

One of the effects of women's under-representation in legislatures is a similar pattern of under-representation in Cabinets and among party leaders. With the exception of Quebec, where Premier Jean Charest has twice appointed a Cabinet with equal representation from the two genders, women comprise less than one-third of Cabinet ministers in all provinces and the federal Cabinet (Equal Voice, 2007). Although several women have served as party leader, only one (Catherine Callbeck of Prince Edward Island) has been elected premier. Another, Rita Johnson, served briefly as premier of British Columbia after winning her party's leadership. The same pattern held for Kim Campbell, who held the post of prime minister briefly before her party lost the 1993 federal election.

What Happens When They Get There?

Despite these barriers to the election of women, the number of women on city councils, in provincial legislatures, and in the House of Commons in Ottawa has increased over the past quarter-century. This raises the question of what happens when they get there. Have women transformed these representative institutions, bringing new perspectives and new issues into the political discourse? Or have they assimilated into the dominant political culture and struggled to gain credibility in a sometimes hostile environment? Increasingly, research on women in politics is on women who have entered the formal political arena.

Evidence of Discrimination

Studies of women who have been elected to serve in legislatures have found evidence that, once elected, they experience discrimination on the part of their male colleagues (for examples of this, see Trimble and Arscott, 2003: ch. 5; and O'Neill, 2002: 45). Clearly, these experiences are not universal and, as in many workplaces, are gradually improving over time. Nonetheless, these accounts are discouraging to those who might consider pursuing political careers.

Joanna Everitt and Elisabeth Gidengil (2003) examine media coverage and public perceptions of female party leaders. Analyzing the content of television coverage of leaders' debates in recent Canadian elections, they found journalists to be more inclined to describe female party leaders' behaviour as aggressive and, consequently, inappropriate for women. Compounding this, they found that female party leaders who avoid engaging in behaviours that might be considered aggressive are not rewarded for this by journalists; rather, they receive very little media coverage at all. In short, the gendered character of media coverage creates a catch-22 for women in politics: they can either engage fully and be mocked and criticized for their behaviour, or they can act in a conciliatory manner and be ignored. In another study, Gidengil and Everitt (2002) used experimental method to determine whether students (standing in for the general public) rated the aggressiveness of fictitious political leaders differently when they used confrontational 'language. They found that female students, but not their male counterparts, were more likely to perceive the hypothetical female leader as aggressive when she used confrontational language. They conclude that this gendered mediation of speech makes it harder for female candidates to appeal to female voters. This, they conclude, has the potential to reverse any positive effect that identification with a candidate of the same sex might have for female candidates. In a similar vein, Sampert and Trimble (2003) found that in the 2000 federal election, the national news media provided less coverage of the female-led NDP than of the comparably placed, but male-led, Progressive Conservative Party. According to their findings, what media coverage there was of Alexa McDonough and the NDP tended not to use the "aggressive action words" otherwise typical of political coverage.

Job Dissatisfaction

There is some evidence that women, once they are elected, find the constraints of political life more frustrating than do many of their male colleagues. In his study of MPs, Docherty (1997: xxiii) notes that "women [in the House of Commons] are less likely to experience satisfying careers. Female MPs tend to enter elected life hoping to participate in policy changes and other substantive activities. As well, the House of Commons is best suited for an adversarial, combative type of debate and does not favour mechanisms of consensus. Many female MPs indicated that they would have preferred to engage in the latter type of debate and found the combative style inefficient and ineffective." This is in keeping with findings reported in studies of legislators in Alberta (Trimble, 1997) and Manitoba (Brock, 1997), which conclude that female legislators tend to focus more on substantive issues and to employ a distinctive, less combative style than their male colleagues.

Do Women Make a Difference? The Substance-Numbers Connection

A key question in the women in politics research centres on the issue of whether the election of women makes a substantive difference. Put in other terms, the question asks whether there is a connection between the numeric representation of women (sometimes also referred to as "descriptive" or "symbolic" representation) and the substantive representation of women's interests. Some feminist scholars argue that pursuing the project of electing women may harm the substantive representation of women's interests because it allows right-wing parties to pursue neoconservative or neoliberal agendas that harm women while legitimizing these actions by promoting the careers of like-minded women (Gotell and Brodie, 1991). In a similar vein, Maillé (1997) argues that, at least in Quebec, the women's movement has been more successful in representing women than have women holding political office, in large part because of the constraints placed upon women who hold formal political office.

This question is itself a source of some controversy: is there such a thing as "women's interests," and if so, what precisely are these interests? This is an intractable problem in the literature. Efforts to define an objective set of common interests shared by all women have ultimately failed. While many women share objective interests stemming from their reproductive role or their shared experience of discrimination in the workplace, these interests are not universal among them. Moreover, even among women who share the same objective interests, there are differences in preference and belief that divide them. Political theorist Anne Phillips (1991: 90) argues that "the representation of women *as women* potentially founders on both the difficulties of defining the shared interests of women and the difficulties of establishing mechanisms through which these interests are voiced." Consequently, efforts to define a set of common interests among women have failed. The most successful arguments hold not that women have a common set of interests, but rather that they share an interest in being represented or in having access to the system (Jonasdottir, 1988; Skjeie, 1988). In her essay "Toward a Feminist Understanding of Representation," Jill Vickers (1997: 44) argues that the representation of women requires that the diverse needs, values, identities, and interests of women be articulated; that women representatives be held accountable to other women; and that women's participation be transformative, not reinforcing of existing hierarchies.

For the most part, scholars working in this field have acknowledged the difficulties inherent in discussing women's representation and have opted to understand representing women's interests as furthering the policy agenda of the women's movement. The issues that are used as litmus tests, then, include support for women's equality, universal child care, and reproductive freedoms. In some studies, this list has been expanded to include women's health issues and measures designed to combat violence against women. This approach is, arguably, defensible as it was the women's movement that prompted the influx of women into the formal political arena; this offers a benchmark of equality that is usable. That said, it must be noted that a substantial proportion of Canadian women do not support the policy agenda of the women's movement and are consequently ignored by a literature that uses this definition. Moreover, as Ship (1998: 318) points out, these liberal feminist issues reflect the concerns of the predominant white and middle-class background of Canadian feminists in the 1970s and 1980s.

Studies of the attitudes and actions of women in political elites have generally found that gender does make some difference. Tremblay (1998) asked MPs about what policy issues they were particularly interested in and the priority that they thought should be given to women's issues. She found that the overall priority placed on women's issues was low but was higher among female MPs than among men. In all five of the major parties, female MPs placed a higher priority on representing women than did men. Several studies of delegates to provincial and federal political party conventions and of candidates running in provincial and federal elections have found consistent patterns of gender difference between women and men in all the parties (Bashevkin, 1985; Brodie, 1988; Tremblay, 1995). Women in these political elites are more favourably inclined towards feminist policy stances and place themselves further left on the political spectrum than do their male counterparts.

That said, in all these studies, differences *between* parties were more substantial that gender differences *within* each party. These findings are in keeping with Tremblay and Pelletier's (2000) conclusion based on their study of candidates in the 1997 federal election. They determine that feminist consciousness, rather than gender, is the strongest predictor of liberal positions on gender-related issues. Candidates who identified as feminists were more likely to be women than men and were more likely to be found in the NDP, the Liberal Party, or the Bloc Québécois than in either of the two right-of-centre parties. Tremblay (1997) and Brock (1997) found similar partisan patterns in their studies of female legislators in Quebec and Manitoba. Based on these findings, they conclude that substantive and descriptive representations of women are not necessarily compatible. If one was interested in feminist policy outcomes, it was more reasonable to support an NDP man than a Reform woman. If, however, the descriptive representation of women was the utmost concern, then the reverse would be true.

Studies of what women do once they are elected are relatively few in number. The strict party discipline and caucus secrecy of the Canadian parliamentary tradition make it difficult to trace the extent to which female legislators intervene on behalf of women behind closed doors. To the extent that studies have focused on legislators, they have found some evidence supporting the numbers-substance connection. At the federal level, Manon Tremblay (1998) studied the interventions of MPs on women's issues in the form of private members' bills, private members' notices of motion, and statements by members. She concluded that female MPs are more likely than their male counterparts to use these opportunities to draw attention to women's issues. She does note, however, that "for both female and male MPs, the total proportion of each of these parliamentary activities devoted to women's issues remains marginal, even insignificant" (1998: 457). At the provincial level, Trimble studied all the interventions made in the Alberta legislation relating to women from 1972 to 1995. She found, first, that women's issues tended not to be mentioned frequently: "the topic of irrigation ditches received more attention than women" (1997: 263). This increased somewhat between 1986 and 1993, a period when there was (by Alberta standards) a strong opposition presence in the legislature. Throughout the study, Trimble found that policy concerns of minority women — immigrant women, foreign domestic workers, Aboriginal women, or disabled women — were effectively invisible from discussion.

Arscott and Trimble (1997: 12), drawing on a series of studies of women's participation in provincial legislatures, conclude that the degree to which women holding political office make a difference for women's representation is dependent on a number of factors, notably the province's political culture; the intensity of political party ideology as it affects women; the character of party competition in the legislature; the location of female representatives in the opposition or government party, Cabinet, or backbenches; and the personal beliefs of the female representatives. Findings like this have caused feminist political scientists to fall back on arguments of justice and equality to support the ongoing effort to increase women's representation.

American research highlights the importance feminist organizations can have in holding female legislators to account on women's issues. Based on a survey of state legislators, Carroll (2003) concludes that ties to feminist organizations, especially feminist groups, "provide affirmation and sustenance for women legislators; they also function as a conscience for these women, providing ... reminders that they have a responsibility to represent women's interests within the institutions in which they serve." The relative absence of membership-based feminist organizations in Canada means that this mechanism of accountability to women's organizations is missing for most female elected officials in Canada.

Conclusion

After more than three decades of women's efforts to enter the world of electoral politics, we can conclude that some progress has been made. The number of women holding elected office has increased from a mere handful of exceptions to almost a quarter of all legislators at the provincial and federal levels. Women have been elected party leaders, regularly serve in high-profile Cabinet posts, and have even been elected as premier and — for a fleeting moment in 1993 — prime minister. But is this progress sufficient? A quarter of the legislature may be better than a handful, but it is far less than women's majority presence in the population. Women remain substantially under-represented in Cabinets, where crucial decisions are made. At meetings of the first ministers (premiers and the prime minister), where essential decisions about the character of the Canadian federation are made, there are currently no women.

Does it matter that women remain excluded from the upper echelons of power in Canada? On one hand, it is important to recall the extent of Canadian women's legal and economic equality and comparatively high standard of living. This speaks to the ability of women outside the formal arena to achieve policy outcomes favourable to their equality. On the other hand, it is difficult to accept that in a country where women have entered and excelled in other highly demanding professions, the world of politics remains foreign territory. Politics matters to women. Governments decide whether women can have access to contraception, whether they can be paid less than men for doing similar jobs, whether abortions are legal and available, whether child care will be regulated or left to the forces of the market, whether they are entitled to have their job back after having a baby, whether health care is private or publicly funded, and how much university tuition will cost. All of these issues matter just as much — if not more — to women than to men. When women abdicate interest in politics, leaving it as a male preserve, they risk having decisions made on their behalf that make their lives more difficult. This does not mean that women must agree on how these kinds of issues are resolved. They quite legitimately disagree among themselves on all these issues and others as well. But surely the diversity of women's views should be represented when public policy is made.

When feminist political scientists started to study women's involvement in electoral politics some 30 years ago, many of them imagined that women's involvement in politics would have a profound influence on how politics was conducted and what public policies were adopted. While we can certainly point to instances in which women have been able to influence the outcomes of political decisions, the larger story is still the relative absence of women from legislatures, from political parties, and from that group of citizens who are interested in and informed about politics. The task for the next generation of researchers is to come to terms with the underlying reasons why women remain ambivalent about something that affects them so personally and profoundly.

References and Suggested Readings

Arscott, Jane, and Linda Trimble. 1997. "In the Presence of Women: Representation and Political Power." In Jane Arscott and Linda Trimble, eds., *In the Presence of Women: Representation in Canadian Governments*. Toronto: Harcourt Brace. 1–19.

Bashevkin, Sylvia. 1985. "Political Participation, Ambition and Feminism: Women in the Ontario Party Elites." *American Review of Canadian Studies* 15, 4: 405–19.

Bashevkin, Sylvia. 1993. *Toeing the Lines: Women and Party Politics in English Canada*. Toronto: Oxford University Press.

Black, Jerome. 2003. "Differences That Matter: Minority Women MPs, 1993–2000." In Manon Tremblay and Linda Trimble, eds., *Women and Electoral Politics in Canada*. Toronto: Oxford University Press. 59–75.

Brock, Kathy. 1997. "Women and the Manitoba Legislature." In Jane Arscott and Linda Trimble, eds., *In the Presence of Women: Representation in Canadian Governments*. Toronto: Harcourt Brace. 180–200.

Brodie, Janine. 1985. *Women and Politics in Canada*. Toronto: McGraw-Hill Ryerson.

Brodie, Janine. 1988. "The Gender Factor and National Leadership Conventions in Canada." In George Perlin, ed., *Party Democracy in Canada*. Scarborough: Prentice Hall. 172–87.

Carbert, Louise. 2002. "Historical Influences on Regional Patterns of Election of Women to Provincial Legislatures." In William Cross, ed., *Political Parties, Representation, and Electoral Democracy in Canada*. Toronto: Oxford University Press. 201–22.

Carroll, Susan J. 2003. "Are US Women State Legislators Accountable to Women? The Complementary Roles of Feminist Identity and Women's Organizations." Paper prepared for presentation at the Gender and Social Capital Conference, St. John's College, University of Manitoba, May 2–3.

Denton, Margaret A. 1984. "Do Female Candidates 'Lose Votes'? The Experience of Female Candidates in the 1979 and 1980 Canadian General Elections." *Canadian Review of Sociology and Anthropology* 21: 395–406.

Docherty, David. 1997. *Mr. Smith Goes to Ottawa*. Vancouver: University of British Columbia Press.

Equal Voice. 2007. *Fast Facts: Women in Provincial Politics*. http://www.equalvoice.ca.

Erickson, Lynda. 1991. "Women and Candidacies for the House of Commons." In Kathy Megyery, ed., *Women in Canadian Politics: Toward Equity in Representation*. Toronto: Dundurn/RCERPF. 101–25.

Erickson, Lynda. 1993. "Making Her Way In: Women, Parties, and Candidacies in Canada." In Joni Lovenduski and Pippa Norris, eds., *Gender and Party Politics*. London: Sage. 60–85.

Erickson, Lynda. 1998. "Entry to the Commons: Parties, Recruitment, and the Election of Women in 1993." In Manon Tremblay and Caroline Andrew, eds., *Women and Political Representation in Canada*. Ottawa: University of Ottawa Press. 219–55.

Erickson, Lynda. 2003. "In the Eyes of the Beholders: Gender and Leader Popularity in a Canadian Context." In Manon Tremblay and Linda Trimble, eds., *Women and Electoral Politics in Canada*. Toronto: Oxford University Press. 160–77.

Everitt, Joanna. 1998. "Public Opinion and Social Movements: The Women's Movement and the Gender Gap in Canada." *Canadian Journal of Political Science* 35: 191–219.

Everitt, Joanna, and Elisabeth Gidengil. 2003. "Tough Talk: How Television News Covers Male and Female Leaders of Canadian Political Parties." In Manon Tremblay and Linda Trimble, eds., *Women and Electoral Politics in Canada*. Toronto: Oxford University Press. 194–210.

Federation of Canadian Municipalities. 2007. *Women in Municipal Politics*. http://www.fcm.ca/english/policy/big.pdf.

Fox, Richard L., and Jennifer L. Lawless. 2004. "Entering the Arena? Gender and the Decision to Run for Office." *American Journal of Political Science* 48, 2: 264–80.

Gidengil, Elisabeth. 1995. "Economic Man — Social Woman? The Case of the Gender Gap in Support for the Canada-US Free Trade Agreement." *Comparative Political Studies* 28: 384–408.

Gidengil, Elisabeth, Joanna Everitt, André Blais, Patrick Fournier, and Neil Nevitte. 2006. "Gender and Vote Choice in the 2006 Canadian Election." Paper presented at the Annual Meeting of the American Political Science Association, Philadelphia, August 31–September 3.

Gidengil, Elisabeth, Matthew Hennigar, André Blais, and Neil Nevitte. 2005. "Explaining the Gender Gap in Support for the New Right: The Case of Canada." *Comparative Political Studies* 38 (December): 1171–95.

Gidengil, Elisabeth, and Joanna Everitt. 2002. "Damned if You Do, Damned if You Don't: Television News Coverage of Female Party Leaders in the 1993 Federal Election." In William Cross, ed., *Political Parties, Representation, and Electoral Democracy in Canada*. Toronto: Oxford University Press. 223–37.

Gidengil, Elisabeth, and Richard Vengroff. 1997. "Representational Gains of Canadian Women or Token Growth? The Case of Quebec's Municipal Politics." *Canadian Journal of Political Science* 30, 3: 513–37.

Gidengil, Elisabeth, Elizabeth Goodyear-Grant, Neil Nevitte, André Blais, and Richard Nadeau. 2003a. "Gender, Knowledge, and Social Capital." Paper prepared for the conference on Gender and Social Capital, University of Manitoba, May 2003.

Gidengil, Elisabeth, André Blais, Richard Nadeau, and Neil Nevitte. 2003b. "Women to the Left? Gender Differences in Political Beliefs and Policy Preferences." In Manon Tremblay and Linda Trimble, eds., *Women and Electoral Politics in Canada*. Toronto: Oxford University Press. 140–59.

Gotell, Lise, and Janine Brodie. 1991. "Women and Parties: More Than an Issue of Numbers." In Hugh G. Thorburn, ed., *Party Politics in Canada*, 6th ed. Scarborough: Prentice Hall. 53–67.

Inter-Parliamentary Union (IPU). 2007. *Women in National Parliaments*. http://www.ipu.org/wmn-e/classif.htm.

Jonasdottir, Anna. 1988. "On the Concept of Interests, Women's Interests, and the Limitation of Interest Theory." In K.B. Jones and A.G. Jonasdottir, eds., *The Political Interests of Gender*. London: Sage. 47–63.

Kushner, Joseph, David Siegel, and Hannah Stanwick. 1997. "Ontario Municipal Elections: Voting Trends and Determinants of Electoral Success in a Canadian Province." *Canadian Journal of Political Science* 30, 3: 539–53.

Maillé, Chantal. 1997. "Challenges to Representation: Theory and the Women's Movement in Quebec." In Jane Arscott and Linda Trimble, eds., *In the Presence of Women: Representation in Canadian Governments*. Toronto: Harcourt Brace. 47–63.

O'Neill, Brenda. 2002. "Sugar and Spice? Political Culture and the Political Behaviour of Canadian Women." In Joanna Everitt and Brenda O'Neill, eds., *Citizen Politics: Research and Theory in Canadian Political Behaviour.* Toronto: Oxford University Press. 40–55.

Phillips, Anne. 1991. *Engendering Democracy.* University Park: Pennsylvania State University Press.

Praud, Jocelyne. 1998. "Affirmative Action and Women's Representation in the Ontario New Democratic Party." In Manon Tremblay and Caroline Andrew, eds., *Women and Political Representation in Canada* . Ottawa: University of Ottawa Press. 171–93.

Praud, Jocelyne. 2003. "The Parti Québécois, Its Women's Committee, and the Feminization of the Quebec Electoral Arena." In Manon Tremblay and Linda Trimble, eds., *Women and Electoral Politics in Canada.* Toronto: Oxford University Press. 126–39.

Sampert, Shannon, and Linda Trimble. 2003. "Wham, Bam, No Thank You Ma'am: Gender and the Game Frame in National Newspaper Coverage of Election 2000." In Manon Tremblay and Linda Trimble, eds., *Women and Electoral Politics in Canada.* Toronto: Oxford University Press. 211–26.

Ship, Susan Judith. 1998. "Problematizing Ethnicity and 'Race' in Feminist Scholarship on Women in Politics." In Manon Tremblay and Caroline Andrew, eds., *Women and Political Representation in Canada.* Ottawa: University of Ottawa Press. 311–40

Skjeie, Hege. 1988. *The Feminization of Power: Norway's Political Experiment.* Norway: Institute for Social Research.

Studlar, Donley T., and Richard E. Matland. 1996. "The Dynamics of Women's Representation in the Canadian Provinces: 1975–1994." *Canadian Journal of Political Science* 29, 2: 269–94.

Tolley, Erin. 2000. *The Higher the Fewer: Assessing the Presence of Women at Three Levels of Government.* Unpublished MA Thesis, University of Western Ontario.

Tremblay, Manon. 1995. "Gender and Support for Feminism." In François-Pierre Gingras, ed., *Gender and Politics in Contemporary Canada.* Toronto: Oxford University Press. 31–55.

Tremblay, Manon. 1997. "Quebec Women in Politics: An Examination of the Research." In Jane Arscott and Linda Trimble, eds., *In the Presence of Women: Representation in Canadian Governments.* Toronto: Harcourt Brace. 228–51.

Tremblay, Manon. 1998. "Do Female MPs Substantively Represent Women? A Study of Legislative Behaviour in Canada's 35th Parliament." *Canadian Journal of Political Science* 31, 3: 435–66.

Tremblay, Manon, and Réjean Pelletier. 2000. "More Feminists or More Women? Descriptive and Substantive Representations of Women in the 1997 Canadian Federal Elections." *International Political Science Review* 21, 4: 381–405.

Trimble, Linda. 1997. "Feminist Politics in the Alberta legislature, 1972–1994." In Jane Arscott and Linda Trimble, eds., *In the Presence of Women: Representation in Canadian Governments.* Toronto: Harcourt Brace. 128–53.

Trimble, Linda, and Jane Arscott. 2003. *Still Counting: Women in Politics Across Canada.* Peterborough: Broadview Press.

Vickers, Jill. 1978. "Where Are the Women in Canadian Politics?" *Atlantis* 3, 2: 40–51.

Vickers, Jill. 1997. "Toward a Feminist Understanding of Representation." In Jane Arscott and Linda Trimble, eds., *In the Presence of Women: Representation in Canadian Governments.* Toronto: Harcourt Brace. 20–46.

Young, Lisa. 2000. *Feminists and Party Politics.* Vancouver: University of British Columbia Press.

Young, Lisa, and William Cross. 2003. "Women's Involvement in Canadian Political Parties." In Manon Tremblay and Linda Trimble, eds., *Women and Electoral Politics in Canada*. Toronto: Oxford University Press. 92–109.

Young, Lisa, and William Cross. 2007. "A Group Apart: Young Party Members in Canada." Canadian Policy Research Networks. http://www.cprn.org/doc.cfm?doc= 1748&l=en.

fifteen
Diversity in Canadian Politics

YASMEEN ABU-LABAN

Introduction

Canada's 2008 national election coincided with an historic American presidential race: Democrat Barack Obama was the first African-American to win the presidential nomination of a major party. That Barack Obama's popularity extended beyond his country's borders was evidenced in polls that found that if it were a possibility, Canadians would actually favour Obama for their prime minister over any of the actual national party leaders (CTV.ca, 2008; Hogben, 2008). Given Obama's cross-border appeal, it is perhaps not surprising that his Canadian-born brother-in-law, Konrad Ng, also generated media attention. Through his marriage to Obama's half-sister Maya Soetaro, Ng had linked his own family tree (his parents having immigrated to Canada from Malaysia) with one that, during the course of the American election, became legendary for its biracial and hybrid character (other members included Obama and Soetaro's white American-born mother, Obama's black Kenyan-born father, and Soetaro's Indonesian-born father) (Jih, 2008). Ng himself served on Obama's Asian American and Pacific Islanders Council during the 2008 campaign (Nolan, 2008).

Unlike Konrad Ng, most Canadians do not have a relative who ran for and won the highest office in the United States while maintaining incredible international popularity too. But other aspects of Ng's family will resonate with many in his country of birth. The 2006 Census alerts us to Canada's demographic heterogeneity. Today, close to 20 per cent of the population are foreign-born (Statistics Canada, 2007) and Canadians are more ethnically diverse than ever. Whereas the 1901 Canadian Census recorded membership in only 25 different ethnic groups, the 2006 Census recorded membership in over 200 (Statistics Canada, 2008: 6). Additionally, there is increasing racial diversity with just over 16 per cent of the population now comprising so-called visible minorities, who are defined by the Canadian government as "persons other than Aboriginal persons who are non-Caucasian in race or non-white in colour" (Statistics Canada, 2008: 11–12). Aboriginal peoples make up a further 5.4 per cent of the Canadian population (Statistics Canada, 2008: 11–12). Many Canadians regularly encounter "diversity" among friends, neighbours, colleagues, and — like Konrad Ng — within their own families. Consider that over 60 per cent of those reporting Aboriginal ancestry also report other origins (Statistics Canada, 2008: 11) and that marriage and common-law relationships between visible minorities and non-visible minorities, as well as between visible minorities of different ethnic origins, are on the rise (Statistics Canada, 2008: 16). These demographic realities underscore why "diversity" — particularly when it comes to place of birth, ethnicity, or race — is a compelling consideration that demands analytic and public policy attention.

This chapter focuses primarily on cultural, ethnic, and racial diversity and its relevance, both historically and currently, in Canadian politics. It examines how these forms of diversity have been addressed both by the Canadian state through its policies and by the contemporary Canadian political science tradition. It argues that diversity is significant for political analyses in both areas because it is relevant to power, a central disciplinary concern. Put differently, whether historic or contemporary, inequalities between identifiable groups are important to political scientists because such inequalities may impact the extent to which all groups feel their voices are heard and their interests are represented in Canadian institutions (what is called legitimacy). More broadly, inequities can tell us about the character of Canadian liberal democracy.

In order to address this argument, this chapter takes a threefold approach. In the first section, major state policies and practices pertaining to diversity are reviewed in relation to Canada's history and evolution. In the second, three different emphases in Canadian political science approaches are highlighted: culture, race, and colonialism. To illustrate how each approach may inform us, the third section offers a close examination of religious diversity, especially as it pertains to both Aboriginal peoples historically and Muslim-Canadians today.

Diversity and the Evolving Canadian State

Canada's history as a settler colony, characterized by pre-existing and distinct Aboriginal societies, European settler colonization, and repeated waves of immigration, is a testimony to the fact that "diversity" is not new. Historically, both the British-origin and French-origin groups attempted to assert dominance over the Indigenous population, although the patterns of colonization of each were distinct (Dickason, 1992). It is, however, Canada's foundation as a so-called white settler colony of Britain that fostered a legacy of group-based inequalities that forms the basis of many grievances and ongoing political struggles. This is because the historic project of modelling Canada after Britain (in political, economic, cultural, and demographic terms) often led to assimilative and discriminatory measures.

The Royal Proclamation of 1763 established the framework by which British administration of the North American territories would take place and served to enforce British sovereignty while at the same time acknowledging Aboriginal tribes and land title rights. In particular, the Royal Proclamation outlawed the expropriation of Aboriginal lands by colonies or by settlers unless treaties with the Crown were completed. This was the beginning of the imperial government's contradictory policy of assimilation and recognition, which was later replicated by Canada (Stasiulis and Jhappan, 1995: 107).

Assimilation and recognition also characterized relations with the French, and these tensions were further woven into the development of liberal democracy and eventually federalism in Canada. The 1774 Quebec Act allowed the freedom to practice the Catholic faith and retained French civil law and seigneurial landholding systems. While it did not say anything about the use of the French language, the appointed council (overseen by a colonial governor) allowed for Roman Catholics to hold office. The 1791 Constitutional Act created Upper Canada (the present-day province of Ontario) and Lower Canada (the southern part of present-day Quebec), governed by bicameral legislatures consisting of elected assemblies with limited powers and more powerful appointed legislative councils that worked on behalf of the colonial governors and the Crown. In both Upper and Lower Canada, reformers fought for responsible government. The response to these struggles, which took the form of armed uprisings in 1837–38, was the 1840 Act of Union that united Upper and Lower Canada into a single colony (Canada) with one parliament and, notably, English as the only official government language. As well, in the 1840s and 1850s, thousands of immigrants, among them a significant number of Irish, were discriminated against by the British authorities (Cardin and Couture, 1996: 208).

In light of pre-Confederation practices, it is unsurprising that the Canadian state also reflected linguistic, ethnic, and racial hierarchies in practices, policies, and laws (Stasiulis and Jhappan, 1995: 96). The founding of the modern Canadian state stemmed from a number of factors, not least of which were fears of an American invasion and the distinctly privileged position of "white settler colonies" to enjoy relative political autonomy within the British empire. With Confederation in 1867, the colonies of British North America — Canada, Nova Scotia, and New Brunswick — were united into a Dominion with British-style political institutions. Unlike Britain, however, and as outlined in the British North America Act/Constitution Act, 1867, Canada adopted a federal system of government. The province of Quebec gained control over education and culture (see Chapter 1 in this volume), and both French and English were to be the languages used in federal (and Quebec) legislative debates and records. The adoption of a federal system was the result of intense struggle by French Canadians, as many British-origin politicians (such as the first Prime Minister, Sir John A. Macdonald) would have preferred a unitary state (Abu-Laban and Nieguth, 2000: 478). Confederation ushered in a new discourse upholding the British and the French as Canada's "two founding peoples" or "two founding races" (Stasiulis and Jhappan, 1995: 110). This discourse held out the promise that the collective aspirations of two collectivities (the British and the French) could be simultaneously accommodated. Yet despite the discourse, and the stated provisions of the Constitution Act, 1867, the promise was never met. As summed succinctly by Richard Day (2000: 180), "the Canadian state ... lived, worked, and most importantly, *dreamed* in English."

As a by-product, the discourse on "two founding peoples" helped legitimize the federal government's assuming jurisdiction over Aboriginal affairs and lands reserved for Aboriginal peoples, paving the way for the seizure of Aboriginal lands by provinces both with and without the use of treaties (see Green, 1995; Green and Peach, 2007). Similarly, except in periods when the pool of labour was insufficient to fuel agricultural or industrial expansion, Canada's immigration policy favoured white, English-speaking, British-origin Protestants (Abu-Laban and Gabriel, 2002: 37–55). Even after the Second World War, Prime Minister Mackenzie King emphasized that Canada did not want immigration from "the orient" since this would negatively alter "the character" of the population (King, 1947). By "the orient" King meant to exclude all areas in the eastern hemisphere beyond Europe; this policy position guided Canada's immigration in-take until 1967.

In 1967 a new immigration policy explicitly banned discrimination on the basis of race or ethnicity and introduced a "point system" of selection. The point system, still in effect today, ranks potential independent immigrants by scoring points on the basis of education and skills. (The point system is not formally used for family members of the principal applicant, nor is it used for refugees.) In addition to immigration, the decade of the 1960s marks an important turning-point for policies in a number of areas. Combined, such changes may be related in part to the international level, where the saliency of the idea of human rights (emphasizing the equal worth and dignity of all persons) coincided with the growing success of many anti-colonial struggles and movements; the growth of the Keynesian-style welfare state, which opened new possibilities of social spending; and the re-mobilization of segments of the Canadian population into identity-based political movements and organizations demanding inclusion in the existing system and, in some cases, self-rule. This was clearly a period in which the inclusiveness of Canada's democracy, inequities in the distribution of power, and the legitimacy of its institutions were put in question.

In response, federal policies were shaped by the resurrection of older discourses and understandings in a new context. For example, in Quebec, the Quiet Revolution was symbolized by the election of the provincial Liberal government of Jean Lesage in 1960. Commitment to a philosophy of *maîtres chez nous* (masters in our own house) led successive Quebec governments to assume greater jurisdictional and fiscal powers for the province as well as to seek federal recognition of the distinct constitutional status of Quebec because the French were a "founding people" at Confederation. Aboriginal people drew on the Royal Proclamation of 1763 that gave them status as "nations within" (or "first nations"); the Royal Proclamation also provided a legal basis for their contemporary and ongoing land and rights claims, including self-government.

In other cases, new federal discourses aiming to foster legitimacy also emerged. The rise of widespread contestation across Canada of French-speaking Canadians, especially in Quebec and New Brunswick (where many young people identified with anti-colonial struggles in Algeria and South America), led the federal Liberals of Prime Minister Lester B. Pearson to form the Royal Commission on Bilingualism and Biculturalism. As a consequence of the findings of this commission, which found that the principle of equality between French and English had been systematically violated in the Canadian federation, the federal Liberal government of Prime Minister Pierre Elliott Trudeau passed the Official Languages Act in 1969. Emerging from its English dream, the Canadian state made clear through this act that English and French were the official languages of Canada, that in many cases public servants could use these languages at work, and that most federal services were to be made available to Canadians in both languages. At the same time, the word "multiculturalism" was introduced as a way for the "third force" (i.e., non-French, non-British, and non-Aboriginal immigrants and their descendants) to be symbolically recognized by the Canadian state. It too was the outcome of a struggle by these groups, especially Ukrainian-origin Canadians in the Western provinces, for representation. By 1971 the Trudeau government announced a policy of multiculturalism within a bilingual framework.

Although the province of Quebec never received the constitutional recognition (or veto power) its leaders sought, the 1982 Canadian Charter of Rights and Freedoms did give recognition to English and French as the two official languages (Sections 16–22), official language minority education rights for French-speakers outside Quebec and English-speakers in Quebec (Section 23), Aboriginal rights as recognized in the Royal Proclamation of 1763 (Section 25), and the multicultural heritage of Canada (Section 27).

The Charter, reflecting the value of human rights, also prohibited discrimination on the basis of race, ethnicity, gender, and mental or physical disability, among other grounds (Section 15). Nonetheless, Section 15 also allowed for the possibility of government programs designed to ameliorate disadvantage experienced by specific groups. This gave constitutional legitimacy to new programs, developed from the mid-1980s, dealing with employment equity for groups deemed to have been historically disadvantaged in the labour market. The specific focus of employment equity is on women, Aboriginal peoples, visible minorities, and persons with a disability. Employment equity seeks to increase the numeric representation of these four groups in federally regulated corporations (such as banks, broadcasting, and airlines). Similar employment equity policies were also adopted in the mid-1980s to increase the numerical representation of the same groups in the public service itself and in companies doing business with the government (so-called federal contractors).

The federal government's prioritizing of certain groups for employment was not entirely new — for instance, in 1918 the Canadian government favoured the recruitment of male First World War veterans for jobs in the civil service. However, the consequences of employment equity for the four target groups have been uneven, depending on the group and the work sector. For example, in the federal public service visible minorities in particular have faced slow progress in achieving increased representation that corresponds to their numbers available for participation in the workforce (Abu-Laban, 2006: 72–73). More broadly, the decade of the 1990s brought new challenges because of the rise of neoliberal ideology. Neoliberalism emphasizes balanced budgets through cuts to social spending, asserts the necessity for individual self-sufficiency, and assumes markets are fair and efficient allocators of public goods. In this context, many identity-based groups (women, minorities, Aboriginal people, etc.) were vilified for being "special interests" out of tune with "ordinary Canadians," and programs faced cuts and re-workings of their terms (Abu-Laban and Gabriel, 2002). As one example, under these new terms it has been impossible to get funding for certain kinds of activities previously funded through multiculturalism, and it has been cumbersome for community groups, many relying on underpaid workers or overworked volunteers, to apply for money. As such, the 1960s-style human rights and equality agenda for ethnic minorities may be seen to have weakened (Abu-Laban and Gabriel, 2002; Kobayashi, 2008).

However, the weakening of the human rights agenda does not mean that real inequality has disappeared. Consider the case of visible minorities. Many, though not all, visible minorities in Canada today were born abroad. Since 1967 Canada has favoured educated and professionally trained immigrants for entry and permanent settlement. Reflecting this, as a group in comparison with the rest of the Canadian population, visible minorities are more likely to have university diplomas, certificates, and degrees and are much less likely to have less than a high school or college education (NVMCLFD, 2004: 12). Yet despite being relatively highly educated, visible minorities have lower employment and higher unemployment rates than the rest of the Canadian population (NVMCLFD, 2004: 19). Visible minorities (foreign- and Canadian-born) also have lower earnings and lower rates of unionization than the rest of the Canadian population (NVMCLFD, 2004: 20–35). Relatedly, visible minorities (both Canadian-born and particularly recent immigrants) have higher rates of poverty than the rest of the Canadian population (NVMCLFD, 2004: 53). The National Visible Minority Council on Labour Force Development (2004) attributes poor labour market outcomes for both Canadian-born and foreign-born visible minorities to racism and discrimination.

Notwithstanding the focus of employment equity on so-called visible minorities, or shifts in the federal multiculturalism policy away from "song and dance" towards fighting racism by the 1980s, for the most part it is ethnocultural and linguistic diversity that are central to how the modern Canadian state has conceptualized "diversity" in its policies (Bloemraad, 2006: 237–38). In other words, "race" (or "racism") is not a primary focus but is secondary to "culture." Just as critically, the two (race and culture) are not automatically linked in policies or policy-making processes. This creates a situation whereby certain groups who cross traditionally conceived divides may fall outside the policy radar — for example, French-speaking visible minorities outside Quebec face compounded disadvantages that have yet to be adequately addressed through federal policy (see M'pindou, 2002).

Likewise, redress for historic injustices and past policies has not been the central focus, though in recent years the Canadian state has engaged, periodically, with redress claims (James, 1999, 2004; Abu-Laban, 2001). This would include the 1988 federal apology and compensation for Japanese-Canadians who experienced internment during the Second World War; the 1996 apology on the part of the federal government for the physical and sexual abuse often suffered by Aboriginal children at residential schools that were run through a partnership of state and church; and the 2006 apology and compensation for Chinese-Canadians who experienced the "head tax." More recently, in 2008 the federal government announced a "Truth and Reconciliation Commission" on residential schools. Its purpose is to offer a space to acknowledge individual experiences and to foster reconciliation between Aboriginal and non-Aboriginal Canadians, thus suggesting the potential value of South Africa's post-Apartheid "Truth and Reconciliation" model for Canada's settler-colonial legacies (Abu-Laban, 2001). Significant as the residential school commission may prove to be, thus far the federal government has dealt with the redress claims of groups in an ad hoc manner — in part because history, including colonial history, is not a primary lens through which policy is framed.

Despite these ongoing features, in comparison with much of Canadian history, policies from the 1960s have a much less overt and blunt assimilative edge. "Angloconformity" as an ideal has given way to human rights and pluralism. In light of shifting federal policy historically and currently, it is clear that the politics of diversity are not static but dynamic and subject to change and ongoing contestation. This is also the case because the population of Canada itself is changing, as the 2006 Census reveals. Such complexities, along with the fact that even in its cultural emphasis federal policy has had to deal with racism and historical redress, may help attune us how best to approach the study of diversity.

Diversity and the Evolving Canadian Political Science Tradition

For much of the postwar period, Canadian political scientists paid uneven attention to issues of diversity, particularly when it came to racial minorities (or majorities), immigrants, and Aboriginal people. However, in 2008 the Canadian Political Science Association (CPSA), the main national body representing political scientists across Canada, issued an e-mail communiqué announcing the creation of a new conference section entitled "Race, Ethnicity, Indigenous Peoples, and Politics/Race Ethnicité, Peuples Autochtones et Politique." The communiqué suggested that the new section intended "to open up space for new emergent disciplinary themes and scholars" (CPSA, 2008). The advent of this new section reflects political scientists' increasing interest in issues of diversity since the late 1980s.

Over this period, Canadian political scientists (both political philosophers and empirical political scientists) have developed distinct approaches to understanding and studying diversity. Perhaps reflecting the dominant emphasis of the Canadian state on themes of culture, "culture" is undoubtedly the central lens through which diversity has been viewed. Less prominent, but equally worthy of consideration, are two other approaches, one emphasizing "race" and the other emphasizing "colonialism." Each approach alerts us to different dimensions of power inequalities experienced by different groups, and as such it may be useful, and indeed desirable, to use them in combination to better understand diversity in Canada.

Turning first to the *lens of culture*, it is notable that in addition to reflecting the dominant organizing unit of the Canadian state, the cultural approach is central to a larger international debate generated by a "Canadian" contribution to political philosophy. In his book *The Rights Revolution* (2001: 11), Michael Ignatieff talks about how Canadians have been at the forefront both politically and intellectually in dealing with the issue of group rights. This intellectual expression of rights philosophy Ignatieff attributes specifically to, among others, Will Kymlicka, Charles Taylor, and James Tully, who defend group-based recognition for cultural minorities.

This body of work is sensitive to *existing* power inequalities based on cultural difference — especially that of groups who fall outside the dominant culture and may utilize the language of nationalism (e.g., in Canada this would include French-Canadians/the Québécois as well as Aboriginal peoples). James Tully, for instance, has noted that demands for recognition by distinct cultural groups are based on a shared sense of longing for self-rule and a belief that the status quo is unjust (Tully, 1997: 4–5). At the heart of the defence of recognition given by philosophers like Taylor and Kymlicka is the view that culture is centrally important to the quality of individual human existence. For example, Kymlicka argues that culture, stemming from a shared language and a shared way of life, "provides people with meaningful options, and with a sense of belonging and identity that helps them negotiate the modern world" (1998: 96). Taylor also suggests that "we become full human agents capable of understanding ourselves, and hence of defining our identity, through our acquisition of rich human languages of expression" (1992: 32). Because belonging to a culture is seen to be so central, it forms the justification for recognizing difference and providing differentiated rights and citizenship.

The emphasis on culture as the basis for rights and difference has generated a particular criticism for opponents of multiculturalism working within the liberal paradigm: the official recognition of group rights on the basis of cultural identity might allow grounds to violate the rights of the individual, and in this respect it is an affront to liberalism (Fierlbeck, 1996: 21). Others have added that the focus on cultural collectivities can strengthen the power of some members within the collectivity over others (e.g., men over women) and as such may be undemocratic. Such Canadian theorists as Avigail Eisenberg (2006) and Monique Deveaux (2006) have taken the lead in exploring and attempting to reconcile such potential tensions as those between gender justice and multiculturalism.

As a totality, the Canadian tradition has cracked open greater space for scholarship on diversity within political science than compared to the 1960s and 1970s. For example, the Royal Commission on Bilingualism and Biculturalism set the stage for what would eventually become Canada's bilingualism and multiculturalism policies, and through the 1960s and 1970s the multidisciplinary field of ethnic studies gained momentum. Yet in comparison with other disciplines, political scientists were not heavily involved (Palmer, 1977: 173). Even in the late 1980s, Gilbert H. Scott observed that "thus far, the study of multiculturalism has been pursued mainly by sociologists, anthropologists and historians. Other social scientists such as political scientists have largely ignored the area" (Scott, 1989: 228).

Given this, the period since Scott's comment is somewhat remarkable, as multiculturalism and diversity moved on to the agenda of Canadian political science because of constitutional politics and the evident demands from ethnic minorities and Aboriginal peoples (Cairns, 1992; Abu-Laban and Nieguth, 2000). After the failure of the Charlottetown Accord in 1992, when constitutional politics shifted to the back burner, issues surrounding diversity did not recede in the discipline's study of Canada. This may be seen to be related to the salience of these issues, underscored by the intellectual contribution of the political theorists discussed above.

On a less positive note, however, there are ways in which the work represented by the Canadian political theory tradition has tended to conflate — under the rubric of culture — race, ethnicity, language, and religion. As such, this work has not directly challenged a larger tendency in the discipline to take "ethnic" or "racial" groups as somehow a natural given. Indeed, in Rupert Taylor's (1999) scathing assessment of political science as an international discipline, whose epicentre lies in the United States, he critiques both the limited extent that ethnicity and race have been studied in the discipline overall and also the manner in which race and ethnicity have been approached in that country. What concerns him are typical election studies that categorize in a very un-nuanced way "ethnic" or "racial" groups (e.g., the "Hispanic vote," the "ethnic vote," the "African-American vote"). For Rupert Taylor, political science cannot advance thinking without a different vision — the vision that has inspired the sociological study of race and ethnicity.

The sociological tradition emphasizes the socially constructed character of ethnic groups, racial groups, and other identity groups, and their contextual and historical variability. In particular, British sociologist Robert Miles (2000) has advanced the argument that race should not be treated as a thing. To this end, Miles favours abandoning the use of the term "race" in favour of looking at the experience of racism and processes of racialization. Racialization is understood as a socially created and historically specific process whereby members (or perceived members) of certain groups are viewed by the majority as inferior by reason of their supposed biology. More recently, culture (and cultural difference or cultural inferiority) has been seen by scholars of race as playing a prominent role in contemporary expressions of racism and processes of racialization. For example, the idea of a "clash of civilizations" between the

West and the Rest, or more bluntly Christianity and Islam (Huntington, 1996), has helped fuel some contemporary examples and discourses used by the far right (Betz, 2002). British political theorist Tariq Modood, who is specifically concerned with the experiences of British Muslims, usefully distinguishes "colour" and "cultural" forms of racism. As he puts it, "there are of course colour or phenotype racisms but there are also cultural racisms which build on 'colour' a set of antagonistic or demeaning stereotypes based on alleged or real cultural traits" (Modood, 2007: 44–45).

Drawing from these international currents, *the lens of "race"* and processes of racialization may be viewed as a second approach taken by Canadian political scientists. For many analysts concerned with racism and racialization, there is a sense that the Canadian policy emphasis on multiculturalism detracts from a focus on the reality of racism (Fernando, 2006; Smith, 2003). Moreover, an emphasis on cultural groups — in so far as this typically implies ethnicity, language, and nation — may be seen to detract from race or its intersection with other forms of diversity that generate inequality (Abu-Laban, 2007; Thompson, 2008; Dhamoon, 2009). For example, there are powerful ways in which "whiteness" has structured intellectual thought and power, as Bruce Baum shows in his genealogy of the meaning of "Caucasian" (2006), a classification still used by the Canadian state. As well, an uncritical emphasis on cultural difference may fuel forms of racialization and differential treatment, especially in the post-9/11 climate (Abu-Laban, 2002, 2004; Abu-Laban and Abu-Laban, 2007).

Political scientists working with race as a central concept have drawn attention to how race has played an important role in Canadian mythology, which ignores Canada's own history with slavery in favour of narratives stressing the role of Canadians in "rescuing" enslaved African-Americans (Bakan, 2008). Likewise, analysts working with the lens of race have underscored its significance in socio-economic differences both in Quebec (Salée, 2007) and Canada as a whole — what Grace Edward Galabuzi refers to as economic apartheid (2006). A distinct aspect of the focus on race (as opposed to simply culture) is that analysts working in this tradition typically also are expressly concerned with identifying popular forms of combating racism (what is also referred to as anti-racism) rather than just taking existing power relations as a given (see, for example, Bakan and Kobayashi, 2007; Abu-Laban, 2007).

While "race" has emerged as an alternative lens to culture, yet another approach to consider would be one that uses the *lens of colonialism* and its legacies. The distinct characteristic of this approach is that it expressly draws attention to how inequalities emerged in the first place and links the past, and narratives of the past, to the present (Abu-Laban, 2001, 2007). Although the themes of colonialism and postcolonialism permeate the work of many scholars dealing with contemporary Quebec and French Canada (Lamoureux, Maillé, and de Sève, 1999; Maclure, 2003; Desroches, 2003; Gagnon, 2004), in recent years it has been Aboriginal scholars in particular who have explicitly insisted on the salience of colonialism as the lens for understanding Aboriginal peoples and politics in Canada. Thus, for Taiaiake Alfred (1999, 2005) Canada remains a colonial state exerting power over the lives of Aboriginal peoples in ways that are obvious (the Indian Act) and less obvious (from self-government arrangements to what food is consumed). This emphasis on colonialism as a lens through which to view both history and the present is also to be found in the writings of Joyce Green (1995) and Kiera Ladner (2008). The value of this perspective is that it automatically draws a clear connection between the history leading up to and emanating from the founding of Canada, as well as informing current inequalities between settlers and the Aboriginal population.

While recently anti-racist scholars have cautioned that the specific struggle of Indigenous peoples against colonialism is distinct from that of racialized immigrants and their descendants against racism (Dua, 2008), it is arguably the case that the scholarly study of diversity needs to consider colonialism and racialization along with culture. Attending to the dominant foci of all three of these approaches can aid in understanding real and ongoing struggles reflective of power differentials. In the next section, religion will be used to illustrate how a multi-pronged approach considering culture, racialization, and colonialism captures the complexity of power relations and policy-making when it comes to "diversity."

Religion, Power and Complexity

Since September 11, 2001, "religion," especially Islam, has emerged as a political flashpoint in international relations because of the American-led "war on terror." Canadian politics has not been immune. Although the presence of Muslims in Canada dates back to the late nineteenth century, since 9/11 their presence has been securitized through the re-working of state border and security policies (Abu-Laban, 2004, 2005). Additionally, after 9/11, media coverage of religion and Muslim-Canadians has increased during elections (Abu-Laban and Trimble, 2006). Media, popular, and partisan debates over "reasonable accommodation" of religious minorities in Quebec in 2007–08 and over faith-based arbitration using Shari'a law in Ontario in 2005 form other examples of the increasing politicization of religious difference. This also was seen in a 2007 federal debate concerning whether Muslim women who wear the *niqab* (a head and face covering worn by a small fraction of Muslim women) could vote without showing their faces.

As this chapter has shown in the preceding historical discussion, religion has been one of many points of difference recognized through policies even prior to Confederation, and thus the twenty-first century emphasis on religion (or religious difference) is not new. Religion, on the face of it, may seem to have everything to do with cultural difference rather than "racism" and how that structures material inequalities between groups or the impact of "colonialism" on historic relations between groups. However, a discussion framed primarily or only in relation to differences in values, beliefs, or culture may have limitations.

Consider, for example, the settler colony of Canada and Aboriginal spirituality. Aboriginal spirituality is tied to life-ways on the land and, as such, might be explored from the vantage of culture and cultural difference in relation to Christianity or secularism. However, an exploration grounded only in relation to culture may miss some key realities. As religious studies professor David Seljak notes, in the Canadian context "no community has suffered more from Christian hegemony than Canada's Aboriginal peoples" (Seljak, 2007: 91). Residential schools epitomized the abuses of church and state, and were fuelled by both colonial practices and racism. The federal apology and compensation for residential schools, and even the new Truth and Reconciliation Commission, may only go so far because the Canadian state has yet to deal with a deeper issue relating to the fact that any recognition of traditional Aboriginal spirituality (tied to the land) inevitably involves recognition of land claims. The failure to address land claims is complex, involving power, colonialism, and racism. As such, "[t]he conflict between Aboriginal peoples' definition of land, property and rights and that of mainstream Canadian society illustrates in the starkest terms the thorny issue of structural discrimination and the connection of the right to religious freedom to a host of broader public policy issues...." (Seljak, 2007: 91).

The relevance of thinking about power and racism also pertains to the post-9/11 period since "what Muslims are up to" abroad and at home has become a national security concern. In this particular climate, debates that may at first glance seem to epitomize the demands for cultural recognition acknowledged by Canadian political theorists may in fact have peculiar features that do not neatly correspond to how analysts might envision group-based claims-making. To illustrate, consider more closely the federal debate over what (not) to wear to the ballot box.

It is extremely rare for the prime minister of Canada to publicly take exception to decisions made by Elections Canada (the independent and nonpartisan body set up by Parliament to oversee federal elections and referenda). Yet on September 9, 2007, Prime Minister Stephen Harper did just that, when he declared his profound disagreement with their decision to allow

Muslim women who wear the *niqab* to vote without showing their faces (CBC News, 2007). In fact, Canada's Chief Electoral Officer was subsequently called before the Procedure and House Affairs Committee of the House of Commons for an explanation. What is perhaps most notable in the question of the ballot box and the *niqab* is that Muslim-Canadian organizations (and Muslim-Canadians themselves) never asked or demanded that this issue be placed on the agenda for discussion (*Globe and Mail*, 2007). Rather, the exchange was given "urgency" because of three federal by-elections taking place in the province of Quebec on September 17, 2007 — even though in the entire province it was estimated that a mere 50 Muslim-Canadian women wear the *niqab* (Sara Elgazzar cited in CBC News, 2007). As such, it is hard to view this debate only through the lens of culture, at least as it concerns the idea of cohesive groups making demands for differentiated rights and citizenship in the way described by many Canadian political theorists.

In the particular discussion of "what not to wear," the way "culture" is important might be better understood by linking it with racialization and its possible fortification through colonial discourses. While the presence of Muslims in Canada spans three centuries, today approximately two-thirds of Canadian Muslims are immigrants (Bramadat and Seljak, 2005: Appendix 240), and the majority are visible minorities under the federal government's definition. Given Modood's idea of the linkage of colour and cultural racism, it is notable that Peter Beyer's 2005 study of religion, education, and income finds that Muslim Canadians who immigrated since the 1970s and their Canadian-born children have among the lowest income levels of all religious groups, even though they have the second highest rate of educational attainment among all religious groups in Canada (Beyer, 2005). Muslim Canadians are also under-represented in major Canadian institutions, such as the Canadian House of Commons (Abu-Laban and Trimble, 2006). However, the ballot box issue was not approached by the Canadian government in relation to issues of power as reflected in socio-economic status (the immigrant status of many Muslim Canadians, their visible minority status, their employment earnings, and their high unemployment rates).

Nor was this debate ever framed in relation to real everyday forms of racial and cultural prejudice or their linkage to older discourses of "orientalism." Orientalism is the term coined by the late Edward Said to explain the formation of Europe and its colonial expansion through stories, policies, and analyses that view the peoples and cultures of "the Orient" as different from and inferior to those of Europe (Said, 1979). Sherene Razack has drawn attention to the relevance of racism and these older discourses of colonialism and empire in her attempt to understand why "in the past, Canadians have had relatively little trouble" with schoolgirls wearing the *hijab* (a head covering), or by extension what women wear to vote, while after 9/11 "the apparently greater ease with different religions and cultures began to disappear" (2008: 174).

Given that the ballot box debate arose without Muslim Canadians making any demand, analysts would do well to consider the insights drawn from discussions of culture alongside race and colonialism/history and, in the case of Muslim Canadians, the possible lingering relevance of orientalism. Such a focus might also invite consideration into how, at the popular level, resistance to these developments is expressed by state and non-state actors (see, for example, Abu-Laban, 2002).

Conclusion

This chapter has addressed different policy responses of the Canadian state to diversity, as well as different approaches used by Canadian political scientists to understand diversity. As argued here, both the study of diversity and the responses to diversity say much about issues of power and the ongoing struggles of collectivities to overturn (or in some cases to reinforce) group-based differences. The responses to such inequalities have much to do with the nature of Canadian democracy and the inclusivity of the practices, policies, and institutions that underpin liberal democracy.

As this chapter has noted, culture has been a dominant frame of reference both for the Canadian state and for Canadian analysts. While culture is important for helping to identify existing inequalities, as this chapter has also pointed out, the demands of some groups also draw attention to racism, processes of racialization, and anti-racism as a means of resistance. Additionally, other approaches draw attention to colonialism as a means for understanding the relationship between history and the present. This would suggest that as political scientists consider ways to best understand the politics of diversity, attention should be given to themes of culture along with race/racialization/ antiracism and colonialism. The value of such a multi-pronged approach will undoubtedly help deal with the constantly shifting terrain of state policies and of understandings of the ways in which people identify and make demands — some of which may have deep resonance in Canadian history. Such a multi-pronged approach may also foster better and more inclusive dialogues across the field of Canadian politics as well as in the sphere of policy-making. As well, a multi-pronged approach may help deal with new perspectives and demands, as well as the new and hybrid forms of identity that Canadians may increasingly exhibit as their colleagues, friends, family, and acquaintances reflect both historic and new forms of diversity that characterize twenty-first-century Canada in a globalizing world.

Not least, such a multi-pronged approach may also alert us to distinguish between actual demands and attributed demands, as in the case of the ballot box and the *niqab*. This is relevant to consider because just as the diversity symbolized by Barack Obama in 2008 made him popular and a symbol of hope for the future for many north and south of the 49th Parallel, for some it also generated tremendous anxiety. Likewise, the study of diversity in Canada may also need to grapple more with the politics of fear. It is hard to adequately begin to address this kind of discussion in the absence of considering how inequalities have come into being, how they show up today, and how they may be potentially transformed.

References and Suggested Readings

Abu-Laban, Yasmeen. 2001. "The Future and the Legacy: Globalization and the Canadian Settler State." *Journal of Canadian Studies* 35, 4 (Winter 2000–01): 262–76.

Abu-Laban, Yasmeen. 2002. "Liberalism, Multiculturalism, and the Problem of Essentialism." *Citizenship Studies* 6, 4 (December): 459–82.

Abu-Laban, Yasmeen. 2004. "The New North America and the Segmentation of Canadian Citizenship." *International Review of Canadian Studies* 29: 17–40.

Abu-Laban, Yasmeen. 2005. "Regionalism, Migration, and Fortress North America." *Review of Constitutional Studies* 10, 1–2: 135–62.

Abu-Laban, Yasmeen. 2006. "Stalemate at Work: Visible Minorities and Employment Equity." In Leen d'Haenens, Marc Hooghe, Dirk Vanheule, and Hasibe Gezduci, eds., *New Citizens, New Policies: Developments in Diversity Policy in Canada and Flanders.* Ghent: Academia Press. 71–87.

Abu-Laban, Yasmeen. 2007. "Political Science, Race, Ethnicity, and Public Policy." In Michael Orsini and Miriam Smith, eds., *Critical Policy Studies.* Vancouver: University of British Columbia Press. 137–57.

Abu-Laban, Yasmeen, and Baha Abu-Laban. 2007. "Reasonable Accommodation in a Global Village." *Policy Options* (September): 28–33.

Abu-Laban, Yasmeen, and Christina Gabriel. 2002. *Selling Diversity: Immigration, Multiculturalism, Employment Equity, and Globalization.* Peterborough: Broadview Press.

Abu-Laban, Yasmeen, and Tim Nieguth. 2000. "Reconsidering the Constitution, Minorities and Politics in Canada." *Canadian Journal of Political Science* 33, 3 (September): 465–97.

Abu-Laban, Yasmeen, and Linda Trimble. 2006. "Print Media Coverage of Muslim-Canadians at Recent Federal Elections." *Electoral Insight* 8, 2 (December): 35–42.

Alfred, Taiaiake. 1999. *Peace, Power, Righteousness: An Indigenous Manifesto.* Don Mills: Oxford University Press.

Alfred, Taiaiake. 2005. *Wasasé: Indigenous Pathways of Action and Freedom.* Peterborough: Broadview Press.

Bakan, Abigail. 2008. "Reconsidering the Underground Railway: Slavery and Racialization in the Making of the Canadian State." *Socialist Studies* 4, 1: 3–29.

Bakan, Abigail B., and Audrey Kobayashi. 2007. "'The Sky Didn't Fall': Organizing to Combat Racism in the Workplace — The Case of the Alliance for Employment Equity." In Genevieve Fuji Johnson and Randy Enomoto, eds., *Race, Racialization, and Antiracism in Canada and Beyond.* Toronto: University of Toronto Press. 51–78.

Baum, Bruce. 2006. *The Rise and Fall of the Caucasian Race.* New York: New York University Press.

Betz, Hans Georg. 2002. "Xenophobia, Identity Politics, and Exclusionary Populism in Western Europe." In Leo Panitch and Colin Leys, eds., *Fighting Identities: Race, Religion, and Ethno-Nationalism. Socialist Register 2003.* London: Merlin Press. 193–210.

Beyer, Peter. 2005. "Religious Identity and Educational Attainment Among Recent Immigrants to Canada: Gender, Age, and 2nd Generation." *Journal of International Migration and Integration* 6, 2 (Spring): 177–99.

Bloemraad, I. 2006. *Becoming a Citizen: Incorporating Immigrants and Refugees in the United States and Canada.* Berkeley: University of California Press.

Bramadat, Paul, and David Seljak, Eds. 2005. *Religion and Ethnicity in Canada.* Toronto: Pearson Longman.

Cairns, Alan C. 1992. *Charter versus Federalism: The Dilemmas of Constitutional Reform.* Montreal: McGill-Queen's University Press.

Canadian Political Science Association. 2008. "CPSA 2009 Conference Section — Race, Ethnicity, Indigenous Peoples, and Politics." POLCAN e-mail communiqué, 16 April.

Cardin, Jean-François, and Claude Couture. 1996. *Histoire du Canada: Espace et différences.* Quebec: Les Presses de l'Université Laval.

CBC News. 2007. "Harper slams Elections Canada ruling on veils," 9 September. http://www.cbc.ca/canada/story/2007/09/09/harper-veil.html?ref=rss.

CTV.ca. 2008. "Canadians prefer Obama over own leaders: Poll," 29 June. http://www.ctv.ca.

Day, Richard J.F. 2000. *Multiculturalism and the History of Canadian Diversity.* Toronto: University of Toronto Press.

Desroches, Vincent. 2003. "Présentation: En quoi la littérature québécoise est-elle postcoloniale?" *Quebec Studies* 30 (Spring/Summer): 3–14.

Deveaux, Monique. 2006. *Gender and Justice in Multicultural Liberal States.* Oxford: Oxford University Press.

Dhamoon, Rita. 2009. *Identity/Difference Politics: How Difference is Produced and Why It Matters.* Vancouver: University of British Columbia Press.

Dickason, Olive P. 1992. *Canada's First Nations: A History of Founding Peoples from Earliest Times.* Toronto: McClelland and Stewart.

Dua, Enakshi. 2008. "Thinking Through Anti-Racism and Indigeneity in Canada." *The Ardent* 1, 1: 31–35.

Eisenberg, Avigail, Ed. 2006. *Diversity and Equality: The Changing Framework of Freedom in Canada.* Vancouver: University of British Columbia Press.

Fernando, Shanti. 2006. *Race and the City: Chinese Canadian and Chinese American Political Mobilization.* Vancouver: University of British Columbia Press.

Fierlbeck, Katherine. 1996. "The Ambivalent Potential of Cultural Identity." *Canadian Journal of Political Science* 29: 3–22.

Gagnon, Alain-G., Ed. 2004. *Québec: State and Society*, 3rd ed. Peterborough: Broadview Press.

Galabuzi, Grace-Edward. 2006. *Canada's Economic Apartheid: The Social Exclusion of Racialized Groups in the New Century.* Toronto: Canadian Scholars' Press.

Globe and Mail. 2007. "Editorial: Why make veils an issue?" 11 September: A20.

Green, Joyce A. 1995. "Towards a Détente with History: Confronting Canada's Colonial Legacy." *International Journal of Canadian Studies* 12 (Fall): 85–105.

Green, Joyce, and Ian Peach. 2007. "Beyond 'Us' and 'Them': Prescribing Postcolonial Politics and Policy in Saskatchewan." In Keith Banting, Thomas J. Courchene, and

F. Leslie Seidle, eds., *Belonging? Diversity, Recognition, and Shared Citizenship in Canada*. Montreal: Institute for Research on Public Policy. 263–84.

Hogben, David. 2008. "British Columbians prefer Obama… for Prime Minister." *The Vancouver Sun*, 23 September. http://www.canada.com.

Huntington, Samuel. 1996. *The Clash of Civilizations: Remaking of World Order*. New York: Simon and Shuster.

Ignatieff, Michael. 2000. *The Rights Revolution*. Toronto: Anansi.

James, Matt. 1999. "Redress Politics and Canadian Citizenship." In Harvey Lazar and Tom McIntosh, eds., *The State of the Federation 1998/99: How Canadians Connect*. Montreal: McGill-Queen's University Press. 247–81.

James, Matt. 2004. "Recognition, Redistribution, and Redress: The Case of the 'Chinese Head Tax.'" *Canadian Journal of Political Science* 37, 4 (December): 883–902.

Jih Soo Ewe. 2008. "Obama has links to Malaysia." *The Star Online*, 21 July. http://thestar.com.

King, Mackenzie. 1947. *Hansard* (Thursday, 1 May). In Canada, Manpower and Immigration, *A Report of the Canadian Immigration and Population Study, Volume Two: The Immigration Program*. Ottawa: Information Canada, 1974. 201–07.

Kobayashi, Audrey. 2008. "Ethnocultural Political Mobilization, Multiculturalism, and Human Rights in Canada." In Miriam Smith, ed., *Group Politics and Social Movements in Canada*. Peterborough: Broadview. 131–57.

Kymlicka, Will. 1998. *Finding Our Way: Rethinking Ethnocultural Relations in Canada*. Toronto: Oxford University Press.

Kymlicka, Will. 2007. "Ethnocultural Diversity in a Liberal State: Making Sense of the Canadian Models." In Keith Banting, Thomas J. Courchene, and F. Leslie Seidle, eds., *Belonging? Diversity, Recognition, and Shared Citizenship in Canada*. Montreal: Institute for Research on Public Policy. 39–104.

Ladner, Kiera. 2008. "*Aysaka'paykinit*: Contesting the Rope Around the Nations' Neck." In Miriam Smith, ed., *Group Politics and Social Movements in Canada*. Peterborough: Broadview. 227–49.

Lamoureux, Diane, Chantal Maillé, and Micheline de Sève. 1999. *Malaise identitaires: Échanges féministes autour d'un Québec incertain*. Montreal: Remue-Ménage.

Maclure, Jocelyn. 2003. *Quebec Identity*. Montreal: McGill-Queen's University Press.

Miles, Robert. 2000. "Apropos the Idea of 'Race' Again." In Les Back and John Solomos, eds., *Theories of Race and Racism: A Reader*. London and New York: Routledge. 125–43.

Modood, Tariq. 2007. *Multiculturalism: A Civic Idea*. Cambridge: Polity Press.

M'pindou, Jacques Luketa. 2002. "La Jeunesse congolaise dans la société canadienne." In Claude Couture and Josée Bergeron, eds., *L'Alberta et le multiculturalisme francophone: témoignages et problématiques*. Edmonton: Canadian Studies Institute.

National Visible Minority Council on Labour Force Development (NVMCLFD). 2004. *Building Our Future Workforce: A Background Paper on Visible Minority Labour Force Development*. Ottawa: NVMCLFD.

Nolan, Daniel. 2008. "Obama's brother-in-law taking it all in stride." *The Hamilton Spectator*, 23 August. http://www.thespec.com.

Palmer, Howard. 1977. "History and Present State of Ethnic Studies in Canada." In Wsevolod Isajiw, ed., *Identities: The Impact of Ethnicity on Canadian Society*. Canadian Ethnic Studies Association, Vol. 5. Toronto: Peter Martin: 167–83.

Razack, Sherene. 2008. *Casting Out: The Eviction of Muslims from Western Law and Politics*. Toronto: University of Toronto Press.

Said, Edward. 1979. *Orientalism*. New York: Vintage Books.

Salée, Daniel. 2007. "The Quebec State and the Management of Ethnocultural Diversity: Perspectives on an Ambiguous Record." In Keith Banting, Thomas J. Courchene, and F. Leslie Seidle, eds., *Belonging? Diversity, Recognition, and Shared Citizenship in Canada.* Montreal: Institute for Research on Public Policy. 105–42.

Scott, Gilbert H. 1989. "Race Relations and Public Policy: Uncharted Course." In O.P. Dwivedi *et al.*, eds., *Canada 2000: Race Relations and Public Policy.* Guelph: Department of Political Studies, University of Guelph: 227–32.

Seljak, David. 2007. "Religion and Multiculturalism in Canada: The Challenge of Religious Intolerance and Discrimination." Report Prepared for the Department of Canadian Heritage. Strategic Policy, Research and Planning Directorate, Multiculturalism and Human Rights Program. Ottawa: Department of Canadian Heritage.

Smith, Malinda. 2003. "'Race Matters' and 'Race Manners.'" In Janine Brodie and Linda Trimble, eds., *Reinventing Canada.* Toronto: Prentice Hall. 108–29.

Stasiulis, Daiva, and Radha Jhappan. 1995. "The Fractious Politics of a Settler Society: Canada." In Daiva Stasiulis and Nira Yuval-Davis, eds., *Unsettling Settler Societies: Articulations of Gender, Race, Ethnicity, and Class.* London: Sage.

Statistics Canada. 2007. *Immigration in Canada: A Portrait of the Foreign-Born Population, 2006 Census.* Catalogue No. 97-557-XIE. Ottawa: Minister of Industry (December). http://www.statscan.ca.

Statistics Canada. 2008. *Canada's Ethnocultural Mosaic, 2006 Census.* Catalogue No. 97-562-XIE. Ottawa: Minister of Industry (April). http://www.statscan.ca.

Taylor, Charles. 1992. "The Politics of Recognition." In Amy Gutmann, ed., *Multiculturalism and the Politics of Recognition.* Princeton: Princeton University Press. 25–73.

Taylor, Rupert. 1999. "Political Science Encounters 'Race' and 'Ethnicity.'" In Martin Bulmer and John Solomos, eds., *Ethnic and Racial Studies Today.* London and New York: Routledge. 115–23.

Thompson, Debra. 2008. "Is Race Political?" *Canadian Journal of Political Science* 41, 3 (September): 525–47.

Tully, James. 1997. *Strange Multiplicity: Constitutionalism in an Age of Diversity.* Cambridge: Cambridge University Press.

PART IV
Canada in the World

sixteen

Globalization and Canada

MARK R. BRAWLEY

When world leaders met in Canada in recent years to discuss the global economy, anti-globalization protesters came out in force. Why does globalization trigger such protests here? Neither academics nor the public agree on an evaluation of globalization's impact, partly because the term encompasses a wide variety of activities but also because any evidence we might use to evaluate claims about globalization will necessarily be complex. The evidence is mixed — countries have had varied results during periods of globalization. To make matters more difficult for us, Canada's experience has arguably been quite unique, forcing us to exercise caution when we consider the relevance for Canada of any insights drawn from the social science literature on globalization. Some findings will be especially pertinent, while some may not be useful at all.

Though the processes making up globalization may be extremely similar across the world, globalization's impact on Canada may be exceptional. Canada's position in the world political economy is quite singular, and its historical development has given it particular traits that determine how globalization has affected it. The Canadian economy is technologically advanced, the country is richly endowed with capital, yet it continues to earn significant amounts by exporting raw materials. Canadian cultural products and artists are world renowned, yet its cultural industry is dwarfed by that of the Goliath to the south. Canada has long been exposed to the turbulence of the world economy; its political economy grew in the shadow of British and then American industries. Nonetheless, Canada's political economy developed unique features, including uniquely Canadian conceptions of its own socio-economic system. Does this make it more vulnerable to threats associated with globalization, or less? Given the contrast between American and Canadian attitudes and practices, the stakes involved are clear — no wonder protestors take to the streets. Yet globalization also has its defenders. Can we distinguish between the possible and the probable? If globalization includes both threats and opportunities, are there ways to manage it, to draw out what Canadians want but avoid the parts we do not want?

Conceptualizing Globalization

Globalization is a process or, more specifically, a number of interrelated processes (Brawley, 2003: chapter 1). In a globalized world, borders no longer act as barriers to the flow of words, pictures, money, goods, services, people, or ideas. Globalization is also supposed to reflect something spanning vast geographic spaces — it represents something more than just countries developing closer ties with their immediate international neighbours. The free flow of money, people, goods, and services triggers changes to the way a country's economy works. Greater flows in communications and individuals can rapidly inject new ideas into society, potentially altering cultural practices. The combined effects can hit all across the spectrum, influencing economic outcomes, policy choices, and social structures. (Note that globalization has been uneven — trade in manufactured goods has become increasingly open in recent decades, while trade in agricultural products remains relatively protected. Capital currently flows across borders with relative ease, but since 9/11, moving people over borders has become more difficult.) On each count, there may be debate over the costs and benefits to such changes — change should not be rejected as automatically bad. Societies and economies are constantly changing. Globalization grabs our attention because it locates the source of change in forces that appear extremely large and powerful as well as global in spread. Sometimes, changes are considered good because they are so wide-ranging. Economists typically encourage globalizing trends, because they see positive aspects to the transformations mentioned above. The greater the economic differences between two countries, the more each might benefit from exchange through trade, for example; drawing more countries into trade might increase the possibilities for developing such gains. Others are more circumspect.

For social scientists, disputes have centred on several specific aspects of the political and economic dimensions to globalization. In particular, research has focused on the economics of opening up to the world economy. This entails evaluating the aggregate gains from financial and trade openness, and assessing immigration. Some research also focuses on the redistributive effects that may go along with aggregate change; even if some changes bring greater wealth to a country overall, the changes may concentrate wealth or jobs in some peoples' hands while denying them to others. Politically, concerns about globalization have centred on whether the new ties impinge on a state's sovereignty (Garrett, 1998; Rodrik, 1998b). Certainly if a state's society and economy become more tightly intertwined with those of its neighbours, its decision-making becomes more complex and potentially fraught with international friction. People have also become concerned about the ability of the state to execute the policies its constituents prefer, especially as the spectre of international economic competition rises in prominence. This latter point is a particular issue in Canada, because of the glaring contrasts between its social policies and those of its most obvious economic competitor, the United States.

Below, there is a brief summary of the current literature on specific dimensions to globalization in several broad categories encompassing economics, politics, and social issues. In each category, globalizing trends can be broken down into more specific processes, making our discussion more manageable and precise. The conclusions derived from broader analyses may not always be so useful for thinking about Canada's situation, however, so the relevance of the research needs to be interpreted from a Canadian perspective. Only by looking at these pieces can we then think about the overall impact of globalization on Canada and reflect on the options Canada (and Canadians) should focus on for the future.

Economic Processes and Outcomes

Much of the social science analysis on globalization focuses on the economic processes at work, because these are so visible and tangible, easy to identify and measure. We can also locate specific policy decisions associated with the lowering of economic barriers to trade, international capital flows, etc., making it relatively easy to search for the impact of globalization over time. Since we can measure the flows of international goods, services, and factors of production (such as capital and labour) and we have well-established economic models predicting what the impact of these changes would likely be, we can compare those expectations with data drawn from a variety of countries.

A number of studies begin with observations about the aggregate impact of trade or financial liberalization on countries, giving an image of the typical impact on a country by looking across broad samples (Chan and Scarritt, 2002; Rudra, 2002, 2004). Overall, the international economy became much more open to trade and then capital flows in the latter half of the twentieth century. Many countries liberalized their international economic policies after the fall of the Soviet Union. Improvements in transportation and communications technologies fostered these changes by making it easier for individuals and firms to coordinate their activities. To participate, countries also had to adopt particular policies. The first breakthroughs came when the members of GATT (the General Agreement on Tariffs and Trade) agreed to lower tariffs on manufactured goods in the 1960s. In the 1970s and 1980s, GATT attracted more members. It eventually evolved into the WTO (World Trade Organization) in the 1990s. The WTO agreement included commitments to extend the liberalization trend into new product ranges, including some services and agriculture.

Capital flows increased in volume beginning in the 1960s, but there was an even more dramatic decline in the barriers to transnational capital flows in subsequent decades. Currently, money moving across borders is worth much more than the value of goods or services exchanged internationally. Money may flow quite rapidly — being pushed and pulled by relatively small differences in the amount of interest it can earn in one place rather than another. Whatever drives expectations of changes in currencies' relative values can trigger significant movements. Rapid flows into economically developing countries — followed by just as rapid exits — have generated boom and bust cycles, as well as international financial crises. Because these financial crises tie together investors from worldwide sources, they represent another way in which economic globalization may offer countries advantages but simultaneously expose them to greater dangers.

The first wave of studies on globalization tried to form some general evaluations of these economic processes. This was often done through a comparison of the economic performance of countries in the first period (the 1950s to 1970s) with their performance in the second period (the 1980s on). This could be done by marking when different countries joined in globalization by liberalizing their foreign economic policies and comparing their individual performances before they joined an agreement to their performance after. Economists expect trade liberalization to increase a country's aggregate wealth, but they also know that trade redistributes wealth within societies. Most studies have shown that trade liberalization and aggregate economic growth have moved together. However, trade brings growth through specialization, and specialization requires altering the mix of goods and services a country produces. Changing production often redistributes wealth within the country — trade produces winners and losers. The winners may choose to assist or otherwise compensate the losers, but that becomes a political question. In any case, we can surmise that the positive economic changes in the aggregate may still prove divisive within the country politically (Rodrik, 1998a). Those who made incomes off older production patterns may stand to lose income as specialization proceeds; their interests get pitted against the interests of those who gain additional income from specialization. Similar battles were fought out during an earlier period of globalization (in the decades before the First World War, culminating in Canada with the election contest over trade arrangements with the United States in 1911). Most economically advanced countries created a series of compensatory policies in the 1930s and 1940s to soften the hardships associated with reopening trade, often referred to as the compromise of "embedded liberalism" (Ruggie,

1982). Embedded liberalism included the creation and implementation of domestic policies such as compensation for unemployment, tax breaks for certain sectors, and so forth. Some sectors remained protected, too.

Studies on globalization examining trade liberalization's impact on social inequality have reached much more mixed conclusions. This probably should not be surprising, since different countries apply quite varied combinations of domestic policies that complement or offset trade's effects. Nonetheless, essential economic models tell us trade over time should increase the return to the factor of production relatively abundant in the national economy. In countries rich in labour but relatively poor in capital (i.e., less industrialized countries), workers' wages should rise when trade is liberalized. Since capital and labour are two significant inputs, and we look at their ratio within the economy to judge which is relatively abundant, the argument leads to the conclusion that freer trade should be popular in poorer countries (Milner and Kubota, 2005). Conversely, freer trade should hurt the income of workers in the richer economies while increasing the returns to owners of capital. In general, labour has been more generally wary of globalization in economically advanced countries and surprisingly receptive in economically developing countries, seeming to confirm this insight (Scheve and Slaughter, 2004). It has proven harder to pin down the preferences of the owners of capital, but this may be because extremely liquid capital may prefer openness, whereas capital fixed in one sector (e.g., in the form of machinery useful for a limited range of purposes) may not.

Economists expect the lowering of barriers to international capital flows to affect borrowing countries by enabling them to increase levels of investment; lending countries presumably make higher profits off foreign investments compared to investing the money at home. Economists therefore also tend to endorse globalization of financial markets.

However, increased capital flows carry increased risks. Both borrowers and lenders must worry about fluctuations in exchange rates, political upheavals, or other risks specific to international investments; these complicate the calculations concerning the profitability of any investment. Yet economists would underline that both borrowers and lenders engage in international lending voluntarily; investors lend money because they expect a return (interest) and borrowers take on debt because they expect to invest it, earn enough profit to pay off the debt plus the interest, and still come out ahead. If both parties make reasonably accurate calculations, the deal should be mutually beneficial. Changing conditions may make those calculations inaccurate, harming one side or the other. Whenever debtors cannot pay back what they borrowed, both sides suffer losses.

On the one hand, the recurrence of international financial crises suggests here too that although participating in economic globalization increases opportunities for gains, it simultaneously raises exposure to problems. Even worse, financial crises in the 1990s seemed to drag in countries where borrowers had taken inordinately high risks and governments made poor decisions, but they also pulled in borrowers in other countries who had not engaged in such risky behaviour or had governments that had made few policy mistakes. The East Asian Financial Crises brought ruin to countries that had mismanaged their currencies and left their domestic financial markets insufficiently regulated (e.g., Indonesia), but the crisis also hit other countries just as hard. It appeared that investors burned by the crisis in one East Asian country simply pulled their funds out of others, reducing their own exposure but forcing the crisis to spread where it need not have.

On top of these concerns, many observers worried that international lenders were exercising pressure (directly or indirectly) on governments. It turns out that governments were among the major international borrowers from the 1970s on, because international banks were offering loans at very low interest rates. Many governments could get money more cheaply if they borrowed from abroad rather than from domestic lenders. When interest rates (and the exchange value of the American dollar) climbed in the early 1980s, debtors' calculations were off — they owed much more than they had expected. Sovereign debtors were particularly hard hit. As governments struggled to pay off past debts, lenders tightened the conditions for contracting new loans. The newer terms often forced governments to reduce expenditures and increase taxes so they could devote more funds to servicing their debts. Higher taxes and less money for services obviously proved unpopular. Social scientists expected lenders to restrict the options of governments everywhere (Mosley, 2003).

These pressures from lenders, reinforced by the heightened competition in trade, led many to predict that economic globalization would compel states to deregulate their domestic economies. Governments would have to restrict services and invest less in their societies; as government activity shrank, competitive pressures would push them to adopt laissez-faire policies. This combination of government austerity and deregulation was imposed on many countries through the Structural Adjustment Programs developed by international financial agencies such as the World Bank and International Monetary Fund (IMF). Many social scientists therefore postulated that governments would "race to the bottom" — compete to deregulate their economies in order to attract employment opportunities and investments as well as to spur on exports.

A second wave of studies questioned whether such a race was indeed taking place. If it has, the race may have included only a handful of extremely indebted countries (Rudra, 2002, 2004). Few if any of the industrialized countries appear to have seriously deregulated their economies; few have actually reduced the size of government (Rodrik, 1998b). This does not mean those industrialized countries were struggling to deal with financial woes in the 1980s and 1990s. Many of the more economically advanced countries were under pressure to balance their budgets or at least significantly reduce their debts. This may have had little to do with globalization and more to do with mounting budget deficits paralleled by rising taxes; constituents, not international lenders, often demanded change.

Follow-up research on this second wave of studies sought to parse out the economic effects of globalization on different kinds of countries, and more thoughtful analyses highlighted some critical assessments about what governments do and the relationship between their actions and economic competitiveness. Competition for direct foreign investments cannot be reduced to a single factor such as low wages or deregulated markets. Some firms require an educated labour force, not merely a cheap one; multinational corporations are not interested in building factories in locales lacking roads or rail networks or suffering from poor services such as intermittent energy supplies. Global economic competition may therefore trigger government investments on infrastructure, education, and other areas, rather than unleashing a race to the bottom. For the most indebted countries, however, servicing past debts still prevents them from undertaking a wider range of activities.

Canada and Economic Globalization

When thinking about how these different findings apply to Canada, several critical points must be kept in mind. First, Canada has held a fairly unique position in the international economy for a long time — trade has consistently contributed significantly to Canada's economy. For countries such as the United States or Japan, the domestic market dwarfed their engagement with the international economy for most of the past century. Those countries face more demanding adjustments, while Canada is continuing on the same path it was already on. Second, Canada's trade has long been concentrated on one partner rather than with the world economy more broadly. Canada's economy is also markedly similar to that of the United States, its main trading partner, which should influence how we interpret the economics of its trade relationship. Third, Canada has developed its own set of domestic policies, geared towards cushioning some parts of the economy even as it has liberalized trade. Have these policies been threatened by globalization in trade, as the "race to bottom" thesis suggests? Or do such policies give Canada an advantage? Fourth, Canada is a relatively rich country in terms of capital, yet its government has held relatively high levels of debt. How have recent trends in economic globalization affected Canada?

Since trade has figured prominently in Canada's economic development, Canada had already focused its economic activities on areas where it has a comparative advantage. These include land-intensive agriculture (think of wheat exports), capital- and knowledge-intensive manufacturing (pharmaceuticals, aerospace, etc.), but also resource-intensive raw materials (such as oil, lumber). Many sectors have relied on exports for decades; therefore, globalization in trade has merely reinforced pre-existing trends in contrast to many other countries where economic globalization reversed past patterns, initiating dramatic changes (Watson, 1998). At the same time, some of these sectors are declining in relative importance in Canada, just as they are in other industrialized societies, as services have expanded.

Canada's trade has also remained focused on the United States, though liberalization has opened up markets for Canadian exports in several new regions. Remember, globalization is supposed to refer to more than an increase in bilateral trade. Canada has increased its trade with Asia in recent years, and with Europe. The United States continues to hold the top ranking as a destination for Canadian exports. This is somewhat curious because Canada and the United States have very similar attributes; this also fuels tensions in trade sometimes, since Canadian exports hit areas where American producers already exist (such as lumber products). It may also mean Canadian exports are driven by factors such as consumer tastes or marketing rather than by the sort of bedrock economic issues focused on in economic models. Interestingly, Canada has become the single largest source of American oil imports in recent years.

For Canada, "embedded liberalism" meant not only the development of policies designed to cushion domestic actors but it also drew limits to trade liberalization. Certain sectors have remained off the negotiating table since the Great Depression. Dairy producers, for example, remain so opposed to liberalization that their stance shaped Canada's policies in the Doha Round of WTO negotiations. Canada also adopted policies assisting people out of work and has explored methods for stimulating growth in regions that are either underdeveloped or where unemployment is high. National health care, government pension plans, and other policies also provide people the opportunity to deal with trade adjustment — it cushions them from some of the costs associated with rapidly shifting production to meet international demands or adjust to world markets. Canadians have become increasingly concerned, however, with the costs associated with such programs. Doubts about their sustainability may have more to do with balancing government outlays with revenues, and less to do with concerns about international competitiveness (more on this below).

The federal and provincial governments together owe some staggering amounts (over $75,000 on a per capita basis) (Palacios *et al.*, 2008). Although the federal and provincial governments have been able to reduce their direct debt in recent years, interest payments on the debt accounted for over 9 per cent of government expenses. Lack of secure funding for government programs means that total government liabilities have risen even as direct debt fell. While the federal and provincial governments maintain good credit ratings because they remain able to generate future income to pay off these debts, the amounts are surprisingly high in per capita terms. If doubts about the ability to service these debts arise, interest rates and conditions on new loans would rise, adding to the debt burden; many people fear that the conditions might include reductions in government spending that would impair essential services such as health care. These remain fears only, for the moment; if anything, the trend has been to increase obligations in these programs as globalization proceeds.

The Political Consequences of Globalization

One of the obvious results of economic globalization is the politicization of foreign economic policies. As more of a country's economy becomes tied to international markets, foreign economic policies become more politicized. In Canada this has been partially recognized by changes in the title and structure of the bureaucracy conducting the country's foreign policy: the Department of Foreign Affairs and International Trade, which has separate Cabinet ministers for each aspect. We would expect international trade negotiations, the value of the currency on exchange markets, and other similar matters to rise in political salience as globalization proceeds. Domestic groups may form around policies that were of little concern decades earlier.

Yet when we think about Canada, does the current trend in globalization represent anything new? Since the Canadian economy has long been exposed to foreign economic influences, issues such as trade and the exchange rate have long mattered to Canadians. Perhaps surprisingly, the dramatic climb in the value of the Canadian dollar versus its American counterpart between 2005 and 2008 generated little interest among the public. Prices of Canadian exports had to rise, making them harder to sell in their prime destination market. Yet exporters voiced few concerns. Instead, consumers proved considerably more vocal. Given the ease with which we can compare similar goods on either side of the border, Canadian consumers noted that prices for imports from the United States did not fall equally; instead, many retailers left imported goods at higher prices, pocketing the difference. Some Canadians responded by crossing the border to purchase goods (ranging from books to automobiles).

Exporters may have been fairly weak to organize, as many may not produce goods so sensitive to price changes in the first place. Agriculture and resources remain important export sectors, but manufacturing and services are the true motors of the Canadian economy. These latter sectors may be largely indifferent to fluctuations in the exchange markets. They are competitive because of the quality of their merchandise or services, and even a 10-15 per cent increase in the wholesale price might not hurt their business. Many firms operate multinationally. With income and assets on both sides of the border, any costs associated with a change in the value of the Canadian dollar would be mirrored by gains elsewhere.

As noted above, trade itself has long mattered, so, unsurprisingly, there are those for and those opposed to further trade liberalization. In general, the supporters of free trade outnumber the opponents. After Conservative governments negotiated and then approved first the Canada-US Free Trade Agreement and then the North American Free Trade Agreement (NAFTA), critics in the Liberal and New Democratic parties campaigned on platforms to overturn those deals. The Liberals split over the wisdom of such a strategy in the 1988 election; when Jean Chrétien led the Liberals to victory in 1993, he famously included a pledge to renegotiate the trade agreements in the party's campaign platform (the "Red Book"). Once in office, however, Chrétien had little incentive to change the deals.

In fact, the trade agreements include a variety of exceptions that keep particular sectors protected. Dairy farming, textiles, and other less competitive sectors located in politically pivotal regions (such as Quebec) received exemptions from liberalization. Since these arrangements might be questioned in any negotiations, only groups with protectionist interests not already covered would desire renegotiation — and they would not find allies among those receiving special treatment already. It therefore appears regional free trade is here to stay. That same balance has placed Canada in some contradictory positions in recent WTO negotiations, however. Agricultural groups in particular are split, some desiring maintenance of the existing barriers on trade, others wishing to push liberalization to match the tariff reductions made much earlier on manufactured goods. In 2008 this pitted wheat farmers and beef ranchers on the one hand versus dairy farmers and egg producers on the other. The government seems pulled between the two.

Neither trade nor international monetary policy seems likely to create the dominant political cleavage in the coming years. Other issues linked to globalization, such as environmental policies, apparent changes in social equality, emerging regional inequalities, or threats to the level of government services (or perhaps, more precisely, the relationship between the level of services, taxes, and the government's debts) are more likely to shape the Canadian electorate. Trade openness can be taken as a given; recent experience also suggests much of the population is insensitive to large swings in the value of the currency *vis-à-vis* Canada's largest trading partner. Canada is already inured to pressures of economic globalization.

As noted above, despite fears that there are pressures on the government to cut programs or services in the name of international competitiveness, there is little evidence to sustain such a perspective when we concentrate on Canada. If anything, the size and scale of government obligations has continued to grow in recent decades. Direct debts have stabilized and even fallen, government regulation remains in place, and the overall size and scale of government does not appear to have shrunk.

Globalization and Canadian Society

While economic processes steal the limelight in academic studies, globalization includes other dimensions. Social connections between countries have also increased dramatically in recent years because the cost of communicating over vast distances has fallen, especially as technology improves (e.g., digitization of mass media entertainment will continue to reshape distribution systems and networks). In one of the most famous books on globalization, Thomas Friedman (1999) used the images of a luxury automobile (the Lexus) and the olive tree to symbolize how many people desired the economic benefits from globalization but feared their cultural identities would be uprooted. Friedman argued that people desire economic advancement (especially for their children) but also want to protect their traditional values. This creates tremendous tensions. From a political science perspective, the greatest opposition to economic globalization comes when those who feel their identities or values threatened are also identified as the losers in the economic changes globalization brings. If those two cleavages reinforce each other, people are more easily mobilized to slow down or even reverse globalizing trends.

Studies in comparative politics have shown how such concerns have risen in salience (Kriesi *et al.*, 2006). (It is a bit harder to measure and evaluate cultural change itself; most studies therefore focus on perceptions of change.) Analyses of the way politicians in Western Europe speak to globalization and the cleavages globalization triggers indicate that voters there have become increasingly concerned with the way globalization affects culture. This has shown up strikingly in anti-immigration sentiments in the Netherlands, in concerns about the pressures on rural life in France, the survival of minority languages or dialects in a number of regions, and so forth.

Canada does not quite fit that pattern, however. It is a nation with a long tradition of accepting immigrants, which continues to this day. Many people living in Canada were born somewhere else, or their parents were. Conversely, Canada also has a large number of people holding multiple citizenships. The fighting in Lebanon in 2006 exposed this in shocking detail, when some 40,000 people living in Lebanon demonstrated they also held Canadian passports. Having so many people with multiple identities ensures various states will have their interests intertwined and overlapping. The same holds for Canada and the United States, who each have large numbers of citizens living within each others' borders.

To understand and evaluate the impact of so many people interacting internationally, moving over boundaries, and holding multiple citizenships, we need more precise theories about multiple loyalties (for some early efforts, see Goff and Dunn, 2004). More research needs to be done to understand how people are handling potential conflicts between their different identities. This is especially relevant for Canadians, since provincial and regional identities remain quite strong. Canadians already have a fairly complicated layering of identities that may reflect metropolitan links ("I'm a Montrealer"), regional origins ("I'm from down east"), ethnic ties ("I'm Acadian"), and provincial ties ("I'm from New Brunswick"), as well as a claim to Canadian identity.

Some scholars expect such trends to produce internal dissension and conflict, as they believe these loyalties will clash. Such ideas are relevant for Canadians given the importance of cultural issues for Quebec separatists. Separatists argue protection of a distinct Quebec identity requires limitation of external influences and ultimately the rejection of a Canadian identity. Other scholars believe such identities can be layered and overlapping — perhaps even reinforcing one another. This interpretation is important for those studying Canada, because it highlights the arguments federalists make concerning Quebec's place in Canada. Those opposed to Quebec separation argue that Quebec plays a central role defining and enriching Canadian society, while the federal system increases the chances for the survival of Quebec's culture in a global context.

Another way to measure social globalization would be to consider the penetration into Canada of cultural products made elsewhere. Most major Canadian cities lie near the American border — close enough that radio and television broadcasts reached them decades ago. Improved technology may in fact have led more people to adopt more regulated forms of mass media (such as cable and satellite feeds), however. In addition, Canada has intense trade ties with the United States. These forces translate into tremendous influence on Canadian culture. Nonetheless, it has often been said that one of the bonds uniting Canadians is their agreement in rejecting particular aspects of American culture (as highlighted in a famous ad campaign produced by Molson). Moreover, one of the more intense splits over identity has been somewhat oddly influenced by globalization. Quebec separatists make note of the potential threats to Quebec's unique attributes coming from globalization, but they also see increased economic globalization as a means to make an independent Quebec viable. By turning to world markets, Quebec can make itself less reliant on the rest of Canada, they argue.

Globalization is supposed to mean something quite specific about global influences affecting everyday life. However, many have noted that many activists actually focus on the dominance of American cultural influences; for instance, French anti-globalization protestor José Bové gained fame by leading demonstrations against McDonald's restaurants. Globalization can mean that ideas and products come in from many countries, of course, but American influence typically draws the most ire. Canada's unique geographic position, as noted before, along with shared cultural attributes and a similar standard of living, may make it especially vulnerable to American cultural influences. Shared use of the English language means that American movies, music, newspapers, magazines, and other products easily find a market in Canada. The two countries have similar histories in many ways, since each developed with settlers moving on a frontier, interactions with Aboriginal populations, waves of immigrants in the late nineteenth and early twentieth centuries, and democratic governments in a federal system. Of course, their histories are also different, with important twists to how their frontiers were settled, how each federal government interacted with First Nations, and so on. Canadians may face an uphill struggle in preserving and promoting the unique aspects of their past in the face of the flood of American ideas and issues.

One response has been to try to regulate the amount of American cultural products being consumed in Canada. Canadians think about cultural products differently than Americans, so these efforts at regulation produced pointed conflicts between the two governments (Goff, 2007). In the Canada–US Free Trade negotiations and then in the NAFTA talks, Canada put in protections for cultural products. Canadians and Americans may define cultural products differently, with Americans more likely to see products such as magazines or movies as commercial rather than cultural. The two have therefore disputed Canadian regulations covering content in magazines, music, and television shows. Canadian artists have both benefited from and chafed under these regulations, since the definitions of Canadian content ultimately become exercises in the application of bureaucratic minutiae.

Political attitudes also distinguish the Canadian and American cultures. Seymour Martin Lipset (1990) noted long ago that Canadians are more def- erential and trusting of government than Americans. This fits with the ideas mentioned above that the government plays a larger role in the economy and provides a wider array of benefits here than in the United States. Others have observed that Canadians are committed more to equality of outcomes, whereas Americans believe more strongly in equality of economic opportun- ity (see Brooks, Chapter 3). This is quite prevalent in attitudes about health care. Canadians are rightly proud of their government-run health insurance program. These differences bring us back to concerns mentioned above about the degree to which globalization may threaten such programs.

Where Does That Leave Us?

Social scientists studying globalization have explored the potential im- pact a number of different processes might have on individual countries. Economically, the evidence suggests that globalization provides opportunities for growth and additional wealth, but it also redistributes wealth internally. Globalized financial markets may have given lenders powerful leverage over borrowers, who must be careful not to trigger exchange crises and capital flight. The ability to take advantage of the economic opportunities varies across countries, with some better placed than others. The domestic upheav- als wrought by economic globalization also vary across countries; in some places, such changes promise to make the distribution of wealth more equal, rewarding the working class. In others, the need for competitiveness may be just as likely to prompt governments to invest in education or infrastructure as it is to spur them to deregulate or provide fewer services. Specific reactions depend on where states believe their economic strengths lie.

Canada is economically competitive across a wide and interesting mix of sectors. It has an industrialized economy with a highly developed infra- structure, well-educated work force, and provincial and federal governments providing a range of services. The country exports manufactured goods and high-tech products, as well as raw materials such as lumber and oil. Canada has proven successful in drawing in international investment. Governments at different levels borrow from international sources with few conditions or constraints imposed, so far. Canada also has a wide variety of domestic policies in place to help soften the economic fluctuations globalization might bring. When thinking about globalization and social policies, Canada seems to have weathered the last two decades well. There is little evidence that

Canadian programs have been reduced due to globalizing forces. On balance, then, Canada has benefited from economic globalization, but that balance could easily tip.

Globalization's impact on Canadian society is harder to decipher. Canadians hold diverse and complex identities. Globalization will add to that complexity and diversity. While we have competing theories about how individuals balance or manage multiple identities, much more work needs to be done. Various identities may prove easy to "nest" one within another, but they may also generate conflicts. The overlap of national identities will undoubtedly present governments with new and daunting challenges. Globalization contributes to both centripetal and centrifugal tendencies here.

Even in a globalizing world, states still have choices. If Canadians desire something with enough intensity, the government will respond. Government policies control the degree to which many aspects of globalization affect Canada. If international lenders exert too much influence, the key would be to rely less on such lenders. Balancing the budget, reducing deficits, and finding sustainable revenue streams would contribute to governments' independence from such pressures. If international markets introduce other forms of volatility, governments need to counter by introducing policies geared to protect Canadians or enhance existing programs that achieve these ends. Services such as government-run health care can be a selling point in international competition, rather than a disadvantage, so long as they are provided efficiently.

Successful strategies for managing globalization often involve cooperation with other actors. Canada actively engages with other leading economies through the G8 to coordinate economic policies in order to help the world economy attain steady growth. Canada has consistently demonstrated its deep commitment to multilateral international institutions. To the extent that these will provide useful solutions to the problems ahead, Canada and Canadians will lead the way.

References and Suggested Readings

Bhagwati, Jagdish. 2004. *In Defense of Globalization*. New York: Oxford University Press.

Brawley, Mark R. 2003. *The Politics of Globalization*. Peterborough: Broadview.

Chan, Steve, and James R. Scarritt, Eds. 2002. *Coping with Globalization: Cross-National Patterns in Domestic Governance and Policy Performance*. London: Frank Cass.

Cline, William. 1999. "Trade and Income Distribution." Policy Brief 99–7. Washington, DC: International Institute for Economics.

Friedman, Thomas. 1999. *The Lexus and the Olive Tree*. New York: Farrar, Straus, Giroux.

Garrett, Geoffrey. 1998. "Global Markets and National Politics: Collision Course or Virtuous Circle?" *International Organization* 52, 4: 787–824.

Goff, Patricia. 2007. *Limits to Liberalization, Local Culture in a Global Marketplace*. Ithaca: Cornell University Press.

Goff, Patricia, and Kevin C. Dunn, Eds. 2004. *Identity and Global Politics, Empirical and Theoretical Elaborations*. New York: Palgrave Macmillan.

Kriesi, Hanspeter, Edgar Grande, Romain Lachat, Martin Dolezal, Simon Bornschier, and Timotheos Frey. 2006. "Globalization and the Transformation of the National Political Space: Six European Countries Compared." *European Journal of Political Research* 45, 6: 921–56.

Lipset, Seymour Martin. 1990. *Continental Divide: The Values and Institutions of the United States and Canada*. New York: Routledge.

Milner, Helen, and Keiko Kubota. 2005. "Why the Move to Free Trade? Democracy and Trade Policy in the Developing Countries." *International Organization* 59, 1: 107–43.

Mosley, Layna. 2003. *Global Capital and National Governments*. Cambridge: Cambridge University Press.

Palacios, Milagros, Niels Veldhuis, and Kumi Harischandra. 2008. *Canadian Government Debt 2008, A Guide to the Indebtedness of Canada and the Provinces*. Fraser Institute Digital Publications. http://www.fraserinstitute.org/COMMERCE.WEB/product_files/CanadianGovernmentDebt2008.pdf.

Rodrik, Dani. 1997. *Has Globalization Gone Too Far?* Washington, DC: International Institute for Economics.

Rodrik, Dani. 1998a. "Globalization, Social Conflict, and Economic Growth." *The World Economy* 21, 2: 143–58.

Rodrik, Dani. 1998b. "Why Do More Open Economies Have Bigger Governments?" *Journal of Political Economy* 106, 5: 997–1032.

Rudra, Nita. 2002. "Globalization and the Decline of the Welfare State in Less Developed Countries." *International Organization* 56, 2: 411–45.

Rudra, Nita. 2004. "Openness, Welfare Spending, and Inequality in the Developing World." *International Studies Quarterly* 48, 3: 683–709.

Ruggie, John Gerard. 1982. "International Regimes, Transactions, and Change: Embedded Liberalism in the Postwar Economic Order." *International Organization* 36, 2: 379–416.

Scheve, Ken, and M. Slaughter. 2004. "Economic Insecurity and the Globalization of Production." *American Journal of Political Science* 48, 4: 662–74.

Watson, William. 1998. *Globalization and the Meaning of Canadian Life*. Toronto: University of Toronto Press.

Wolf, Martin. 2004. *Why Globalization Works*. New Haven: Yale University Press.

seventeen

Canadian International Environmental Policy: Context and Directions

PETER J. STOETT

There was once a time, not long ago, when we could summarize environmental politics as an emerging field of study consigned largely to the sphere of national politics. While ecology evinces a transnational perspective, Canadian analyses have usually paid token respect to the international dimensions of environmental policy formation and implementation. Clearly, with climate change as the dominant ecopolitical issue, this is an untenable position in 2009. Indeed, as argued elsewhere (Gore and Stoett, 2008), we live in what can be termed a *glocal condition* today, where local environmental needs and global biospheric imperatives meet, clash, synthesize, and produce new currents of concern, opportunity, and governance.

There has been no guiding arc to Canadian international environmental policy-making in the preceding four decades, and it is unlikely that the electoral outcome of fall 2008 will significantly alter this characterization. Economic competitiveness has always been the central pillar of Canadian foreign policy, though it has wrestled with periodic bouts of enthusiasm for collective and human security (and seemingly forgotten efforts to link human security and sustainable development — see Axworthy, 1997). The environment has never been a central factor, though public concern with climate change has at least ensured it is squarely on the agenda today. However, it has never been entirely absent, either, and has on occasion become a serious distraction from business as usual. This was clearly the case in the early 1970s, when the United Nations (UN) Stockholm Conference took place; the early 1990s, when the UN Conference on Environment and Development occurred in Rio de Janeiro; and again in the mid-2000s, when extreme weather events and spiralling fuel costs cast the spotlight on climate change talks in Bonn, Montreal, Bali, and elsewhere. Arguably, external events have been as important as Canada's own ecological challenges in provoking both public and governmental responses to the demands of contemporary environmental diplomacy.

This chapter will present a broad overview of the Canadian context, including the predominant structures and trends that are forming the glocal ecopolitics of the twenty-first century. I argue that we need to contextualize

Canada's international environmental policy with regard to its natural characteristics and the threats to biosecurity caused by a century of industrialization, agriculture, urbanization, and climate change. Nor can we ignore the historical legacy and contemporary reality of a staples-based economy; the overarching continental dimension, and particularly the significance of Canadian-American trade; the impact of globalization, in terms of both global governance efforts/regimes and transnational normative trends; and the omnipresent constraints of Canadian federalism. Within this context, public environmental concern continues to grow, though whether this will force Canadian governments to play a forceful role in international efforts is another issue. Sub-national actors will continue to play increasingly key roles on the international stage, regardless of who is in power in Ottawa. Two concrete areas where Canada can move towards a lasting impression of leadership are in the provision of Canadian expertise abroad and in committing to the ethical obligations that will attend climate change, and I turn to these before concluding the chapter.

Natural Characteristics, Biosecurity, and Climate Change

The geographical features of any governed area will to a large extent determine the nature of ecopolitical issues and related foreign policy options. While it is relatively straightforward to think of Costa Rica as blessed with incredible biodiversity, Namibia as largely semi-arid desert, or Switzerland as largely mountainous, countries such as Canada are more geographically complex. Not only is there easily notable divergence in terms of the geo-physical landscape as one moves across the country but the science of climate change suggests this landscape is in a period of accelerated alteration.

Canada, the world's second-largest country, has ample supplies of freshwater, oil, natural gas, forests, agricultural land, and other natural bounties. It has Arctic, sub-Arctic, riparian, coastal, prairie, boreal, and mountainous regions. In fact, it would take a geographer a lifetime just to study the many bioregions within Canadian borders, and its growing urban landscapes are also important features with expanding ecological footprints.

This has immediate political impact. For example, Canada's northern latitude makes it a circumpolar region, and, spurred by fears that climate change will make Arctic economic activity irresistible to the rest of the world, the present Canadian government takes a much stronger interest in the Arctic than it did even in the days of the infamous Manhattan icebreaker voyage (Kirton and Munton, 1987). Melting ice has long been recognized as a sovereignty issue for Canada (Huebert, 2003). Canada played a key role in the creation of the eight-country Arctic Council, which has a limited mandate but nonetheless represents a visible forum for circumpolar diplomacy and the dissemination of reports on Arctic environmental conditions (Stoett, 2000). The Council also gives the Inuit Circumpolar Conference a voice at the table, though it is not a voting voice (it is a "permanent observer"). A recently completed (and impressively thorough) Arctic climate impact assessment concluded that air temperatures in Alaska and Western Canada have increased as much as three to four degrees Celsius in the past 50 years, leading to an estimated 8 per cent increase of precipitation across the Arctic; as this falls as rain it increases snow melting and the dangers of flash flooding. Melting glaciers, reductions in the thickness of sea ice, and thawing of permafrost are all occurring, and they will in turn exacerbate the warming trend, threatening wildlife such as polar bears and those people whose sustenance is dependant on it.[1]

While the abundance of natural areas and national parks has earned Canada its international image as a great place to fish and hike, it is somewhat anachronistic, superseded by the negative connotations associated with Canadian intransigence on several key areas such as climate change. Yet when Canadian negotiators attend meetings related to the hundreds of bilateral and multilateral agreements the country has signed or is working towards, they must keep this varied and demanding geography in mind. For example, Canada's northern location also means that seasonal weather variation will ensure an energy-intensive future, since heating and transportation costs rise inexorably in winter months. When combined with a staples economy (see below) and the sheer distance that must be traversed for intra-country trade, the weather demands heavy machinery and fossil fuel consumption for resource extraction and distribution, which in turn makes living up to international commitments to reduce heat-trapping greenhouse gas emissions (GHGEs) that much more difficult. This does not entail a necessary rejection of the Kyoto targets on climate change, but until significant improvements in eco-efficiency and alternative energy provision take place, realism dictates that Canadian cuts in GHGEs will be limited by the need to warm homes in winter and drive long distances throughout the year.

But decision-makers must also bear in mind the impact of climate change on Canada's geography, wildlife, and general biosecurity. For example, the symbioses between globalization and global warming are increasing the likelihood of bio-invasions at both the microbial and species levels, causing shifts in pathogenic virulence. There is evidence that warming trends will induce species migration northward, and this raises concerns about disease

---

1. The report is the 2004 *Arctic Climate Impact Assessment's Scientific Report,* which is available at http://www.acia.uaf.edu/pages/scientific.html and was published in hard copy by Cambridge University Press in 2005.

and threats to native species. Such "unassisted migration" will prove difficult for rare species of plants and trees, necessitating adaptation or extinction.

Not so for insects: for example, warming patterns have vastly extended the range of the mountain pine beetle, ravaging Yoho National Park in British Columbia and threatening forests in Washington; officials in Alberta are "setting fires and traps and felling thousands of trees in an attempt to keep the beetle at bay." The pine beetle has swept across British Columbia and scientists fear it will "cross the Rocky Mountains and sweep across the northern continent into areas where it used to be killed by severe cold … U.S. Forest Service officials say they are watching warily as the outbreak has spread." The United States is less vulnerable because it "lacks the seamless forest of lodgepole pines that are a highway for the beetle in Canada."[2] (One former government official involved in the negotiations over softwood lumber tariffs mentioned the possibility that the agreement reached in 2006, which was certainly not in tune with the Canadian government's initial demands, was provoked at least partly by the pine beetle — or, rather, the urgent need to clear forests before infestation and, as a result, the need to resume large-scale exports.)

In the case of the zebra mussel, which has clogged up parts of the Great Lakes and beyond, we might see northward migration as appropriate reproduction temperatures are more common. Flooding, often associated with global warming, could also expand zebra mussel territory even further. In general, it is believed that "…climate change will affect the incidence of episodic recruitment events of invasive species, by altering the frequency, intensity, and duration of flooding [and] by allowing aggressive species to escape from local, constrained refugia" (Sutherst, 2000: 224). It is especially difficult to predict the impact of climate change on biosecurity for Canada's north, since the Arctic is such a vulnerable ecosystem.

Canada is not immune from a rise in endangered species and the prospect of species extinction; habitat protection is the most important element of species conservation, and environmental change is the greatest threat to habitat. Even relative success stories are problematic: though Canada has cut sulphur dioxide emissions in half since 1980, acid rain remains a serious problem. Environment Canada estimates a further 75 per cent cut in nitrogen oxide emissions would be necessary to protect all the lakes and forests in Eastern Canada (Gorrie, 2004). Indeed, combined with daily reminders such as the blistering European heat wave of summer 2003 and repeated hurricanes in the Caribbean, the threats associated with global warming are often enough to convince concerned citizens that the move towards renewable energy sources, such as hydro, solar, and wind power, is a necessity.

---

2. Quotes from Doug Struck in an article written for the *Washington Post* and reprinted in the *Montreal Gazette*, "Our forests are a feast," 5 March 2006: A10.

These threats include radical shifts in weather patterns, seashore flooding with rising sea levels, increased drought and inland flooding, disease transmissions, reduced agricultural production (but increases in other areas), human dislocation, further wildlife habitat destruction (in both biodiverse and polar regions), and other effects. While it can be argued that we are witnessing many of these effects at the present time, it is difficult to make long-term predictions. The fact that Canada has three accessible coastlines (Pacific, Arctic, and Atlantic) means not only that the work of the Coast Guard is demanding but that related opportunities for aquaculture, shipping, and oil drilling are a constant source of both optimism and concern (salmon and trout farming for export is increasingly popular but remains under-regulated and a threat to ocean ecology and other fish species). It also exacerbates preceding tensions between provincial and federal governments over jurisdictional issues. The spectre of rising sea levels — whether the rise is one, two, three, or more metres in upcoming decades — is a serious threat to Canadian territory. Since an international effort is needed to curb climate change, as well as many other threats to biosecurity, it is self-evident that investment in international environmental diplomacy is not optional for a state such as Canada.

The Staples Economy Continued

The reliance on the extraction of staple resources for the growth of the Canadian economy is more than just history; it has international repercussions on trade relations, Canada's image abroad, and national security. While it may be wise for Canadian leaders to discuss managing, or at least surveying, what Thomas Hutton refers to as the "normative dimensions of the post-staples state" (2008: 54), a realistic view of the Canadian economy would not conceal the fact that the normative milieu of a staples economy still dominates most of Canadian industry and commerce. As Judith McKenzie writes, this relies on a utilitarian perspective of nature, which "sees land as an inert commodity that can be surveyed, subdivided, and zoned. As a commodity, it may be valuable, but it is no more 'sacred' that a stack of cedar logs [or] a heap of coal ..." (2002: 41). This is often contrasted with Aboriginal and First Nation perspectives (see Knudston and Suzuki, 1992), though these groups are quite often associated with extractive activities today.

Though Canadians are more likely to buy products made in Asia than Canada, and there is certainly a well-developed high-technology sector in most provinces, it is quite premature to declare that Canada has moved into a post-staples era. Despite both market and natural perturbations, the economy is still very reliant on natural resource extraction, from forestry, to natural gas, to fisheries, to uranium. Most pointedly, the Alberta tar sands have become nothing short of an oil rush, drawing capital and further entrenching Canada's dependence on the American economy, and there is no end in sight (for critical analyses, see Pratt, 1976; Woynillowicz, 2005; and Clarke, 2008). The 1995 goal of producing a million barrels of oil per day was surpassed in 2004; five million barrels a day is projected for 2030. According to the Canadian Association of Petroleum Producers, the tar sands now account for 30 per cent of Canada's oil production.[3] Meanwhile, deep oil sands development will even outstrip the extent of surface mining for conventional tar sands, scarring thousands of acres of the boreal forest and contaminating ground water in the process. The American oil market will remain voracious for decades to come, and the Canadian economy under NAFTA remains highly dependent on this source of income. Fears of a new National Energy Plan and federally imposed carbon taxes (as proposed by the Liberals under Stéphane Dion's leadership) fuel Albertan alienation and helped the Harper government to a near-blanket win in the West in the federal election of 2008.

The consequences of the continuation of a staples economy are fairly straightforward when it comes to foreign policy-making. Business lobbies have always had a large role to play in both federal and provincial legislative processes, and resource industries have certainly been no exception (see Boyd, 2003). Indeed, much of non-urban Canada remains highly dependent on resource extraction for local employment, while industrial employment in urban areas has been subject to the usual vagaries of globalization. Lobby groups abound, from the Canadian Association of Petroleum Producers and the Canadian Petroleum Products Institute, to the Canadian Renewable Fuels Association. Environmental groups such as the Sierra Club and Greenpeace are vocal participants, as are think-tanks such as the Pembina Institute and the David Suzuki Foundation. But it is fairly self-evident that, as the world's third-largest producer of natural gas and ninth-largest producer of crude oil, and the largest supplier to the United States, the petroleum industry has a considerable and enviable impact on the decision-making process, as do interests in uranium mining and forestry.

No doubt, this colours (but does certainly not determine) Canada's international environmental diplomacy. The contradictions between the Canadian government's energy and climate policies clearly identified by Mark Winfield (2008) and others have been less pronounced under a Conservative administration, since grandiose climate policy design has not been a guiding factor in its foreign or domestic policy development. Yet the continued, indeed expanding, fossil fuel economic base makes it increasingly difficult to take

---

3. http://www.capp.ca/default.asp?V_DOC_ID=6.

Canadian rhetoric at meetings of the UN Framework for Climate Change (UNFCC) and other summits seriously. Similar images of an environmental laggard emerge at talks related to forestry and fisheries conventions, though to be fair Canadian efforts are complex and often underestimated.

Nonetheless, we can certainly argue that Canada protects its interests with some consistency and that international agreements that challenge the sovereign prerogative over natural resource policy decisions are not welcome. Indeed, on occasion, we witness periodic flourishes of aggressively protective policies that contravene international convention, such as the seizure of a Spanish trawler fishing off the Grand Banks in the turbot dispute of 1995 (see Stoett, 2001), or the conflict over Pacific salmon among British Columbian fishermen, Aboriginal peoples, and Americans (Barkin, 2006), or efforts to stem the tide towards total bans of substances such as asbestos, or insist on labelling for genetically modified organisms (GMOs).

The Continental Dimension

Beyond its natural characteristics and base staples economy, a third structural factor, often termed the *continental dimension* (Munton and Castle, 1992; VanNijnatten, 2003), is fundamental to any rudimentary understanding of the external pressures faced by Ottawa. The simple fact is that the Canadian economy is primarily reliant on trade with the giant to its south; that ideological winds blowing from Washington will fill or becalm sails in Ottawa; and that cross-border resource sharing, trade arrangements, and pollution control will always be central to the ecopolitical agenda of all three members (Canada, the United States, and Mexico) of NAFTA.

Canadian political parties have strong, if fluctuating, views on the appropriate level of coordination and integration with the American political system and economy, but none can deny its centrality in short or long-term planning. In biophysical terms, there are many trade-offs: prevailing winds send American pollution northward, but invasive species entering the continent through the St. Lawrence Seaway affect American ecology and commerce. Largely because of its economic and security dimensions, the environment has been central to Canadian-American relations. The two countries share a 9,000-kilometre-long border that cuts through a wide diversity of ecosystems, such as shared river basins and the Great Lakes, mountain ranges, Arctic wilderness, coastal zones, and old-growth forest. Prevailing winds mean that air pollution from the Midwest finds its way to New England and the Canadian East. Native Americans and First Nations Canadians are often more prone to recognize this ecosystemic continuity than they are any borderline negotiated by Europeans (startling findings of PCBs and other toxic pollutants in the breast milk of Inuit mothers in the late 1980s offered evidence of this interdependence and the asymmetrical vulnerability it reflects). And the similarities between Canadian and American economic systems, with their intensive consumption of resources and careless disposal of waste, make differences in environmental health and policy much less pronounced than is often assumed.

The ecopolitical relationship with the United States is long and varied (Le Preste and Stoett, 2006). There is a significant history of cooperation on transborder issues, in particular the Great Lakes (see Bilder, 1972), where the International Joint Commission (IJC) has worked since 1909 to promote mutually agreeable action to protect the lakes. Bulk water exports remain a hotly contested issue, but the Great Lakes Water Quality Agreement, and efforts to curb air pollution, have emerged as major achievements of the 1970s and 1980s; the Commission for Environmental Cooperation (CEC) of NAFTA, with its Secretariat in Montreal, may also be viewed as an innovative, if rather weak, institution.

Most of the bilateral ecopolitics animating relations between Canada and the United States have involved resources and trade. Disputes over softwood lumber, Pacific salmon, diversion plans for Devil's Lake in Manitoba, and mad cow disease have threatened to sour the relationship. The decision to diverge from Washington is never an easy one; Canada withdrew from the International Whaling Commission in 1982 in order to avoid voting against it and has been threatened with sanctions over renewed Inuit bowhead whale hunting. But it was the Canadian government's decision to sign and ratify the Kyoto Accords that caused the greatest public rift in recent history. A low point was Prime Minister Paul Martin's 2005 speech at the Montreal Conference of the Parties to the UN Framework for Climate Change Convention, in which he lambasted the Americans for their intransigence on climate change and accused them of acting without a "global conscience," even though Canada remained woefully unprepared to implement the necessary cuts to attain its own Kyoto commitment (6 per cent cuts in GHGE from 1990 levels). Stephen Harper's Conservative minority government — with its strong political base in Western oil-producing provinces — has relieved this diplomatic strain considerably by putting climate change on the policy backburner, irking both Canadian environmentalists and Canadian nationalists in the process.

Globalization and Global Environmental Governance

A fourth structural factor is the continuing path of globalization and Canada's entanglement in both international trade and global governance. This extends beyond the limitations of the continental question and further propels us towards a glocal level of analysis. Again, Canadian politicians may be more or (much) less enamoured with the prospects of globalization; they may embrace mythologies that see it as the neoliberal panacea for, or as the root cause of, all that troubles the Canadian citizen today. The central fact remains that Canada is a political player on the multilateral stage and has a plethora of related commitments to institutions with a direct impact on environmental policy — including the World Trade Organization, the International Monetary Fund, and the UN Environment Program (UNEP) — along with diverse cultural and economic interests including the Commonwealth, la Francophonie, and the United States. It also has an active, highly connected citizenry accustomed to relatively free speech. This adds considerable complexity to the policy context.

Part of this structural exigency, we should note, is an increasingly transnational environmentalism that pits the materialistic results, good and bad, of a continental staples economy against an ecological perspective that eschews mass production and reliance on carbon-intensive industry and agriculture. The contestation over old-growth logging and sealing policies, for example, reflects fundamental differences in values between resource-based local economies and urban consumer proclivities.

This is not uncharted territory for a staples-based economy, but previous Canadian leadership initiatives only enhance the image of lost opportunities for many environmentalists. Under Brian Mulroney's leadership Canada was the first country to sign the Convention on Biological Diversity (CBD); it played a prominent role in establishing the Secretariat for the Montreal Protocol on ozone layer protection and the Arctic Council; and its support for the UN Environmental Program was rarely questioned. Today, this multilateral environmentalism is in disarray, as Canadian commitments are arguably less clear and certain than ever before. Of course, global environmental governance efforts face many challenges to their legitimacy and efficacy, and those predisposed against them will stress their downsides, including the threats they pose to sovereignty, the fear of moral hazard, unnecessary repetition by different institutions, and of course the constant issue of finding adequate financing. The Kyoto Protocol has several embedded problems that suggest a premature demise, such as the lack of participation by key states with rapidly expanding economies including China, India, and Brazil; lack of American leadership; and a reliance on market mechanisms to control emissions with insufficient infrastructure or regulations to avoid corruption. But Canadian diplomats are well aware of these problems and of the fact that Canada is slowly losing its status as a respected advocate of global governance.

Globalization also raises the stakes of not pursuing active international cooperation. A hot topic since the 1990s, infectious diseases — microbial pathogens — receive increasing attention by security analysts today, though much of it is fixated on the bioterrorist threat. However, the main threat here to human health and industry stems not from deliberately released anthrax spores or smallpox but the incidental spread of disease in a highly interconnected global society. The threats posed by other highly infectious diseases may, if anything, be commonly underestimated. In late 2004 influenza experts warned of a possible "perfect storm" of infection that could easily kill millions. Certainly the experience of the so-called Spanish flu, which killed some 40-50 million people during and following the First World War, suggests that another such catastrophe is possible.[4] As of March 2005, the H5N1 avian influenza virus has killed over 50 people in Asia, and scientists worry that the flu could mutate into a strain that can spread rapidly among humans. This has the potential to make the SARS virus, which shocked Canadians in 2003, look innocuous in comparison. Meanwhile, the HIV/AIDS pandemic, itself a byproduct of globalization, has taken over 20 million lives and devastated entire communities in sub-Saharan Africa and elsewhere. Canada has yet to emerge as a leading state in the global fight against HIV/AIDS, despite its capacity to do so.

Resolution of these interlinked problems — environmental degradation, unequal access to health care, and exposure to toxic chemicals, climate change, and others — all demand a multilateral approach. Canada has signed and ratified many international agreements, including the 1916 Convention between the United States and Britain for the Protection of Migratory Birds in Canada and the United States; the 1973 Convention on International Trade in Endangered Species of Wild Fauna and Flora; the 1989 Basel Convention on the Control of Transboundary Movements of Hazardous Wastes and Their Disposal; the 1995 UN Agreement on Straddling Fish Stocks and Highly Migratory Fish Stocks, and many others. Canada has often played a key role in the negotiation and implementation of these agreements. Though it is common to label Canada a "petro-dinosaur" at climate change talks today, it has a robust history of international environmental diplomacy to draw upon if a serious effort to renew its reputation is made. This does not imply such an effort is forthcoming, however. We live in the midst of globalization, for better or worse, and Canadian foreign policy on biosecurity issues will reflect the complexity of this context. It will also reflect the

---

4. "Flu experts warn 'prefect storm' of infection could kill millions," *Montreal Gazette* 21 November 2004: IN6. There were in fact three influenza pandemics in the twentieth century, of which the first was by the far the deadliest: 1918–19, 1957–58, and 1968–69.

complexity of the Canadian political system itself, most notably the exigencies of federalism.

Federalism

A final structural factor, the federal political nature of Canada, is incontestably vital to understanding environmental policy formation and the awkwardness of Canada's international environmental diplomacy. Ottawa is inevitably consigned to playing two-level games without adequate authority to impose agreements on the provinces once a position has been reached. This dualism is not as pronounced in the American context, but it is clear there as well that sub-national governments, particularly states such as California intent on introducing carbon pricing and renewable energy requirements in spite of federal intransigence under the Bush Administration, have made substantial headway.

To some extent, there is a perpetual leadership gap in the governance of environmental policy in Canada, since the Constitution does not explicate such policy jurisdiction. Though the federal government is assumed to have paramountcy in most environmental matters, it is clearly the case that, "since before the Second World War, many environmental functions, including resource management, pollution regulation, wilderness and species regulation, and parks services, have been legislated and administered largely at the provincial level" (McKenzie, 2002: 107). For example, each province and territory has its own interests in the energy production field, reflecting geographic opportunities, while facing unique challenges regarding the impact of global warming and emissions reductions. The federal government retains international treaty negotiation rights — which is why Kyoto could be ratified in the first place — but this does not imply it has the authority to enforce treaty implementation with impunity. Indeed, provincial disharmony has been a constant complicating factor in Canadian climate change policy, since the provinces differ in terms of their resource and energy production bases.

Quebec's historically contentious relationship with Ottawa will only be exacerbated if a carbon trading system does not recognize its lower emission base and investment in hydro power. In Canada the lead-in to Kyoto is often referred to as a textbook example of how *not* to conduct the complex interplay between foreign affairs commitments and federal-provincial relations. Arguably, it was a squandered opportunity for serious cooperation. There are of course several interpretations of this, with some portraying the provinces' recalcitrance as the main culprit and others insisting Ottawa made all the wrong moves in its lackluster effort to achieve provincial harmony (see Winfield and Macdonald, 2008, for an excellent and concise analysis). The

1995 National Action Program in Climate Change, resulting from federal-provincial ministerial dialogue, did nothing to decrease emissions, which were almost 10 per cent above 1990 levels in 1999. A 1997 agreement, *sans* Quebec, to stabilize emissions by 2010 had some promise, but the federal government unilaterally declared its intention to agree to a 3 per cent reduction instead of stabilization at Kyoto. Once there, it went a step further, effectively doubling that commitment to 6 per cent below 1990 levels. No doubt this description misses much of the nuance behind the process, but it remains an event that most provincial historians note as a federal betrayal (MacDonald and Smith, 2000).

As always, relations between Canada and the United States and their public optics are interesting facets of the story. Much of the Canadian federal oscillation during the Kyoto negotiations seemed to be predicated on shifts within the Clinton administration in the United States. Likewise, Prime Minister Harper was tagged with the popular suspicion that his approach was based largely on the Bush administration approach to energy policy. Also constant are concerns that a majority government will be impossible to achieve if the rest of Canada perceives the government as excessively Albertan. But open consultation and, on some key issues, negotiation with the provinces will be as essential as it will be strained. A *rapprochement* between Ottawa and Quebec in 2007 (after several initiatives to court the favour of Québécois concerned with their cultural identity) will be put to an interesting test in this regard; Quebec's assumption of the moral high ground on the climate issue (afforded by its immense hydro power development) is particularly irksome to Westerners.

There is more than mere territorial politics involved here. When it comes to GHGE reductions, common terminology may be found, but common understandings will be a much more difficult and localized process. For example, Manitoba has claimed it is well on the path to exceed Kyoto commitments, but there remains ample controversy over the exact level of GHG contributions made by hydro power, a fact that Quebec often ignores in its self-congratulatory assessment of its leading role. Indeed, it is often assumed that we have commonly agreed-upon methodologies for measuring emissions, and even this is false (certainly on a global scale, but also across a large country such as Canada). Similarly, debates over carbon sequestration and sinks leave much room for both innovation and compromise. Canada should develop its expertise in this vital scientific field, through the UNFCC's Subsidiary Body for Scientific and Technological Advice and through the promotion of educational programming in Canadian universities. A March 2007 cost-sharing agreement between Alberta and Ottawa to implement the technology in the tar sands region is simultaneously promising to some and viewed as a stalling tactic or federal favouritism towards Alberta by others.

One ray of hope here is that a national emissions cap and trading regime can be established that will unite provincial jurisdictions (though under the current government this will entail intensity-based caps only), and efforts to establish a Montreal Exchange futures market for carbon dioxide emissions (a joint venture with the Chicago Climate Exchange) have been promising, with the Exchange beginning operations in late spring of 2008.[5] This should be taken cautiously, however. The promise of a robust international emissions trading regime has generated an entirely new field of economics, based almost entirely on derivatives and futures. The idea is borrowed from American efforts to cap air pollution, but in its Kyoto variation it has spawned a virtual feeding frenzy of potential investors, chartered accountants, financial advisers, and lawyers. It has, in short, already taken off at astronomical speed towards becoming a major industry in itself.

Sub-national Actors in International Policy

Export of carbon-based fuels and uranium is still a major means of generating economic wealth in Canada, and it is unlikely that signing more international treaties will alter this fact. Local efforts to mitigate the effects of lightly regulated industrial activity, however, will have a lasting and perhaps internationally inspiring impact.

If climate change is the central global environmental issue of our time, and if the Kyoto process of negotiations have produced yardsticks with which we measure policy success, Canada has indeed proven a dismal failure. The "Bali roadmap," based on the latest round of negotiations where Canada's rejection of Kyoto commitments was routinely denounced by environmental groups, calls for reductions in industrialized countries' emissions to 25–40 per cent below the 1990 level by 2020, while Canada in 2008 has increased its emissions over 20 per cent since 1990, leaving it very far indeed from the lowest of the Bali yardsticks.

As this chapter has suggested, there are many reasons why serious action at the federal level has not taken place. But a more encouraging trend, with global antecedents and implications, is towards sub-national actors taking proactive stances regarding environmental policy, often in cross-border or transnational fashion. Provinces are free to use international trends and market opportunities to shape their own environmental policies, whether it entails highly publicized visits from state governors or selling renewable energy to

---

5. *Financial Post*, 14 March 2008. http://www.financialpost.com/story.html?id=376054.

power-hungry states with green quotas. First Nations in Canada also have navigated the international system to promote their concerns; in 1992 the Cree of Northern Quebec paddled down the Hudson River to New York to protest a deal between Hydro-Quebec and New York State, which would see the expansion of the James Bay hydro project and the flooding of Aboriginal land along the Great Whale River. This action resulted in the governor of New York cancelling the deal with Hydro-Quebec. More recently, Sheila Watt-Cloutier served as the Chair for the Inuit Circumpolar Conference, and her leadership and activism surrounding the impacts of persistent organic pollutants and climate change on the Inuit of the Arctic has earned her many domestic and international honours. Political leadership takes many forms on the many biosecurity issues that traditionally combine grassroots activism and local governance disputes with transnational pressures for change. There are many sound reasons why leadership on environmental issues rarely emanates from the centre of political power in Ottawa, and sporadic attempts — such as the Chrétien government's decision to sign on to Kyoto without provincial consent — can prove highly problematic.

Given the leadership lacuna at the federal and pan-Canadian level, a decentralized vision and strategy has begun to emerge. This remains a sensitive political issue. For example, if much of the action on climate change will take place at the municipal level, the federal government needs to find innovative ways to support local initiatives without inciting provincial territorialism. This is easier said than done. Nonetheless it is evident that mayoral leadership in the United States is impressive: some 231 mayors representing over 45 million Americans have signed the US Conference of Mayors Climate Protection Agreement; 20 Canadian counties, towns, and cities (including Calgary and Edmonton) belong to the International Council for Local Environmental Initiatives.

Actions at the provincial level have been more attuned to the spirit of the Kyoto Protocol. Carbon taxes have been introduced in Quebec and British Columbia; the latter has joined Manitoba in the Western Climate Initiative, along with several American states; Ontario has joined with several North-Eastern states in the Regional Greenhouse Gas Initiative; and in early June 2008, Quebec and Ontario signed a Memorandum of Understanding (which they have left open for others to join) on a cap and trade initiative based on reductions in GHGE from 1990 levels, explicitly rejecting intensity-based reductions and the federal government's proposed move to 2006 as the baseline year. While it is far too early to gauge the effectiveness of such sub-national regimes, it is clear that leadership on this issue has come from the provinces. No doubt, the conflict between provinces on these issues will exacerbate with time; for instance, Quebec's firm belief that it should be rewarded for investing in hydro power infrastructure clashes with Alberta's insistence on its right to develop its oil and gas based economy. Similarly, there is no coordinated provincial standard for vehicle emissions or mileage or methane releases from landfill sites. A Pembina Institute survey concluded in uncertain terms regarding the extant of long-term provincial commitment (see Winfield, 2008: 10; he also suggests that provinces need to strengthen energy efficiency provisions).

Transgovernmental approaches will similarly hold greater promise than multilateral ones at this stage. For example, in 2001 the New England governors and the Eastern Canadian premiers adopted a joint Climate Change Action Plan, committing to reduce GHGE to 1990 levels by 2010 and 10 per cent below 1990 levels by 2020 (see Selin and VanDeveer, 2006). This commitment was renewed as recently as May 2006. It is time to recognize that most leadership on this issue is not national but regional and municipal and that concerned Canadians would be foolish to assume the inevitability of national leadership. Nonetheless, if the latter is to proceed, it will be within the realm of consultative relations with the provinces.

Canadian Expertise Abroad

Uncertainty retains a central role in policy development, as the debates over the safety of innovations in biotechnology, genetically modified organisms (GMOs), nanotechnology, and other areas demonstrate, and specialized knowledge is in high demand. Canadian expertise in these areas, in terms of the science, values, and policies that accompany them, has grown exponentially in recent decades, and though Canadians are often found on important bodies such as the Intergovernmental Panel on Climate Change, more could be done to ensure Canadian scientific contributions are forthcoming. In the biosecurity issue realm, the "front-line worker" has become an essential element in the chain of response. As we now have a small cadre of wildlife management experts monitoring invasive species, and health professionals experienced in dealing with highly contagious pathogens, and many farm workers experienced with avian flu and mad cow containment, we can perhaps begin to build upon this resource for future generations both within and outside of Canada, making sure we incorporate Aboriginal peoples' knowledge in the process. The latter has much to contribute to the Convention on Biological Diversity, as well as the Convention on International Trade in Endangered Species, the Basel Agreement on Hazardous Waste, and many other forums. Further, proper environmental impact assessment (EIA) should now be considered an element of customary international law, a position based largely on the widespread rhetorical acceptance of the precautionary principle, and Canadian environmental engineers and other specialists have a long tradition of conducting EIA.

I would suggest also that Canada is not doing enough to sell renewable energy abroad, despite the economic opportunities this entails. Though undoubtedly improving, Canadian commitment to solar power, wind power, geothermal activities, and hydrogen fuel cell development has been limited. While wind technologies are beginning to penetrate utility markets and catch the eye of domestic policy-makers, and companies such as Ballard have emerged as world leaders in the development and employment of fuel cell technologies, the Canadian International Development Agency (CIDA) remains actively engaged in developing the oil and gas sector abroad, from Bolivia to Kazakhstan. Given the immense potential for solar power and biomass development in Africa and elsewhere, it might be wise at this juncture to investigate more seriously the option of redirecting resources into these emerging fields.

The assumption that developing states must pass through a fossil-fuel dependent stage in their paths towards "modernity" discourages more creative efforts to facilitate development. Given the potential contribution Canada can make with technology transfers, and the fact that any global agreement based on emissions reductions will indeed prove futile in the face of expanding industrialization in Asia and Latin America, it would appear obvious that Canadians can best pursue their long-term interests by encouraging states to either limit or rapidly bypass the oil-based technological culture that characterized North American and European development. The Harper government's obvious disdain for the (admittedly problematic) Clean Development Mechanism and Joint Implementation (which reward industrialized states for investing in energy conservation development projects abroad) need not preclude more creative, non-Kyoto based efforts to promote clean energy technologies abroad. For example, many Canadian firms are moving towards carbon-neutrality in their productive activities by planting trees to offset emissions. Surely this can be encouraged, if not required, activity by Canadian companies with international resource extraction and production investments.

Global Ethical Obligations: Concluding Remarks

Meanwhile, it will remain a federal prerogative and duty to address the thorny questions related to compensating those suffering the adverse effects of climate change. The highest costs of adaptation will be largely born by those least able to pay, and who made the least contribution to GHGE. The role that Canada and other Western states play here will be highly controversial and probably expensive; yet there is also a clear moral imperative.

The legal codification of such an ethic will remain elusive, however. There have been small measures of success in this regard. For example, the legal campaign by the Alliance of Small Island States has at least drawn public attention to their potentially disastrous plight. Articles 4.8 and 4.9 of the UNFCC have led to the creation of the Special Climate Fund. Articles 8(1) and 8(2) of the Rome Statute give the International Criminal Court jurisdiction for intentional "widespread, long-term and severe damage to the natural environment" in war that exceeds military objectives. The 1991 Espoo Convention on Environmental Impact Assessment in a Transboundary Context, negotiated under the auspices of the UN Economic Commission for Europe (UNECE), and the Espoo Kiev Protocol on Strategic Environmental Assessment, as well as the 1998 Aarhus Convention on Access to Justice in Environmental Matters, explicate the need for environmental justice and planned adaptation measures. So does the Lugano Convention on Civil Liability for Damage Resulting from Activities Dangerous to the Environment and the 1998 Strasbourg Convention on the Protection of the Environment Through Criminal Law. None of these measures amounts to a firm legal context, but they may be seen by future legal historians as the beginning of more robust international law on the environment.

It is increasingly difficult for northern governments to avoid these public policy questions or the suffering of millions of victims in the south. Biosecurity threats referred to as "neglected diseases" by the World Health Organization (WHO) and other UN agencies "affect almost exclusively poor and powerless people living in rural parts of low-income countries"; Chagas' disease, sleeping sickness and river blindness, and malaria and yellow fever, among other tropical diseases, remain serious health threats in many states also struggling to deal with the AIDS pandemic, land and forest degradation, and civil or international military conflict (see Hunt, 2007: 3). These are, at heart, human security issues, and Canadian foreign policy may yet again turn to human security as a central theme. Indeed, there is an increasing recognition of the right to a healthy environment in international law (see Schrijver and Weiss, 2004). For example, members of the UN Economic Commission for Europe signed the Aarhus Convention in 1998, which not only pledges signatories to pursue sustainable development paths but guarantees greater citizen input (see Giorgetta, 2004). Of course, this is but a formal convention, and security specialists are under no illusions about the actual enforceability of conventions. Nonetheless, health issues related to environmental ones are on the international agenda. Canada's multilateralist tradition would suggest that it will support the development of international legal mechanisms and institutions — such as the UNEP, the WHO, and the CBD — to deal with invasive species, major micro-environmental issues such as AIDS and avian flu, and other threats to biodiversity and human security. But it would be at best premature to rely on such mechanisms.

Nor should the oft-cited inevitability of globalization and massive economic growth in Asia or elsewhere resign us to an ethical void. The fact remains that global warming is being caused not by globalization per se but by the type of globalization rich states and transnational elites have decided to pursue. Rather than succumb to what Hirst and Thompson refer to as "potentially destructive arguments about the emergence of a global economy dominated by ungovernable market forces, which is at variance with the evidence" (2000: 58), we can simply observe the absurdity of billions of public dollars being funnelled into what are, essentially, subsidized large "final emitter" industries, such as coal and oil. While the practice of subsidizing carbon intensity has received widespread condemnation in Europe and elsewhere, it is still a convenient political device. The time to accept the ethical obligations that will result from climate change is already here — and Canada can take concrete steps in this direction, even if it does not significantly curtail its own GHGEs at home — with commensurate financial commitments.

The competing strains of influence will continue to produce rather fuzzy policy directions, but we should expect little else in the glocal context of environmental policy in the twenty-first century. There are no simple or permanent regulatory or technological solutions, but the urgency of the biosecurity threats posed by climate change, air and water pollution, species reduction, invasive species, and many other issue areas should not only keep the environmental policy agenda at the forefront of international concerns but continue to animate the broad range of actors engaged in ecopolitical discourse. Canada has a key role to play in advancing international efforts to protect the environment; it certainly has the public will, engaged actors, exportable expertise, and economic means to make a significant and lasting contribution. However, any realistic assessment of the limitations imposed by geography, the crucial relationship with the United States, the threats to biosecurity posed by globalization, and the political demands of federalism should temper our expectations.

References and Suggested Readings

Axworthy, Lloyd. 1997. "Sustainable Development and Human Security." *Canadian Speeches* 11, 1 (April): 43–47.

Barkin, Samuel. 2006. "The Pacific Salmon Dispute and Canada-U.S. Environmental Relations." In Philippe LePrestre and Peter Stoett, eds., *Bilateral Ecopolitics: Continuity and Change in Canadian-American Environmental Relations*. New York: Ashgate. 197–210.

Bilder, Richard. 1972. "Controlling Great Lakes Pollution: A Study in U.S.-Canadian Environmental Cooperation." *Michigan Law Review* 70: 469–556.

Boardman, Robert. 1992. "The Multilateral Dimension: Canada in the International System." In Robert Boardman, ed., *Canadian Environmental Policy: Ecosystems, Politics, and Process*. Toronto: Oxford University Press. 224–45.

Boyd, David. 2003. *Unnatural Law: Rethinking Canadian Environmental Law and Policy*. Vancouver: University of British Columbia Press.

Clarke, Tony. 2008. *Tar Sands Showdown: Canada and the New Politics of Oil in an Age of Climate Change*. Toronto: James Lorimer.

Coward, Harold, and Andrew Weaver, Eds. 2004. *Hard Choices: Climate Change in Canada*. Waterloo: Wilfrid Laurier Press.

Giorgetta, Sueli. 2004. "The Right to a Healthy Environment." In Nico Schrijver and Friedl Weiss, eds., *International Law and Sustainable Development*. Leiden: Martinus Nijhoff. 379–404.

Gore, Chris, and Peter Stoett. 2008. *Environmental Challenges and Opportunities: Local-Global Perspectives on Canadian Issues*. Toronto: Emond Montgomery.

Gorrie, Peter. 2004. "Hydrilla Plant: alien in search of a predator." *Toronto Star*, 22 August. http://www.thewaterhole.ca/press/news/20040822.htm.

Hirst, Paul, and Grahame Thompson. 2000. "Global Myths and National Policies." In Barry Holden, ed., *Global Democracy: Key Debates*. London: Routledge. 47–59.

Huebert, Robert. 2003. "The Shipping News Part II: How Canada's Arctic Sovereignty is on Thinning Ice." *International Journal* 58, 3: 295–308.

Hunt, Peter. 2007. *Neglected Diseases: A Human Rights Analysis*. Geneva: WHO.

Hutton, Thomas. 2008. "The Reconstruction of Political Economy and Social Identity in 21st-Century Canada." In Michael Howlett and Keith Brownsey, eds., *Canada's Resource Economy in Transition: the Past, Present and Future of Canadian Staples Industries*. Toronto: Emond Montgomery. 39–60.

Kirton, John, and Don Munton. 1987. "The Manhattan Voyages and Their Aftermath." In Franklyn Griffiths, ed., *Politics of the Northwest Passage*. Montreal: McGill-Queen's University Press. 67–97.

Knudston, Peter, and David Suzuki. 1992. *Wisdom of the Elders*. Toronto: Stoddart.

LePrestre, Philippe, and Peter Stoett, eds. 2006. *Bilateral Ecopolitics: Continuity and Change in Canadian-American Environmental Relations*. New York: Ashgate.

Macdonald, Douglas, and Heather A. Smith. 1999–2000. "Promises Made, Promise Broken: Questioning Canada's Commitments to Climate Change." *International Journal* 55, 1: 107–24.

McKenzie, Judith. 2002. *Environmental Politics in Canada: Managing the Commons into the Twenty-First Century*. Oxford: Oxford University Press.

Munton, Don, and Geoffrey Castle. 1992. "The Continental Dimension: Canada and the United States." In Robert Boardman, ed., *Canadian Environmental Policy: Ecosystems, Politics, and Process*. Toronto: Oxford University Press. 203–23.

Paehlke, Robert, and Douglas Torgerson, Eds. 2005. *Managing Leviathan: Environmental Politics and the Administrative State*. Peterborough: Broadview.

Pratt, Larry. 1976. *The Tar Sands: Syncrude and the Politics of Oil*. Toronto: Hurtig.

Schrijver, Nico, and Friedl Weiss, Eds. 2004. *International Law and Sustainable Development*. Leiden: Martinus Nijhoff.

Selin, Henrik, and Stacy VanDeveer. 2006. "Canadian-U.S. Cooperation: Regional Climate Change Action in the Northeast." In Philippe LePrestre and Peter Stoett, eds., *Bilateral Ecopolitics: Continuity and Change in Canadian-American Environmental Relations*. New York: Ashgate. 93–114.

Sproule-Jones, Mark. 2002. *Restoration of the Great Lakes: Promises, Practices, Performances*. Vancouver: University of British Columbia Press.

Stoett, Peter. 2000. "Mission Diplomacy or Arctic Haze? Canada and Circumpolar Cooperation." In Andrew Cooper and Geoff Hayes, eds., *Worthwhile Initiatives? Canadian Mission-Oriented Diplomacy*. Toronto: Irwin. 90–102.

Stoett, Peter. 2001. "Fishing for Norms: Foreign Policy and the Turbot Dispute of 1995." In Rosalind Irwin, ed., *Ethics and Security in Canadian Foreign Policy*. Vancouver: University of British Columbia Press. 249–68.

Sutherst, Robert. 2000. "Climate Change and Invasive Species." In A. Mooney and R. Hobbs, eds., *Invasive Species in a Changing World*. Washington, DC: Island. 211–40.

VanNijnatten, Debora. 2003. "Analyzing the Canada-U.S. Environmental Relationship: A Multi-Faceted Approach." *American Review of Canadian Studies* 33, 1: 93–120.

Winfield, Mark. 2008. "Climate Change and Canadian Energy Policy: Policy Contradiction and Policy Failure." *Behind the Headlines* (Canadian International Council) 65, 1: 1–19.

Winfield, Mark, and Douglas Macdonald. 2008. "The Harmonization Accord and Climate Change Policy: Two Case Studies in Federal-Provincial Environmental Policy." In Herman Bakvis and Grace Skogstad, eds., *Canadian Federalism: Performance, Effectiveness, and Legitimacy*, 2nd ed. Toronto: Oxford University Press. 266–88.

Woynillowicz, Dan. 2005. *Oil Sand Fever: The Environmental Implications of Canada's Oil Sand Rush*. Calgary: Pembina Institute.

eighteen

Redefining the Core Ingredients of Canadian Foreign Policy: Afghanistan as the Main Game

ANDREW F. COOPER

Afghanistan is at the top of the agenda for Canada's foreign policy. Indeed, despite being overshadowed by the details of Canada's operational involvement, Afghanistan is at the core of a contested search for a redefinition of Canadian foreign policy. The traditional master narrative that defines Canadian foreign policy has been that there is a partisan, ideological, and conceptual consensus. This view holds that even if there has not been a conceptual agreement that Canada has the status of a middle power, there is a consensus that Canada has been obsessed with its status in the international order and its ranking in the international system and that there should be a mix of liberal internationalism and small "c" conservative "limitationalism," whether termed functionalism or niche diplomacy.

Canada's foreign policy agenda can be viewed by using various lenses, offering different perspectives and reasons for its actions and concerns. A *normative* lens highlights Canada's concern with institutional order from the late 1940s to the late 1990s, to the point where Canada is often termed the quintessential joiner. A *practical* or *political* lens showcases how Canadian prime ministers shift to accommodate this consensus. Certainly there have been some historical exceptions to this consensus-orientation. On the 1956 Suez crisis, most notably, there was a bitter split between the Progressive Conservatives (in support of Britain, which with France and Israel had moved to control the Suez Canal) and the Liberals (in support of a United Nations (UN) peacekeeping force). But this sort of open division has been few and far between.

The core theme of this chapter is that in the contemporary landscape of Canadian foreign policy the image of the traditional narrative of consensus is severely bent, albeit, it is also important to note, still not completely broken. This narrative is bent, rather than broken, because there are signs that Prime Minister Stephen Harper, like earlier prime ministers, is moving towards some embrace of the earlier consensus.

A clear example of Harper's move towards consensus has been his own significant endorsement of the middle power notion. In an address to the Council on Foreign Relations on September 25, 2007, Harper noted that "with other middle powers, Canada can and Canada is making a real contribution to protecting and projecting our collective interests, while serving as a model of a prosperous, democratic and compassionate society, independent yet open to the world" (Harper, 2007). It is through these actions that Canada is seen to be leading by example. Yet amidst this type of declaratory statement, the strong current of polarization concerning Canadian foreign policy — even pre-dating Harper's Conservative government — should not be overlooked. In the place of the consensus orientation, what is playing out is a rich but decisive clash, whether it is described as a clash of narratives or perspectives.

Intellectually, the consensus has been torn by two strong currents, which are both maximalist in orientation. From one side, most traditional voices argue that Canada's aspirations need to be routed through another fork in the road, not as a pathfinder state but as a state that should bond with those countries it has long been comfortable with — above all, the Anglo sphere. Such a division highlights, among other things, the completely different use of historical analysis or narratives. The traditional perspective looks back to the glories of the past, such as Canada's involvement in the two world wars of the twentieth century, when it was seen as standing tall in the world. Most notably, these moments are played out through remembering battles in which Canadian soldiers played a large role, such as Vimy Ridge and the D-Day Invasion.

From another side, there are those that argue Canada is not and should not be a middle power, but rather a Model Power with ambitions that find outlets in dramatic initiatives/connections with transnational society. A primary example of this thrust is a book by Jennifer Welsh from Oxford University, *At Home in the World: Canada's Global Vision for the 21st Century* (2004). *At Home in the World* is framed by the aspiration that Canada should be a model international citizen. Another example of this idea comes from Michael Byers, of the University of British Columbia, in his *Intent for a Nation: What is Canada For?* (2007). Although this is more robustly stated in Byers than in Welsh, both posit that the model citizen looks to a post-colonial Canada, with a deep distrust for followership. They advocate a mode of cosmopolitan globalism, where Canadians as individuals transcend state-centric nationalism.

In policy terms, the clash of analysis cuts across all the major intersecting areas of Canadian foreign policy, rehearsed in the 1990s but magnified in the period since 9/11. The first sign of where the narratives departed in the multilateral arena is on the so-called Axworthy Doctrine with its emphasis on mixed coalitions, soft power, and human security. Its most dynamic expressions come on the issues of land mines and the International Criminal Court. The narrative of the Axworthy Doctrine puts orthodox conceptions of security and national interest on the defensive; at the same time it is an implicit criticism of the traditional Pearsonian conception of middle power diplomacy, as it regards this as being too slow and too cautious.

There was vocal opposition to the Axworthy Doctrine; voices of defence reacted vigorously to an approach that they saw as a sham. As Denis Stairs proclaimed, the doctrine meant that Canada would "speak loudly and carry a bent twig" (Stairs, 2001). For some, this narrative betrayed Canada's alternative allies — preferring the small and the virtuous to the robust and reliable. For others it was perceived hypocrisy, in that Canada was viewed as running down its military when in cases — such as Kosovo where human security was on the line — the military was required. The force of this backlash became so strong that new organizations began to spring up, especially the Canadian Defence and Foreign Policy Institute, which encompasses the most robust of the traditionalists, including David Bercuson and Jack Granatstein, and more nuanced observers, such as Kim Nossal, Denis Stairs, and Gordon Smith, in their ranks.[1]

The second clash of narratives straddles the time before and after 9/11 and is focused on the Canadian border with the United States. The narrative of consensus extended to this domain, with a discourse championing the longest undefended border in the world. While Liberals might oppose the free trade agreements with the Americans, they have in their legacy various examples of cooperating and ceding to American interests, including the Auto Pact that managed trade between major automobile companies with production plants on both sides of the border. With the pressure for increasing border security, however, once again the narratives diverged.

The model citizen advocates resisted most, if not all, forms of accommodation to this emerging agenda — a tendency that became magnified after 9/11. Calls for responses that reflected the realities of the security situation were met with strong opposition to several sensitive items, including armed guards on planes and finger printing. Alternatively, traditionalists — or realists — called for new forms of security perimeters, calls that were amplified by leading members of the business community.

It must be acknowledged here that, as on the middle power declaratory statements, the consensus narrative re-exerted itself in this arena through the use of the language of the Canada-US Smart Border Declaration in 2003[2] and with sophisticated work by John Manley, the Finance Minister and later Deputy Prime Minister, and some members of the Canadian bureaucracy, including Peter Boehm, the former Assistant Deputy Minister for North

---

1. For more information, see http://www.cdfai.org/index.htm.
2. For the full text of the Declaration, see http://www.dfait-maeci.gc.ca/anti-terrorism/actionplan-en.asp.

America. However, stresses on this consensus continue and are reinforced by the perceived needs of the model citizen advocates for more attention to human rights issues, punctuated by the backlash against renditions (most notably the Maher Arar case, where a Canadian of Syrian descent was stopped in transit in New York and then transported via Jordan to a Syrian jail where he was tortured) and ethnic profiling, as well as the perception of the need to fill cracks in the security perimeter through arming officials on the border.

It must also be acknowledged that another clash of narratives occurred, although this one can be exaggerated. Purportedly over the weight given to values versus national interest in Canadian foreign policy, this was in many ways a false debate, as shown by the Harper government's preference for values on many foreign policy issues — the values of democracy and human rights, especially.[3] Certainly it is noteworthy how often Harper has invoked these values in the context of the Afghan mission. On the day after the 2006 federal election he said, "We will continue to help defend our values and democratic ideals around the world — as so courageously demonstrated by those young Canadian soldiers who are serving and who have sacrificed in Afghanistan" (Kirton, 2006). In other ways this was simply an echo of the larger debate, juxtaposing "Mars" and "Venus" — over a Canada that can be counted on in tough situations versus a more moralistic Canada.

Yet, if exaggerated, the intensity of this debate should not be discounted. On the one side, a model citizen advocate such as Michael Byers could underscore the power of imagination — the foundation of what he terms "Intent for a Nation." On the other side, traditional realists scoffed at what they considered the pretense of such sentiments. As Jack Granatstein termed it, "We want our nation to be a good international citizen, but it can't if we have no resources to employ abroad … It is time to put our nation's interests first" (2007b: 4). Such a call was echoed firmly by the so-called Wise men of the older generation of diplomats, most notably Derek Burney and Alan Gotlieb (both Canadian ambassadors to the United States).

If all these issues are significant in highlighting the clash of analysis in Canadian foreign policy, it is on the current mission in Afghanistan that these tensions come out most boldly. Although this chapter will not do full justice to the theme, it is on Afghanistan that references to different types of historical narratives are most explicit. John Kirton, from the University of Toronto, offers support for the traditionalist narrative about Afghanistan being in keeping with Canada's historic military tradition:

---

3. Prime Minister Harper's position in this regard is reflected in his dealings with China, where he has advocated for human rights and democracy at the expense of deeper trade integration. For more information, see Devau and Laghi, 2005.

There have been moments in the life of the world where Canada
has stood in first place in the most deadly and dangerous part of
the international politics game, going to war: back in 1944 — the
liberation of Europe — there were only three countries that had
beaches when we hit the shore of Normandy; Canada was one of
them. So when we go forward to the most deadly and dangerous front
of Afghanistan, in the south, [it is] not surprising that Canada is there
[as] one of the top three or four troop contributors (Kirton, 2007).

For the model citizen advocates, though, the crucial narrative about Anglo-
sphere solidarity — the common element of which has been Canada supporting the United States and Britain — is one of neo-colonialism. One
such alternative narrative showcases not the glories of D-Day but the defeats
of earlier interventions in support of Britain, such as in the Anglo-Boer war.
Another narrative compares the argument in support of the Afghan mission
to support for joining the Vietnam War in the 1960s.

Afghanistan also most clearly brings in the element of high politics to
Canadian foreign policy. As eminent Canadian political scientist Donald
Savoie notes, prime ministers have little space for engaging with more than a
few issue-areas at once: "prime ministerial time is the rarest of commodities
in Ottawa ... The flip side of having most key channels of public policy
in Canada coming to him is that he can hardly find the time to give each
the proper attention it deserves" (1999: 87). The usual practice therefore
has been a high degree of delegation both to ministers and to state officials.
Illustrations are varied, but in the forefront of this model are those initiatives associated with the so-called Axworthian diplomacy on land mines, the
International Criminal Court, etc.

What Afghanistan has done is make the "Governing from the Centre" ap-
proach far more explicit, both because of the stakes and sensitivity involved. It
needs to be acknowledged that this was somewhat true under Prime Minister
Paul Martin. But as a highly detailed book by Janice Gross Stein and Eugene
Lang, *The Unexpected War*, reaffirms, Martin's decision-making approach on
Afghanistan was highly reactive: he did not grab ownership of Afghanistan.
Afghanistan was, in the words of Martin's former chief of staff Tim Murphy,
"something we had to do more than something we wanted to do" (quoted
in Turley-Ewart, 2008).

What we have seen in the life of the Harper government is a desire to
contrast its own approach with that of Martin on a number of significant
criteria. Whereas the Martin approach was hyperactive across a diffuse set of
policy initiatives, the Harper government has chosen to concentrate on core
concerns. And if the Martin government's weak point was its tendency to

"review not do," the Harper government wanted from the outset to re-brand Canada in a more stand-up image as a country that is action-oriented and muscular.

In his paper "Mr. Harper Goes to War: Canada, Afghanistan and the Return of 'High Politics' in Canadian Foreign Policy" (2007), Duane Bratt has explored the question of how and why Prime Minister Harper was prepared to ramp up the Canadian mission, as much symbolically as instrumentally, to the point where it is often called "Mr. Harper's War." The how is very connected with Harper's willingness to go to the front lines in Afghanistan, complete with his statements that "we don't make a commitment and then run away at the first sign of trouble" (Harper, 2006). Moreover, he kept to this approach by his determination to both extend and expand the mission. For one thing, he took the initiative to have Parliament lengthen Canada's commitment to the International Security Assistance Force (ISAF) around Kandahar from 2007 to 2009 and again until 2011. For another thing, he increased the scale and nature of the Canadian Force's commitment, including the addition of a tank squadron in September 2006.[4]

The motivating principle that shaped the worldview of the Martin government was that of the Responsibility to Protect (R2P), a concept put into play in large part by Canadian entrepreneurship and intellectual support via the Commission on State Sovereignty and Intervention.[5] Indeed, R2P is a rare case where an issue has been passed on from one government to another: it was introduced by Lloyd Axworthy under the Chrétien government and taken up by Paul Martin (former Prime Minister Chrétien's arch rival). Potential and performance, however, remained two different matters. On the R2P, there was little tangible to show for this ambitious approach. For all of its good talk, above all the push for humanitarian intervention in Darfur, Martin's government was widely judged to have generated far more promises than delivery by the time of its electoral defeat in 2006.

Where the Martin government deserved credit was in its attempt to formulate a new operational framework for dealing with big issues such as Afghanistan from a bureaucratic perspective, the so-called 3D approach — with the three "D's" being Defence, Diplomacy, and Development. It is an over-statement to say that under the Harper government the 3D approach has been transformed into one big D, with Defence as the only D that counts (Regehr, 2006).

---

4. For more information, see http://www.forces.gc.ca/site/newsroom/view_news_e. asp?id=2065.

5. For more information and to read the full report, see http://www.iciss.ca/menu-en. asp.

Development, judged at least in terms of the budget for the Canadian International Development Agency (CIDA), has held up quite well, an analysis reinforced by ongoing infusions of new monies for reconstruction and development programs in Afghanistan — $200 million was promised for 2007 alone. Nor, at least judging by the presence of individual state officials as core policy-makers, has diplomacy been downgraded. To give the most explicit illustration, David Mulroney, Associate Deputy Minister in the Department of Foreign Affairs and International Trade (DFAIT), is not only the government's overall coordinator on Afghanistan but the prime minister's choice for Canadian Sherpa[6] at the 2007 G8 (Clark, 2007). In addition, a number of Canadian diplomats (and former diplomats) have been prominent on the ground: for instance, Canadian Ambassador Christopher Alexander and Michel de Salaberry, a civilian coordinator and Canada's representative in Kandahar. If the image of the Harper government is one that puts defence in a privileged position, this appearance needs to be nuanced.

For one thing, the key military figure that has re-branded the image of the Canadian military — General Rick Hillier — was appointed by the Martin government. The Harper government provided General Hillier with a great deal of additional space to pursue this re-branding process, as the Canadian military pushed for and received greater responsibilities in Afghanistan. The fact that General Hillier epitomizes a military commander who leads by example has shone considerable light on the component of his career that he spent training with the American military, in particular his role as the first Canadian Deputy Commanding General of III Corps, US Army in Fort Hood, Texas, from 1998 to 2000.

Yet, although Hillier's background is significant, it is also necessary to say that he was restrained by the power of the centre, that is to say the Prime Minister's Office. Although it has been widely suggested in the Canadian media that Hillier wanted his three-year appointment as Chief of Canada's Defence Staff to be extended to allow his exit to coincide with the previously scheduled departure of the Canadian troops in February 2009, the Harper government demurred, leading to speculation that despite the mutual benefits that both the government and Hillier have received from his tenure, the mood has changed. Certainly Hillier was not afraid to step on political toes, including those of the former Conservative Defence Minister Gordon O'Connor.[7]

---

6. A Sherpa is the official appointed by a government to discuss arrangements, policies, statements, and other work in advance of summits such as the G8 conference.

7. During July 2007 there were reports that General Hillier and Defence Minister O'Connor were "out of step" on issues regarding the mission in Afghanistan to the point that O'Connor felt the need to publicly respond to the claims. For more information, see CTV News, 2007.

Analysis of the political dimension inevitably turns the focus back onto the purpose of the Afghan mission. Much of the Liberal government's original motivation to "up the ante" in terms of Canadian engagement in Afghanistan was a pragmatic one, to balance participation in that theatre of conflict with non-participation on the war in Iraq. Yet it would be wrong to ignore the fact that sections of Canadian society have continually laid out a strong normative claim for "doing something" in Afghanistan. This sentiment has been especially strong within mainstream women's groups, as the oppressive nature of the Taliban's own gender war becomes more visible (Armstrong, 2003). To some extent, nonetheless, this idealism has been complicated by the increasingly polarized view of the mission. To the opponents of the extension of the mission, the idealism has been contaminated. For them the hopes of the Bonn process to bring democracy to Afghanistan — with its framework for power-sharing, a constitution, elections, and other expressions of a democratic impulse — seem a very distant memory.

Michael Byers, to return to the perspective of one of the most vociferous critics of Canada's Afghan policy, takes issue with any positive interpretation of the Karzai government. In a presentation he made to members of Parliament, Byers stated, "some of the most important posts in the Afghan government are held by former warlords. Some of them stand accused ... of heinous crimes, and of siphoning of billions of dollars of foreign aid" (Byers, 2006). Byers, in a more sustained fashion, also expresses his disdain for some of the practices he takes Canadian forces to have overlooked if not actively participated in, such as the transfer by Canadian Special Forces of detainees to American custody without scrutiny or approbation.

In taking on this line of argument, links are made, rightly or wrongly, between normative deficiencies at home — as found most notably in the Arar case — and abroad.

Defenders of the mission believe that Canadian feminists, in particular, should lend support to the Canadian mission. The controversial 2009 Afghan marriage law shows the divergence of Canadian norms and the Afghan legislature. Outrage followed the law, which made it illegal for Shiite women to refuse sex to their husbands and prevented them from leaving their houses without the permission of a male relative. Canadian Foreign Affairs Minister Lawrence Cannon, along with other international governments, pushed the Afghan government to rework the legislation, which is set for review (Clark, 2009).

Jack Granatstein pointedly asks why there should be so much enthusiasm for other forms of intervention — above all on Darfur (an enthusiasm that Michael Byers shares) — and not on Afghanistan. In his own reflections on this differentiation, Granatstein suggests that "there are a number of pathologies at work here. One is that Darfur [is to] be a UN peace enforce-ment mission, and the United Nations and peacekeeping in any variety are, by definition, good. Afghanistan, by contrast, is seen on the left as a US war, aided and abetted by NATO" (2007a).

Such a view also merges the re-branding efforts by analysts (such as Granatstein) with those of key practitioners (such as General Hillier) to dispel the image of Canada as a UN-centric peacekeeper and its replacement, or a return, to a more militaristic reputation. The motor for this re-branding approach was national pride when Canada moved in its deployment in Afghanistan to become part of NATO's inner circle, as the ISAF gradually spread its coverage beyond Kabul.

Still, bureaucratic self-interest was married to national interest: Canada was back and so was the Canadian military. The opportunities open to the Department of National Defence in terms of both prestige and material resources by going big into Afghanistan are obvious. After years of being held back by their political masters and instead of being lectured by NATO offi-cials about Canada's under-performance, Canada could lecture other NATO members about the need to pull their weight (CBC News, 2007).

With big opportunities come big risks, however. At the forefront of these risks is the physical danger faced not only by the Canadian military but also by Canadian state officials more generally, as the death of Glyn Berry from DFAIT in Kandahar is stark testimony (Pardy, 2006: 20–21). It is well publi-cized that the Canadian military engagement in Afghanistan — as showcased both by the decision in August 2005 to send 2,300 military personnel as part of Task Force Afghanistan to Kandahar and the onset of Operation Archer — is the largest since the Korean War. Less publicized, at least outside of Canada, is the fact that Canada's losses of military personnel are of a disproportionate number (118 by latest count, plus one diplomat and two aid workers; see CBC News, 2009) to the level suffered by other states that have engaged in both Afghanistan and Iraq. The comparative example is Australia, which outside of one case of suicide in its military ranks has not faced one fatal casualty while maintaining a high reputation in terms of commitment and capabilities.[8]

Another potential risk is underestimating the complexity or the possible timeline of the Afghanistan engagement. Facing the spring 2007 offensive from the Taliban in southern Afghanistan was difficult enough, but dealing

---

8. If, however, Retired Maj.-Gen. Lewis MacKenzie is correct, Canada is required to pay a higher price in terms of physical risk, precisely because it is seen as a country that scaled back on these risks for too long: "You don't get credit on these missions unless the potential is there to bleed … You've got to be on the ground, you've got to be there taking high risk" (quoted in Harris, 2006).

with the combined threat of the Taliban and Al Qaeda in the porous and sovereignty-free environment of an increasingly fragile Pakistan is another measure altogether. It is in some ways a positive, albeit sobering, trend that the NATO engagement in Afghanistan is now deemed a counter-insurgency. Yet experts in the field point to the reality that such counter-insurgencies are highly protracted (on average up to 14 years) and bitter affairs. This is especially true when loyalties on the ground (the so-called hearts and minds) are shaped by historical and ethnic ties that are extremely deep and intricate.[9]

To these external risks must be joined the internal political and societal risks, as Canada becomes increasingly divided over the costs and benefits of the Afghan mission. As referred to above, it is wrong-headed to suggest that the Harper government only sees Afghanistan in defence or military terms — as one big D not as a 3D approach. In a manner analogous to the use of middle power status, the Harper government has increasingly indicated its preference for a "whole of government" approach. This was reinforced by the targeting of added resources for development and some areas of diplomacy *vis-à-vis* Afghanistan. At least in terms of resources, CIDA has been well taken care of, with its budget increased well beyond the $200 million originally promised for 2007. Canada's aid is the fourth largest in percentage terms after the United States, Britain, and Germany.

If the upside is a high degree of generosity, the downside has been on-going tensions between the military and the development community. The Regional Commands and Provincial Reconstruction Teams do some excellent work, above all connecting roads, but they remain state-centric. And, for that matter, they are structures that highlight the dominance of the military, with teams of 220 personnel heavily weighted to the military side. Although the asymmetry of this approach can be justified, with respect to the partnership with DFAIT, CIDA, and the RCMP, the almost total detachment (and in some cases estrangement) of non-governmental organizations (NGOs) from this structure is a marked deficiency both on legitimacy and efficiency grounds.

In principle, there is a recognition that both the military and NGOs operate in shared space with an interdependent skill set. In practice, though, enormous gaps exist between how they view humanitarian interventions. The military see themselves as the "lead" actor whose activities to secure the environment enables other actors to operate; they certainly do not perceive themselves as "social workers with guns" (Evrarie, 2004). Coordination means

---

9. A recent Senate Committee report asked, "Are Canadians willing to commit themselves to decades of involvement in Afghanistan, which could cost hundreds of Canadian lives and billions of dollars, with no guarantee of ending up with anything like the kind of society that makes sense to us?" (Canada, 2007).

ensuring the priorities defined by the military. NGOs for their part want a strict compartmentalization of the military role, with no intrusion into their domains and responsibilities. As Nancy Gordon of CARE Canada has put it bluntly, "We're not in the security-providing business and the military is not as effective as we are at providing humanitarian relief and development assistance ... those of us working in humanitarian relief can get tarred with an impartial brush" (Thorne, 2004).

In a variation of this theme, there are tensions between the Canadian government and the Senlis Council think-tank about the ability of development and aid workers to access the south of Afghanistan. The Senlis Council says that area has become a "no-go" area while Canadian state officials strongly dispute this claim (ICOS, 2006). There is also some apparent controversy about the role of the Canadian Forces Strategic Advisory Team, a group made up of approximately 20 high level planners embedded in the Afghanistan government. For some observer/participants, diplomats and development officials should be given a more prominent role. For others, especially those in defence-related industries, such as Alain Pellerin of the Conference of Defence Associations, diplomats needed to be more operational.

One result of all this is that Afghanistan will loom as the main, if increasingly contested, game in Canadian foreign policy. This prospect is indelibly linked to the more controversial aspects of the conflict. An image through this lens is the association of Canada with an increasingly unpopular war. A September 2008 Environics poll confirms that fewer Canadians now support the mission in Afghanistan than ever before, with only 41 per cent of respondents approving (CBC News, 2008b). Such unpopularity is related to the high risks, but it is also connected to other negative images — reliance on warlords, corruption by the Karzai government, and the contamination with what many see as a narco-state. Faced with what could become an even more precarious situation, Canada inevitably finds itself faced with problematic choices.

One of these is to increasingly adopt tactics that are at odds with acceptable behaviour. The other is to do deals with some insurgents, trying to split "moderate" members of the Taliban from hard-liners. This theme was picked up, out of many others, from the report authored, with a team of experts, by Gordon Smith for the Canadian Defence and Foreign Affairs Institute, "Canada in Afghanistan: Is it Working?" in March 2007. Politically, this had the potential to create a decisive — and ill-tempered — battle between the advocates and opponents of the Afghan mission, centred on controversy over the extension of the Canadian mission after the end of its commitment in February 2009. This scenario, which showcases the partisan divide among Canadian political parties, was given a boost by the Harper government's

Throne Speech in late 2007 that suggested an extension of the mission to 2011. These partisan tensions were overcome, however, as on March 13, 2008, a vote in the House of Commons saw the Harper government and the Liberal Party voting together on a compromise motion that extended the mission until 2011 (Campion-Smith, 2008).

There is another scenario, however: not restoring consensus to Canadian foreign policy will help to further ease the tensions. From this perspective Canada will be able to take some glory from its robust support of the mission (albeit with some considerable blood and sacrifice), while gradually disengaging from Afghanistan and beginning to focus again on other core foreign policy issues. Among other things, this movement would be sensitive in terms of American politics. And it almost certainly would not be a complete disengagement. After all, a bi-partisan commission led by former Liberal Foreign Minister and Deputy Prime Minister John Manley has recommended that Canada's commitment towards robust activities in southern Kandahar should be made conditional above all on an upgraded effort by other members of the NATO alliance (Manley *et al.*, 2008).

Moreover, from all indications it appears likely that the Americans will take on this increased NATO burden. The Obama administration has made it a point to increase the American presence in Afghanistan, following up on the Bush administration's injection of American marines into southern Afghanistan in April 2008 (Associated Press, 2008) and the decided preference for local allies to play a role. There also have been calls by Robert Gates, who remains as the American Defense Secretary under Obama, for Canada to reassess its plan to withdraw in 2011. The initial stance of the Harper government, however, has been to affirm its commitment to end Canada's combat mission in 2011 (CBC News, 2008a). Former Harvard professor and leader of the opposition Liberal Party, Michael Ignatieff's connections with members of the Obama administration give the impression that Canada's role in Afghanistan will continue to generate debate in the House of Commons (Goodman, 2009).

Any shift *vis-à-vis* the Afghan mission will not end the new polarization about foreign policy, either in political or intellectual/academic circles. The legacy of "going big" in Afghanistan will continue to influence the discourse in other areas as commentators such as Granatstein and Byers continue to see the world, and the Canadian role, in completely different ways.

However, going big in Afghanistan may temper the major point of divisiveness in Canadian foreign policy and allow a more constructive, if not completely consensual, approach. Through this policy-oriented lens, there will be a mixture of elements of liberal globalism, extending out from the middle power perspective, and small "c" conservatism, with a sense of limitations. Taking on an ambitious military operation in Afghanistan will not soon stimulate an appetite for another big military-oriented engagement, such as an initiative in a situation such as Darfur. Yet the positive virtue of going big in Afghanistan may not in fact be only the re-invigoration of the Canadian military but the opening up of more potential space in other areas of foreign policy. After taking on the risks of Afghanistan, Canada will be free of complaints about being a free rider in the security domain. With an enhanced reputation because of its onerous obligations in Afghanistan, for the first time since 9/11, Canada will have some more discretionary room to do what it wants in some select — and more diverse — areas of foreign policy.

References and Suggested Readings

Armstrong, Sally. 2003. *Veiled Threats.* Toronto: Penguin Canada.

Associated Press. 2008. "US marines return to fight in southern Afghanistan." *International Herald Tribune*, 27 April. http://www.iht.com/articles/2008/04/27/asia/helmand. php.

Bratt, Duane. 2007. "Mr. Harper Goes to War: Canada, Afghanistan, and the Return of 'High Politics' in Canadian Foreign Policy." http://www.cpsa-acsp.ca/papers-2007/ Bratt.pdf. Paper presented at the 79th Annual Conference of the Canadian Political Science Association, 30 May-1 June. http://www.cpsa-acsp.ca/template_e. cfm?folder=conference&page_name=session31am.htm.

Byers, Michael. 2006. "Afghanistan: Wrong Mission for Canada." Speech to MPs and senators, 5 October. http://thetyee.ca/Views/2006/10/06/Afghanistan/.

Byers, Michael. 2007. *Intent for a Nation: What is Canada for?* Vancouver: Douglas and MacIntyre.

Campion-Smith, Bill. 2008. "MPs vote to extend Afghan mission to 2011." *Toronto Star*, 13 March. http://www.thestar.com/News/Canada/article/345835.

Canada. 2007. "Canadian Troops in Afghanistan; Taking a Hard Look at a Hard Mission." Interim Report of the Standing Senate Committee on National Security and Defence (February).

CBC News. 2006. "Canada committed to Afghan mission, Harper tells troops," 13 March. http://www.cbc.ca/world/story/2006/03/13/harper_afghanistan060313.html.

CBC News. 2007. "Canada handling more than its share in Afghanistan: O'Conner," 7 September.

CBC News. 2008a. "MacKay declines Gates's suggestion to extend Afghanistan mission," 11 December. http://www.cbc.ca/world/story/2008/12/11/gates-soldiers.html.

CBC News. 2008b. "Public support for Afghan mission lowest ever: poll," 5 September. http://www.cbc.ca/canada/story/2008/09/05/poll-afghan.html.

CBC News. 2009. "Afghanistan, In the line of Duty: Canada's Casualties." http://www. cbc.ca/news/background/afghanistan/casualties/list.html.

Clark, Campbell. 2007. "PM appoints point man for Afghan mission; foreign affairs advisor takes on new role." *Globe and Mail*, 27 January.

Clark, Campbell. 2009. "Afghan rape-law review to take months." *Globe and Mail*, 7 April.

CTV News. 2007. "O'Connor, Hillier out of step on issues: critics," 31 July; "O'Connor downplays differences with Hillier," 1 August.

Devau, Scott, and Brian Laghi. 2005. "PM says he won't sell out human rights." *Globe and Mail*, 15 November. http://www.theglobeandmail.com/servlet/story/RTGAM. 20061115.wchina1115/BNStory/National.

Evrarie, Richard J. 2004. "Remarks by Lieutenant-General Richard J. Evrarie (Ret'd), Chairman Conference of Defence Associations (CDA) to the Subcommittee on Human Rights and International Development of the Standing Committee on Foreign Affairs and International Trade." Ottawa, 25 November. http://www.cda-cdai.ca/presentations/chairmans_remarks_FAIT_sub_committee.htm.

Goodman, Lee-Anne. 2009. "Ignatieff raises concerns about Napolitano in US talks." *Toronto Star*, 23 April.

Granatstein, J.L. 2007a. "The left, feminists, and Afghanistan." *Hamilton Spectator*, 15 January.

Granatstein, J.L. 2007b. *Whose War Is It? How Canada Can Survive in the Post-9/11 World.* Toronto: HarperCollins.

Harper, Stephen. 2006. Speech to Canadian troops, Kandahar, 13 March 2006.

Harper, Stephen. 2007. Address to the Council on Foreign Relations, 25 September. http://www.cfr.org/publication/14315/conversation_with_stephen_harper_rush_transcript_federal_news_service.html.

Harris, Kathleen. 2006. "Sitting with the big boys: Harper recasts foreign policy." *Winnipeg Sun*, 7 September.

ICOS. 2006. "The tide has turned: Taliban have retaken control of southern Afghanistan — Support from local population for central government and international military presence has been lost." News Release, 6 June. http://www.senliscouncil.net/modules/media_centre/press_releases/62_news.

Kirton, John. 2006. "Canada's New Government's Foreign Policy and the G8 St. Petersburgh Summit." http://tspace.library.utoronto.ca/bitstream/1807/4819/1/kirton_060125.html.

Kirton, John. 2007. "Canada's Engagement with Afghanistan," 30 October. http://www.canadainternational.gc.ca/canada-afghanistan/media/video/kirton.aspx.

Manley, John, Derek H. Burney, Jake Epp, Paul Tellier, and Pamela Wallin. 2008. *Independent Panel on Canada's Future Role in Afghanistan.* Ottawa: Ministry of Public Works and Government Services (January).

Pardy, Gar. 2006. "When Diplomacy Turns Deadly." *Diplomat & International Canada* (May-June).

Regehr, Ernie. 2006. "Afghanistan: From Good Intentions to Sustainable Solutions." *Project Ploughshares Briefing* (1 August).

Savoie, Donald J. 1999. *Governing from the Centre: The Concentration of Power in Canadian Politics.* Toronto: University of Toronto Press.

Smith, Gordon. 2007. "Canada in Afghanistan: Is it Working?" Ottawa: Canadian Defence and Foreign Affairs Institute (March).

Stairs, Denis. 2001. "Canada in the 1990s: Speak Loudly and Carry a Bent Twig." Institute for Research on Public Policy. http://www.irpp.org/po/archive/jan01/stairs.pdf.

Stein, Janice Gross, and Eugene Lang. 2007. *The Unexpected War: Canada in Kandahar.* Toronto: Viking Canada.

Thorne, Stephen. 2004. "New Canadian foreign policy blurs line between military, development roles." *Brockville Recorder and Times*, December 29.

Turley-Ewart, John. 2008. "Manley report takes a dig at Paul Martin." *The National Post*, 22 January. http://network.nationalpost.com/np/blogs/fullcomment/archive/2008/01/22/john-turley-ewart-manley-s-report-takes-a-dig-at-paul-martin.aspx.

Welsh, Jennifer. 2004. *At Home in the World: Canada's Global Vision for the 21st Century.* Toronto: HarperCollins.

The Constitution Act, 1982

Enacted as Schedule B to the Canada Act 1982, (UK) 1982, c. 11.

PART I

Canadian Charter of Rights and Freedoms

Whereas Canada is founded upon principles that recognize the supremacy of God and the rule of law:

GUARANTEE OF RIGHTS AND FREEDOMS

1. The *Canadian Charter of Rights and Freedoms* guarantees the rights and freedoms set out in it subject only to such reasonable limits prescribed by law as can be demonstrably justified in a free and democratic society.

Rights and freedoms in Canada

FUNDAMENTAL FREEDOMS

2. Everyone has the following fundamental freedoms:

Fundamental freedoms

 a) freedom of conscience and religion;
 b) freedom of thought, belief, opinion and expression, including freedom of the press and other media of communication;
 c) freedom of peaceful assembly; and
 d) freedom of association.

DEMOCRATIC RIGHTS

Democratic rights of citizens

3. Every citizen of Canada has the right to vote in an election of members of the House of Commons or of a legislative assembly and to be qualified for membership therein.

Maximum duration of legislative bodies

4. (1) No House of Commons and no legislative assembly shall continue for longer than five years from the date fixed for the return of the writs of a general election of its members.

Continuation in special circumstances

(2) In time of real or apprehended war, invasion or insurrection, a House of Commons may be continued by Parliament and a legislative assembly may be continued by the legislature beyond five years if such continuation is not opposed by the votes of more than one-third of the members of the House of Commons or the legislative assembly, as the case may be.

Annual sitting of legislative bodies

5. There shall be a sitting of Parliament and of each legislature at least once every twelve months.

MOBILITY RIGHTS

Mobility of citizens

6. (1) Every citizen of Canada has the right to enter, remain in and leave Canada.

Rights to move and gain livelihood

(2) Every citizen of Canada and every person who has the status of a permanent resident of Canada has the right

a) to move to and take up residence in any province; and
b) to pursue the gaining of a livelihood in any province.

Limitation

(3) The rights specified in subsection (2) are subject to

a) any laws or practices of general application in force in a province other than those that discriminate among persons primarily on the basis of province of present or previous residence; and
b) any laws providing for reasonable residency requirements as a qualification for the receipt of publicly provided social services.

(4) Subsections (2) and (3) do not preclude any law, program or activity that has as its object the amelioration in a province of conditions of individuals in that province who are socially or economically disadvantaged if the rate of employment in that province is below the rate of employment in Canada.

Affirmative action programs

LEGAL RIGHTS

7. Everyone has the right to life, liberty and security of the person and the right not to be deprived thereof except in accordance with the principles of fundamental justice.

Life, liberty and security of person

8. Everyone has the right to be secure against unreasonable search or seizure.

Search or seizure

9. Everyone has the right not to be arbitrarily detained or imprisoned.

Detention or imprisonment

10. Everyone has the right on arrest or detention

Arrest or detention

  a) to be informed promptly of the reasons therefor;
  b) to retain and instruct counsel without delay and to be informed of that right; and
  c) to have the validity of the detention determined by way of *habeas corpus* and to be released if the detention is not lawful.

11. Any person charged with an offence has the right

Proceedings in criminal and penal matters

  a) to be informed without unreasonable delay of the specific offence;
  b) to be tried within a reasonable time;
  c) not to be compelled to be a witness in proceedings against that person in respect of the offence;
  d) to be presumed innocent until proven guilty according to law in a fair and public hearing by an independent and impartial tribunal;
  e) not to be denied reasonable bail without just cause;

f) except in the case of an offence under military law tried before a military tribunal, to the benefit of trial by jury where the maximum punishment for the offence is imprisonment for five years or a more severe punishment;

g) not to be found guilty on account of any act or omission unless, at the time of the act or omission, it constituted an offence under Canadian or international law or was criminal according to the general principles of law recognized by the community of nations;

h) if finally acquitted of the offence, not to be tried for it again and, if finally found guilty and punished for the offence, not to be tried or punished for it again; and

i) if found guilty of the offence and if the punishment for the offence has been varied between the time of commission and the time of sentencing, to the benefit of the lesser punishment.

Treatment or punishment

12. Everyone has the right not to be subjected to any cruel and unusual treatment or punishment.

Self-crimination

13. A witness who testifies in any proceedings has the right not to have any incriminating evidence so given used to incriminate that witness in any other proceedings, except in a prosecution for perjury or for the giving of contradictory evidence.

Interpreter

14. A party or witness in any proceedings who does not understand or speak the language in which the proceedings are conducted or who is deaf has the right to the assistance of an interpreter.

EQUALITY RIGHTS

Equality before and under law and equal protection and benefit of law

15. (1) Every individual is equal before and under the law and has the right to the equal protection and equal benefit of the law without discrimination and, in particular, without discrimination based on race, national or ethnic origin, colour, religion, sex, age or mental or physical disability.

(2) Subsection (1) does not preclude any law, program or activity that has as its object the amelioration of conditions of disadvantaged individuals or groups including those that are disadvantaged because of race, national or ethnic origin, colour, religion, sex, age or mental or physical disability.

Affirmative action programs

OFFICIAL LANGUAGES OF CANADA

16. (1) English and French are the official languages of Canada and have equality of status and equal rights and privileges as to their use in all institutions of the Parliament and government of Canada.

Official languages of Canada

(2) English and French are the official languages of New Brunswick and have equality of status and equal rights and privileges as to their use in all institutions of the legislature and government of New Brunswick.

Official languages of New Brunswick

(3) Nothing in this Charter limits the authority of Parliament or a legislature to advance the equality of status or use of English and French.

Advancement of status and use

16.1 (1) The English linguistic community and the French linguistic community in New Brunswick have equality of status and equal rights and privileges, including the right to distinct educational institutions and such distinct cultural institutions as are necessary for the preservation and promotion of those communities.

English and French linguistic communities in New Brunswick

(2) The role of the legislature and government of New Brunswick to preserve and promote the status, rights and privileges referred to in subsection (1) is affirmed.

Role of the legislature and government of New Brunswick

17. (1) Everyone has the right to use English or French in any debates and other proceedings of Parliament.

Proceedings of Parliament

(2) Everyone has the right to use English or French in any debates and other proceedings of the legislature of New Brunswick.

Proceedings of New Brunswick legislature

18. (1) The statutes, records and journals of Parliament shall be printed and published in English and French and both language versions are equally authoritative.

(2) The statutes, records and journals of the legislature of New Brunswick shall be printed and published in English and French and both language versions are equally authoritative.

19. (1) Either English or French may be used by any person in, or in any pleading in or process issuing from, any court established by Parliament.

(2) Either English or French may be used by any person in, or in any pleading in or process issuing from, any court of New Brunswick.

20. (1) Any member of the public in Canada has the right to communicate with, and to receive available services from, any head or central office of an institution of the Parliament or government of Canada in English or French, and has the same right with respect to any other office of any such institution where

a) there is a significant demand for communications with and services from that office in such language; or

b) due to the nature of the office, it is reasonable that communications with and services from that office be available in both English and French.

(2) Any member of the public in New Brunswick has the right to communicate with, and to receive available services from, any office of an institution of the legislature or government of New Brunswick in English or French.

21. Nothing in sections 16 to 20 abrogates or derogates from any right, privilege or obligation with respect to the English and French languages, or either of them, that exists or is continued by virtue of any other provision of the Constitution of Canada.

22. Nothing in sections 16 to 20 abrogates or derogates from any legal or customary right or privilege acquired or enjoyed either before or after the coming into force of this Charter with respect to any language that is not English or French.

Rights and privileges preserved

MINORITY LANGUAGE EDUCATIONAL RIGHTS

23. (1) Citizens of Canada

Language of instruction

   a) whose first language learned and still understood is that of the English or French linguistic minority population of the province in which they reside, or

   b) who have received their primary school instruction in Canada in English or French and reside in a province where the language in which they received that instruction is the language of the English or French linguistic minority population of the province,

have the right to have their children receive primary and secondary school instruction in that language in that province.

(2) Citizens of Canada of whom any child has received or is receiving primary or secondary school instruction in English or French in Canada, have the right to have all their children receive primary and secondary school instruction in the same language.

(3) The right of citizens of Canada under subsections (1) and (2) to have their children receive primary and secondary school instruction in the language of the English or French linguistic minority population of a province

Continuity of language instruction

   a) applies wherever in the province the number of children of citizens who have such a right is sufficient to warrant the provision to them out of public funds of minority language instruction; and

Application where numbers warrant

   b) includes, where the number of those children so warrants, the right to have them receive that instruction in minority language educational facilities provided out of public funds.

ENFORCEMENT

Enforcement of guaranteed rights and freedoms

24. (1) Anyone whose rights or freedoms, as guaranteed by this Charter, have been infringed or denied may apply to a court of competent jurisdiction to obtain such remedy as the court considers appropriate and just in the circumstances.

Exclusion of evidence bringing administration of justice into disrepute

(2) Where, in proceedings under subsection (1), a court concludes that evidence was obtained in a manner that infringed or denied any rights or freedoms guaranteed by this Charter, the evidence shall be excluded if it is established that, having regard to all the circumstances, the admission of it in the proceedings would bring the administration of justice into disrepute.

GENERAL

Aboriginal rights and freedoms not affected by Charter

25. The guarantee in this Charter of certain rights and freedoms shall not be construed so as to abrogate or derogate from any aboriginal, treaty or other rights or freedoms that pertain to the aboriginal peoples of Canada including

    a) any rights or freedoms that have been recognized by the Royal Proclamation of October 7, 1763; and

    b) any rights or freedoms that now exist by way of land claims agreements or may be so acquired.

Other rights and freedoms not affected by Charter

26. The guarantee in this Charter of certain rights and freedoms shall not be construed as denying the existence of any other rights or freedoms that exist in Canada.

Multicultural heritage

27. This Charter shall be interpreted in a manner consistent with the preservation and enhancement of the multicultural heritage of Canadians.

Rights guaranteed equally to both sexes

28. Notwithstanding anything in this Charter, the rights and freedoms referred to in it are guaranteed equally to male and female persons.

Rights respecting certain schools preserved

29. Nothing in this Charter abrogates or derogates from any rights or privileges guaranteed by or under the Constitution of Canada in respect of denominational, separate or dissentient schools.

30. A reference in this Charter to a Province or to the legislative assembly or legislature of a province shall be deemed to include a reference to the Yukon Territory and the Northwest Territories, or to the appropriate legislative authority thereof, as the case may be.

Application to territories and territorial authorities

31. Nothing in this Charter extends the legislative powers of any body or authority.

Legislative powers not extended

APPLICATION OF CHARTER

32. (1) This Charter applies

Application of Charter

a) to the Parliament and government of Canada in respect of all matters within the authority of Parliament including all matters relating to the Yukon Territory and Northwest Territories; and

b) to the legislature and government of each province in respect of all matters within the authority of the legislature of each province.

(2) Notwithstanding subsection (1), section 15 shall not have effect until three years after this section comes into force.

Exception

33. (1) Parliament or the legislature of a province may expressly declare in an Act of Parliament or of the legislature, as the case may be, that the Act or a provision thereof shall operate notwithstanding a provision included in section 2 or sections 7 to 15 of this Charter.

Exception where express declaration

(2) An Act or a provision of an Act in respect of which a declaration made under this section is in effect shall have such operation as it would have but for the provision of this Charter referred to in the declaration.

Operation of exception

(3) A declaration made under subsection (1) shall cease to have effect five years after it comes into force or on such earlier date as may be specified in the declaration.

Five year limitation

(4) Parliament or the legislature of a province may re-enact a declaration made under subsection (1).

Re-enactment

<table>
<tr><td>Five year
limitation</td><td>(5) Subsection (3) applies in respect of a re-enactment made under subsection (4).</td></tr>
</table>

CITATION

<table>
<tr><td>Citation</td><td>34. This Part may be cited as the Canadian Charter of Rights and Freedoms.</td></tr>
</table>

PART II

Rights of the Aboriginal Peoples of Canada

<table>
<tr><td>Recognition of
existing aboriginal
and treaty rights</td><td>35. (1) The existing aboriginal and treaty rights of the aboriginal peoples of Canada are hereby recognized and affirmed.</td></tr>
<tr><td>Definition of
"aboriginal peoples
of Canada"</td><td>(2) In this Act, "aboriginal peoples of Canada" includes the Indian, Inuit and Métis peoples of Canada.</td></tr>
<tr><td>Land claims
agreements</td><td>(3) For greater certainty, in subsection (1) "treaty rights" includes rights that now exist by way of land claims agreements or may be so acquired.</td></tr>
<tr><td>Aboriginal and
treaty rights are
guaranteed equally
to both sexes</td><td>(4) Notwithstanding any other provision of this Act, the aboriginal and treaty rights referred to in subsection (1) are guaranteed equally to male and female persons.</td></tr>
<tr><td>Commitment
to participation
in constitutional
conference</td><td>35.1 The government of Canada and the provincial governments are committed to the principle that, before any amendment is made to Class 24 of section 91 of the "Constitution Act, 1867", to section 25 of this Act or to this Part,</td></tr>
</table>

  a) a constitutional conference that includes in its agenda an item relating to the proposed amendment, composed of the Prime Minister of Canada and the first ministers of the provinces, will be convened by the Prime Minister of Canada; and

  b) the Prime Minister of Canada will invite representatives of the aboriginal peoples of Canada to participate in the discussions on that item.

PART III
Equalization and Regional Disparities

36. (1) Without altering the legislative authority of Parliament or of the provincial legislatures, or the rights of any of them with respect to the exercise of their legislative authority, Parliament and the legislatures, together with the government of Canada and the provincial governments, are committed to

Commitment to promote equal opportunities

a) promoting equal opportunities for the well-being of Canadians;
b) furthering economic development to reduce disparity in opportunities; and
c) providing essential public services of reasonable quality to all Canadians.

(2) Parliament and the government of Canada are committed to the principle of making equalization payments to ensure that provincial governments have sufficient revenues to provide reasonably comparable levels of public services at reasonably comparable levels of taxation.

Commitment respecting public services

PART IV
Constitutional Conference

37. [Repealed. See section 54.]

PART IV.1
Constitutional Conferences

37.1 [Repealed. See section 54.1]

PART V
Procedure for Amending
Constitution of Canada

*General procedure
for amending
Constitution
of Canada*

38. (1) An amendment to the Constitution of Canada may be made by proclamation issued by the Governor General under the Great Seal of Canada where so authorized by

a) resolutions of the Senate and House of Commons; and

b) resolutions of the legislative assemblies of at least two-thirds of the provinces that have, in the aggregate, according to the then latest general census, at least fifty per cent of the population of all the provinces.

*Majority of
members*

(2) An amendment made under subsection (1) that derogates from the legislative powers, the proprietary rights or any other rights or privileges of the legislature or government of a province shall require a resolution supported by a majority of the members of each of the Senate, the House of Commons and the legislative assemblies required under subsection (1).

*Expression
of dissent*

(3) An amendment referred to in subsection (2) shall not have effect in a province the legislative assembly of which has expressed its dissent thereto by resolution supported by a majority of its members prior to the issue of the proclamation to which the amendment relates unless that legislative assembly, subsequently, by resolution supported by a majority of its members, revokes its dissent and authorizes the amendment.

*Revocation
of dissent*

(4) A resolution of dissent made for the purposes of subsection (3) may be revoked at any time before or after the issue of the proclamation to which it relates.

*Restriction on
proclamation*

39. (1) A proclamation shall not be issued under subsection 38(1) before the expiration of one year from the adoption of the resolution initiating the amendment procedure thereunder, unless the legislative assembly of each province has previously adopted a resolution of assent or dissent.

(2) A proclamation shall not be issued under subsection 38(1) after the expiration of three years from the adoption of the resolution initiating the amendment procedure thereunder.

Idem

40. Where an amendment is made under subsection 38(1) that transfers provincial legislative powers relating to education or other cultural matters from provincial legislatures to Parliament, Canada shall provide reasonable compensation to any province to which the amendment does not apply.

Compensation

41. An amendment to the Constitution of Canada in relation to the following matters may be made by proclamation issued by the Governor General under the Great Seal of Canada only where authorized by resolutions of the Senate and House of Commons and of the legislative assembly of each province:

Amendment by unanimous consent

a) the office of the Queen, the Governor General and the Lieutenant Governor of a province;

b) the right of a province to a number of members in the House of Commons not less than the number of Senators by which the province is entitled to be represented at the time this Part comes into force;

c) subject to section 43, the use of the English or the French language;

d) the composition of the Supreme Court of Canada; and

e) an amendment to this Part.

42. (1) An amendment to the Constitution of Canada in relation to the following matters may be made only in accordance with subsection 38(1):

Amendment by general procedure

a) the principle of proportionate representation of the provinces in the House of Commons prescribed by the Constitution of Canada;

b) the powers of the Senate and the method of selecting Senators;

c) the number of members by which a province is entitled to be represented in the Senate and the residence qualifications of Senators;

d) subject to paragraph 41(d), the Supreme Court of Canada;

e) the extension of existing provinces into the territories; and

f) notwithstanding any other law or practice, the establishment of new provinces.

Exception

(2) Subsections 38(2) to (4) do not apply in respect of amendments in relation to matters referred to in subsection (1).

Amendment of provisions relating to some but not all provinces

43. An amendment to the Constitution of Canada in relation to any provision that applies to one or more, but not all, provinces, including

a) any alteration to boundaries between provinces, and

b) any amendment to any provision that relates to the use of the English or the French language within a province,

may be made by proclamation issued by the Governor General under the Great Seal of Canada only where so authorized by resolutions of the Senate and House of Commons and of the legislative assembly of each province to which the amendment applies.

Amendments by Parliament

44. Subject to sections 41 and 42, Parliament may exclusively make laws amending the Constitution of Canada in relation to the executive government of Canada or the Senate and House of Commons.

Amendments by provincial legislatures

45. Subject to section 41, the legislature of each province may exclusively make laws amending the constitution of the province.

Initiation of amendment procedures

46. (1) The procedures for amendment under sections 38, 41, 42 and 43 may be initiated either by the Senate or the House of Commons or by the legislative assembly of a province.

Revocation of authorization

(2) A resolution of assent made for the purposes of this Part may be revoked at any time before the issue of a proclamation authorized by it.

Amendments without Senate resolution

47. (1) An amendment to the Constitution of Canada made by proclamation under section 38, 41, 42 or 43 may be made without a resolution of the Senate authorizing the issue of the proclamation if, within one hundred and eighty days after the adoption by the House of Commons of a resolution authorizing its issue, the Senate has not adopted such a resolution and if, at any time after the expiration of that period, the House of Commons again adopts the resolution.

(2) Any period when Parliament is prorogued or dissolved shall not be counted in computing the one hundred and eighty day period referred to in subsection (1).

Computation of period

48. The Queen's Privy Council for Canada shall advise the Governor General to issue a proclamation under this Part forthwith on the adoption of the resolutions required for an amendment made by proclamation under this Part.

Advice to issue proclamation

49. A constitutional conference composed of the Prime Minister of Canada and the first ministers of the provinces shall be convened by the Prime Minister of Canada within fifteen years after this Part comes into force to review the provisions of this Part.

Constitutional conference

PART VI
Amendment to the Constitution Act, 1867

50. [The amendment is set out in the Consolidation of the Constitution Act, 1867, as section 92A thereof.]

51. [The amendment is set out in the Consolidation of the Constitution Act, 1867, as the Sixth Schedule thereof.]

PART VII
General

52. (1) The Constitution of Canada is the supreme law of Canada, and any law that is inconsistent with the provisions of the Constitution is, to the extent of the inconsistency, of no force or effect.

Primacy of Constitution of Canada

*Constitution
of Canada*

(2) The Constitution of Canada includes

    a) the Canada Act 1982, including this Act;

    b) the Acts and orders referred to in the schedule; and

    c) any amendment to any Act or order referred to in
        paragraph (a) or (b).

*Amendments
to Constitution
of Canada*

(3) Amendments to the Constitution of Canada shall be
made only in accordance with the authority contained in the
Constitution of Canada.

*Repeals and
new names*

53. (1) The enactments referred to in Column I of the schedule
are hereby repealed or amended to the extent indicated in
Column II thereof and, unless repealed, shall continue as law in
Canada under the names set out in Column III thereof.

*Consequential
amendments*

(2) Every enactment, except the Canada Act 1982, that refers
to an enactment referred to in the schedule by the name in
Column I thereof is hereby amended by substituting for that
name the corresponding name in Column III thereof, and
any British North America Act not referred to in the schedule
may be cited as the Constitution Act followed by the year and
number, if any, of its enactment.

*Repeal and
consequential
amendments*

54. Part IV is repealed on the day that is one year after this Part
comes into force and this section may be repealed and this Act
renumbered, consequentially upon the repeal of Part IV and this
section, by proclamation issued by the Governor General under
the Great Seal of Canada.

54.1 Part VI.1 and this section are repealed on April 18, 1987.
[Repealed.]

*French version
of Constitution
of Canada*

55. A French version of the portions of the Constitution of
Canada referred to in the schedule shall be prepared by the
Minister of Justice of Canada as expeditiously as possible and,
when any portion thereof sufficient to warrant action being taken
has been so prepared, it shall be put forward for enactment by
proclamation issued by the Governor General under the Great
Seal of Canada pursuant to the procedure then applicable to an
amendment of the same provisions of the Constitution of Canada.

56. Where any portion of the Constitution of Canada has been or is enacted in English and French or where a French version of any portion of the Constitution is enacted pursuant to section 55, the English and French versions of that portion of the Constitution are equally authoritative.

English and French versions of certain constitutional texts

57. The English and French versions of this Act are equally authoritative.

English and French versions of this Act

58. Subject to section 59, this Act shall come into force on a day to be fixed by proclamation issued by the Queen or the Governor General under the Great Seal of Canada.

Commencement

59. (1) Paragraph 23(1)(a) shall come into force in respect of Quebec on a day to be fixed by proclamation issued by the Queen or the Governor General under the Great Seal of Canada.

Commencement of paragraph 23(1)(a) in respect of Quebec

(2) A proclamation under subsection (1) shall be issued only where authorized by the legislative assembly or government of Quebec.

Authorization of Quebec

(3) This section may be repealed on the day paragraph 23(1)(a) comes into force in respect of Quebec and this Act amended and renumbered, consequentially upon the repeal of this section, by proclamation issued by the Queen or the Governor General under the Great Seal of Canada.

Repeal of this section

60. This Act may be cited as the Constitution Act, 1982, and the Constitution Acts 1867 to 1975 (No. 2) and this Act may be cited together as the Constitution Acts, 1867 to 1982.

Short title and citations

61. A reference to the "Constitution Acts, 1867 to 1982" shall be deemed to include a reference to the "Constitution Amendment Proclamation, 1983".

References

Index

S

Saada, Jacques, 240
Said, Edward, 314
Saint-Laurent, Louis, 118
Sampert, Shannon, 292
Saskatchewan
    founding settlers, 79
    "notwithstanding" clause, 205
Sauvé v. Canada (Chief Electoral Officer)
    [2002], 210, 216
Savoie, Donald, 363
Sayers, Anthony, 240
Schmitter, Philippe, 271
Scott, F.R., 163
Scott, Gilbert H., 310
Secession Reference, 14–15
Sechelt Band, 191
sector-specific agreements, Aboriginal
    governance, 192
secularism, 65–66
security, post 9/11, 361–362
self-government, Aboriginal. *See*
    Aboriginal self-government
self-government narratives
    coexisting sovereignty, 185–187
    delegated authority, 183–184
    inherent right, 184–185
self-government rights, 27–31
    differentiated citizenship, 40–41
    integration, 40–41
    nationalism, 41–42
    Quebec in the Constitution, 28
    representation, 34–35
    United States, 41
    women, 37–38
self-regulation, 271
Seljak, David, 313
Selling Illusions: The Cult of
    Multiculturalism in Canada
    (Bissoondath), 59
Senate
    composition, 149–150
    reform, 33, 112, 149–151, 243–244
    regional representation, 85–86

seats and diversity, 33–34
    women, 33, 37–38
Senlis Council, 369
September 11, 2001. *See* 9/11
settler societies, 24, 302–303
Sévigny, Pierre, 127
Seyd, Patrick, 252
Shils, E., 73
Ship, Susan Judith, 294
Siegfried, André, 66
"The Significance of the Frontier in
    American History" (Turner), 74
Simeon, R., 71
    "Regional Political Cultures in
    Canada," 79
Smiley, Donald, 47, 106, 164
Smith, Gordon, "Canada in
    Afghanistan: Is it Working?," 369
social capital, 64
social policy and programs, intergov-
    ernmental agreements, 171–172
social union, 171–172
Social Union Framework Agreement
    (SUFA), 112, 171–172
Soetaro, Maya, 301
sovereignty, Aboriginal, 185–187
sovereignty-association, 112–113,
    166–167. *See also* referendums on
    sovereignty-association
special committee of the House
    of Commons on Indian
    Government (1983), 184–185
special representation rights, 33–35
    integration, 39, 40–41
Sponsorship Scandal, 242
Stairs, Denis, 361
standing committees, 146–147
Statement on Indian Policy, 12, 179, 182
Status Indian reserves, devolution of
    power, 31
Stein, Janice Gross, *The Unexpected
    War*, 363
strategic action, by interest groups,
    268–269